Download Forms on Nolo.com

You can download the forms in this book at:

 www.nolo.com/back-of-book/RIPER.html

We'll also post updates whenever there's an important change to the law affecting this book—as well as articles and other related materials.

More Resources from Nolo.com

 Legal Forms, Books, & Software
Hundreds of do-it-yourself products—all written in plain English, approved, and updated by our in-house legal editors.

 Legal Articles
Get informed with thousands of free articles on everyday legal topics. Our articles are accurate, up to date, and reader friendly.

 Find a Lawyer
Want to talk to a lawyer? Use Nolo to find a lawyer who can help you with your case.

8th Edition

Getting Permission

Using & Licensing Copyright-Protected Materials Online & Off

Attorney Richard Stim

EIGHTH EDITION	OCTOBER 2022
Design and Production	SUSAN PUTNEY
Proofreading	IRENE BARNARD
Index	RICHARD GENOVA
Printing	SHERIDAN

Names: Stim, Richard, author.
Title: Getting permission : using & licensing copyright-protected materials
  online & off / Attorney Richard Stim.
Description: 8th edition. | El Segundo : Nolo, 2022. | Includes index.
Identifiers: LCCN 2022019338 | ISBN 9781413330076 (paperback) | ISBN
  9781413330083 (ebook)
Subjects: LCSH: Copyright licenses--United States--Popular works. |
  Trademark licenses--United States--Popular works.
Classification: LCC KF3002 .S75 2022 | DDC 346.7304/82--dc23/eng/20220714
LC record available at https://lccn.loc.gov/2022019338

This book covers only United States law, unless it specifically states otherwise.

Please note

Accurate, plain-English legal information can help you solve many of your own legal problems. But this text is not a substitute for personalized advice from a knowledgeable lawyer. If you want the help of a trained professional—and we'll always point out situations in which we think that's a good idea—consult an attorney licensed to practice in your state.

Acknowledgments

Thanks to all the Dear Rich blog readers who have provided helpful advice.

About the Author

Richard Stim is an attorney and the author of several Nolo books, including *Music Law: How to Run Your Band's Business, Patent Pending in 24 Hours,* and *Patent, Copyright & Trademark: An Intellectual Property Desk Reference.* He is also the author of the Dear Rich blog (www.dearrichblog.com).

Table of Contents

Your Legal Companion

From the Indies to the Andes, what a mission
Stopping only now and then to do some fishing
And he went without a copyright permission
What a very daring thing to do.

> "From the Indies to the Andes in His Undies"
> by Lawrence Royal, Ernie Burnett, and William E. Faber
> © Rialto Music Publishing.

These whimsical song lyrics, written more than 80 years ago, express a basic truth about copyright law: Using someone's creative work without permission can be a very daring move. An unhappy copyright owner may sue you for monetary damages, prevent you from publishing your work, or both. On the other hand, by simply obtaining permission, you gain lawsuit-free access to the work you need.

But how do you obtain permission? It often seems as if the task of acquiring rights is too tricky, troublesome, or time-consuming. And in some cases, the hassle of the permission process may outweigh any benefits of legal security. But for most permission situations, the task can be quite simple and direct, and—surprise, surprise—you may learn that permission is not even required.

This book will reduce your risks by guiding you through the permissions process and explaining how to obtain the appropriate rights when using other people's creative work. Information is provided about locating copyright owners, asking for permission, assessing the conditions of the permission agreement, and avoiding potential disputes.

The information in this book deals with the three basic questions in the permissions process:

- Is permission necessary?
- What type of work do you want to use?
- How do you plan to use the work?

Depending on which question you're concerned with, you may need to review different chapters of this book as outlined below. For example, the following chapters discuss how to evaluate whether permission is necessary.

- Academic permissions. Chapter 7 explains when permission is not required for academic and library uses.
- The public domain. Chapter 8 deals with materials that are not protected by copyright law and fall into what's called the "public domain."
- Fair use. Chapter 9 provides information about "fair use," the copyright principle that enables limited uses of materials without permission.
- Releases. Chapter 12 discusses when permission is needed to use a real person's image.
- Copyright research. Chapter 13 explains how to research whether copyright protection exists, and, if so, who owns the copyright.
- Acquiring ownership. Chapter 15 provides information on acquiring ownership of copyrighted material, not merely getting permission to use it.

There are a variety of materials for which you may seek permission—text, photographs, artwork, music, trademarks, characters, and images of real people. The type of material you wish to use affects the type of permission you need, the fee you must pay, and your permissions process. For example, the rules for permission are different for using trademarks than for using copyrighted material. If you know what type of material you wish to use, you can proceed directly to the relevant chapter:

- Chapter 2 discusses using text.
- Chapter 3 discusses using photographs.
- Chapter 4 is about using fine art, graphic art, stock art, and cartoons.
- Chapter 5 is devoted to using music and song lyrics.
- Chapter 10 helps if you are using trademarks and trademarked characters (for example, Mickey Mouse).
- Chapter 12 deals with using an image of a real person, including in news articles and ads or promotional materials.

The medium in which you use the material and the rights that you need for that use also affect the permissions process. The rights you obtain may create certain limitations, including how long you may use the material, where you may distribute your project, and whether you have exclusive use of the material. The following chapters discuss the rules for specific uses:

- Chapter 6 describes some special rules for use of materials online.
- Chapter 7 explains unique rules for academic permissions.
- Chapter 11 discusses rules for using copyrighted works on merchandise.

As you can see, we've already done much of the groundwork for you. Using this book—and the *Getting Permission* companion page online at www.nolo.com (see the appendix for the exact link) which contains many useful permission agreements—should enable you to accomplish most permissions tasks easily and with the knowledge that you have protected yourself and your company.

The Dear Rich Blog

Dear Rich: An Intellectual Property Blog (www.dearrichblog.com) operates as an online companion to this book. The Dear Rich blog provides answers to common questions regarding permissions, copyright, trademark, and related areas of law. Many Dear Rich questions are included in this book.

Introduction to the Permissions Process

This chapter offers an overview of the whole process, explaining the purpose and legal basis for permission, as well as the potential risks of operating without permission. It also serves as a guide to using this book.

Permission: What Is It and Why Do I Need It?

Obtaining copyright permission is the process of getting consent from a copyright owner to use the owner's creative material. Obtaining permission is often called "licensing"; when you have permission, you have a license to use the work. Permission is often (but not always) required because of intellectual property laws that protect creative works, such as text, artwork, or music. (These laws are explained in more detail in the next section.) If you use a copyrighted work without the appropriate permission, you may be violating—or "infringing"—the owner's rights to that work. Infringing someone else's copyright may subject you to legal action. As if going to court weren't bad enough, you could be forced to stop using the work or pay money damages to the copyright owner.

As noted above, permission is not always required. In some situations, you can reproduce a photograph, a song, or text without a license. Generally, this will be true if the work has fallen into the public domain, or if your use qualifies as what's called a "fair use." Both of these legal concepts involve quite specific rules and are discussed more fully in subsequent chapters.

In most cases, however, permission is required, so never assume it's okay to use a work without permission.

Many people operate illegally, either intentionally or through ignorance, when it comes to the use scenario. They use other people's work and never seek consent. This may work well for those who fly under the radar— that is, if copyright owners never learn of the use, or don't care enough to take action. The problem with this approach—besides its questionable ethics—is that the more successful the project becomes, the more likely a copyright owner will learn of the use. So, if you want your project to become successful, unauthorized use becomes an obstacle.

Some people avoid getting permission because they don't understand the permissions process, or they consider it too expensive. But the process is not difficult, and the fee for use of text, photo, or artwork is often under $200 per use. In some cases, it's free. On the other hand, the legal fees for dealing with an unauthorized use lawsuit can easily cost ten to 50 times the average permission expense—or more!

The Basics of Getting Permission

This section outlines the basic steps for obtaining permission. Subsequent chapters provide more detailed information about the process for each type of permission you may be seeking, whether for text, photographs, music, or artwork.

In general, the permissions process involves a simple five-step procedure:

1. Figure out if permission is needed.
2. Identify the owner.
3. Identify the rights needed.
4. Contact the owner and negotiate whether payment is required.
5. Get your permission agreement in writing.

Each step is described in more detail below.

Figure Out If Permission Is Needed

The first step in every permission situation is to determine whether you need to ask for permission. In other words, do you need an agreement or can you use the work without permission? Figuring out whether to ask for permission depends on the answers to two questions:

- Is the material protected under the law?
- Would your use of the material violate the law?

Unfortunately, it is not always possible to answer these questions with a definitive "yes" or "no." Sometimes, you may have to analyze the risk involved in operating without permission. Below are some basic legal principles you'll need to know. Later chapters explore these principles in more depth.

Is the Material Protected Under Intellectual Property Law?

You should always start with the presumption that, if the creative work you want to use was first published after 1923, U.S. copyright law protects it. There are only two ways that a work published after 1923 is not protected: Either the owner of the work made a mistake (such as failing to renew the copyright) or the work does not meet the minimum standards for copyright protection. Later chapters on the permission rules for particular types of creative works provide guidelines to determine if the work you intend to use is protected.

A work that isn't protected by intellectual property laws is in the public domain and can be used without asking for permission. Most works that fall into the public domain do so because of old age, but public domain status can also result from other factors discussed in Chapter 8.

> EXAMPLE: Bill wants to include his recording of the song "Give My Regards to Broadway" on his website. Because the song was first published in 1904, it is in the public domain and Bill can use it without obtaining permission.

Would Your Use of the Material Constitute a Violation of Law?

If a creative work is protected under intellectual property laws, your unauthorized use may still be legal. This is because there are exceptions to each of the laws protecting creative work—situations in which authorization is not required. For example, under copyright law, a principle known as "fair use" permits you to copy small portions of a work for certain purposes, including scholarship or commentary. Under the fair use doctrine, you could reproduce a few lines of a song lyric in a music review without getting permission from the songwriter (or whoever owns the copyright in the song). Chapter 9 discusses fair use in greater depth.

What Is the Risk of Not Asking for Permission?

The goal of this book is to minimize your risk of being sued. This risk hinges not only on your particular use, but on factors such as the likelihood that the use will be spotted, whether you are a "worthy" target for litigation, or whether the other side is inclined to sue.

This book recommends a conservative approach. Unless you are certain that the material is in the public domain or that your use is legally excusable, seeking permission is worth your time. If you are not sure, you'll have to either make your own risk assessment or obtain the advice of an attorney knowledgeable in copyright or media law.

> EXAMPLE: I wanted to use the lyrics from the song "From the Indies to the Andes in His Undies," featured in the "Your Legal Companion" section at the front of this book. I located information about the writers of the song from a compilation recording of country music. Then, I located the name of the publisher (Rialto Music, Inc.) from the American Society of Composers, Authors, and Publishers (ASCAP), which informed me that the owner had ended its affiliation with the organization in 1975. I searched online to no avail for the songwriters, and for Rialto Music. I also checked the online Library of Congress records but found no reference, either because the song was never registered or the song was written before the date their online computer records began. I contacted the Harry Fox Agency, another agency that controls rights, which gave me a reference for Rialto in Providence, Rhode Island. I tried using operator assistance but could find no listing. I decided to proceed without permission because my limited use of the lyrics (four lines) for purposes of commentary, combined with my good-faith attempt to find the owner, probably qualifies as a fair use.

Dear Rich: Plagiarism or Infringement

I am a romance novelist and occasionally I borrow material from other books for my historical romances. I'm confused about the difference between plagiarism and infringement.

A plagiarist is a person who poses as the originator of words he did not write, ideas he did not conceive, or facts he did not discover. "Plagiarism" is not a legal term; it's an ethical term. You can plagiarize someone without infringing. For example, if a plagiarist only copies public domain materials, he can't be sued for copyright infringement. And you can infringe without plagiarizing. For example, this whole answer is pretty much lifted from Stephen Fishman's Nolo book, *The Public Domain*. (See ... I've provided attribution; let's hope he doesn't sue— :-).) Which is worse? A whiff of plagiarism can damage a romance novelist's reputation, while infringement means dealing with lawyers and hefty judgments.

Identify the Owner

Identifying the owner of the work you want to use is crucial to obtaining permission. Sometimes, this task is simple. Often, you may be able to locate the rights owner just by looking at the copyright notice on the work. For example, if the notice reads "Copyright 1998, Jones Publishing," you would start by finding the Jones Publishing company. Sometimes, more detailed research is required. Copyright ownership may have passed through several hands since your copy of the work was published.

In addition, some kinds of art, such as film and recorded music, can involve multiple owners, each with a separate right to different underlying works. For example, in order to use a Johnny Cash recording, you would have to obtain permission from the record company, the music publisher (the owner of the song), and, in some cases, from Mr. Cash's estate.

You'll find that the method of identifying owners differs from industry to industry. For example, photographic reproduction rights are often owned by stock photo organizations, while many music performance rights are owned by performing rights societies. Later chapters on the permission rules for particular types of creative works will include tips on locating owners. And in Chapter 13 we'll explain how to search for owners in Copyright Office records.

Identify the Rights You Need

The next step in getting permission is to identify the rights you need. Each copyright owner controls a bundle of rights related to the work, including the right to reproduce, distribute, and modify the work. Because so many rights are associated with copyrighted works, you must specify the rights you need. This can be as simple as stating your intended use—for example, you want to reproduce a photograph in your magazine or display a cartoon in your PowerPoint presentation.

Asking for the proper rights can be a balancing act. You don't want to pay for more than you need, but you don't want to have to return for a second round of permissions. Sometimes this requires negotiating with the rights owner to find a middle ground for fees.

Besides identifying the type of intended use, you'll need to figure out a few key details concerning your use of the material. Specifically, your permissions agreement will need to address three common variables: exclusivity, term, and territory.

Exclusive or Nonexclusive

All permission agreements are either exclusive or nonexclusive. A permission agreement is exclusive if you are the only person who has the right to use the work as described in the agreement. For example, if you enter into an agreement with the owner of a photograph for the exclusive use of the photograph in a cookbook, no one else could use the photograph in another cookbook. Exclusivity can be as narrow or as broad as you choose. For example, you could expand the exclusivity of your permission agreement by obtaining the exclusive right to print the photo in any book, not just any cookbook.

Most permission requests are nonexclusive, meaning others can use the material in the same way as you. For example, if you have a nonexclusive agreement to use a photo in your cookbook, the same photo could be used in someone else's cookbook (provided permission was granted). The permission agreements included throughout this book offer you the option to choose exclusive or nonexclusive rights.

Term of Use

The length of time for which you are allowed to use a work is often referred to as the "term." Your rights under a permission agreement will often be limited in duration. For example, if you are licensing the right to display a photograph on a website, the copyright owner may limit the length of your use to one year. Or you might obtain what's called a "one-time use," meaning you can only use the material in one edition of a magazine, not in subsequent editions. If there is no express limitation on the use, you are allowed to use the material for as long as you want or until the copyright owner revokes the permission. Some agreements prohibit the copyright owner from putting an end to use rights by stating that permission is granted "irrevocably." Sometimes an agreement states that it is "in perpetuity," which means that rights are granted without time limits. In reality, the copyright owner can only grant permission for as long as the owner's copyright protection lasts. After that, anyone can use the material without permission.

Territory

Your rights under a permission agreement may be limited to a geographic region, referred to as the "territory." For example, the copyright owner of a book might grant you permission to reprint a chapter only in the United States and Canada.

Plan Ahead for Permission

Expect getting permission to take anywhere from one to three months. Permission should be obtained before you complete your work. It is sometimes more difficult and more expensive to obtain permission after a book, film, or recording is complete. If the copyright owner becomes aware that you have a vested interest in obtaining permission (for example, your book is already in production), the price may rise. In addition, if you can't obtain permission, you'll have to redo the work, which can be expensive and time consuming. The best policy is to start seeking all required permissions as soon as possible.

Negotiate Whether Payment Is Required

The primary issue that arises when seeking permission is whether you will have to pay for it. Sometimes, the owner of the work will not require payment if the amount of the work you wish to use is small, or if the owner wishes to contribute to an educational or nonprofit effort. In some cases, an artist or musician eager for exposure may agree to suspend payment unless the work becomes profitable, or may condition payment on other factors.

> **EXAMPLE:** Sam is making a low-budget documentary film in which he wants to include photographs of vintage accordions. He contacts the copyright owner of the photographs who, in return for a credit at the end of the film, signs an agreement allowing use of the photographs in the film. However, the agreement also provides that, if Sam uses the photographs in a poster or an advertisement for the film, he must make an additional one-time payment of $1,500.

Although many uses of works may be free, you should usually expect to pay something—even a minimal fee—for copyright permission. For example, the evolving world of stock photos has made it possible to get some photo permissions for around $5. Or it could be a fairly hefty payment. For example, using a song in a commercial usually requires a payment of several thousand dollars.

What If You Hire Someone to Create a Work?

Most of the situations described in this book deal with obtaining permission to use an existing work. But it's possible to hire an artist or other creative person to create the work for you. If the creative person qualifies as your employee, you will automatically own all rights to the work they create on your behalf, and no permission is required. The Supreme Court has established standards for determining whether a creative person is an employee. These standards include factors such as whether the person is given weekly or monthly payments (instead of being paid by the job), whether you withhold employee taxes for the person, and whether they receive employee benefits.

If the person creating the work is not an employee, they are an independent contractor. In this event, your ownership of the person's work is not automatic. To guarantee your ownership of an independent contractor's work, you should use either a work-for-hire agreement (if your commission meets the requirements) or an assignment. Chapter 15 covers these agreements. For a thorough analysis of acquiring rights from independent contractors, see *The Copyright Handbook*, by Stephen Fishman (Nolo).

Generally, permission fees are linked to the size of the audience your work will reach. For example the fees for online uses may depend upon the number of visitors to a website or other data. In each chapter, we will discuss the likelihood of payment and the current rates for common uses. However, these figures can vary widely, as the copyright owner has discretion when charging a fee.

Cashing "Payment in Full" Check

I'm having a dispute with a company for which I granted permission to use an image. The contract says that they owe me $350. They claim I didn't do the photos the way they wanted. Then, they sent me a check for $250 that says "Payment in full for photo rights." Is it true that if I crossed out the "payment in full" and wrote "under protest," I could deposit the check and still go after the other $100?

Court rulings are not always consistent on this, but the majority of courts say that if there is a dispute as to what is owed, and the party receiving the check knows that it's intended as "payment in full," depositing the check ends the dispute (known as "accord and satisfaction"). The rule doesn't apply if there is no dispute (in which case the "payment in full" is meaningless) or if the dispute is not "honest"—for example, one party deceives the other, making it difficult to figure out what's owed. Finally, if there is a dispute but the check is cashed inadvertently, the rule might not apply (courts are split on that issue). If you have deposited the check and wish that you hadn't, most state statutes give you 90 days to repay the check and get back into the dispute. Check your state's Uniform Commercial Code (UCC Section 3-311).

Get It in Writing

Relying on an oral agreement or understanding is almost always a mistake. You and the rights owner may have misunderstood each other or remembered the terms of your agreement differently. This can lead to disputes. If you have to go to court to enforce your unwritten agreement, you'll have difficulty proving exactly what the terms are. Get written permission agreements—do not rely on oral agreements.

That said, an oral permission may be legally enforceable if it qualifies as a binding agreement under general contract law principles. And even if you have no explicit oral agreement, you may still have a right to use a work if permission can be inferred from the conduct of the parties.

> **EXAMPLE:** Sam is writing a book and asks for permission to reproduce Tom's photo. Tom quotes Sam a fee of $100, which Sam sends to Tom. After receiving the payment, Tom sends the photograph to Sam. Although they never put an agreement into writing, a permission agreement may be inferred from Tom's conduct.

Overview of Intellectual Property Laws

A wide body of federal and state laws protects creative property such as writing, music, drawings, paintings, photography, and films. Collectively, this body of law is called "intellectual property" law, which includes copyright, trademark, and patent laws, each applicable in various situations and each with its own set of technical rules. When obtaining permission to use creative works, you're concerned primarily with copyright law. However, trademarks, trade secrets, and publicity and privacy rights sometimes come into play when permission to use certain types of works is sought. Below is a summary of the various types of intellectual property laws that are relevant to the permissions process (later chapters provide more details as needed):

- **Copyright.** Federal copyright law protects original creative works such as paintings, writing, architecture, movies, software, photos, dance, and music. A work must meet certain minimum requirements to qualify for copyright protection The length of protection also varies depending on when the work was created or first published. (See Chapter 8 for an explanation of copyright duration.)

- **Trademark.** Brand names such as Nike and Apple, as well as logos, slogans, and other devices that identify and distinguish products and services, are protected under federal and state trademark laws. Unlike copyrighted works, trademarks receive different degrees of protection depending on key variables, including consumer awareness of the trademark, the type of service and product it identifies, and the geographic area in which the trademark is used. (See Chapter 10.)

- **Right of Publicity.** A patchwork of state laws known as the "right of publicity" protect against the unauthorized use of a person's name or image for commercial purposes—for example, the use of your picture on a box of cereal. The extent of this protection varies from state to state. (See Chapter 12.)

- **Trade Secrets.** State and federal trade secret laws protect sensitive business information. An example of a trade secret would be a confidential marketing plan for the introduction of a new software product or the secret recipe for a brand of salsa. The extent of trade secret protection depends on whether the information gives the business an advantage over competitors, is kept a secret, and is not known by competitors. (See Chapter 10.)

- **Right of Privacy.** Although not part of intellectual property laws, state privacy laws preserve the right of all people to be left alone. Invasion of privacy occurs when someone publishes or publicly exploits information about another person's private affairs. Invasion of privacy laws prevent you from intruding on, exposing private facts about, or falsely portraying someone. The extent of this protection may vary if the subject is a public figure—for example, a celebrity or politician. (See Chapter 12.)

Permission Tools: Licenses and Releases

Obtaining permission to use a protected work requires entering into an agreement with the owner of that work. Your agreement may give you the right to use the work (a "license") or it may be a promise that the owner will not sue you for an unauthorized use (a "release").

Licenses and Clearances

A license is the legal right to do something that you would not otherwise be permitted to do. For example, you need a driver's license to give you the right to drive a car. The owner of a copyrighted work can authorize someone else to use the work by granting a license to the user. For example, the owner of a photograph copyright can grant a license to someone else who wants to reproduce the photograph on greeting cards. If no license has been given, the copyright owner can sue for the unauthorized use of the work, referred to as "infringement."

The terms "license" and "permission agreement" are often used interchangeably. You may also find that, in some situations, a license or permission agreement is referred to as a "clearance agreement." "Clearance" is a general term used to describe the process by which permission is granted.

> EXAMPLE: Don is writing a book on British horror films and wants to reproduce an image from a 1950s film. Don must obtain a license to reproduce the image from the owner of rights in the film.

Releases

A release is an agreement in which someone releases you from legal liability for a particular activity. In essence, the person is agreeing ahead of time to give up (or release) any right to sue you that may arise from a specific situation. Releases are often used to avoid lawsuits involving someone's right of privacy (the right to be left alone) or right of publicity (the right to control how one's image, voice, or persona will be used to sell things). A release may also protect against claims of defamation (a false statement that injures someone's reputation). Releases are discussed in more detail in Chapter 12.

> EXAMPLE: *Makeover* is a TV show in which audience members are selected for beauty and fashion makeovers. Any audience member selected must sign a release before appearing on the show. The release protects the TV show from any potential lawsuits by disgruntled participants who are unhappy with the results of their makeovers and seek damages for legal claims such as infliction of emotional distress or defamation.

CAUTION

Don't rely on the title of an agreement. In many cases, licenses and releases overlap. For example, a release agreement may contain license language and vice versa. Despite what it says at the top of the agreement, either type of contract can be used to grant rights or to prevent lawsuits. Because of this overlap, the title of an agreement is less important than the content. Always review any agreement carefully (and compare it to the model agreements in this book) before assuming what rights it covers.

2

Getting Permission to Use Text

This chapter covers how to get permission to use text—whether it's found online or in print (including books, magazines, newspapers, newsletters, and journals). We'll help you identify the company or person who owns the rights to the text (the "rights holder") and offer suggestions for making your permissions request. We'll also discuss special situations that can crop up when using text from interviews, speeches, or print publications. At the end of the chapter, you'll find two sample text permission agreements: a short-form agreement and a longer, more detailed agreement.

This chapter does not cover permission to use song lyrics or literary characters, or to create academic coursepacks. Here's where to skip ahead for information on these materials:

- For song lyrics, refer to Chapter 5.
- For literary characters, refer to Chapter 10.
- For academic coursepacks, refer to Chapter 7.

Experiences of a First-Time Permissions Editor

For an introduction to the permissions process, you might find it helpful to read the following Q&A with Marcia Stewart, the co-editor of an anthology, *Sisters! Bonded by Love and Laughter.* The book, published by the Erma Bombeck Writers' Workshop in 2021, includes poems, letters, Q&A's, original essays, interviews, blog posts, magazine and newspaper articles, book and website excerpts, lyrics, lists, and quotes. In all, the book contains more than 100 individual works for which permission decisions had to be made.

Did you have any experience with permissions before working on this book?

Not really. I had a vague idea that I could use photos or quotes I found on the Internet for personal use. I also felt it was okay to cite a section from a book or magazine article, as long as I attributed the source. I didn't understand what the public domain or fair use meant. Basically, I was pretty clueless.

I worked closely with the Erma Bombeck Writers' Workshop, a program of the University of Dayton. We were self-publishing the book, and did not have the legal staff of a traditional publisher to advise on permissions and licensing issues.

Experiences of a First-Time Permissions Editor (continued)

Was there any particular aspect of the permission process that surprised you?

There were many surprises, including:

- How difficult it sometimes was to find the right person responsible for granting permission for material I wanted to reprint. In a few cases, I wanted to license a funny piece written by a freelance writer; I found the freelancer, but then they were unable to get approval from the copyright owner. Tracking down the licensing department for magazine articles was especially challenging (sometimes impossible) because several magazines have gone out of business or have been purchased by a large corporation. Happily, with some persistence, I was able to find and secure permissions for the majority of material I wanted to include in *Sisters!*

- How long it took (typically six to 12 weeks) to get permission, from a magazine, book, or music publisher, especially because a few publishers needed to contact the author for permission to grant reprint rights.

- How little relevant material I could find in the public domain. The only piece I used that was in the public domain was a poem by Emily Dickinson.

- How much information publishers typically required before quoting a price or granting reprint permission. This included the book's number of pages and word count; estimated unit sales by format (paperback, ebook, audiobook); pub date; where exactly the reprinted material would be used in the book (what was going before and after the piece); and where (in what territory) we planned to distribute *Sisters!* Since we were self-publishing the book and doing it print on demand (POD), I didn't have advance sales figures and couldn't quote an estimated print run, like a traditional publisher would. And we were holding off setting a cover price until we had a better sense of how long the book was going to be and how much we would have to spend on content for the book. So, I had to do ballpark estimates for much of the info requested by licensing departments.

- How much easier it was to hire an artist to draw celebrities, rather than license celebrity photos. I originally wanted to include photos of sisters from popular TV shows and movies, or of celebrity sisters, such as Beyoncé and Solange, but I didn't like what was available in the public domain or stock photos. The prices for photos I did want were way too high. Fortunately, I hired a great book designer who did original illustrations for the book, which I was really happy with.

Experiences of a First-Time Permissions Editor (continued)

- How much publisher contracts varied in terms of the fee charged for a reprint; the territory where the book could be distributed (such as U.S. only); the limit on sales (i.e. 3,000 print or 1,000 ebooks) for using the reprinted material; prohibitions against using the author's name for promotional purposes; and the term of the agreement (usually from one to five years) before renewal would be required.

Did you start with a budget?

I was pretty confident I could get a lot of material free (see the next question), and I set a ballpark figure of $500 for reprints. I naively (and incorrectly) assumed that I would be able to get reprint rights for little or no money, because I was doing *Sisters!* with a nonprofit (the Erma Bombeck Writers' Workshop with the University of Dayton). I was primarily contacting large publishers for this anthology, and only asking for relatively little content (such as a page of text from an Amy Schumer book), and there was no negotiation on fees.

One of the reasons I didn't have a set budget for reprints was I wasn't sure how much I would need. When I started planning *Sisters!*, I primarily planned to include only original content, including essays from winners of Nickie's Prize for Humor Writing, a writing competition I cosponsored with the Erma Bombeck Writers' Workshop; pieces from and interviews with well-known writers and humorists; and material I wrote myself. I didn't consider getting reprinted material, until it was clear I needed another 30 or 40 pages for the book to be the length I wanted (about 250 pages), and to include diverse pieces for each of the book's main themes, such as the sisterly pecking order in older-younger sister relationships.

Were any rights holders willing to grant permission without requiring a fee?

Happily, I did not need to pay for the majority of the content in *Sisters!* This included the 21 winners of Nickie's Prize for Humor Writing; original essays contributed by well-known writers and humorists, such as Laraine Newman and Peggy Rowe; interviews that my co-editor, Teri Rizvi, and I did with sister experts, such as Carol Saline, and comedians, such as Wendy Liebman; and reprints from online blogs or websites, including Gretchen Rubin's and Jenny Lawson's.

I only needed to pay for a few excerpts, including a poem by Billy Collins and one page from a memoir by Amy Schumer; celebrity sister Q&As from *Vanity Fair*; and lyrics, such as to Carly Simon's song, "Older Sister." I exceeded my estimated $500 budget for reprints, but it was really worth it.

You dealt with many book publishers like Simon & Schuster and Random House. Any tips you can provide about obtaining these types of permissions?

My main advice is to think carefully about what content your book needs, how you plan to use it, and whether the costs and restrictions are worth it in terms of marketing and selling your book. For example, the market for *Sisters!* is limited to the U.S., because of restrictions by a few large publishers to this territory. Even though the U.S. is the book's major market, *Sisters!* would appeal to people outside this country, but we can't sell it elsewhere. And if something is too pricey for your budget, consider alternatives, especially if the item won't enhance the sales potential of your book.

And based on my answers to your second question, be sure to know all relevant details—such as estimated length and cover price of your book—before seeking permissions, because you're going to need this information. You won't be getting permission overnight, so build in at least six to eight weeks in your planning process.

If there is some content you really want, be persistent. Don't give up if you can't find the right licensing person or group. Just don't expect any special deals or personal concessions based on your book or material. While the person responsible for licensing content at one publisher might love your idea (as was the case with *Sisters!*), this doesn't necessarily mean you'll get a special deal (at least I didn't).

Be organized, because you'll need to make sure you comply with many contract terms, such as how you credit a particular piece, and when it'll be time to renew the contract (and pay an additional fee).

Finally, ask a lawyer if you have any questions. Fortunately, I had a good lawyer to turn to with issues big and small, on everything from legal agreements with the book's illustrator and contributors to specific permissions questions. I recommend that all authors—especially those self-publishing and doing any kind of anthology such as *Sisters!*, or planning to use a lot of others' content or design material—line up an intellectual property lawyer from the start.

Experiences of a First-Time Permissions Editor (continued)

You have several pieces from *Vanity Fair*. What was it like seeking permission from Condé Nast?

Unlike some other big magazine publishers, it was pretty easy to find the licensing department at Condé Nast, and the terms and information they requested (brief description of *Sisters!* and the estimated print run) were reasonable. And their staff were very friendly and helpful. I was thrilled with the reprints I was able to get for *Sisters!* including Q&As with famous sisters, such as Stella and Mary McCartney, from a special issue of the magazine on sisters.

Was it a challenge to track down lyric permissions?

Yes! It was harder to do this than find the licensing departments for book publishers. I hit a lot of dead ends, but ultimately I found the music publisher (Hal Leonard being the main one) authorized to give permission to reprint lyrics I wanted from songs, such as "My Sister." In a few cases, I was unable to track down the responsible copyright holder for lyrics I wanted to include, so I didn't use them.

The book includes many original pieces. Did you negotiate an arrangement with each author?

Yes, but it was pretty easy, because of the book's association with the Erma Bombeck Writers' Workshop. Most of the well-known contributors were familiar with and fans of the workshop, having been faculty members in previous years, so they were happy to contribute an essay or do an interview at no fee. The subject of the book (funny stories about sisters) appealed to the contributors, all of whom had good relationships with their sisters and were delighted to write about them. Many were moved that I was doing the book to honor my deceased sister. A key selling point was that proceeds from book sales of *Sisters!* were going to the workshop's endowment fund, which is used to keep the workshop affordable for writers. Teri Rizvi, the Director of the Erma Bombeck Writers' Workshop, and my co-editor on *Sisters!*, had personal relationships with many of the authors, and was clear from the start that the book was a labor of love and would be benefiting the workshop.

The essays from Nickie's Prize for Humor Writing were a focal point of *Sisters!*. The 21 winners each received $300 for their essay, and agreed to include their piece in a book, understanding there would be no additional payment or royalties.

Experiences of a First-Time Permissions Editor (continued)

In all cases, contributors to *Sisters!* signed an "Agreement to Reproduce Work in *Sisters!*" form that my lawyer drafted, which clarified the terms, including the fact that the contributors would retain copyright, and they'd agree to let the workshop use their name or image to promote *Sisters!* On the other hand, as mentioned above, many of the publishers of reprinted material explicitly prohibited use of the reprinted material for promotional purposes.

How did you keep track of all the permissions? Did you create a spreadsheet?
I followed this book's advice to always seek permission and to get all attempts (whether successful or not) in writing. I dealt with dozens of individuals and organizations, so being organized was crucial. I kept paper and electronic copies of all notes and agreements. I also found the "Permissions Tracking Sheet" included in this book useful. It helped to have everything in one place in terms of contract details, such as the specific rights granted and the term of the agreement.

If you were doing it all over again, what would you do differently?
I would definitely allow more time to plan *Sisters!* and identify early on the table of contents and design, estimated market, and the like. If we had not been self-publishing the book, we would have done this kind of advance planning before submitting a proposal to a traditional book publisher. Doing an anthology like *Sisters!*, we weren't exactly sure what we needed (in terms of content and illustrations) or what was available and at what cost. Mainly we had a hard deadline for publication, but could have used more time to develop the book and get even more content. I am especially fortunate that so many writers were willing to contribute material at no charge, and under a tight deadline. Also, that I chose a book designer/illustrator who was not only creative, but really easy to work with and willing to try many different designs, again under tight deadline. If I had more time to solicit original materials from outside writers, or write myself, I wouldn't have needed as many reprints. It will definitely be easier next time!

Who Owns the Text?

The first step to obtain permission is to make sure you're asking the correct entity. The owner of the text may be the company that published it, the author of the text, or no one at all. Who owns the text depends on how the rights were negotiated between publisher and author. The law and industry traditions can also factor in.

CAUTION
Before seeking out the copyright owner, confirm whether permission is necessary. No permission is required if the text you want to use is in what's known as the "public domain." Also, many uses of text are permitted without permission under a principle of copyright law known as "fair use." The public domain is discussed in Chapter 8, and fair use is covered in Chapter 9.

Shifting Ownership of Articles

Before the 1980s, the author of an article was usually the primary rights holder. At that time, periodicals traditionally only asked for first "North American serial rights"—the right to publish the article once in the United States and Canada. However, in the past four-plus decades, content providers (online publications, magazines, journals, and other periodicals) have increasingly obtained reprint, syndication, and other primary rights from authors. Therefore, when multiple publishers have published an article in the last 40–45 years, your starting point for permission will be the original publisher of the article. For older articles, your best bet is to start by contacting the author.

Shifting Ownership of Electronic Database Reprints

The rules for ownership of electronic rights to written works changed dramatically in June 2001. That's when the U.S. Supreme Court decided that freelance writers must be compensated when their works are placed online or in electronic databases, such as LexisNexis. The Court, in the case of *The New York Times v. Tasini*, 533 U.S. 483 (2001), found that *The Times* and other publishers committed copyright infringement when they resold freelance newspaper and magazine articles through electronic databases without asking permission or making additional payments to the freelancers. The ruling applies to any freelancer who sold an article without expressly transferring the electronic rights to the publisher.

If you are seeking electronic rights to an article written by a freelancer before 1995, chances are good that the freelancer has retained the electronic rights, and you should start by contacting the freelancer. After 1995, publishers routinely obtained electronic rights from freelance authors, and you're best off contacting the publisher first.

Dear Rich:

Who Owns a Tweet?

What are the legalities regarding tweets inserted in a biography that I am writing?

Copying individual text tweets is unlikely to trigger a lawsuit. That's because reproducing an individual tweet is likely to qualify as fair use, or because the tweeter may have difficulty demonstrating sufficient originality and creativity to qualify for copyright protection (a difficult task when considering the brevity of tweets). Retweeting is also not going to cause a problem as that type of reproduction is permitted under Twitter's license. However, you might run into problems with your biography if you reproduced Twitter threads—tweets that are joined together to make longer statements—or if you collected a group of tweets by one person. These collections may constitute protectable works. There is no quantitative measurement as to what constitutes infringement (or fair use) so when in doubt, seek permission or legal advice.

Copyright Clearance Center (CCC) Permission Services

The Copyright Clearance Center (CCC) (www.copyright.com), has simplified the process of obtaining text permissions. If the work is part of the service's online database, you can usually obtain permission within one or two days (sometimes immediately).

The CCC represents over 10,000 print publishers, including *The New York Times* and *The Wall Street Journal*. Acting as the agent and broker for publishers and authors, CCC allows you to pick and click your way through millions of works, including books and journal and magazine articles.

Publishers set the fees with CCC—for example, a national newspaper, via CCC, may charge $400 to reprint an article in a book and $600 to reprint an article in a national magazine. These prices are similar to those for permissions granted without the use of an online service—but if you wish to comparison shop, you can contact the copyright owner directly following the suggestions below.

The CCC's online procedure is often far easier than the traditional system of locating and calling a publisher, negotiating permission, and signing a written agreement. If a service does not represent a publisher—that is, the publisher's works are not designated in the database—you can still use the service to inquire about the use of works on your behalf.

You can obtain permission for the following activities:

- **Photocopying.** This includes photocopy permissions for newspaper and magazine articles, books, journals, research reports, or other published documents.
- **Email.** CCC grants rights to email an online article or PDF.
- **Electronic uses.** CCC allows you to post digital content on your corporate website, intranet, and extranet.
- **Printouts.** CCC facilitates your ability to print out Web-based and other digital content onto paper and overhead slides.
- **Republication.** CCC permits you to republish content in a newsletter, book, or journal.
- **Digital rights.** CCC grants rights to scan printed material into digital form when an electronic version is not readily available.

To use the CCC's service, visit the website and create an account (most likely you'll want a pay-per-go account and not an annual subscription). Complete the registration, and you will be directed how to start using your pay-per-use account. There's a helpful online search page in which you can choose the type of permission wanted, and search for the publication by title, publisher, ISBN, author, or editor. When you find the material you're seeking, CCC will provide you with the terms for licensing or, if necessary,

CCC may provide you with a direct contact to the rights holder to negotiate terms. The latter functionality is triggered when CCC handles some, but not all rights for a certain publisher. In other cases, CCC may contact the rights holder for you and get back to you in a few days with a quote. Much of CCC's permission process is channeled through the CCC service, Rightslink (www.copyright.com/publishers/rightslink-permissions).

If you're having trouble at any point in the CCC's process, FAQs and a useful demo on the site can help you. (The CCC's primary competitor, iCopyright.com, folded in 2018.)

And Don't Forget About the Creative Commons ...

Creative Commons, a nonprofit organization, is designed to support the free exchange of copyrighted materials, that is, to eliminate permissions for many uses. If you see text (or artwork) marked with the Creative Commons logo (two "c's" in a circle) then the material is subject to a Creative Commons license, which often means that most forms of reproduction are free, provided you abide by the license requirements. We discuss the Creative Commons more in Chapter 8.

Locate the Publisher

If you cannot obtain permission through the Copyright Clearance Center, or if you think you'll get a better rate for permission by negotiating directly with the copyright owner, you'll need to search the old-fashioned way. The first step is to locate the publisher—the company that produced and distributed the work. For example, Nolo is the publisher of the book you're reading now. In the case of a quote from a magazine or journal article, the publisher is the company that produces and distributes the magazine or journal.

Permissions Departments

Many publishers have permissions departments or a person who handles reprints, permissions, and clearances. Information about the permissions department is usually found on or near the copyright page of a book, or on a magazine or journal's masthead page. Online magazines and book publishers' websites generally include copyright and permissions information on the introductory webpage (the index or home page).

If the book, magazine, or journal contains no specific information about permissions, direct your inquiries to the "Permissions Department" at the publisher's main business address, usually listed in the first or last few pages of a publication.

Are You Under Contract to Write a Book?

Have you signed a contract to write an article or a book? Publishing contracts usually indicate who has responsibility for obtaining permission for anything you use in your article or book, either the author (you) or the publisher. Your publishing contract may also specify the language to be used in any permission agreement you obtain. Inquire whether your publisher has its own permission form you can use.

Locating Publishers

You can usually find contact information for publishers with the aid of Google or another online search engine. If not, you can search *Books in Print* (www.bowker.com) online for a fee. The print publications *Literary Marketplace* and *Writer's Market* also provide publisher info.

For information on locating periodical publishers, try an online search or consult Mediafinder (www.mediafinder.com). If you're looking for information on academic publishers, check out the Association of American University Presses Directory, published by the University of Chicago Press (www.press.uchicago.edu).

Distributing Photocopies at Work May Be an Infringement

Many businesses save money by photocopying an article from a journal, periodical, or book for employees or outside clients. For example, an insurance company that subscribes to a legal newsletter might make 200 photocopies and distribute photocopied newsletters to employees and customers. Though common, such photocopying is a violation of copyright law if done without permission. This rule was established in 1995, when an oil company was found liable for unauthorized photocopying of academic and scientific journals. (*American Geophysical Union v. Texaco, Inc.*, 60 F.3d 913 (2d Cir. 1995).)

If a company gets caught, illegal photocopying can turn out to be no savings at all. In 1999, a national law firm paid out over $100,000 when confronted with a charge of illegal photocopying. How do publishers learn about this type of infringement? Often from disgruntled employees or from informants paid by publications that offer payments (sometimes as high as $10,000) for tipoffs.

Permission to photocopy and distribute materials can be acquired directly from the publisher or from the Copyright Clearance Center (www.copyright. com). The CCC provides individual-permission services (as well as "repertory" or "blanket" licensing services), including its basic Transactional Reporting Service. In some cases, a business can obtain an annual blanket license that permits unlimited photocopying from the CCC's collection of 1.75 million works. These blanket licenses are based on the type of industry and the number of employees for whom photocopies will be made. For example, law firms might pay a blanket license fee of $150 per year for each professional employee.

Certain types of photocopying for educational purposes do not require permission. However, this does not extend to the wholesale copying of articles for classroom use in coursepacks. The CCC has a special program that assists educators in obtaining permission for coursepacks. For details, see Chapter 7.

Dear Rich:
Do We Ask the Publisher or the Author?

I work for a small nonprofit with offices in the UK and California. Our mission concerns the protection of both biological and cultural diversity. In an effort to fulfill this mission, our group created a community study program that includes a reader featuring works written by leading ecological scholars and

*activists. We're updating the curriculum and most of the authors have agreed
enthusiastically to let us use their material for free. However, a few of them do not
hold rights to their work and the publishers are asking for fees that are prohibitive.
We're trying to find substitutes. Do we need to get both the authors' and the
publishers' permission if the books attribute copyright only to the authors?*

The short answer is that the copyright owner is usually—but not always—the
person who should give permission. The reason we need to provide a longer
answer is that often the author retains copyright ownership but grants exclusive
rights to a publisher. So even though the book's title page says something like
"Copyright 2019 Dear Rich," the publisher still controls all rights and can even file
an application for copyright registration as the owner of those exclusive rights.

How can you tell who owns what? Usually, you need to ask the publisher. As
a very general rule, authors of articles in scholarly journals and other periodical
publications traditionally retain subsequent print publication rights. Also, as a
general rule, most authors of books do not control the right to copy portions of
their published books, since print reproduction rights are one of the exclusive
rights universally granted to book publishers. (Note, in the event that the
publisher stops selling the book, these rights commonly revert to the author—or
at least they used to in the old days of publishing....) So even though the author
may be enthusiastic about including the work (and may be listed as copyright
owner), the publisher may be the one who has to okay the use.

When There Is More Than One Publisher

Different publishers may print the same book in different versions. For
example, one book may be published first in hardcover, later published in
paperback by a different publisher, and then published outside the United
States in a foreign language by yet a third publisher. Articles may be printed
in magazines and then reprinted in digests or books by different publishers.

In cases of multiple publishers, you must find out who controls the right
to reprint the work in another publication (known as "reprint rights").
The person or company who controls a work's reprint rights is known as
the "primary rights holder." Often, the first publisher is the primary rights
holder. In the case of a book, this is usually the hardcover publisher. You
can find the name of the hardcover publisher by searching an online

bookstore such as Amazon (www.amazon.com) or Barnes & Noble (www.barnesandnoble.com) using the title and/or author of the book.

If the hardcover publisher tells you that it does not have the right to reprint the work, ask if the publisher knows whom you should contact. If the publisher doesn't know, contact the author.

Also, keep in mind that the primary rights holder may only control rights in one country. If you intend to reproduce a work outside that country, you may need to seek additional permission. For example, one rights holder may have the right to publish a work in the United States, another in Great Britain, and yet another in Canada. If the work for which you're seeking permission will be distributed in the United States, Britain, and Canada, you will need permission from all three rights holders. The primary rights holder can often lead you to foreign rights holders.

Check the Copyright Notice

Information about the publisher or other rights holders is often located in the publication's copyright notice. The notice has three elements: the word "Copyright," or a "C" in a circle (©), the name of the copyright owner, and the year of first publication of that version of the work.

EXAMPLE: © 2022 Nolo

While the name in the copyright notice will indicate the rights holder as of the date of publication, remember that ownership may have been transferred since the notice was published. For example, the original publisher may have been acquired by another, or the copyright owner may have designated someone else to handle permissions. In either case, the name in the notice provides a starting point.

Text first published before March 1, 1989 without a copyright notice may be in the public domain. For more information, see Chapter 8.

Regional Rights Versus Foreign Language Rights

The territory in which a publication is distributed and the language in which it is published involve two separate rights. In other words, reprint rights are sold language by language and territory by territory. When dealing with U.S. publishers, unless you specifically ask for reprint rights in a foreign language, you will only be given the right to reprint the work in English in the territory specified. This means, for example, that acquiring "world" rights is not the same as acquiring rights in all languages. Rather, it means you have the right to publish the work in English throughout the world.

Be specific in your requests and permission agreements and keep the fees you must pay low by asking for only the rights you need. If your work will only be published in English, don't ask for foreign language rights. For example, if your magazine is distributed primarily in the United States and Canada, you probably only need one-time North American rights—the right to publish the work one time in the United States and Canada in English. However, if you print a French language edition for Canadian readers, you would need one-time North American rights and French language rights.

Contact the Author

If the publisher doesn't own the rights you need, it may be able to put you in contact with the author by forwarding your request to the author or, if the author is deceased, to the author's estate. For privacy purposes, it's unlikely that the publisher will give you the author's address or phone number.

You may be able to locate an author using public sources, such as the Authors Registry (www.authorsregistry.org), which maintains a directory of authors and will search for one or two names, usually free of charge. Information about over 1,000 nonfiction writers may be found through the American Society of Journalists and Authors (www.asja.org).

Also, the University of Texas (https://norman.hrc.utexas.edu/watch) maintains a searchable database entitled WATCH (Writers, Artists, and Their Copyright Holders). This database contains the names and addresses of copyright holders or contact persons for authors and artists whose works are housed in libraries and archives in North America and the United Kingdom. The WATCH database also contains limited information on whether an author's or artist's copyrighted work has entered the public domain.

If the rights for the text are owned by two or more authors, you will need to obtain permission from only one of them—provided that your use is nonexclusive and for U.S. or North American rights. "Nonexclusive" means that other people can use the text for the same purpose as you. If you obtain permission from one of several coauthors, your permission agreement should include a statement that the rights holder has the authority to grant the rights in the agreement. For example, include a statement like, "Licensor warrants that it has the right to grant permission." (This language is included in the sample licenses at the end of this chapter.) This provision places you in a better legal position if a dispute arises over your right to use the material.

You will need permission from all of the coauthors if you want:

- to use the text on an exclusive basis—meaning you are the only person who can use the text for a specific purpose
- to use the text on a worldwide, nonexclusive basis—because some countries require consent of all co-owners even for nonexclusive uses, or
- to use the text for a commercial purpose, to sell a service or product— for example, you want to include a quotation from a book in an advertisement (but simply using the text in a book or article you're writing for money is not considered to be a commercial purpose).

Educational Copying and Coursepacks

Some types of photocopying for educational purposes are allowed without requiring permission. However, this does not extend to the wholesale copying of articles for classroom use in coursepacks. The Copyright Clearance Center (CCC) (www.copyright.com) has a special program that assists educators in obtaining permission to include works in coursepacks. The rules for using copyrighted material in academic coursepacks are discussed in detail in Chapter 7.

Special Situations: Interviews, Letters, Speeches, and More

Finding rights holders for certain types of text, such as syndicated columns, speeches, interviews, and letters, may prove a little tricky. Below are suggestions for getting permission to use these types of works, as well as unpublished and out-of-print texts.

Interviews

If you want to use an interview from a magazine or book, contact the publisher. To use a written transcript of an interview from a radio or television show, contact the network or station that originally aired the show. For interviews first published on a website, contact the owner of the site, usually indicated on the bottom of the home or index page.

If you want to use a transcript of a television or radio interview, most stations have permissions departments that will furnish you a printed version. Sometimes you can download interview transcripts from the station's website. If you want to use the actual audio or audiovisual recording of an interview, you will need to obtain the consent of the person or company that recorded the material, often the radio or television station that initially broadcast it. (If you are interviewing someone yourself, for example —doing a live interview on your podcast, and want to make sure you have the necessary rights to publish the content of the interview, see Chapter 12, "Releases.")

Syndicated Text

Rights for works by columnists such as Miss Manners and Dear Abby are usually controlled by national syndicates (the name of which appears somewhere in or near the text). For example, to acquire permission to reprint a "Dear Abby" column for use in a book with an initial printing of 5,000 copies, you would first look at the column in a newspaper or online to find the syndicate's name (in this case, Andrews McMeel Universal) and then seek permission from them online (http://syndication.andrewsmcmeel.com/text_features/dearabby).

If the publisher, website owner, or television or radio station is not the rights holder and cannot lead you to the rights holder, try to locate the interviewer through one of the author resources listed in the previous section.

On occasion, determining the rights holder of an interview can get messy. In some cases, such as celebrity interviews, the interview subject may have placed restrictions on the use of interview material. In other situations, the interview subject might seek to prevent republication of the interview, claiming copyright ownership of their responses. A publication might write to you stating something like: "We are unable to grant your request because our publication holds no rights to the reuse of this material. Quotations that appear within the text remain proprietary to the speaker."

Unfortunately, sometimes a publication will provide you the interview text even if they don't own the rights to it. If you reprint the text, the interview subject could sue you for unauthorized reproduction of their remarks. To head off this possibility, when seeking permission to reprint an interview, ask if there is a written consent by the interview subject on file and, if so, ask for a copy. If there is no release, ask if the rights holder is willing to sign a written assurance that it has the authority to grant the rights you need. Such a document should state: "Licensor warrants that it has the right to grant permission." This will not shield you from liability as effectively as a signed release from the interview subject, but it does provide you with some legal protection. If the interview subject later files a lawsuit, you will have a stronger case against the licensor (the rights holder) for breach of the written assurance it gave you. If you are still worried about whether you have the right to reproduce the interview, your only option is to seek a release from the interview subject. A sample interview release is provided in Chapter 12.

Dear Rich:

Using Scientist Interviews

I have a question. I am a science journalist and I've recorded interviews with many famous scientists. I've used this material in books and articles and would now like to use these on a website for free, open-access listening. Someone has suggested that I obtain permissions from all my subjects or their estates. I believe that no permissions are required because the subjects implicitly granted me permission to use the interview material as I saw fit when they sat down with me and my tape recorder and pad.

You are navigating through one of the grayer areas of copyright law, so in answering we'll have to use a lot of equivocating language, such as "likely," "may," and "probably." If you don't have time to read all of that stuff, the bottom line is that you are probably okay to do what you plan to do. The courts and legal scholars are not a beacon of clarity when it comes to divvying up the rights for interviews.

From the limited case law available, it's likely that a court will consider an interview to consist of two separate works: one work created by the interviewer's questions, and the other created by the subject's responses. These works could be protected under traditional copyright principles (or they might be protected under what's referred to as "common law copyright"). Under that "two-separate works" approach, you'd need permission to reproduce the subject's answers. That permission may be implied by the subject's consent to the interview. In fact, one court—dealing with an interview with Ernest Hemingway—hinted that Hemingway's failure to limit usage at the time of the interview implied unlimited use.

Some legal scholars argue that a better approach is that the interviewer and subject jointly create one work. Under that analysis, the interviewer and the subject are joint authors. In that case, either author can use the interview for any purpose provided that the party using the interview accounts to the other for any profits. If this approach were applied to your case, your use should be fine since you are distributing the interviews for free and (assuming you are not making money off the website) no accounting would be necessary. Also, as you are probably aware, if you proceed without permission, you would have a strong fair use argument for distributing these interviews based on their historic and scientific value.

The whole thing becomes more complicated if you are making money from the sale or licensing of the recordings—a situation that could trigger a right of publicity claim or (if you and the subject are considered joint authors) an accounting of moneys earned to the interview subject. Finally, there is some question as to whether federal copyright protection extends to a recorded interview, since simultaneous recording of the performance of a work of authorship (that is, not being broadcast) is not considered to be fixed. That means that the interview is not protectable under copyright law (hence the need to use common law copyright, as described above). There's no guarantee that this will all play out as described. A lawyer would advise you that the only completely safe course is to obtain permissions. But we think your chances of avoiding hassles are good, and we look forward to listening to the interviews. There is always so much to learn about our scientific heroes.

Letters

The writer of a letter is usually the owner of the copyright in the text. However, there are two exceptions to this rule: Letters written by employees within the course of employment are owned by the employer; and letters written by federal employees within the course of employment are in the public domain.

Don't assume that the recipient of the letter owns the rights you need. The recipient owns only the physical letter itself. For example, the owner of a letter written by Elvis Presley could sell the physical letter itself, but only the Estate of Elvis Presley could grant rights to reproduce the text of the letter. And don't assume you can use an unpublished letter, no matter how old, without permission.

Dear Rich:

Who Owns a Letter to the Editor?

I contribute to an online site that provides public domain books, documents, etc. A question came up about the definition and copyright status of newspapers' "Letters to the Editor" and what are often defined as "open letters." I was wondering whether you are aware of any guidance or directions on such material. Who would hold the copyright? Is copyright ceded from the author to the newspaper publisher?

As a general rule—sorry, we hate to start with that phrase—letters are literary works and the author retains copyright. Unless (a) published before 1927, (b) published before 1964 but not renewed, or (c) dedicated to the public, the letters are not in the public domain.

What's unique about letters? By their nature, letters must be given to someone else—in this case, the newspaper publisher. That doesn't automatically transfer copyright ownership; it just transfers ownership of the physical letter. According to the Dear Rich Staff, it's possible that a publisher would acquire copyright under a written agreement or, in the case of an online publication, a click-to-agree agreement transferring rights. Check the fine print in the publication. Otherwise (and unless excused by fair use), the letter writer can prevent duplication or further publication.

Speeches

Not all speeches are protected by copyright. Copyright law only protects a speech if it is written down or recorded ("fixed") and if the writing or recording was done with the speechwriter's permission. If a speaker improvises a speech and their words are not written down or recorded with their authority, the speech has no copyright protection. Both criteria, fixation (recording) and authorization, are necessary. If the text of a speech is not fixed with the authorization of the speaker, you are free to use it without violating copyright law.

Dear Rich: **Using Speeches by Foreign Leaders**

Are speeches given by leaders in other countries in the public domain or are they owned by the government of that particular country?

The short answers to your questions are "It depends on the country," and "It depends on the country." You're probably already aware that speeches by U.S officials are in the public domain, as are works created by federal employees in the course of their employment. (One exception to this principle is that independent contractors can assign their copyrights to the U.S. government.) However, generally, you should feel free to create your own mashups of presidential speeches. But you can't do the same with Tony Blair's speeches as prime minister. Those are protected under Crown Copyright, as are government works in most British Commonwealth nations. Crown copyright is subject to a number of exceptions, which vary country-to-country. Some other nations (and the U.N.) also reserve the rights to their leaders' pronouncements. We're not sure why you're asking the question, but if you're considering republishing these speeches for purposes of scholarly analysis, criticism, or other commentary, the Dear Rich Staff feels that it's likely that a fair use defense will protect your U.S. publication. (Note: We're only discussing the use of the speech itself, not television coverage, which triggers additional copyrights.)

The Right to Use Monica's Words

Monica Lewinsky's infamous telephone conversations with confidante Linda Tripp about President Clinton are not protected under copyright law because they were recorded by Tripp without Lewinsky's authorization. On that basis, Lewinsky has no claim against Tripp or any of the companies that have published the conversations. It's possible that her statements may be protected under principles known as "state common law" copyright, but, as a practical matter, it's difficult to enforce such claims.

This does not mean that you can lure an interview subject into a phone interview, tape it, and use it without the subject's authorization. Twelve states, including California, have laws prohibiting the recording of telephone conversations without the consent of both parties. In addition, publication of such conversations may trigger claims of invasion of privacy.

Determining Whether a Speech Has Been Published

If a speech is protected by copyright, it's important to determine whether the text of the speech has been published, because works that have not been published enjoy longer periods of copyright protection. Giving a speech or lecture in public does not amount to "publication." Legally, publication only occurs when copies of the speech or lecture are distributed to the public.

This rule was fortified in a case involving Martin Luther King Jr.'s "I Have a Dream" speech. A federal court of appeals ruled that Reverend King's 1963 performance of the speech to 200,000 people (and simultaneous broadcast over radio and television) did *not* amount to publication of the speech. (*Estate of King v. CBS, Inc.*, 194 F.3d 1211 (11th Cir. 1999).)

Who Owns the Copyright?

If a speech is written down before it's given, the author usually owns the copyright (assuming the author also delivered the speech—see below for rules on ghostwriters). However, if the speech was written as part of an employment obligation—for example, a speech written by the president of General Motors for a shareholders' meeting—the author's employer owns the speech. If the speech was written by a federal government employee as part of their employment—for example, a speech by the Secretary of the Treasury to Wall Street investors—it is in the public domain. If the speech was ghostwritten—written by someone other than the speaker— the ghostwriter owns the rights, unless the ghostwriter was the speaker's employee or transferred the rights to the speaker (or someone else) under a written agreement.

If the speech was given extemporaneously (improvised, not written down in advance) but recorded with the speaker's permission, the author/speaker usually owns the copyright in the speech itself, the same way as if it was written down (as described above). However, the recording of the speech belongs to the people who recorded it—for example, a TV station news crew or a newspaper reporter. A video, film, or sound recording of a speech is a copyrighted work in its own right, owned by the person who made the work. However, a verbatim written transcription of the speech—made, for example, by a newspaper reporter at the scene—is not separately copyrightable since the author/speaker owns the speech (but not the recording of it).

If the speech was recorded, to use the recorded copy of the speech you'll need to obtain permission from both the author/speaker and the recorder of the speech. The same rule holds true whenever you want to use a sound recording, film, or video of a speech, instead of the written text.

If you cannot locate the speaker, contact the organization that sponsored the event. Often you can find the full text of a speech reprinted online, so a search engine may help you locate the rights holder.

Titles and Short Phrases May Be Protected Under Trademark Law

In Chapter 8, we explain that titles and short phrases are not protected under copyright law. However, despite their public domain status, names, titles, and short phrases may be protected under trademark laws. Take, for example, the slogan "Just Do It." Because the phrase does not qualify for copyright protection, you can use it in a song lyric, movie, or book. However, because Nike has a trademark for the phrase, you cannot use it in a manner that is likely to confuse consumers into thinking that you are associated with Nike, or in a way that tarnishes Nike's reputation. For more information on using something that is trademarked, see Chapter 10.

Stump the Booksellers

When all else fails, you may want to try Stump the Booksellers (www.logan berrybooks.com/stumpthebookseller), a website that will try to answer questions about books, authors, editors, and publishers at $4 a pop. P.S. The $4 fee can be applied to the purchase of the book you're seeking.

Out-of-Print Works

Just because a book or magazine is out of print doesn't mean that its copyright has run out. Your use, without permission, may still amount to an infringement. Therefore, if you intend to use text from an out-of-print publication, start by contacting the publisher. A good way to find the name of the publisher is through online bookstores such as Amazon and Barnes & Noble, who have extensive listings of out-of-print books and publishers.

Locating the copyright owner of out-of-print works becomes more complicated if the publisher no longer exists. Authors often own the rights to their out-of-print works because publishing contracts often return rights to the author if the publisher stops selling the book. You should research the author's whereabouts using the resources described above. If your search for the publisher and author lead to dead ends, you will have to perform more extensive copyright research or hire a copyright search firm to determine the current owner. (See Chapter 13 for more on copyright research.)

There is no comprehensive source that lists all books out of print, so in order to determine publication status, you can check whether the book is "in print," either by searching online for a fee at *Books In Print* (www.bowker.com) or for free at online book stores. The ISBN number (see "ISBNs and ISSNs" below) located on or near the title page may help locate the book. You may find information as to whether a book is out of print at the following websites:

- Bookfinder (www.bookfinder.com)
- Alibris (www.alibris.com)
- AddAll (www.addall.com), and
- AbeBooks (www.abebooks.com).

Unpublished Text

As with an out-of-print work, do not assume that an unpublished work is free to use. The rules regarding copyright protection for unpublished works depend on if and when the author died, and, in the event the work was ultimately published, the date of publication. Below are some general rules regarding unpublished works such as letters, diaries, and manuscripts.

Unpublished works created after January 1, 1978 are protected for the life of the author plus 70 years. Unpublished works created after January 1, 1978 that were made for hire or written under a pseudonym or anonymously are protected for 120 years from their creation or, in the event the work was ultimately published, 95 years from first publication, whichever comes first.

ISBNs and ISSNs

ISBNs (International Standard Book Numbers) and ISSNs (International Standard Serial Numbers) identify books and magazines and are sometimes required when seeking permission. ISBNs are used for books; ISSNs are used for magazines, journals, newsletters, and other serial publications. These numbers can be found on or near the title or copyright page or near the publication's UPC bar code. Since several numbers may be printed on the bar code, look for the number preceded by either "ISSN" or "ISBN."

If an unpublished work was created before January 1, 1978:
- Copyright expires 70 years after the death of the author, unless the author died more than 70 years ago. In that case, protection expired on January 1, 2003.
- Regardless of when the author died, the copyright in an unpublished work created before 1978 but published before January 1, 2003 will not expire before December 31, 2047.

EXAMPLE: Jane Austen died in 1817, but someone discovered an unpublished Austen manuscript in the 1990s. If the book remained unpublished, it would be in the public domain. However, the book was published in the 1990s, so it will be protected in the United States through December 31, 2047—230 years after Austen's death.

For more information on copyright protection for unpublished works, see Chapter 13.

As you can imagine, it can be quite difficult to locate copyright owners for unpublished works because there is no publisher to contact. Copyright Office records may help, if the unpublished work was registered. Determining ownership for unpublished works is especially difficult if the author is deceased and the author's estate or heirs are hard to track down. The WATCH database may help you track down the author of an unpublished work. Review the research techniques suggested in Chapter 13.

Dear Rich:

Using One-Liners From Email List

I edit an annual photography book, sold to raise money for charity, which accepts photos from members of an email list. We have a "click-wrap" agreement for the photo upload system. But the book also includes a few pages featuring a compilation of the wittiest quips that have appeared on the mailing list over the past year. I get the quotations either directly from the emails that go out on the list server or through third-party websites that archive all the content that appears on the mailing list. Are there any copyright issues I should be aware of in taking one-line quotations like this?

The short answer is that you're probably fine. Most short statements are hard to protect under copyright for various reasons. So, you're generally good to go when you take a one-liner from an online source. Issues are more likely to arise if you take several one-liners from a single source, or if your one-liners are actually three- or four-liners.

What about attribution? The Dear Rich Staff could go either way on this one so you can make the call. For many people attribution is a validating experience; others may prefer anonymity. Also, we probably don't need to say it—but we can't help ourselves since we're in the legal business—you probably want to avoid defamatory or privacy-invading one-liners. In the future, you can consider adding a "permission statement" to your mailing list terms and conditions, indicating that some statements may be included in the annual photo book.

What Does "Publication" Mean?

"Publication" occurs for copyright purposes when the copyright owner, or someone acting with the copyright owner's authority, distributes one or more copies of the work to the general public or offers the work for distribution, public display, or public performance. Copies do not need to be sold for publication to occur—they can be leased, rented, loaned, or even given away, so long as the work has been made available to the general public.

Publication does *not* occur when:

- Copies of the work are made but not distributed.
- The text of the work is performed publicly (for example, a speech is presented).
- The text of the work is displayed (for example, in a slide presentation or on television).

A "limited publication" is also not considered a publication. A limited publication occurs if copies are distributed only to:

- a selected group of people
- for a limited purpose, and
- without the right of further reproduction, distribution, or sale.

For example, it is not a publication when an author sends copies of a manuscript to several publishers seeking publication.

Using Text From Advertisements

Text in advertisements is usually owned by the corporate sponsor of the ad. However, in some cases it may be owned by the advertising agency or publication that prepared the ad. To locate an ad agency or corporate advertiser, try using an online search engine or search online for a fee at Winmo (www.winmo.com).

Using advertising text will trigger many of the same issues raised by using a corporate trademark. For detailed guidance on trade-related permissions, see Chapter 10, "Getting Permission to Use Trademarks."

Dear Rich:

Using Trial Transcript as the Basis for a Play

I'm a young aspiring playwright and am interested in writing a one-act play based on the transcript from a trial that took place earlier this year. The defendant was found guilty of misdemeanor manslaughter and I've received the transcript directly from the AG office. Can I use the transcript liberally (adding my own lines here and there but basically using what was actually said)? And then who is the play copyrighted to? Is it credited to me as the writer and "based on the transcript of..."?

The Dear Rich Staff thinks you'll be able to pull it off (and hopes you give it a shot) but we can't guarantee freedom from legal liability. (We know that sounds legalese but it's the best we can do.) We've been here before. We previously explored a similar issue regarding the Nuremberg Trials transcripts, and we start with the same principles—copyright does not protect spoken testimony, only fixed versions of that testimony. The "author," for copyright purposes, is typically "the fixer"—in this case the court reporter. And as we also noted, at least one case has held that court reporters are not authors of courtroom testimony because the mechanical process of transcribing does not demonstrate sufficient originality. We're unable to find any case law that grants copyright in trial transcripts. Although laws currently exist providing common law rights to spoken statements, it's not clear whether they could be successfully asserted against you. If we were a betting blog, we'd bet that you would be okay—under copyright law—to use the transcripts.

What about other legal theories? Are you in danger of defaming, invading anyone's privacy, or infringing a right of publicity? As you're probably aware, many great plays have been based on trial transcripts, often years after the final gavel sounded—for example, *Inherit the Wind* and *The Crucible*. Using a more current case may anger living participants especially if (1) you add additional dialog that slanders an individual, (2) you include false facts (or facts not introduced as public evidence), or (3) the trial is about someone famous and you use that fame as a basis for promoting your play. To further protect yourself, we recommend that you "fictionalize" the trial—for example, change the names and other identifying facts so that parties are not identifiable (this may be tricky if it is a locally publicized case).

Who gets credit? You get credit as author, at least as to the original material you contribute and your organization of the material and stage directions. You have no obligation to attribute the source (and it may even be wise to avoid doing that if you've fictionalized). When registering the work at the Copyright Office, you would disclaim the material from the trial transcript.

If the Text Contains a Trademark

A trademark is any word, photograph, or symbol that is used to identify specific products or services. Permission is not required to use a trademark if your use:

- is for informational or editorial purposes—for instance, you use the trademark as part of an article or story, or
- is part of accurate comparative product statements.

You do need to obtain permission if any of these apply:

- Your use is commercial and likely to create confusion among consumers of the trademarked product or service.
- Your use is commercial and reflects poorly on or "tarnishes" the trademark.
- You modify the trademark.

See Chapter 10, "Getting Permission to Use Trademarks," for an explanation of trademark rights and rules.

When You Can't Find the Rights Holder

If you've used the techniques discussed in this chapter and cannot find the person or business whose permission you need, you have a few options. You could try to delve deeper into copyright records at the Copyright Office. These records may help you determine who owns the work currently because many copyright transfers are recorded with the Copyright Office. Copyright Office renewal records will reveal if the publisher has failed to renew the copyright in the work—which puts the work in the public domain if it was published before 1964. Chapter 13 offers guidance on the three most common methods of searching Copyright Office records: hiring a search firm, paying the Copyright Office to do the search for you, or searching the Copyright Office records online.

If you still cannot locate the rights holder, it may be time to consider using the material without permission. As you might imagine, this poses risks. If the rights holder finds out about your use, you (or your publisher) may receive a letter from the rights holder or an attorney demanding that you stop using the material (known as a "cease and desist letter").

Before you use any material without permission, you should answer two questions:

- How likely is it that the rights holder will see your work?
- What is your potential legal liability if you are subject to a claim of copyright infringement?

Likelihood of Discovery

The likelihood that the author or rights holder will discover your unauthorized use depends on the extent of the distribution of your work and the popularity of the rights holder's work. For example, if you use an excerpt from an obscure writer's work in a book that sells under 2,000 copies, the odds are in your favor that the writer will not learn of your use. On the other hand, if you use a well-known quote from a famous play in an article for a major magazine that sells millions of copies, your use has a much greater chance of being discovered. The more likely it is that the rights holder will see your use of the copyrighted work, the more caution you should take in proceeding without the owner's permission.

Potential Liability

When using material without authorization, there is always a risk of potential liability—meaning, under the law, you might have to pay money damages and/or change your work. The amount of risk depends on several factors, described below. Generally, if you can show that you made a good-faith effort to search for the copyright owner, you will probably only have to pay the rights holder the standard fee within the trade for a similar use. However, there are exceptions to this general rule. A disgruntled copyright owner may refuse to grant permission and insist that you halt distribution of your work. Alternatively, a copyright owner may demand an exorbitant payment and drag you into court.

Consider the following risk factors when proceeding without permission:

- **The investment in the project using the copyrighted work.** The more money spent on your project, the greater risk if you need to halt publication. It may not be worth risking a $100,000 project for the sake of using one unauthorized illustration.

- **The diligence of your copyright search.** The more diligently you searched, the less risk. A thorough search demonstrates that you acted in good faith, and may show that it's not possible to locate the copyright owner.
- **The nature of your work and how easy it would be to remove the offending portion.** There is less risk involved if it is easy for you to remove the unauthorized material from your work. For example, a photo posted on a website can be easily removed, while one printed in a book cannot, at least not without wasting any remaining inventory and reprinting the whole thing.
- **The nature of the copyrighted portion and how easy it is to replace.** Although not as important as the other factors, your risk analysis should incorporate how hard it will be to replace the material in the event that you must remove it.

EXAMPLE: Jim publishes a newsletter for seafood restaurants and wants to use material from a cookbook entitled *Steamed Eels*, published in 1977. Jim was unable to locate the publisher; his letters to the publisher were returned with a notice that the company had moved with no forwarding address. Jim later learned from a distributor that the publisher had gone bankrupt in 1983. Jim paid the Copyright Office to perform a search, which turned up only an address for the author who died in 1986. Jim wrote to the author's last known address, but his letter was returned as undeliverable. Jim searched online for people with the same last name as the author and posted requests for information at several cooking websites. Jim documented this search and then researched the standard fee for a similar text license. Based on this, Jim proceeded to use the material without permission, citing *Steamed Eels* and its author in his work. In the event that the copyright owner turns up, Jim is prepared to pay a reasonable fee for using the work. Jim's risk is relatively low because his search was very diligent and, given the obscurity and relatively low value of the work he's copying, the financial risk for infringement is low.

When weighing risk factors, consider the expense and aggravation of the two worst-case scenarios—litigation and halting distribution of your work:

- **Litigation.** Any "wronged" party can file a lawsuit regardless of the merits of their claim. A frivolous lawsuit can drag on for months, and the attorneys' fees can amount to several thousand dollars. Even worse, a lawsuit based on a nonfrivolous claim (one in which there is a reasonable basis for the claim) could go on for years, and your attorneys' fees can soar into the tens of thousands of dollars.

- **Halting distribution.** If a copyright owner forces you to halt distribution, you face losing the money spent on the printing or distribution of the work, as well as the additional expenses to reprint and redistribute it. In addition, your costs may include recovery of unsold copies from distributors, notification to purchasers, and loss of revenue from advertisers.

Paraphrasing, Omissions, and Facts

If you use someone's copyrighted work but don't copy it exactly, do you need permission? This can be a tricky question. When you paraphrase a work, omit text, or use facts taken from a text, there are no fixed rules regarding whether permission is necessary. Instead, you'll have to look to general guidelines fashioned from language in the Copyright Act and court decisions.

 RESOURCE
For more detailed information on paraphrasing and other issues covered in this section, refer to *The Copyright Handbook,* by Stephen Fishman (Nolo).

Paraphrasing

Paraphrasing means using different wording to summarize or restate existing text. There are two general rules about permission when paraphrasing that you should understand:

- Paraphrasing will not always prevent a claim of copyright infringement.
- Paraphrasing may be prohibited by a permission agreement.

Paraphrasing May Not Avoid Infringement

Some writers believe they can avoid a claim of copyright infringement if they alter a text's wording instead of copying the words verbatim. This can work if the wording is changed so much that it is not recognizable as having been copied from the prior work. In the words of one court, "Copying so disguised as to be unrecognizable is not copying." (*See v. Durang,* 711 F.2d 141 (9th Cir. 1983).)

However, don't assume that paraphrasing is always a cure-all for infringement. There is no bright-line test that clearly tells you when paraphrasing is or is not an infringement. In one case, the author of a biography of novelist J.D. Salinger paraphrased many copyrighted letters. The biographer identified Salinger as the author, but, in an attempt to skirt copyright law, paraphrased the original letters. In one letter, Salinger had written, "She's a beautiful girl, except for her face." The author paraphrased this as: "How would a girl feel if you told her she was stunning to look at but that facially there was something not quite right about her?" The court held that the author's paraphrase infringed upon Salinger's original letter—and the court took offense at how inadequately the paraphrasing had been performed. The court further determined that many readers would have had the impression they had read Salinger's words. (*Salinger v. Random House*, 811 F.2d 90 (2d Cir. 1987).) In other words, even though the paraphrasing was dissimilar, it was considered infringement by the court because it was so poorly accomplished that it reflected negatively on the original author.

Permission Agreements May Prohibit Paraphrasing

Many publishers prohibit paraphrasing. A permission agreement may include a statement—such as "You may not alter or adapt this material"—to preserve the author's work as written and guarantee that the text will not be misconstrued.

Why would you paraphrase a work if you had permission to use it? Sometimes an editor wants to shorten the text because of space limitations. It is possible that some paraphrasing may be excused as a fair use. However, if you paraphrase in violation of a permission agreement, you may be subject to a claim of breach of contract. If possible, always clear any major paraphrasing with the rights holder.

Omitting Text

As with paraphrasing, consult your permission agreement to determine your right to omit part of the text that you have licensed. For example, one permission agreement reviewed for this book included the following statement: "You may not alter the material. You may omit up to 5% of a story by marking the omission with ellipses." A simple solution is to ask permission for only the material you want to use. Otherwise, your omissions may violate the permission agreement and subject you to a breach of contract claim.

Using Facts

If you wish to use text that is primarily factual, you may or may not have to obtain permission, depending on your use. In general, you don't need to ask for permission if you are using facts or fact-based theories themselves.

> EXAMPLE: The author of a book on the gangster John Dillinger uncovered certain facts and concluded that Dillinger did not die in 1934, but was alive in California as of 1979. A television series incorporated this theory and the supporting facts into one of its episodes. When the author sued, a federal court ruled that the television show was free to use the author's facts and theories. (*Nash v. CBS, Inc.*, 691 F.Supp. 140 (N.D. Ill. 1988).)

Copying Facts Versus Expression

Although you can copy facts themselves, you cannot copy the unique words by which a writer expresses those facts. For example, anyone is free to use facts about the life of Abraham Lincoln. However, you cannot copy the exact language Carl Sandburg used to express those facts in his biography of Lincoln.

> EXAMPLE: A company translated and summarized financial business and news articles from a Japanese newspaper. These summaries were offered to the public as abstracts. The Japanese newspaper sued the abstract company, and the court ruled that the creation of the abstracts was an infringement. The court found that 20 of the abstracts were literal translations of portions of the articles. The abstract company had copied more than the facts—they had copied the newspaper's protectable expression of them as well. (*Nihon Keizai Shimbun, Inc. v. Comline Business Data, Inc.*, 166 F.3d 65 (2d Cir. 1999).)

A major exception to this rule is when there are a limited number of ways to express the facts. For example, you are probably permitted to copy the expression, "The U.S.S. *Spiritualized* sank on June 12, 1944 as a result of an explosion in the galley" because there are only so many ways of expressing these facts. This is referred to as the "merger doctrine" because the fact and the expression are merged or inseparable.

Dear Rich: How Many Facts Make Up a Compilation?

*In a previous entry you mentioned that a lot of things that can be
protected by copyright, like short quotes, facts, and material in the public
domain, can be protected if they are compiled together in some way. Is there any
way to quantify this? How many facts do you need to collect to get protection?*

We're hesitant to give any numbers or proportions, as these issues usually
are decided by the quality or novelty of the organization and choice not the
numbers. Nevertheless, number crunchers might enjoy two relatively recent
cases. In *Bensbargains.net, LLC v. XPBargains.com*, a website (www.bensbargains.
com) compiled some of the best shopping deals on the Web. A competitor
(XPBargains.com) copied the Bensbargains deals. A California federal court held
that the Bensbargains compilations were copyrightable and set a numerical (and
novel) threshold of 70% for infringement—that is, infringement occurred if 70%
of all Bensbargains' deals appeared at the XPBargains site. In a second case, *New
York Mercantile Exchange v. Intercontinental Exchange*, the New York Mercantile
Exchange ("NYMEX") sought to enforce a copyright in its settlement prices—
numbers that are used when trading energy futures. NYMEX claimed copyright
in these numbers (not in their compilation or collection). "Claimed" would be
the key term here, since it's a basic premise of copyright law that protection
won't be granted for individual numbers. (The Copyright Office refused the
NYMEX registration.) Nevertheless, NYMEX pursued this lawsuit and lost. The
court relied on the merger doctrine—a principle that copyright won't protect
ideas when they're inseparable from the manner in which they're expressed.

Copying Compilations of Facts

Although individual facts are not protectable, a creatively organized
collection of facts such as the "Harper's Index" is protectable because the
editors of the "Harper's Index" (https://harpers.org/departments/harpers-
index) organize their facts in a unique manner that creates connections in
the reader's mind. You may be infringing copyright if you copy a collection
of facts from such a compilation.

There is no clear line as to how many facts you can use from a fact compilation without permission. In some cases, courts have held that people were free to copy an entire factual database, such as a phone book or a compilation of codes used on dental bills. In other cases, courts have prevented copying any facts from compilations. For example, a compilation of used car values was held protectable by a court because the values were arranged by locales, equipment, and mileage, making the information sufficiently original to be protected by copyright. (*CCC Info. Servs. v MacLean Hunter Mkt. Reports,* 44 F.3d 61 (2d Cir. 1994).)

Copying "Fictional" Facts

You cannot freely copy "fictional facts" such as the plot elements and characters of a television show. If, for example, you are writing a book that summarizes the plots and characters of the 1970s show *Charlie's Angels,* you will need to acquire permission from the production company that owns the copyright in the show.

For example, in 1997, a publisher was sued after releasing a book of trivia questions about the events and characters on the television series *Seinfeld.* The book included questions about 84 *Seinfeld* episodes, and actual dialog from the show was quoted in 41 of the book's questions. The defendant argued that all that was taken were facts; however, the court ruled that the events and characters on the television show were fiction, not fact, so copying was an infringement. (*Castle Rock Entertainment v. Carol Publishing Group Inc.,* 955 F.Supp. 260 (S.D.N.Y. 1997).)

Unfortunately, it is not uncommon for the owners of television and motion pictures to sue the creators of works that summarize or celebrate popular shows. This can be an intimidating tactic, especially when the rights holder is a well-funded motion picture studio. It is possible that a trivia book may be permitted if a court judges it to be a fair use (see Chapter 9 for an explanation of fair use principles), but if a book or website is primarily trading off the popularity of a movie or television show, the copyright owner is likely to send a "cease and desist" letter requesting the publisher to stop making references to the show.

When Facts Become Fiction

What if the author of a nonfiction work sues someone for infringing material claimed to be fact but at trial the author claims they were "fictionalized" facts? That was the strategy employed by the copyright owner of a biography of the singing group The Four Seasons. The author argued that the producers of a musical about the singing group borrowed more than facts from the biography because he made up some of the facts. The Ninth Circuit ruled against the author, holding "Copyright protects the creative labor of authors; it does not protect authors' post-completion representations about the lack of veracity of their own avowedly truthful work." (*Corbello v. Valli*, 974 F. 3d 965 (9th Cir. 2020).)

Negotiating Text Permission and Fees

Obtaining permission to use text involves a four-step process:

1. You must clearly and specifically identify what material you want to use and how you want to use it.
2. You must send a permission request letter to the publisher or rights holder.
3. You and the publisher or rights holder must negotiate a permission fee, if any.
4. You must get a signed permission agreement—your permission request letter may do, or you may need to draft a separate permission agreement.

The View From the Permissions Desk: Be Specific

From the point of view of people who grant permissions, the biggest problem with permission inquiries is vagueness. "The biggest tip [for obtaining permission] is simply that people should provide as much specific information as possible," says Richard Vittenson, former Director of *Copyrights & Contracts* (American Bar Association Publishing). "It's surprising how often people request permission without giving their name, an address or fax number to which we can respond, the organization that will be publishing our information, or the title or issue number of the publication from which they wish to reprint."

Bill Hammons, former manager of rights and permissions for *Newsweek* magazine, agreed. "Definitely, one suggestion I would give is to provide concrete details. A lot of times we would get people who didn't have issue dates or page numbers, or they didn't know how many copies there would be or how many uses." If requesting permission for use on a website, be prepared to provide information about the site and its use. "A publisher may ask for a report on the number of hits per month or the commercial uses of the site," said Hammons. "It's not just the number of hits [the publisher is interested in] but how the site is being used."

Identify the Material and Rights You Need

Your first task is to identify the material you want to use and the rights you will need. You can do this by completing the following worksheet.

 FORM
You can download this form (and all other forms in this book) from Nolo.com; for details, see the appendix.

What Is an "Edition"?

An edition is a new version of a book, distinguished from a reprinting, which is simply a new press run to produce more copies of the book. A new edition signifies a publication in which substantial changes have been made to the text.

Make a Request to the Rights Holder

After you identify the material and rights you need, send a letter to the rights holder requesting permission to use the material. Your permission request letter should provide all of the details about the text you want to use, how you expect to use it, and the permission you seek.

There are two different types of request letters you can use:

- One simply informs the rights holder of your needs and anticipates that you and the rights holder will later complete and sign a separate permission agreement.
- The other serves as both a request and a simple permission agreement for your use of the material. The copyright owner reviews the request and gives you permission by signing and returning the letter. This approach is recommended for simple requests to reproduce text.

The second type of letter—which serves as both a request and an agreement—is discussed later in this chapter. This section looks at a basic permission request letter that contemplates that the parties will negotiate and sign a separate permission agreement letter.

Whichever type of request letter you use, include a copy of the text that you wish to reproduce with your letter.

Keep Your Rights Request Simple

Most text permission requests are for the right to reproduce all or part of a work. For example, say you want to reproduce text in your magazine or on your website. If that's all you need, keep your rights request short and simple.

EXAMPLE: Chris wants to reprint a newspaper column on his website. The request he sends is basically as follows: "I am creating a website for the Association of Barking Dog Observers (ABDO) and would like to post the Jan. 20, 2022 Dan Fields column at our site for one month. I would like to know how much it would cost to post this column. Also, I would appreciate it if you could fax or email me a sample permission agreement."

Text Permission Worksheet

Material You Want to Use: The "Selection"

Title of text you want to use: _____

Name of author: _____

Source publication or product from which it came: _____

If from a periodical, indicate the ISSN, volume, issue, and date: _____
_____

If from a book, indicate the ISBN: _____

If from the Internet, indicate the entire URL address (the website address that starts with "http" or "https") as it appears when viewing the document: _____

Number of pages or segments to be used (actual page numbers are helpful). If you can, provide a word count, since some permission fees are based on word use:
_____

Your Intended Use: The "Work"

Title of your publication, program, product, or website: _____

Name of publisher or sponsor: _____

Type of work in which the selection will appear (book, website, periodical, podcast, or handout): _____

If a website, the average number of visitors to the site per month: _____

Estimated number of copies to be printed or produced. If a book, include the estimated first print run: _____

If copies are to be sold, indicate the price. If copies are free to attendees of an event, indicate the cost of event: _____

The date the material will be distributed (for example, the estimated publication date of your book): _____

Rights needed (for example, right to reproduce a work, translate a work, or modify the agreement): _____

Sample Permission Request Letter

Dear Ms. Hitchcock:

I am writing to you about your article, "Why I Hate Surround Sound." *New Audio Magazine* informed me that you were the owner of rights in the article. I'm writing a book entitled *DDA: Death to Digital Audio,* and I'd like to use an abridged version of your article in the book. The details are as follows:

Title of Your Article (the "Selection"): "Why I Hate Surround Sound"

Author: Michelle Hitchcock

Source of Article: *New Audio Magazine*

Volume, Issue, ISSN: Vol 23, No. 6, ISSN 1099-8722

Number of Pages: 4

My intended use of the Selection is as follows:

Title (the "Work"): *DDA: Death to Digital Audio*

Publisher: Cumberland Books

Type of Publication: Book (trade paperback)

Rights Needed: 1) the right to shorten or modify the Selection (I'll send you a copy of the abridged version for your approval); and 2) the nonexclusive right to reproduce the Selection in all editions of the trade paperback book, *DDA: Death to Digital Audio.*

Estimated First Print Run: 6,000

Expected Price $12.95

Projected Published Date: January 2023

I'm seeking these rights for myself and my publisher, Cumberland Books, and for any company that might acquire my rights to the book in the future. Please review this request and let me know the terms for licensing rights as well as the required credit. Once you let me know, I can prepare a permission agreement. Thank you very much.

Sincerely,

Roberta Weston

Negotiate Permission Fees

Next you'll need to work out how much you'll have to pay for the rights you've requested. The publishing industry does not have standard rates for using text. Some magazine and newspaper publishers use fixed rates for common permission situations and can furnish you with what is known as a "rate card" listing such fees. In other instances, the owner won't be able to assess the fee until after reviewing your request. Below, we've summarized some fee information.

Using Text in a Book

The fees for using text in a book are commonly affected by:

- the number of copies to be printed; pricing is often calculated at print runs of 5,000, 10,000, and 100,000 copies.
- the price of the book
- territorial and language rights; world rights may cost double or triple the cost of U.S. rights alone. A rights holder may charge 25% more for permission to reprint in a second language.
- whether the use is for a nonprofit purpose, and
- placement of the text within the book; for example, a half-column quote placed at the beginning of a chapter or book may result in a higher fee.

Generally you should expect to pay anywhere from $100 to $400 for use of text in a book, depending on the size of the print run and your rights request. By way of example, one national magazine charges $100 per column of text (there are three full columns to a standard page) for use in a book with a print run over 5,000 copies, and $125 for print runs over 100,000. Sometimes, the fees may seem high. For example, a professor who sought to use four lines from a poem by Emily Dickinson was quoted a fee of $200 by a university press. (Note, because of copyright rules regarding unpublished works, not all of Dickinson's works were in the public domain at the time of the request.)

Using Text on Your Website

The fees for website uses are evolving—meaning nobody is quite sure how much to charge. The fees are affected by:

- the extent of advertising on the website

- whether the site is intended primarily to provide information to the public (sometimes referred to as an "editorial" purpose); the rights holder may want to know whether the purpose of the site is to provide information or sell products or services.
- whether the organization sponsoring the site is a nonprofit
- the estimated number of visitors, listeners, or readers of the text per day, and
- whether the text will be used in a print publication as well as the website; for example, will you use the text in a print magazine and on the magazine's website?

A national magazine may charge between $100 and $500 to allow you to post an article on a website, with higher fees being charged for popular commercial sites—for example, posting a review of a movie at a high-traffic Hollywood studio website.

Giving Credit Where It Is Due

Your permission agreement will detail your obligation to include a written credit for the author or publisher. Make sure the credit is correct as required in your permission agreement. This is a serious subject between you and the rights holder. Unless otherwise required under your permission agreement, you can group credits together on the copyright page. For example:

"Elvis's Toothbrush" originally appeared in *Meet the Stars* © 2018, by Missy Laws. Reprinted by permission of Ross Books.

"You Can Collect Toilet Paper" originally appeared in *Antique and Collecting Magazine* © 1990, by Harriet L. Rinker. Reprinted by permission of the author.

Minimizing Fees

It's possible to get fees lowered or avoid them entirely by doing any combination of the following:

- Seeking a one-time nonexclusive use, as long you are not planning to write future editions or different versions of your work.
- Narrowing your permission request. The narrower your request, the less you may have to pay. For example, don't ask for "worldwide rights, all languages" if you only need "United States rights, English."

- Acquiring multiple items from one publisher. Often, you can reduce your per-item fee by licensing more than one work from the same publisher.
- Paying up front. You may be able to lower the fee by offering to pay up front instead of waiting 30 or 60 days.

Execute a Permission Agreement

Once the rights holder has agreed to grant permission and you've agreed on a fee, you need to complete and sign a written text permission agreement. There are two ways you can go about this:

- You can convert your permission request letter into a permission agreement (a "permission letter agreement").
- You can draft and execute a detailed permission agreement that should suffice for most text-licensing situations (a "permissions agreement").

This section provides samples of each.

Does the Agreement Have to Be in Writing?

Unless you have an "exclusive" agreement, your license or permission agreement does not have to be in writing to be valid. A nonexclusive oral permission may be enforceable as long as it qualifies as a contract under general contract law principles. However, there are limits on oral agreements. For example, in most states, an oral agreement is only valid for one year. Also, it can be very difficult to prove that an oral agreement exists, not to mention to prove its terms. Because of these limitations, do not rely on an oral licensing or permission agreement—get it in writing.

Sample Permission Letter Agreement

This short-form agreement is similar to those used by many magazines. It is intended for authors and publishers who only want to reprint text, whether in printed form or on a website. This approach—turning the request letter into an agreement—is recommended if your request is simple and you have agreed upon the terms. For example, if you want to include several paragraphs from an essay on your website, newsletter, or book, this form should be sufficient.

FORM
You can download this form (and all other forms in this book) from Nolo.com; for details, see the appendix.

What If the Copyright Owner Furnishes the Permission Agreement?

Many publishers' permissions departments and other copyright owners will provide their own permission agreements. If the permission agreement provided is short, you can probably comprehend its terms. If not, review Chapter 11, which explains how to review an agreement.

Instructions for Permission Letter Agreement

If you use this form, you don't need a separate request letter (as discussed in the previous section). Complete the agreement as if you were preparing the worksheet or a request letter. Below are some additional explanations for various sections:

- At the end of the **Licensor Information** section is a section the licensor—the person from whom you are requesting permission—should fill in if he or she does not own the rights you need. If this section is filled in, the licensor cannot grant you the necessary permission, so you will need to obtain permission from whomever the licensor indicates in the blank.
- The **Licensor's Approval of Request** section is a combination of the warranty and grant of rights, both discussed in Chapter 11.
- It is possible that the licensor will only want to grant rights for a specific print run or for a specific period of time. Or, the licensor may not want to grant you permission to transfer the rights to someone else. In this event, modify the grant to reflect these requests—for example, strike the language regarding "successors, licensees, and assigns."
- It's possible that you will want more rights than are granted in this letter agreement. For example, you may need rights for all foreign translations and derivative rights and you may want these rights in all media. If you want a broader grant of rights, you can use the **Licensor's Approval of Request** language below to replace the language in the agreement above. Be aware that the licensor may object to such a broad grant, causing a delay in the permissions process.

Text Permission Letter Agreement

To _____ ("Licensor"):

I am writing to you to request permission to use the following material.

Licensor Information

Title of Text (the "Selection"): _____

Author: _____

Source publication (or product from which it came): _____

If from a periodical, the ISSN, volume, issue, and date. If from a book, the ISBN:

_____

If from the Internet, the entire URL: _____

Number of pages (or actual page numbers) to be used: _____

If you are not the copyright holder or if worldwide rights must be obtained
elsewhere, please indicate that information: _____

Licensee Publication Information

The Selection will appear in the following work(s) (the "Work"): _____

_____

Title: _____

Name of publisher or sponsor ("Licensee"): _____

Author(s): _____

Type of work: _____

If print publication, estimated print run: _____

If print publication, projected publishing date: _____

If print publication, expected price: $ _____

If website, or podcast, the URL: _____

If website or podcast, estimated monthly visitors or listeners: _____

If website or podcast, the posting date: _____

Rights needed: _____

Fee

Licensee shall pay a fee of $ _____ to Licensor at the following address _____ upon publication of the Work or within six months of executing this agreement, whichever is earlier.

Credit

A standard credit line including your company name will appear where the Selection is used. If you have a special credit line you would prefer, indicate it below:

_____

Samples

Upon publication, Licensee shall furnish _____ copies of the Work to Licensor.

Signed by Licensee: _____

Name: _____

Title: _____

Address: _____

Date: _____

Licensor's Approval of Request

I warrant that I am the owner of rights for the Selection and have the right to grant the permission to republish the materials as specified above. I grant to Licensee and Licensee's successors, licensees, and assigns the nonexclusive worldwide right to republish the Selection in all editions of the Work.

Permission Granted By: _____

Signed by Licensor: _____

Name: _____

Title: _____

Address: _____

Date: _____

Licensor's Approval of Request. I warrant that I am the owner of rights for the Selection and have the right to grant permission to republish the materials as specified above. I grant to Licensee and Licensee's successors, licensees, and assigns the nonexclusive worldwide right to adapt and republish the Selection in all languages, in all editions of the Work, and in all versions derived from the Work in all media now known or hereafter devised.

TIP

Make the process convenient for the copyright owner. When sending your permission letter agreement, always enclose a stamped self-addressed envelope for the licensor's convenience.

Sample Permission Agreement

The permission agreement below is intended for authors and publishers who are negotiating for more than basic reproduction rights—for example, assembling an anthology of short stories, assembling contributions for an online database, or acquiring multiple or foreign rights to reproduce a work.

FORM

You can download this form (and all other forms in this book) from Nolo.com; for details, see the appendix.

Instructions for Permission Agreement

- In the introductory paragraph, insert the names of the licensor (the party who owns the material) and the licensee (you or the person who is seeking permission).
- In the **Licensor Information** and **Licensee Publication Information** sections, complete the blank spaces as if you were filling out the worksheet.
- In the **Grant of Rights** section, complete the grant to reflect the rights that you have negotiated. More information on the rights associated with grants is provided in Chapter 11, "Art and Merchandise Licenses."

Text Permission Agreement

_____ ("Licensor")
is the owner of rights for certain textual material defined below (the "Selection").
_____ ("Licensee")
wants to acquire the right to use the Selection as specified in this agreement
(the "Agreement").

Licensor Information

Title of Text (the "Selection"): _____

Author: _____

Source (or product from which it came): _____

If from a periodical, the ISSN, volume, issue, and date. If from a book, the ISBN:

_____

If from the Internet, the entire URL: _____

Number of pages or actual page numbers to be used: _____

Licensee Publication Information

The Selection will be reproduced in the following work(s) (the "Work"): _____

_____

(_Check if applicable and fill in blanks_)

□ book—title: _____

□ website or podcast—URL: _____

□ periodical—title: _____

□ event handout—title of event: _____

Name of publisher or sponsor: _____

Author(s): _____

Estimated date(s) of publication or posting: _____

Estimated number of copies to be printed or produced (if a book, the estimated first
print run): _____

If for sale, the price: $ _____

If copies are free to attendees of a program, the cost of program: _____

If a website, the average number of visitors per month: _____

Grant of Rights

Licensor grants to Licensee and Licensee's successors and assigns, the:

(*Select one*)

☐ nonexclusive

☐ exclusive

right to reproduce and distribute the Selection in:

(*Select all that apply*)

☐ the current edition of the Work.

☐ all editions of the Work.

☐ all foreign language versions of the Work.

☐ all derivative versions of the Work.

☐ all media now known or later devised.

☐ promotional materials published and distributed in conjunction with the Work.

☐ other rights _____ .

Territory

The rights granted under this Agreement shall be for _____
(the "Territory").

Fees

Licensee shall pay Licensor as follows:

(*Select one and fill in appropriate blanks*)

☐ **Flat Fee.** Licensee shall pay Licensor a flat fee of $ _____ as full payment for all rights granted. Payment shall be made:

☐ upon execution of this Agreement.

☐ upon publication.

☐ **Royalties and Advance.** Licensee agrees to pay Licensor a royalty of _____ % of Net Sales. Net Sales are defined as gross sales (the gross invoice amount billed customers) less quantity discounts and returns actually credited.

Licensee agrees to pay Licensor an advance against royalties of $ _____ upon execution of this Agreement. Licensee shall pay Licensor within 30 days after the end of each quarter. Licensee shall furnish an accurate statement of sales during that quarter. Licensor shall have the right to inspect Licensee's books upon reasonable notice.

Credit and Samples

(Check if applicable and fill in blanks)

☐ **Credit.** All versions of the Work that include the Selection shall contain the following statement: _____

☐ **Samples.** Upon publication, Licensee shall furnish _____ copies of the Work to Licensor.

Warranty

Licensor warrants that it has the right to grant permission for the uses of the Selection as specified above and that the Selection does not infringe the rights of any third parties.

Miscellaneous

This Agreement may not be amended except in a written document signed by both parties. If a court finds any provision of this Agreement invalid or unenforceable, the remainder of this Agreement shall be interpreted so as best to effect the intent of the parties. This Agreement shall be governed by and interpreted in accordance with the laws of the State of _____ . This Agreement expresses the complete understanding of the parties with respect to the subject matter and supersedes all prior representations and understandings.

Licensor | Licensee

By: _____ | By: _____

Name: _____ | Name: _____

Title: _____ | Title: _____

Address: _____ | Address: _____

Date: _____ | Date: _____

| Tax ID # _____

- Complete the **Territory** section to reflect the regions in which you have acquired rights—the world, the United States, Canada, or whatever region you have agreed upon. For more help, review Chapter 11.
- In the **Fees** section, indicate what type of fee has been negotiated, check the appropriate boxes and complete the information. For more information on fees, particularly regarding the nuances of royalty payments, review Chapter 11.
- Complete the **Credit and Samples** section per your agreement with the licensor. For more information, review Chapter 11.
- A warranty is a contractual promise made by the licensor. Some licensors do not want to make promises, particularly promises that the work does not infringe any third parties' copyright or other rights. You may have to modify the **Warranty** section or strike it entirely if the licensor objects.
- If you believe you have the bargaining power to get the licensor to agree, you may want to include an indemnity provision in the agreement. Indemnity is a financial punishment if the licensor breaks its promises. Indemnity provisions are not included here. If you wish to add such a provision, samples and explanations are provided in Chapter 11.
- Explanations for the **Miscellaneous** section (also called "boilerplate" provisions) are provided in Chapter 11. If you believe you have the bargaining power to get the licensor to agree, you may want to include a provision that covers attorneys' fees or arbitration.

CAUTION

Commercial uses are more complex. If you are seeking permission to use text on behalf of an advertising agency or a company selling a product or service (for example, Nike or American Airlines), your use is more likely to be categorized as a commercial endorsement, which will trigger additional legal issues. Review Chapter 12 regarding releases you may be required to obtain.

Getting Permission to Use Photographs

This chapter explains how to obtain permission to use existing photographs published online, in magazines, or available through image banks. (If you are interested in obtaining rights for "assignment photography"—that is, when you hire a photographer to create a specific image—see Chapter 15.)

The most common method of obtaining rights for an existing photograph is to license a stock photo from an image bank. Millions of existing photographs are available for license from image banks, which often specialize in different subjects, such as images of nature, food, or historical eras. The agreement (license) you'll enter into with an image bank depends on the type of image you want to use—whether the image is rights protected or royalty free.

Rather than seeking out an image bank to provide the photo you need, you may already have found a specific photograph—say, one you've clipped from a magazine—that you want to use. In this case, you'll need to find the owner of the photograph to obtain permission to use it.

This chapter explains how image banks work, how to find the photos you need, how to locate photo owners and negotiate rights with them, and how to work with photo researchers (people who hunt down photographs and obtain permission to use them). At the end of the chapter you'll find pricing information and a sample photograph permission agreement to use when licensing stock photographs.

RELATED TOPIC

Merchandising involves different rules. If you want to use a photo on a poster, cup, T-shirt, or other merchandise, skip ahead to Chapter 11, "Art and Merchandise Licenses."

CAUTION
Review public domain rules. Any photograph first published in the United States before 1927 is in the public domain, so you can use it without asking for permission. Photos published after 1926 and before 1964 are in the public domain if the owner failed to renew the copyright. A photograph may also be in the public domain if it was published between January 1, 1927 and March 1, 1989, and did not include copyright notice.

Don't assume that photographs published without copyright notices are in the public domain. And don't assume that you can use public domain works for free. You may have to pay a fee to obtain a copy of the photograph.

For more information on public domain issues, refer to Chapter 8.

CAUTION
What's in the photo may trigger other rights. If the photo you want to use contains trademarks, copyrighted artwork, or a person's image, you may need to obtain additional permissions or releases.

The World of Stock Photos

A stock photograph is any photo available to the public for license. Stock photos encompass every conceivable subject—celebrities, science, entertainment, sports, travel, and history—and conjure up every imaginable occasion and emotion. Stock photos are typically handled by agencies known as image banks (also known as stock photo agencies), that control the right to license the stock photos in their databases. Image banks sometimes specialize in certain types or themes of photos, such as nature, vintage Hollywood, or race car images. We provide a list of image bank resources at the end of this chapter.

In addition to the general selection of stock photographs, the entertainment industry has a vast selection of promotional photos and movie stills. If you're looking for an image of a celebrity figure, chances are there's a promotional photo available for license.

"Royalty Free" and "Rights Protected"

Two terms commonly used in the stock photo world are, "royalty free" and "rights protected." Both are a bit misleading.

Rights protected. To some extent, all stock photos are rights protected (sometimes also called "rights managed") because the owner has rights that are protected under copyright law. However, this term commonly refers to photos for which specific rights are negotiated—for example, when you negotiate the right to use a celebrity photo in a film or on a book cover. That is, your use is for a limited time and for specific purposes. Most photo licenses from high-end stock photo sources (such as Getty Images) involve "rights-protected" photos.

Royalty free. In a broad sense, "royalty free" refers to the fact that you do not need to make ongoing payments for your continued use of a photo. More commonly, the term "royalty free" means that the uses are (relatively) unrestricted. That is, once you either buy the collection of photo art, or pay for the rights to a photo, you can do whatever you want with it, except perhaps sell the photo, sell the image on merchandise or posters, or sell the photo as part of a photo collection.

It used to be that the quality and variety of choice was always better with rights-protected photos, compared with royalty-free photos. For example, most historic, news, celebrity, and entertainment photos are available as rights protected. At the same time, royalty-free stock was generally considered less expensive and more useful for standard corporate and advertising imagery, especially because of the large number of lifestyle, business, and scenic travel photos available for unrestricted uses. In some cases, those two axioms are still true, but there is also a growing "mid-high range" of stock photos that have relatively unrestricted uses and which are free of royalty obligations—for example, the vast collection and range at iStock.

Thumbnail Reproductions Are Fair Use

In a 2003 case, a court ruled that permission was not needed to reproduce thumbnail copies of photographs on a website. (A "thumbnail" is a small reproduction of an image, normally linked to a larger version.) Arriba Soft Corporation operated a search engine that displayed thumbnails copied from other websites. Kelly, a photographer, discovered that his photographs were part of Arriba's database and filed suit for copyright infringement. The Court of Appeal held that using thumbnail reproductions of copyrighted photographs on a website was a fair use because the use was "transformative" and did not interfere with the photographer's economic expectations. (*Kelly v. Arriba Soft Corporation*, 336 F.3d. 811 (9th Cir. 2003).) A similar result was reached by the Ninth Circuit in a case involving Google. The Court of Appeals determined that Google's use of thumbnails was permitted as a fair use in a case involving reproductions of images from an adult men's magazine website. (*Perfect 10, Inc. v. Amazon.com, Inc.*, 508 F.3d 1146 (9th Cir. 2007).)

Not All Image Banks Are Alike

Not all image banks are created equal. Large corporations run most image banks, while individual photographers manage others. Some image banks specialize in particular genres (for example, travel photos or American history), while others provide a more general, broad range of imagery. To give you an idea of how image banks work, we profile a few of the largest.

iStock

One choice for royalty-free (unrestricted use) stock photos is iStock (www.istockphoto.com), which pioneered a new approach to stock photography known as "microstock" (a system for very inexpensive licensing). The prices (based on a micropayment model) can be as low as $5 per image, and the company provides a wide variety of imagery and indexing. (iStock is owned by Getty Images.)

iStock has built its business around a user-generated content business plan. This crowd-sourcing model has created a massive database of stock photos mixing amateur and professional photography. As a result, even the most low-budget enterprise can license and use high-quality photography, often for a few dollars per photo. (At the same time, iStock has set some professional photographers to grumbling that the world of stock photo sales is open to anyone with a digital camera and a computer.) Regular users can purchase subscriptions or credits. The license agreement permits generally unrestricted usage, except of course for merchandise, posters, and sale of individual images.

GettyImages

GettyImages (www.gettyimages.com), founded in 1995, is the undisputed leader in the stock photography market. It was the first company to license imagery via the Web, and was the agent for moving the entire stock photo industry online. Getty has also acquired many stock companies, including Hulton Archives, a well-known collection of historic photos, iStock, Jupiter Images, and most recently Corbis, a stock photo company with a reputation for a wide professional photo selection, including the Bettmann Archive of 16 million images documenting 20th-century civilization. Getty's buying spree included the vast photo archive of Time Life, consisting of hundreds of thousands of images from that company's stable of magazines (including *Time*, *Life*, *People*, and *Sports Illustrated*) and its Mansell Collection of over one million historical illustrations, prints, and photographs.

Stock Photo Aggregator Sites

Photo aggregator sites enable you, via subscription or other payment system, to access a variety of images at various stock photo sites. Check out sites such as BigStock (www.bigstockphoto.com) and Fotosearch (www.fotosearch.com).

Creative Commons

Creative Commons is not an image bank, but it offers a similar service—
millions of royalty-free photos for your use, provided you abide by the
licensing requirements.

> EXAMPLE: You are in need of a photo of a pelican for your Powerpoint
> presentation, and you would prefer not to spend any money. In that case you
> might want to look for a Creative Commons photo license, since most of these
> photos are available for free, provided that you include proper attribution
> (always read the reuse requirements). Start at the Creative Commons Search
> page, now called "Openverse" (https://wordpress.org/openverse). Although
> Creative Commons does not operate a search engine, it links to other photo
> search engines such as Google, Flickr, and Wikimedia. Before choosing the
> search engine, you can indicate whether you want something that you can use
> for commercial purposes and/or modify and adapt. If, for example, you choose,
> "Use commercially" under "Filters"/"Filter by" and "Use" and type "Pelican" in
> the search box, you will be able to choose among several hundred Creative
> Commons licensed pelican images. For example, you may choose "Pelican in
> Water," a nicely composed color photo of a pelican standing in water. According
> to the license information, you are free to use the photo provided that it is
> properly attributed to the photographer, listed as J RAWLS. (If you don't see the
> licensing information, click on the Creative Commons symbol.)

Photo: by J RAWLS, used pursuant to a
Creative Commons Attribution License.

Dear Rich:

Using Old Company Photos

I recently took a public relations accreditation test that included the question below. The answer was D. If the photos were in company files why can't it be argued they were paid for? If the photos were 20 to 100 years old does the copyright still hold?

To celebrate its 100th anniversary, your company wants to publish a coffee-table book of photos depicting the company's history. You dig through the files and old annual reports and find many photos, some of which have never been published. Some of the unpublished photos are dated and stamped on the back with the name of a photography studio that has been out of business for 20 years. When you consult with your publisher about the most effective way to reproduce these particular prints, the publisher says they cannot reprint them without the original photographer's permission. You are unable to find the original contract between the company and the photographer. Can you reprint the photos without the original photographer's permission?

    A. Yes, if you pay the publisher a fee to reproduce the photos.

    B. Yes, the company paid for the photography and therefore owns the prints.

    C. Yes, you can reproduce the photos if you give proper credit to the photographer.

    D. No, the photographer or heirs own the copyright and must grant permission to reproduce the unpublished photographs.

        The answer to your question within a question is that D is the best (or "most correct") answer. We understand your desire to argue the point—that's one of the reasons that the Dear Rich Staff quit teaching—but unless there is documentation showing that the photographer transferred rights to the company, the photographer retains copyright. The act of paying for a service such as photography does not, by itself, grant copyright.

A better and much more long-winded answer would have been:

    E. Probably not. If the photos were subject to a work-for-hire arrangement executed before January 1, 1978, it's possible that the republication would be permitted since such agreements are interpreted more "loosely" than under the current Copyright Act. However, as a general rule, photos are protected for the life of the author plus 70 years (although if the United States ever passes Orphan Works legislation, this whole question will be moot).

CAUTION
Always ask whether the image bank possesses all rights for the stock photo. It may seem odd, but there are occasions when an image bank possesses a stock photo but not its licensing rights. This is sometimes the case for rare photos or movie stills. In such scenarios, you need to contact the rights holder to obtain permission to reproduce the photo.

Public and Private Institutions

You can also obtain photographs of historical interest (people or events) and of works of art from museums, foundations, art galleries, libraries, and historical societies. These institutions function much like image banks when licensing works in their collection and may have unusual, very old, or obscure photos not obtainable from image banks. Locating these institutions requires the same research techniques used to locate image banks. You can also get information on obtaining photos of artworks at many art museums from the *Image Buyers' Guide*, available from the Visual Resources Association (www.vraweb.org).

Digital Watermarks

Some image banks allow you to view stock photos online, but attempt to prevent piracy by encoding the photos with a digital watermark. This may take two forms: a visible watermark (usually the name of the stock agency imprinted across a portion of the photo) or an invisible digital watermark that is buried in the software code of your digital photo. Sometimes, the watermark appears only when you print the photo. In 1998, Congress passed legislation making it a violation of copyright law to remove digital watermarks.

If You Can't Budge the Budget
Your choice of image bank probably depends on your budget if you—as opposed to your publisher—are paying the fees for acquiring photo rights. Review stock photo prices and prepare a budget before beginning your photo search. And don't forget to check for photos that may be available for free under a Creative Commons license.

Obtaining Rights to a Photo You've Found

If you've already come across a photo that you want to use (instead of searching for an image at a stock photo company) your task is to find out who owns the copyright in the photo, and obtain their permission.

This procedure is usually simple. First, find the photo credit—the phrase that lists who owns the copyright in the photo. If the photo appeared in a book or magazine, the credit is usually on the same page as the photograph, although in some cases photo credits are listed on one page near the beginning or end of the publication. If the photo credit is for a publication, contact the publisher's rights and permissions department. If the photo credit refers to a company or an image bank (for example "Photo: Reuters"), locate the image bank using the information and resources described in this chapter. If there is no photo credit, contact the publication in which the photograph was reproduced. If the photo is from a website and no credit is listed, use the "contact" email form found at most websites to ask about ownership and rights.

If the credit is for a photographer—that is, the photographer retained rights—contact the photographer, their estate (if the photographer is deceased), or the photographer's representative. You can locate a photographer three ways:

- Contact the publication in which the photograph appeared.
- Search online using the photographer's name as a keyword.
- Contact photographer trade organizations.

You'll find a list of photographer trade organizations at the end of this chapter.

> EXAMPLE: I sought to locate photographer Bobby Neel Adams, whose work had been featured on the cover of *Life* magazine, to obtain permission to print one of his photographs in this book. I didn't have much luck contacting representatives of Time, Inc., owners of the now-defunct *Life* magazine, and after several unreturned phone calls I began an online search. Eventually, I found an agency called Focal Point F8 that represented Adams. This company was able to provide contact information for him and arrangements were made for permission.

Photo credit: Self-Portrait (Age-Map Series) © 1989, Bobby Neel Adams (www.bobbyneeladams.com). Reprinted with permission of the photographer.

Google Image Searching

If you've located an image online but can't find anything about ownership, consider using Google Image search. This will enable you to find all uses of that image on the Internet, one of which may contain attribution or ownership issue. To use Google Image Searching, first locate the image on the Web. Right-click the image and select Copy Image Address. Visit https://images.google.com or click the camera icon in the search box on any Images results page. Paste the URL you copied into the box. That should provide you with other reproductions or similar images.

Celebrity Photos and Movie Stills

In addition to the vast libraries of photos at image banks, the entertainment industry is a rich source of photos, with thousands of promotional photographs and stills from motion pictures and television programs. Whether you are looking for a photo of Jay-Z or Jay Leno, you can bet there's a promotional photo available.

There are two basic types of celebrity or entertainment photographs available. One type is created by freelance photographers (paparazzi) and sold to the media, such as a photo of Meryl Streep walking into the Cannes Film Festival. Stock photo houses and magazines usually own these photos. The other type is prepared by the entertainment industry as a promotion for a specific project (a film, music recording, or television show), such as a picture from the film *Groundhog Day* or a portrait of Katy Perry.

Most likely, in order to reproduce the image, you will need to contact the rights holder—the photographer, stock house, or entertainment production company that owns the rights to the photo. If the photo includes a photographer credit—particularly if it indicates that the photographer retained the copyright (for example, "Copyright 2022 Roberta Barley")—contact the photographer using the methods described in the previous section.

If there's no credit associated with the photo, you may still be able to track down either an image bank or a production company that owns the copyright or can direct you to who does. Certain image banks specialize in entertainment-related stock photos. You could try contacting them to ask if they represent the photo you want to use. You'll find a list of image banks, including those that specialize in entertainment photos, at the end of this chapter. In some cases, particularly for rare motion picture and television stills, image banks may not control the copyright but can direct you to the production company or photographer for permission.

If the photo is from a television show or movie, you can locate the name of the production company via the Internet Movie Database (www.imdb.com), a searchable bank of thousands of films and television shows. You can also find entertainment production companies online or in the New York,

Nashville, or Los Angeles telephone listings. When you contact the production company, ask for the publicity, media relations, or public relations department.

If you don't have a copy of the photo you want to use but you know that you need a photo of say, Cate Blanchett in *Ocean's Eight,* you must either contact an image bank that has the photo you need or find the production company that owns the rights to such a photo. Search image banks that specialize in the proper type of entertainment (here, movies) or use the resources described in this chapter (such as IMDb) to find the company that produced the movie or show in question.

> EXAMPLE: I sought to locate stills from the 1974 film *The Conversation.* I started my search by contacting movie still sites such as Star File Photo and the Motion Picture & Television Photo and Archive, but none had stills for this film.
>
> Next, I tried the Internet Movie Database (www.imdb.com) and located the production company for the film—Paramount Pictures. I found the phone number for Paramount online. Paramount directed me to the Paramount Pictures Stock Footage & Stills Library, which licenses stills and footage from Paramount movies, including *The Conversation.*

CAUTION

Commercial uses can get tricky. The permissions situation may become more complex if you are using the photograph as part of an advertisement or to sell a product. Chapter 12 discusses these uses.

Dear Rich:

Disneyland Pix in Travel Book

I am writing a travel book. I would like to include photographs of items that are subject to a Disney trademark, such as the Disneyland castle. If I own the copyright to the photograph, would I need to get a license to include it in my book? Are there any issues with discussing these items, but without including photographs? What about other places in the Disney parks that are on Disney property, but probably not subject to any trademarks, such as a building on Main Street or a trash can?

First, we're not sure that the Disney World trash cans lack trademarks. As for the remainder of your questions, Disney creates some hurdles for travel publishers.

"We Appreciate Your Understanding." A member of the Walt Disney staff wrote to the Dear Rich Staff and explained that:

"All requests to use materials which are copyrighted by The Walt Disney Company (e.g. photos, logos, characters, etc.) must be directed, in writing, to the following address: Walt Disney World Legal Department, Attn: Requests, Post Office Box 10000, Lake Buena Vista, FL 32830-1000. Due to the volume of third-party requests that we receive and in view of the consideration process that these requests are subject to, please know that it may take up to eight weeks for a response to be provided. As such, any requests that are received indicating the need for an immediate response are automatically declined and returned to the sender. We appreciate your understanding."

In short, if you are asking for assistance, whatever you do, don't tick off the WDW staff by asking that they expedite your request. You can learn more about Disney photo rules at the Disney photography site and its forum, the Disney photo forum. We've never been to WDW or Disneyland so we're not sure if the purchase of a ticket incorporates photo rules as well, but a visit to Disney property is a visit to private property, so you may have signed away your rights on this one, just by purchasing a ticket. You can discuss the parks (in textual form) without worrying about trademark issues. And arguably, under First Amendment principles (and possibly trademark fair use principles), you can reproduce those trademarks for editorial purposes. We recommend you consult other travel books and see how they've handled it, since Disney is an active and high-profile enforcer of its IP rights.

Using Photo Researchers

Think of a photo researcher as an art detective who can track down an elusive image. If you perform photo licensing regularly—for example, if you are a website designer or a photo acquisitions editor—you may want to consider using a photo researcher as a matter of course. Many photo researchers have specialties—for example, Chicago-based photo researcher Mary Goljenboom of Ferret Research (www.ferretresearch.com) has expertise in science, business, and historical images, particularly women's history.

Photo researchers are usually paid per day (approximately $250), although some charge by the hour. A researcher will prepare a budget for your needs and may also be able to arrange photo shoots for materials located in archives. The American Society of Picture Professionals (aspp.com) publishes a directory of members along with their specialties, and can help you find the right researcher for your purposes. Additional resources for locating photo researchers are listed at the end of this chapter.

Photo Fees

A picture may be worth a thousand words, but is it worth a thousand dollars? How about $450 or $225? As soon as you start pricing photographs, you'll discover that stock photo prices vary widely. The minimum fee for using a stock photo from a high-end agency is usually $150 and may rise to several thousand dollars, especially if the agency charges reuse fees (additional payments you must make when you reprint the book or article in which the photo first appeared). Some midpriced image banks, such as iStock, charge lower rates ($5–$100 or subscription rates) and might not seek reuse fees. At the low end of the pricing tier are sources that often advertise as being royalty free or copyright free.

Some of the factors that affect pricing are described below. If you perform photo clearances on a regular basis, you may want to consult one of several books listed at the end of this chapter that focus exclusively on photo pricing guidelines.

As we discussed earlier, there are two categories of stock photos: rights protected and royalty free. Each type has its own rules regarding fees.

Fees for Rights-Protected Photos

Fees for rights-protected photos vary widely and are closely tied to your intended use of the photo, which must be clearly disclosed to the licensor up front. As a general rule, the more intended uses you have for the photo, the more you'll have to pay. For example, you could be charged according to the length of time you use a photo on your website, or the size of a print run for a book in which a licensed photo appears. If you want to use the photo for a different purpose in the future, you will likely have to pay an additional reuse fee.

For the most part, the image bank or photographer is concerned with how many people will see the image. The larger the viewing audience, the higher the fee for your use. The worksheet below lists the information an image bank will typically require from you to calculate its fee and grant you permission.

 FORM
You can download this form (and all other forms in this book) from Nolo.com; for details, see the appendix.

Fee Multipliers

Some image banks use a multiplier system to determine the fee. Here's how it works: The image bank starts with a minimum fee, usually the lowest amount they accept for a use. For most image banks, the minimum fee is between $150 and $200 (the amount charged for reproducing the photo on a quarter of a page in a 5,000-edition book). Every other use has a multiplier that determines the fee. For example, the multiplier for using a photo on a magazine cover is 4. If the minimum fee is $150, the cover use fee would be $600. The highest multipliers are for national advertising uses. For example, the multiplier for a full-page photo used on the back cover of a national magazine could be 20, raising the $150 minimum fee to $3,000.

Advertising Fees

If you intend to use a rights-protected photo in an advertisement, the fee an image bank will charge you will be based on the circulation and placement of your advertisement. Expect to pay $1,000 to $5,000 to use a photo in a full-page ad in a national magazine and at least $1,000 for a quarter-page ad inside. Rates may be based on the number of insertions—meaning when an ad is placed in each edition of a magazine. An image bank may charge reuse fees for subsequent insertions. Rates may be lower for advertising for nonprofit organizations or for "advertorials"—advertisements dressed up to look like news articles.

Photo Permission Worksheet

Photographic Use

Title of publication (book, periodical, handout), program, product, or website in which the photograph will appear: _____

Name of publisher or sponsor: _____

Estimated number of copies to be printed or produced. If a book, include the estimated first print run: _____

If copies are to be sold, indicate the price. If copies are free to attendees of an event, indicate the cost of event: _____

The date the material will be distributed (for example, the estimated publication date of a book or the posting date of a website): _____

Will the publication be in any language other than English? ☐ yes ☐ no

If yes, identify which language: _____

Website uses:

　Does the site include advertising? ☐ yes ☐ no

　Is the site commercial or editorial? ☐ commercial ☐ editorial

　Will the photo be used on a ☐ home page or an ☐ internal page?

　The number of visitors or hits per day: _____

Will the photograph be used in both a print publication and a related website (for example, in a magazine and on the magazine's website)? ☐ yes ☐ no

If using in a presentation, the sponsor of the presentation, the number of attendees, and the cost of attendance: _____

Rights needed:

　(1) reproduction of the photograph

　(2) display of the photograph

　(3) modification of the photograph

Territory (for example, North American or world rights): _____

The format in which you will need the photograph: scan, print, transparency, or digital (if digital, what DPI and file format): _____

The date you need the photo: _____

If for a film or TV show, the context of the use (supply a synopsis of the plot):

_____

Color Versus Black-and-White Fees
Don't expect to pay less for black-and-white photos. Some image banks claim it costs as much, or more, to reproduce quality black-and-white prints.

Corporate Use Fees

Image banks charge more for corporate uses—using photos in corporate brochures, annual reports, and in-house publications—than for editorial uses. For example, an image bank may charge $500 for a quarter-page photo in a corporation's annual report with a distribution of 50,000, versus $250 for a similar use in a magazine with a similar circulation.

Digital Photograph Quality

Fees may also be affected by the resolution of the photo—meaning the number of dots per inch (DPI) that make up the photo. The denser the dots, the higher the DPI, the better the resolution, and the more expensive the photo. In some cases, the quality of the reproduction is expressed as a combination of the DPI and the size of the image. For example, a 72 DPI that is 4 x 5 inches will have a lesser image quality than the same image at 72 DPI and 8 x 10 inches. A low-resolution photo (72 DPI) is usually suitable only for use on websites or for nonprofessional uses. Graphics professionals prefer high-resolution photos (300 to 600 DPI). Some stock houses will furnish bundles of low-resolution images as royalty-free or copyright-free. Other image banks may charge on a sliding scale—for example, $50 for low resolution (72 DPI) to $250 for high resolution (300 DPI or higher).

As you may be aware, resolution also affects the size of the file on your computer. A 72 DPI photo may take up only 500K in disk space. The same photo at 300 DPI may take up 10–20 MB of space.

> ## Drum Scans Versus Flatbed Scans
>
> Quality can vary widely when it comes to scanned photographs. If you need high-quality scans—for reproduction in a coffee-table book, for example— you should ask for drum scanning, which is a higher quality scanning process compared with standard flatbed scanners. If the image bank doesn't indicate the type of scan used, ask.

Rights-Protected Website Use Fees

Fees for using an image on your website can vary widely. *Selling Stock* (www.selling-stock.com), a website for the stock photo industry, reports that the fee for using a 4x4-inch stock photo on one major corporate home page was $1,000 for six months.

Most rights-protected image banks base fees for website uses on the following factors:

- the sponsor of the site (who is paying for it)
- whether the photo will reside on the home page or a secondary page
- the prominence or size of the photo
- how long the photo will be displayed, and
- whether the photo will be used on any additional sites.

Image banks may want to know how long the image will be stored on the site, even if it is a relatively short period of time. Some image banks determine fees based on the number of visitors to the site or other site use ("traffic") data. Sometimes, website use fees can be waived if the online use is ancillary to use in a printed work. For example, a website use fee may be waived if a magazine has licensed the photograph for a print publication and also wants to use the photo in its online edition.

Additional Fee Factors

In addition to standard fees, the following factors may increase the fees you're required to pay to use a rights-protected photo:

- **Exclusive or nonexclusive rights.** Obtaining an exclusive right to use a photo means that no one else can use that photo in the same manner as you're using it. Exclusive rights are always more expensive than nonexclusive rights. An exclusive rights arrangement often means getting exclusive rights for a specific use—for example, the exclusive right to reproduce the photo in Canada or the exclusive right to use the photo in automobile advertising.

- **Reuse fees.** An image bank might only grant you rights for a specific print run or for a specific time period. If you are planning subsequent uses, you may be charged a reuse fee, usually a reduced version of your original fee. Some image banks charge reuse fees for new editions, not reprintings. (A new edition is a significant revision of a book, as opposed to a simple reprint when inventory runs out.) There may be an additional fee (similar to a reuse fee) when a work is converted to a new medium—for example, when a documentary film is reproduced for sale in video format. Find out the cost for a one-time fee for all potential uses and compare that to the cost of a series of reuse fees.

- **North American or world rights.** Worldwide rights are more expensive than U.S. rights. For example, if you had to pay $100 for North American rights for a quarter-page photograph inside a textbook with a print run of 5,000 copies, you might have to pay $150–$300 for world rights. Note, there is a difference between world rights in all languages and world rights in only one language (in Chapter 2, see "Regional Rights Versus Foreign Language Rights").

Fees for Royalty-Free Photos

In contrast to rights-protected fees, fees for royalty-free photos are not based on use and are less expensive (often under $20). While the rights granted are broad for royalty-free photos, there are usually some limitations, like a prohibition on using the images on merchandise. (Merchandise uses are discussed in Chapter 11.) As long as your use falls within the rights granted, you do not have to pay anything extra for your use of the photo. This means, for example, that you may use the photo several different times in various ways for the one-time fee.

Since the scope of royalty-free rights may vary, you must review the written documentation that accompanies your purchase of the images. If you obtain the images from a website, the legal limitations on your use may be presented in a click-wrap agreement, which is a screen that appears when you prepare to download the images. For more information on the enforceability of click-wrap agreements, see Chapter 4.

Photo Permission Agreements

Permission agreements to use photographs vary quite a bit depending on whether you're using a rights-protected or royalty-free image. Agreements to use royalty-free photos are generally much less specific than agreements to use rights-protected photos. Typically, once you pay an access fee for a website containing royalty-free photos, you can use the images within the general limitations outlined.

If you're using a rights-protected photo, however, you'll generally need to enter into a more specific agreement that outlines the terms of your use. This section outlines the terms commonly found in licenses for rights-protected photos and offers a sample photo permission agreement with explanations of its terms.

CAUTION

Check the print or slide for more conditions. When an image bank furnishes you with physical photos, always review the back of the photos or the mounts of the slides for additional limitations on the license—for example, a requirement to provide a specific photographer credit. These limitations become a condition of your photo license agreement.

Agreement Terms

After agreeing upon a fee for a rights-protected photo, the image bank will usually furnish you with the images (transparencies, prints, scans, or digital images) along with a permission agreement outlining the terms of your license. Alternatively, you may receive an invoice that functions as a permission agreement. The invoice or agreement will list the terms of your license, and should include the following:

- the photograph (identified by title or catalog number)
- the nature and length of use (for example, the name of the publication or website in which the photo will be used)
- your name or the name of your publisher or sponsor (the company paying for the publication or website)
- the photographer's name or other photo credit requirements
- the fee, to whom it should be paid, and when, and
- whether you are required to furnish samples of your work when the photo is published.

The Small Print

The bottom or the back of the invoice will ordinarily contain additional terms and conditions for your use of the photos. These conditions often include the following:

- **Additional fees.** Image banks that furnish prints (not digital copies) request that you return the print. Usually, you can retain the originals for a period of 30 to 90 days, sometimes referred to as the "approval period." After you have copied the image for your use, you must return the images to the image bank before the end of the approval period. In some cases, a late fee may be charged ($1 or more per day). If you lose or damage the photo you might be stuck with a fee of $50 to $1,500, depending on your agreement.
- **Late fees.** You may also have to pay late fees if your payment doesn't arrive on time. If your agreement states that "time is of the essence,"

you will have a harder time getting out of these late fee obligations. Despite the fact that you have a signed agreement, your failure to pay the fee on time may terminate your right to use the photo.

- **Model releases.** A model release is an agreement between the model and the photographer allowing use of the model's image without violating the model's rights of privacy or publicity. (Model releases are discussed in detail in Chapter 12.) If the photo you're licensing includes a model's image, make sure the image bank has a model release on file. If the image bank says it has such a release, include this statement somewhere in the permission agreement. Since many photo permission agreements are invoices (with contract language on the back), ask that the model release claim be stated on the invoice. For example, add language such as:

  "Image Bank warrants that a model release is on file for the licensed photograph."

  In addition, if possible, have the image bank provide you with a copy of the release so that you can compare it to the model release sections in Chapter 12, where we discuss how to analyze a release. These rules should apply regardless of whether the photo is rights protected or royalty free.

- **Warranties and representations.** The image bank may want to protect itself from any legal claims resulting from unlicensed use of the photos or uses that are not included in the model release. To that end, your agreement might include language such as "hold harmless" or "indemnify." For more information on these provisions, see Chapter 11. Review royalty-free shrink-wrap and click-wrap agreements for indemnity provisions as well.

- **Dispute resolution, attorneys' fees, and jurisdiction.** The agreement may provide for methods of dealing with disputes, including arbitration or payment of attorneys' fees. In addition, the agreement may establish in what state you may have to bring or defend a lawsuit. For more information on these dispute provisions, review Chapter 11. These provisions usually are not included in royalty-free agreements.

Modifying a Photograph

Unless your agreement prohibits it, you can make minor modifications to the photograph, such as changing its size or resolution. However, major modifications—for example, colorizing a black-and-white image or digitally removing elements of a photo—require permission under copyright law, and usually under the license agreement too. If the image bank or photographer discovers that you have made a major change without permission, it may decide to chase you for copyright infringement. In this event, it's possible that you could defend yourself under fair use principles, arguing that you had a right to make changes to the image. However, this is an unpredictable defense. In addition, if you are distributing the work of a European photographer in Europe, you may violate certain moral rights (special European copyright rights) if you tinker with the photographer's aesthetic judgment.

To avoid a lawsuit, notify the rights holder of your intent to modify the photo when you seek permission.

Respect Photo Credits

Your agreement could require that you include certain credit information along with the photo. Recent court cases have held that a failure to provide proper credit may justify a lawsuit. Make sure that your credits conform to the requirements of your agreement.

Basic Photo Permission Agreement

Below is a simple all-purpose photo permission agreement for rights-protected photos. Note that the included agreement lacks some provisions (such as dispute resolution and alternative payment systems) that may be included in more complete artwork agreements, omitted here because it is often easier to negotiate and obtain permission using short agreements. An explanation of the various provisions follows.

FORM

You can download this form (and all other forms in this book) from Nolo.com; for details, see the appendix. Most likely, the image bank will provide you with its own agreement. In that case, you can still use the sample agreement below to help you understand the image bank's version. Or, the image bank may not furnish its own agreement, in which case you can use this version.

Explanation for Photo Permission Agreement

- In the **introductory paragraph,** insert the names of the licensor (the party who owns the material) and the licensee (you or the person who is seeking permission).
- In the **Licensor Information** and **Licensee Publication Information** sections, complete the blank spaces.
- In the **Grant of Rights** section, complete the grant to reflect the rights you have negotiated. More information on the rights associated with grants is provided in Chapter 11, "Art and Merchandise Licenses."
- Complete the **Territory** section to reflect the regions in which you have acquired rights. For more information about territory, review Chapter 11.
- In the **Fees** section, indicate what type of fee has been negotiated by checking the appropriate box(es) and completing the information.
- Complete the **Credit and Samples** section to reflect your agreement with the licensor.
- A warranty is a contractual promise made by the licensor. Some licensors do not want to make promises, particularly promises that the work does not infringe any third parties' copyright or other rights. You may have to modify the **Warranty** section or strike it entirely if the licensor objects.
- If you believe you have the bargaining power to get the licensor to agree, you may want to include an indemnity provision in the agreement. Indemnity is a financial punishment if the licensor breaks its promises. Indemnity provisions are not included here. If you wish to add such a provision, samples and explanations are provided in Chapter 11.

Photo Permission Agreement

_____ ("Licensor")

is the owner of rights for the photograph described below (the "Selection").

_____ ("Licensee")

wants to acquire the right to use the Selection as specified in this agreement (the "Agreement").

Licensor Information

Title of work (the "Selection"): _____

Catalog number (if applicable): _____

Photographer_____

Licensee Publication Information

The Selection will appear in the following publication(s) (the "Work"):

(*Check if applicable and fill in blanks*)

☐ book—title: _____

☐ website—URL: _____

☐ periodical—title: _____

☐ event handout—title of event: _____

If to be used on a website, the Selection will appear on:

(*Check if applicable*)

☐ home page

☐ internal page

Name of publisher or sponsor (if different from Licensee): _____

Estimated date(s) of publication or posting: _____

If applicable, the estimated number of copies to be printed or produced (if a book, the estimated first print run): _____

If for sale, the price: $ _____

If copies are free to attendees of a program, the cost of program: _____

If a website, the average number of visitors per month: _____

Grant of Rights

Licensor grants to Licensee and Licensee's successors and assigns, the:

(*Select one*)

☐ nonexclusive

☐ exclusive

right to reproduce and distribute the Selection in:

(*Select all that apply*)

☐ the current edition of the Work.

☐ all editions of the Work.

☐ all foreign language versions of the Work.

☐ all derivative versions of the Work.

☐ all media now known or later devised.

☐ promotional materials published and distributed in conjunction with the Work.

☐ other rights _____ .

Territory

The rights granted under this Agreement shall be for _____ (the "Territory").

Fees

Licensee shall pay Licensor as follows:

(*Select payment option and fill in appropriate blanks*)

☐ **Flat Fee.** Licensee shall pay Licensor a flat fee of $ _____ as full payment for all rights granted. Payment shall be made:

☐ upon execution of this Agreement.

☐ upon publication.

☐ **Royalties and Advance.** Licensee agrees to pay Licensor a royalty of _____ % of Net Sales. Net Sales are defined as gross sales (the gross invoice amount billed customers) less quantity discounts and returns actually credited. Licensee agrees to pay Licensor an advance against royalties of $ _____ upon execution of this Agreement. Licensee shall pay Licensor within thirty (30) days after the end of each quarter. Licensee shall furnish an accurate statement of sales during that quarter. Licensor shall have the right to inspect Licensee's books upon reasonable notice.

Credit and Samples

(Check if applicable and fill in blanks)

☐ **Credit.** All versions of the Work that include the Selection shall contain the following statement: _____

☐ **Samples.** Upon publication, Licensee shall furnish _____ copies of the Work to Licensor.

Warranty

Licensor warrants that it has the right to grant permission for the uses of the Selection as specified above and that the Selection does not infringe the rights of any third parties.

(Check if applicable)

☐ Licensor warrants that a model release is on file for the Selection.

Miscellaneous

This Agreement may not be amended except in a written document signed by both parties. If a court finds any provision of this Agreement invalid or unenforceable, the remainder of this Agreement shall be interpreted so as best to effect the intent of the parties. This Agreement shall be governed by and interpreted in accordance with the laws of the State of _____ . This Agreement expresses the complete understanding of the parties with respect to the subject matter and supersedes all prior representations and understandings.

Licensor	Licensee
By: _____	By: _____
Name: _____	Name: _____
Title: _____	Title: _____
Address: _____	Address: _____
Date: _____	Date: _____
	Tax ID # _____

- Explanations for the **Miscellaneous** (also known as "boilerplate") provisions are provided in Chapter 11. If you believe you have the bargaining power to get the licensor to agree, you may want to include a provision that covers attorneys' fees or arbitration.

What About Movies, Videos, GIFs, and Animations?

If you're interested in acquiring rights for film, video, GIFs, or animations, all of the rules in this chapter apply to these moving images as well. Use permission for these kinds of works can be complicated if the content includes separately protectable components—for example, a video may contain a copyrighted song or still photograph. As a general rule, the principles described below will apply to both moving and still images. For more information on music and film, see Chapter 5. For information about public domain film and fair use, see Chapters 8 and 9, respectively.

CAUTION

Commercial uses are more complex. If you are seeking permission to use a photograph on behalf of an advertising agency or a company selling a product or service (for example, Nike or American Airlines), your use is more likely to be categorized as a commercial endorsement, which will trigger additional legal issues. Be sure to review Chapter 12 regarding the different releases you may be required to obtain.

When the Photograph Contains Art, Trademarks, or a Person's Image

What if the photograph you intend to use contains copyrighted artwork, a trademark, or a person's image? In that case you may need to obtain more than one permission, because commercial uses of people and trademarks may trigger additional legal rights and claims. In addition to copyright permission from the photographer, you may need permission from the copyright owner or trademark owner of the subject of the photograph, or from the person appearing in it. This section offers a brief explanation of these issues. You also may want to refer to Chapter 10, "Getting Permission to Use Trademarks," and Chapter 12, "Releases."

When the Photograph Contains Copyrighted Art

You may need two permissions if you want to reproduce a photograph that contains a copyrighted work of art. For example, if you want to use a photo that includes a mural by Diego Rivera in the background, you may need permission from the copyright owner of the Rivera mural as well as from the owner of the photograph. Whether permission is in fact required from the owner of the artwork depends on whether your use of the artwork within the photo would be considered a fair use under copyright law. Fair use principles are discussed in more detail in Chapter 9.

Generally speaking, you might not need permission if the artwork is incidental to your photo, such as artwork that appears in the far background of a street fair. A minimal use such as this may be deemed a fair use not requiring permission. For example, a court has ruled that the momentary appearance of an artist's work in a motion picture did not require permission. In another case, however, the appearance of a copyrighted poster in a television show did require permission. As explained in Chapter 9, relying on fair use principles can be risky, as the final word can only come from a judge.

RELATED TOPIC

Chapter 4, "Getting Permission to Use Artwork," provides information **on the relationship of photos and artwork** and discusses how to locate the copyright owners of artwork.

Dear Rich:

Reproducing a Photo of a Statue

As I understand copyright, if I visit a park and take a photo of a statue, I own the copyright to the photo and I can use it in a book. But if I open a magazine and take a photo of an illustration, I still own the copyright to the photo, but using it in a book would be a copyright violation. Why is it different?

Actually, they're not different. It's true you own the copyright in both photos but your copyright only extends to what you contributed, for example, the choice of subject matter, composition, lighting, etc. Your copyright does not extend to the statue itself. If the statue and the image are protected by copyright, it would be a violation to reproduce them in your book (unless permitted under fair use principles). And, if you register your photos with the Copyright Office, you're required to disclose (and exclude) those items in your application because they are not original to you.

In some countries (Canada, for example) art that is permanently situated in a public place or building can be photographed and reproduced without permission. Not so in the U.S., where unauthorized reproduction of a photo of a public statue can be costly, as the U.S. Postal Service learned. (The USPS mistakenly used a photo of a Las Vegas imitation of the Statue of Liberty—one with "a more contemporary, fresher face than the original"—and the sculptor of the Vegas statue sued and recovered $3.5 million.) The reverse principle—it is a violation of copyright law to create a sculpture of a photograph—has also been followed by the courts.

Few photographers of publicly-viewable statues need to worry about copyright lawsuits. The incidental appearance of a statue, for example, in a travel photo, a news photo, or an educational lesson is not likely to trigger a dispute, and if it did, the reproduction would probably qualify as fair use. In addition, many statues are in the public domain and do not require permission.

Q: Why Wasn't Warhol Sued?
A: He Was

Copyright is one of my favorite subjects, as I work with students who will soon be schoolteachers. Here is a question my students have been exploring. Considering all the problems Shepard Fairey had because of his derivative poster based on a photo of Barack Obama, I wonder, did Andy Warhol's use of photos of Campbell's soup cans and Marilyn Monroe get him into trouble with the owners of those original works?

The short answer to your question is that Warhol's art has triggered some lawsuits. Patricia Caulfield, the photographer whose work was used as the basis of Warhol's flower prints, sued in November 1966 and settled for cash and artwork. Warhol's 1964 work, *16 Jackies,* was the subject of a lawsuit brought against the Warhol Foundation in 1996 by the photographer of the original Jackie photos. That led the Foundation to sue Warhol's insurer. Warhol was never sued over his Marilyns, which were based on a publicity still of Monroe. Campbell's Soup Company didn't litigate; they exploited the efforts of their most famous chicken-noodle fan. The company even offers an Art of Soup contest in collaboration with the Warhol Museum. In 2022, the U.S. Supreme Court is expected to hear an appeal by the Warhol Foundation regarding whether a Warhol print featuring Prince was a fair use of a photograph of the musician.

When the Photograph Contains Trademarks

A trademark is any word, photograph, or symbol that is used to identify a specific product or service for sale. Familiar trademarks include Tesla, McDonald's, and Apple. Under trademark law, you do not need permission to reproduce a trademark if your use is "editorial"—or informational. An example of an editorial use is using the trademark to illustrate a newspaper article, magazine feature, or other literary statement. You do not need permission to use a trademark when making accurate, comparative product statements.

On the other hand, you are much more likely to need permission to use a trademark in a commercial context. You will probably need to get permission under any of the following circumstances:

- **Your use is likely to create confusion among consumers.** For example, your use of a photo of a jogger wearing a Nike shirt in an ad for your sports equipment website may confuse viewers as to whether Nike is associated with or endorses your site. You would need permission from Nike to use its logo or name (which appears in the photo).

- **Your use tarnishes or diminishes the strength of the trademark.** A rule known as the "dilution doctrine" prohibits the use of a trademark that weakens another famous mark by chipping away at its distinctiveness. In other words, the more just anyone is allowed to use the term "Nike," the less customers will make an automatic association between the term and actual Nike products. In addition, you might not be allowed to use a trademark if your use reflects poorly upon the trademark (also known as "tarnishing"). For example, if you use a photo of a woman wearing a Nike shirt on an adults-only website, the Nike company could stop the use.

- **You have modified the trademark.** Comparative advertising uses of trademarks are legal, but it is not permissible to modify the trademark when making comparisons. For example, a tractor company was found liable for animating the trademark of the John Deere Company in a television commercial.

It can be quite tricky to figure out whether or not permission may be required in a given situation. Even if you are legally entitled to use a trademark, some trademark owners—particularly owners of famous marks—will sue first and review the legal rules later.

For more information on trademark rules, review Chapter 10, "Getting Permission to Use Trademarks."

Dear Rich:

I Want to Create a *Superman* Coffee Table Book

I am working on a Superman *movie coffee table book that will be photo heavy and likely self-published. The photos come from my own collection, many of which were never seen by the public (and were not going to be used in publicity because they are production photos and not posed stills). I have run a website, www.capedwonder.com, for many years. It is a favorite among fans, and has been enjoyed by many in the* Superman *world over the years (including the late* Superman *director Richard Donner and the late Christopher Reeve). Warner Bros. has even bought photos from me for their DVD art. I am told that I have more photos than Warner's does in their vaults! My question is, do I need to get permission from Warner Bros. to publish these ultrarare photos? I don't need anything material-wise from WB since it's all in my archives. The photos were shot by various set photographers between early 1977 and the end of 1978.*

Somebody owns the copyright in the photos and we're guessing that it's Warner Brothers/DC Comics who acquired rights from whoever employed the set photographers. Even though WB paid you for access to your collection, they're probably the ones from whom you would need permission.

What about the *Superman* trademark? Besides copyright, Warner Brothers can hassle you if you're using trademarks to confuse fans into thinking that your book comes from or is endorsed by WB. One way to limit that claim is with appropriate disclaimers. In 1998, a publisher offered a *Godzilla* filmography book that included a brief disclaimer on the back cover. Toho, the company that owned rights to *Godzilla*, sued and won. According to the court, an appropriate disclaimer would have been: "The publication has not been prepared, approved, or licensed by any entity that created or produced the original Toho *Godzilla* films," and the disclaimer would be printed on the front cover and spine of the book in a distinguishing color or typestyle. In other words, to avoid trademark hassles, make your disclaimers clear and prominent.

The year copyright law changed. By the way, copyright law changed on January 1, 1978. Photos created after that date are subject to the new law, the Copyright Act of 1976, and photos before that date are subject to the old one, the 1909 Act. That shouldn't make much difference unless the set photographers were independent contractors and not employees.

From the FYI Dept. If you go ahead without permission, we'd suggest offering your book as a print-on-demand title. That way, if challenged, you can halt production without destroying inventory (often a request in copyright infringement lawsuits).

When the Photograph Contains a Person's Image

In general, you don't need permission to use a photograph of a person if your use is editorial and does not defame or invade the person's privacy (see below). An editorial use is an informational use, in which the photo is used to elaborate or illustrate an article or story. For example, no permission is necessary to use a photo of a paratrooper in an article about the Vietnam War. However, you do need permission (known as a "release" or "consent" in the context of people), for the uses described below. (Releases are discussed in Chapter 12.)

- **Your use is for commercial purposes—to advertise or sell a product or service.** Under "right of publicity" laws, you cannot use a person's name or image for commercial purposes without obtaining a release. For example, if you sell sweaters from your website, you would need permission to use a photo of a model wearing one of your sweaters. This right of publicity can survive a person's death, sometimes for as long as 50 years depending on state law. There are some exceptions to these rules. If your use is editorial—for example, a photo of a fashion model in a book about the fashion industry—you can use the photo to advertise the book without obtaining a release.

- **Your use invades a person's privacy.** Every person has the right to be left alone. If you are using a photograph that was taken surreptitiously (for instance, using a hidden camera on private property) or if your photo depicts very personal or potentially embarrassing activities (for example, medical treatment), you should obtain a release. Without a release, your use might violate state "right of privacy" laws. Keep in mind that a person's right to privacy only exists while they are alive. This is not true of the right of publicity that survives death in some states.

- **Your use is defamatory.** If your use of a photograph creates a false impression injuring someone's reputation, you could be liable for defamation, sometimes known as libel. For example, say you use a stock photo of two doctors to illustrate an article on physician-assisted suicide. If you did not obtain a release for that specific use, you may be subject to liability if the doctors sue you for damaging their reputations. There are some exceptions to defamation rules for public figures, such as politicians and celebrities, who have voluntarily thrown themselves into the public eye and, to a limited extent, for people who have become subject of a public controversy. For these people, you will only be liable if the public figure can prove that you acted with actual malice or reckless disregard for the truth—for example, you knowingly printed a damaging lie about someone. For non-public figures, if what you said is true, you are protected from liability—truth is an absolute defense. Keep in mind, however, that dredging up old (but truthful) facts may invade a person's right to privacy. A more in-depth explanation of these principles is provided in Chapter 12.

Stock Photo Resources

This section lists the many companies, directories, organizations, and other entities that may be able to help you obtain photographs and the rights to use them.

Image Banks

The image banks listed below are all accessible online. Some are rights-protected, some are royalty-free, and some offer both. Selection may vary from company to company, so check out a few to find the company that suits your needs.

Rights-Protected Image Banks

- AP/Wide World Photos: www.apimages.com
- Getty Images: www.gettyimages.com

Royalty-Free Image Banks

- iStock: www.istockphoto.com
- Shutterstock: www.shutterstock.com
- Dreamstime: www.dreamstime.com

Celebrity and Entertainment Image Banks

The image banks listed below have extensive collections of promotional photos, including images of celebrities, events, and movie stills:

- The Everett Collection: www.everettcollection.com
- Photofest: www.photofestnyc.com
- Motion Picture & Television Photo Archive: www.mptvimages.com

Image Bank Aggregators/Locators

- BigStock: www.bigstockphoto.com
- Fotosearch: www.fotosearch.com

Resources for Locating Photographers

- The American Society of Media Photographers: www.asmp.org
- Professional Photographers of America: www.ppa.com
- National Press Photographers Association: https://nppa.org
- American Photographic Artists: https://apanational.org

Resources for Locating Picture Researchers

- American Society of Picture Professionals: aspp.com

Getting Permission to Use Artwork

This chapter explains how to obtain permission to reproduce artwork—meaning fine art or graphic art. Fine art includes one-of-a-kind or limited edition works, such as a limited edition silkscreen print by Andy Warhol, a mobile by Alexander Calder, or a painting by Georgia O'Keeffe. Graphic artwork is any art intended for commercial reproduction, such as an illustration, design, icon, clip art, cartoon, or comic. This chapter addresses these types of works together because the process of obtaining permission to use them—and the ways in which they are used—are similar, and the rights are sometimes controlled by one company.

This chapter also offers tips for finding clip art (existing images available for license) and sample agreements. At the end of the chapter you'll find two model agreements: a basic license for acquiring permission to use artwork in a publication or website, and an agreement for using artwork in films and videos.

Acquiring Rights to Artwork

If you need to reproduce a specific item of artwork that's not in the public domain—for example, a painting by Pablo Picasso—you will need to negotiate with whoever owns copyright in the artwork (in this case, Picasso's estate) for the right to reproduce it. If, on the other hand, you want to use a fine art painting that is in the public domain—the *Mona Lisa*, for example—you won't have to acquire the rights to reproduce the work, because public domain works are free to copy. Keep in mind that if you want a high resolution copy of a public domain work and you can't take the photo yourself—for example, photographic access is denied—you might have to seek the rights from a gallery or artist rights organization that controls access.

If you do not need a specific artwork and have a suitable budget, you may want to specially commission artwork and acquire rights to use it. For example, if you need illustrations for a book, you can hire a graphic artist and acquire exclusive and unlimited rights to the artwork. Ownership can be acquired under an employment arrangement, by an assignment, or by using a work-for-hire agreement (acquiring ownership is explained in Chapter 15).

Many artists prefer not to convey all rights and instead convey limited rights by granting a license. A sample license agreement is provided at the end of this chapter. When graphic artwork is used on merchandise such as T-shirts or ceramic cups, a special artwork merchandise license agreement is used (see Chapter 11) that provides for ongoing royalty payments to the artist.

If your budget is small, you may prefer to use clip art. The term "clip art" simply refers to existing graphic art images that are available either for a fixed fee or for free. Clip art can often be used for unlimited purposes, so a permission agreement is not required. However, some clip art collections have limitations on use, so you should examine the shrink-wrap or click-wrap agreement accompanying the artwork.

Dear Rich:

Can I Reproduce Covers of Magazines?

My company is launching a magazine on the subject of marketing. One of the news stories in the mag talks about how luxury print advertising is expected to increase this year. We've included a quote from a publisher who talks about how some of their household name magazines are experiencing good success. I'd like to know if it's okay to illustrate our editorial feature with some images of the front covers of the magazines referenced in the story.

There are a few questions that should be asked when someone reproduces a magazine cover:

- **Are you infringing the magazine's trademark?** In your case, no, because you are using it for editorial purposes (as we explain in Chapter 10).
- **If there is a person on the cover, are you violating that person's right of publicity?** Not based on your use (see Chapter 12).
- **Are you violating the magazine's copyright by reproducing the cover without permission?** Yes, reproduction without permission is infringement. However, you're likely to be excused as a fair use because you're commenting on the magazine and especially if the reproduction is a reduced or thumbnail size (see more on fair use in Chapter 9).

Fine Art: Paintings, Sculptures, and Limited Editions

The main thing to remember when seeking permission to use fine art is that one permission may not be enough. As with other forms of creative work, fine art is protected by a number of rights that may be held by different owners. To use just one work, you may need to obtain permission from two or more people or businesses, including:

- **The copyright owner of the artwork.** If the artwork is copyright protected, you need permission from the copyright owner—usually the artist or the artist's estate (if the artist is deceased). Copyright protection for foreign works may last longer than works protected under U.S. law. If you are unsure whether a work is protected under copyright, review Chapter 8.

- **The copyright owner of a photograph of the artwork.** If you are using photographs of artwork, you may need permission from the copyright owner of the photographs as well as from the copyright owner of the artwork itself.

- **The people who appear in, or the owners of, trademarks or copyrighted art included in the fine art.** Depending on your use, you may need a release for any people, trademarks, or copyrightable art included in the artwork. (Review Chapters 10 and 12.)

- **The owner of the artwork.** If you want to photograph a work of fine art, you may have to get access from its owner, usually a museum or a private owner. Many museums won't allow you to photograph their art; instead they hire a photographer and charge you for the photograph.

When seeking permission to use fine art, always ask what rights you are obtaining from the person granting you permission. Never assume the person who "rents" you a fine art image controls the copyright in the underlying artwork, as that's often not the case.

Obtaining Photos of Fine Art

Photographs of fine art may be obtained from the museum or gallery exhibiting the work or through museums affiliated with the Smithsonian Institution. Gallery resources are provided at the end of this chapter. Image banks (companies that license photos and artwork) also supply high-quality copies of copyrighted and public domain fine art. Getty Images (www.gettyimages.com) has an extensive collection of fine art images. In addition to these sources, the Artists Rights Society (ARS; www.arsny.com; discussed in more detail just below), can, for a fee, help you locate high-quality photographs of public domain works.

Getting Permission to Use Copyrighted Fine Art

The Artists Rights Society (ARS), represents the intellectual property rights of more than 80,000 visual artists and their estates. (In 2018, ARS absorbed its major competitor, VAGA (Visual Artists and Galleries Association).) The ARS can grant permission for reproduction of copyrighted works for most common uses such as publications, websites, advertisements, and merchandise.

To locate the rights holder of copyrighted fine art, start by contacting ARS. In the case of a fine artist who is not represented by ARS, the best starting point is the institution or gallery in which the artist's work is exhibited. Often, the gallery can refer you to the rights holder.

EXAMPLE: In 2010, I sought to reproduce a black-and-white copy of *Monogram*, a fine artwork by Robert Rauschenberg. I wanted to use the artwork in a book with an initial printing of 5,000 copies. A VAGA (now ARS) representative explained that the fee for my use would be $75. (That fee was subsequently waived for this use.)

Monogram © Robert Rauschenberg Foundation

Dear Rich:

Can I Reproduce Images From the Crystal Bridges Museum?

I live near Crystal Bridges Museum. We here in Northwest Arkansas are so excited to have access, free access in fact, since the museum has been given an endowment by Wal-Mart that will allow the nonprofit museum to be forever free to the public, to see great American art from colonial times to the present. Many of these artworks are early works (pre-1927) and are part of the public domain. I have a new website I'm developing for public domain images. Crystal Bridges allows photographs to be taken of the art as long as a tripod or flash is not used. However, their photography policy states that photos of the art are only to be used for personal use. I take this to mean that they cannot be used on my site that shares images with the whole wide Web world. Am I correct in my assumption that they don't have the right to restrict the use of my photographs of their public domain artworks? I am not trying to claim copyright of the photographs, since they will be merely reproductions of public domain works.

Whether you can reproduce imagery that's in the public domain really depends on one thing: Did you enter into an agreement with the museum not to reproduce the images? You're probably thinking, "I didn't enter into any agreements with Crystal Bridges." But obtaining an admission ticket, if the ticket contains certain terms and conditions, may qualify as the type of agreement we're talking about. This may seem incredibly creepy—to condition admission into the museum based on your promise not to reproduce public domain imagery—but it's not uncommon in the copyright world and these so-called licenses are generally enforceable. Here's what public domain expert Steve Fishman has to say about the practice in his excellent public domain guide.

"Many copyright experts believe that licenses imposing copyright-like restriction on how the public may use public domain materials should be legally unenforceable. This is because the federal copyright law preempts (overrides) state contract law and prevents people from using contracts to create their own private copyrights. Moreover, there are sound policy reasons for holding such license restrictions unenforceable—their widespread use diminishes the public's access to the public domain. However, almost all courts have ignored the experts and enforced these licenses."

What's a valid license? To have a valid license, you and the museum must assent to the terms and conditions, typically at the time when you enter. If the admission ticket contains no restrictive provisions and you never assented knowingly to such conditions, there probably is no license in place. For example, it's unlikely that an after-the-fact assertion of rights—a sign on the way out of the museum that tells you that you cannot reproduce the imagery—is legally enforceable as a contractual license.

What about the Crystal Bridges website? Each page of images at the Crystal Bridges website contains the statement:

Works of art in Crystal Bridges' collection are protected by copyright and may not be used without permission. For more information visit Rights and Reproductions.

That sounds foreboding but we're not sure that statement creates a binding license. It reminds us more of a tip jar, left in view to trigger a hoped-for result. The museum would have a much stronger argument that its terms and conditions are binding if the user had to assent to these terms and conditions— that is, click a "Yes, I Agree" button to access the works. The fact that the site includes "copyrighted" photographs of public domain artworks also doesn't affect your ability to copy and reproduce that artwork. Courts have held that "slavish copying" of public domain works does not make the photographs protectable under copyright law. Although we're not a betting blog, if we had to bet, we'd place our money on the fact that currently public domain images at the site can be copied and reproduced without permission.

One last thing. Just because a painting was created before 1927 doesn't mean it's in the public domain. It must have been published before 1927. You may be surprised to learn that displaying a painting in a museum, for example, does not amount to publication. Publication refers to reproduction of the image, for example in a magazine, postcard, or book. To learn more about these tricky public domain rules, check out Stephen Fishman's tome, *The Public Domain* (Nolo).

One other last thing. We're not encouraging you to get chased by the museum and we appreciate the fact that great art is being made available to the masses at no charge. But is it really free? The driving force behind these efforts to restrict reproduction is a desire to jack up gift shop sales and generate licensing revenue. We hope the museum rethinks its desire to reclaim and restrict rights to artwork that our government has designated to be freely available to the public.

Photographs of Fine Art

Sometimes you must get (and pay for) two permissions to reproduce a photograph of copyrighted artwork: one to use the artwork and a second to use the photograph of the artwork. This practice is derived from the principle that a photograph of an artwork and the artwork itself are two separate copyrighted works. Unfortunately, it's not always easy to figure out if a photograph is protected by copyright and whether a separate permission is necessary.

One factor used to make this determination is whether the subject of the photograph is itself protected by copyright. Another factor, which can be very subtle and difficult to measure, is the way in which the subject was photographed, including aspects such as lighting and camera angle.

In cases involving public domain works, the federal courts have ruled that "slavish" (nearly identical) copies of public domain works don't merit copyright protection. *(Hearn v. Meyer,* 664 F.Supp. 832 (S.D.N.Y. 1987).) In other words, a photographer cannot acquire protection for a perfect photographic reproduction of the *Mona Lisa. (Bridgeman Art Library Ltd. v. Corel Corp.,* 36 F.Supp.2d 191 (S.D.N.Y. 1999).)

Unfortunately, there have not been enough court decisions to allow photographers, artists, and academics to determine conclusively when a photograph of a painting acquires separate protection. In general, the more the photo is an exact reproduction of the original, the less likely it is protected by copyright (meaning you don't need permission to use the photograph). On the other hand, if the photograph has original elements in it such as unusual colored lighting, special effects, or other additions to the piece of art itself, it's more likely that the photographer owns copyright in the photo and that you need permission to use it.

Regardless of the copyright rules (and regardless of whether the work is in the public domain), you may have to pay to use a photo owned by a museum, gallery, or image bank. In some cases, you may have to sign an agreement promising that you won't reproduce the photographic image other than for the agreed purposes. Such an agreement might not be legally enforceable—for example, if you use an exact photographic reproduction of a public domain work without anything added by the photographer to create a separately copyrightable work. However, as a practical matter, you probably want to avoid the expense and aggravation of a lawsuit on the issue. For that reason, paying for photo reproductions of artwork is often a practical necessity.

Graphic Art

Graphic art is any illustration intended for commercial reproduction, whether in magazines, books, advertisements, or online. As with other types of artwork, how you obtain the right to use graphic art depends on whether you have the art created specifically for your use, or you use existing artwork.

Obtaining Rights to Works Created for You

If an artist creates a work for you, your right to use the work will be based on an assignment, a work-for-hire agreement, or a license:

- An assignment is a transfer of copyright ownership. In return for a payment (or ongoing payments) you acquire copyright ownership in the artwork. Acquiring ownership is explained in Chapter 15.
- A work made for hire is owned by the hiring party, not the artist. Works made for hire are created in a number of ways. If the artist is your employee and creates the work within the course of employment, the work will be a work for hire. A work for hire can also be created if: (1) You commissioned the work; (2) the work falls into certain categories; or (3) you entered into a written work-for-hire agreement. Assignments and works made for hire are discussed in Chapter 15.
- A license is the right to use the artwork for a specific purpose. A license does not transfer copyright ownership.

Obtaining Rights to Existing Artwork

If you want to use graphic art that already exists and was not created for your use, you can usually acquire the rights you need by license. Start by contacting the publisher (magazine, newspaper, or website, for example) in which the graphic art appeared. Since publishers generally try to acquire all rights from graphic artists, it's possible that the publisher may own the rights you need. If the publisher doesn't own the rights or is unable to help, you'll have to search for the graphic artist. Searching online may do the trick, or you could try contacting the Graphic Artists Guild (GAG) (www.graphicartistsguild.org). The GAG has an artist locator service and publishes the *Graphic Artists Guild Handbook*.

Reproductions of Architecture

Under a copyright amendment passed in 1990, some works of architecture were granted copyright protection. You cannot reproduce the architectural plans or the architect's renderings (illustrations of the building) or mock-ups (the miniature constructions of the building). However, you can photograph a copyrighted building if it is visible from a public place, and you can reproduce your photograph without infringing copyright.

> EXAMPLE: Ronald has acquired copyright protection for the architectural design of his new casino, Ace Towers. The building is visible from the public beach in Atlantic City. Shirley photographs the building and sells her photographs in postcard reproductions. Shirley is not infringing Ronald's architectural copyright.

It is also possible that a unique building design may serve as a trademark—for example, the novel shape and appearance of a White Castle restaurant. In this event, the commercial reproduction of the trademarked appearance of the building may trigger a lawsuit for trademark infringement. This is precisely what happened when a photographer shot and reproduced pictures of the Rock and Roll Hall of Fame—which the owners claimed was protected by trademark. A federal appeals court ultimately ruled that the use was not a trademark infringement. For more information on this case and trademark laws, review Chapter 10, "Getting Permission to Use Trademarks."

Dear Rich: **Do You Need Permission to Publish Pictures of Buildings?**

I have a question. Do I need to ask permission to publish a picture that I took that contains several local buildings and a city cultural monument?

If you took the picture, you own the copyright (with exceptions, if you were hired to take it). As for the copyright in the buildings, it's true that architecture created after 1990 is protected under copyright law, but that's not an issue for you because there is an exception that permits you to photograph and publish constructed buildings that are publicly viewable. (That's not true if you must trespass on private property to photograph the building.) Even if the building contains sculptural elements like vampire figures, you can still photograph those elements and even use them as part of the backdrop in a Batman movie. (Check Copyright Office Circular 41—*Copyright Registration of Architectural Works*—for more information.) The city monument (considered as a work of art), may be a different copyright issue. If it has been around for more than 85 years, it's most likely in the public domain (and even if it's newer than that, it may be PD as well). Post-1926 monuments may be protected under copyright law, in which case, you can expect to get hassled (though public pressure can always change public policy). Generally, you don't need to worry about a lawsuit over photos of public art unless your use is blatantly commercial—for example, in a movie, TV show, or on a poster.

There's a minor hiccup when it comes to trademark law. Building owners have claimed building appearances as a trademark when used in connection with the sale of goods and services—think White Castle and the Sears Tower. But in order for a trademark owner to stop you, the following would have to be true: (1) the building would have to have an identifiable, distinctive appearance; (2) the building would have to be publicly associated with certain goods or services; (3) your use would have to be commercial (not editorial); and (4) your use would have to be linked to an offer or endorsement of similar goods or services. For example, you will run into problems if you use a picture of the Transamerica Pyramid in an ad for another company's financial services. Generally, this strategy hasn't always fared so well for trademark owners, and you probably won't need to worry about it. If you are concerned—for example, you're working for an ad agency or movie company—obtain a release for your photography.

Actually, the biggest hurdle for photographers in public spaces is a national paranoia following 9/11, as exhibited by building owners, employees, and security guards. Photographers of public spaces are now considered suspect even when taking pictures of their own kids. Anyway, feel free to come by and photograph the Dear Rich Building anytime—the Dear Rich Staff will even take you on a guided tour.

Children's Book Illustrators

If you're looking for a graphic artist who has illustrated a children's book, contact the Society of Children's Book Writers and Illustrators (SCBWI), who can put you in touch with any member illustrator. Contact information for this organization appears in the resource section at the end of this chapter.

Reproducing U.S. Postage Stamps

The United States Postal Service (USPS) owns the copyright to all stamps issued after 1977. In other words, you are free to reproduce U.S. postage stamps issued before 1978. However, if you reproduce pre-1978 public domain postage stamps in color, the reproduction must be at least 50% larger or 25% smaller than the original stamp. Black-and-white reproductions can be any size.

For stamps issued after 1977, you can learn more about the licensing requirements for commercial and nonprofit use of postage stamps at https://about.usps.com/doing-business/rights-permissions/welcome.htm.

Comics and Cartoons

Comics and cartoons include a variety of graphic artwork. Comics may be in strip or book form, both of which involve a series of drawings telling a story. Single-panel drawings telling a joke or gag are often called cartoons. Animated cartoons include TV shows like *The Simpsons*, movies like *Toy Story* or *Frozen*, and old series like *Bugs Bunny* or *Daffy Duck*. Below we explain the process of obtaining rights to use various types of print or animated comics.

Comic Books

To obtain rights to reproduce images from comic books, start with the publisher, who typically owns the rights to the comic books it publishes. Rights for underground, experimental, or other types of comics may be owned by either the publisher or the individual artists. Sometimes, the name located in the copyright notice indicates ownership. If the artist's name is in the notice, for example, "Copyright 2022 Steve Purcell," then the artist has probably retained reprint rights.

Determining the rights for comic books published before 1965 may prove complex, as many comic publishers have folded, sold rights to other companies, or failed to renew their copyright. Comicon (www.comicon.com) is a good source of comic book information and links. A number of major comic book publishers are listed at the end of this chapter.

Comic Strips, Editorial Cartoons, and Single-Panel Cartoons

Reprint rights for most newspaper comic strips and for many editorial cartoons (also known as political cartoons) are controlled by syndicates. Editorial cartoons or comic strips not owned by a syndicate are probably owned by the individual newspaper or magazine employing the cartoonist. Contact the syndicate or publication for information regarding permission. You'll usually find the name of the cartoonist and the syndicate printed vertically between the panels of the strip.

Besides the syndicates and publications, other resources exist to help you find cartoonists. For example, a site called Politicalcartoons.com provides email addresses for many editorial cartoonists. For your reference, a list of syndicates, as well as other resources for finding editorial cartoonists, appears at the end of this chapter.

Single-panel cartoons (not comic strips or editorial cartoons) are often owned by the publications in which they appear. If you're seeking to use a single-panel cartoon from a magazine, start by contacting that magazine's permission department. If calling the publication does not provide leads, you may be able to get contact information for the cartoonist through the National Cartoonists Society. If you're interested in *New Yorker* cartoons, Cartoonbank.com (www.cartoonbank.com) is a great one-stop source for licensing rights.

In the past few years, syndicates have streamlined the licensing process and can accommodate a broad range of licensing requests. Fees for a comic strip or single-panel cartoon range from $35 to several hundred dollars depending on the type of use.

Animated Cartoons

Rights to an animated cartoon series such as *The Simpsons* or *The Flintstones* are usually owned by an entertainment production company. If the cartoon series is in syndication, you can find the production company by reviewing the credits at the end of any episode. Quite often, this is the last or next to last credit. The production company can also be determined online at the Internet Movie Database (www.imdb.com), a searchable database of thousands of films and television shows.

Most entertainment production companies can be found online or in the New York, Nashville, or Los Angeles telephone listings. When you contact the company, ask for the publicity, media relations, or public relations department.

CAUTION
Reproducing cartoon characters may raise additional issues. If you want to obtain permission to use a particular cartoon character such as Superman or Andrea Anaconda, review Chapter 10, "Getting Permission to Use Trademarks."

Medical Illustrations

Do you need medical or anatomical imagery? Medical illustrators specialize in anatomical and health-related illustrations. Rights for illustrations are often controlled by publishers. If the publisher is unable to help, you can find a specific medical illustrator by contacting the Association of Medical Illustrators. You can also find medical clip art on the Web. One of the largest CD collections is provided by LifeART (www.fotosearch.com/lifeart), which offers medical clip art images at a cost of approximately $70 per image. Other websites offering medical images can be located using the search term "medical clip art."

Dear Rich:

Can I Reproduce Images From *Gray's Anatomy*?

I found a website that includes a huge number of wonderful illustrations from the original 1918 printing of Gray's Anatomy of the Human Body *that I'd like to use. The pitfall is our research librarians aren't certain if we are allowed to utilize any of the online imagery since it's saying the company renewed the copyright in 2000. If I use the reproduced 1918 digitized illustrations from the site am I violating any copyright? Or am I well within the public domain period to use these images without permission or attribution?*

Copy all you want from the 20th edition of *Gray's Anatomy*. You're free to copy it from the site where you found it, or if you're uncomfortable with that, use any of the 1,247 graphic plates from the book that have been digitized and posted at the Wikimedia site. When you click on any image there, you'll see an expanded reproduction and the following explanatory tag on the bottom of the page.

> *This faithful reproduction of a lithograph plate from* Gray's Anatomy, *a two-dimensional work of art, is not copyrightable in the U.S. as per* Bridgeman Art Library v. Corel Corp. ...

What's that mean? It means that the original image in the book is in the public domain in the U.S. and that slavish digitized reproductions (exact copies) are also in the public domain, as decided by a New York federal court in the case of *Bridgeman Art Library v. Corel Corp.*, 36 F.Supp. 2d 191 (S.D.N.Y. 1999). Because you're only asking about print rights in the U.S., we don't address worldwide rights (and we are not sure that you can rely on Wikimedia's conclusions regarding worldwide use, as well. You'd be better off consulting Steve Fishman's *Public Domain* book).

What about the site's terms of use? The terms of use might claim something like, "All materials published and provided on the [site] are protected by copyright. ..." That kind of wishful thinking is popular at a lot of sites that publish public domain works. It's true that the 21st through the 30th editions of *Gray's Anatomy* are protected, but the 20th edition published in 1918—the one featured on the site you found—is safely in the PD in the U.S. (and probably in the rest of the world as well). Unless the site has done something original to the works, for example, added distinctive coloring and titles, there is no claim the site can make to the images.

Royalty-Free and Public Domain Clip Art

An alternative to paying licensing fees to use artwork is to use public domain artwork or artwork offered on a royalty-free basis. This type of artwork is sometimes referred to as clip art, or royalty-free or copyright-free artwork, and is sold in books, digital bundles, or distributed free through websites.

The Terms

The terms clip art, public domain, royalty free, and copyright free are often used interchangeably (and confusingly):

- **Clip art** is a general term used to refer to any artwork that is available in a collection, either in a book, or in digital form. Clip art may be in the public domain or royalty free.

- **Public domain** art is not protected by copyright. Many publishers, such as Dover Books, specialize in offering collections of public domain art. This image of the man and dog is from a Dover publication entitled *Humorous Victorian Spot Illustrations*. You are free to copy and use the individual artwork in a public domain collection without permission. However, you are not free to copy and sell the collection.

- Unlike public domain art, **royalty-free** art is protected under copyright law and cannot be used for free. However, once you buy the collection or pay for access to a website that contains royalty-free artwork, your license to use the images is largely unlimited, so you can usually use the works numerous times for a broad range of uses. Use for merchandising or commercial endorsements, however, is usually not allowed—the major exception to the rule that you can use royalty-free images any way you like. See Chapter 11 for special rules surrounding merchandising and commercial uses.

- Because it can mean several things, the term **copyright free** can be confusing. Some people use it to refer to public domain artwork; others use it to refer to royalty-free artwork. Often, it's used to describe artwork that websites offer for free to the public—whether the works are public domain works or royalty-free works. This book does not use the term "copyright free," but instead sticks with the terms "royalty free," for artwork that can be licensed for a wide range of uses, and the term "public domain work," for artwork that can be used for free.

Finding and Using Clip Art

Clip art is often downloadable from the Web. To find websites that offer clip art, use the keywords "clip art," "royalty free," or "copyright free" in any search engine. Many of the royalty-free photo resources listed in Chapter 3 also provide royalty-free clip art.

> **Dear Rich:**
>
> **Source for Hard-Copy Public Domain Clip Art**
>
> *My sister and I are planning on writing a small book about our mom. I plan on illustrating the book. What is a good source of clip art that I can use without worrying about copyright infringement ? I actually want a hard copy of images that I can physically cut out the old-fashioned way.*
>
> The short answer is that one of the best sources of hard-copy clip art is CLIPART (www.clipart.com). You can also find a great deal of public domain art (and inspiration) at The Public Domain Review (https://publicdomainreview.org).

Clip art—which generally includes royalty-free and public domain artwork —is fine for most standard business and personal uses. The only significant drawbacks to using this type of artwork are that the quality varies and that competitors are free to use the same image by accessing the same website. If you are seeking exclusive rights to artwork, you should either hire an artist (see Chapter 15) or enter into an exclusive license to use a graphic work.

Sometimes clip art is sold for a flat fee or a subscription fee. Use is limited only by the terms of the shrink-wrap or click-wrap agreement (discussed below).

EULAs and Click-Wrap Agreements

To impose restrictions, many clip art publishers use a contract known as an end-user license agreement (EULA), also known as a "click-wrap agreement," or "browser-wrap agreement." Typically, the user enters into the agreement online and must click to accept the conditions before accessing a website or using software. Review the EULA that accompanies a clip art collection before clicking "Okay" or "I Agree." These agreements contain a list of dos and don'ts—sometimes a more restrictive list than required under copyright law.

For example, the following is a list of conditions you might see in a click-wrap agreement for clip art:

This software contains original clip art that is fully protected by copyrights. The original purchaser of the software is authorized to use individual items to produce copyright-free art for the printing of newsletters and the like. However, this collection may not be reproduced in whole or in part as a collection or individually as stock engravings, prints, negatives, positives, stock printing, and the like.

In other words, you are free to use the clip art as a book illustration or in an ad, but you cannot reprint the collection in its entirety or sell individual images.

EXAMPLE: A company downloaded several volumes of fire-fighting clip art and then offered clip art packages at its website. The company was found liable for copyright infringement for copying the three volumes of software clip art and placing it on a website for downloading, without the authorization of the clip art owner. (*Marobie-Fl, Inc. v. National Association of Fire Equipment Distributors,* 983 F.Supp. 1167 (E.D. Ill. 1997).)

Although only a few courts have reviewed the legality of click-wrap and shrink-wrap agreements, the majority of these courts have enforced them. In other words, if you do business with artwork owners who insist on these types of agreements, they'll probably be able to enforce them against you in court if you violate the terms.

Searching for Art

There's a wide range and variety of art indexed online. If you're looking for a particular artist or work, the simple solution would be to use a search engine like Google. Your goal is to find a means of contacting the artist, the artist's estate, or whoever controls the rights to the artist's work.

But what if you don't have a specific artist or work in mind and you'd just like to see what's available for your use? It used to be that search engines typically searched based on the type of file—for example, GIF and JPG—and were unable to distinguish as to the content.

In recent years, however, the major search engines have done a relatively decent job of sorting out graphic clip art from photos. Google's Advanced Search features (see below) enable a user to search solely for clip art, and even to filter it further based on images that are available for commercial use, black and white, or other variables.

EXAMPLE: We wanted to find an image of an angel, and began our search using Google's Advanced Image Search. We typed in the word "angel," and chose the "Black and White" option. We looked for images that were available for commercial reuse. We found the image, "An angel swooping in to save the day." The image is available under a Creative Commons license and our only requirement for republication is to attribute the image to eyehook.com.

Google

Advanced Image Search

Find images with...		To do this in the search box
all these words:	|	Type the important words: `winter hoarfrost`
this exact word or phrase:		Put exact words in quotes: `"frost flower"`
any of these words:		Type OR between all the words you want: `trees OR weeds OR grasses`
none of these words:		Put a minus sign just before words you don't want: `-windows`

Then narrow your results by...

image size:	any size	Find images in any size you need.
aspect ratio:	any aspect ratio	Specify the shape of images.
colors in image:	● any color ○ full color ○ black & white ○ transparent ○ this color:	Find images in your preferred colors.
type of image:	any type	Limit the kind of images you find.
region:	any region	Find images published in a particular region.
site or domain:		Search one site (like `sfmoma.org`) or limit your results to a domain like `.edu`, `.org` or `.gov`
SafeSearch:	Show most relevant results	Tell SafeSearch whether to filter sexually explicit content.
file type:	any format	Find images in the format you prefer.
usage rights:	not filtered by license	Find images you are free to use yourself.

Advanced Search

Millions of Images: The Smithsonian

The Smithsonian Institution in Washington, DC, is more than a single institution —it's an umbrella organization for national museums, libraries, and archives. It provides an invaluable link to millions of photographic, fine art, and historical images from sources such as the Archives of American Art, Freer Gallery of Art, Gem & Mineral Collection, Harvard-Smithsonian Center for Astrophysics, National Air & Space Museum, National Museum of African Art, National Museum of American Art, National Museum of American History, National Museum of Natural History, National Museum of the American Indian, National Portrait Gallery, and the National Postal Museum.

Unfortunately, there is no comprehensive Smithsonian guide that explains how to locate various materials. You may need to make several telephone calls until your request arrives at the correct curatorial or collecting unit. (The collecting unit is the museum or gallery that controls the rights to the work.) Permission to publish a photograph of an item can only be granted by the Smithsonian collecting unit that holds the original object or image. That unit also provides you with the Smithsonian negative number, a necessary element if you need a copy of a photograph. To locate the right collecting unit, use the Public Inquiry Mail Service, the Smithsonian telephone book, or one of the various Smithsonian websites that explain where collecting units are located. These resources are listed below.

The Smithsonian and its affiliated institutions are not considered to be U.S. government agencies for copyright purposes. This means they are allowed to claim copyright in images they make of works in their collections.

The resources below can help you locate images affiliated with the Smithsonian Institution:

- Smithsonian Institution Archives: https://siarchives.si.edu
- Smithsonian Institution Research Information System (SIRIS): https:// siris.si.edu. At this site you can search the holdings of the Smithsonian Institution Libraries, several Smithsonian archival repositories, and other special collections areas.

As we discussed in Chapter 3, one of the most popular alternatives to paying for image licensing is to use imagery that's subject to a Creative Commons license. Images that are associated with a Creative Commons license display the Creative Commons logo (two C's in a circle) and usually state which rights are associated with the artwork. Typically, most commercial uses are permitted, provided there is attribution. In many cases, the artists permit the creation of derivatives based on their artwork.

Using Picture Researchers

If you are having difficulty locating a particular artwork item, consider using the services of a professional picture researcher. Picture researchers are skilled at digging into a variety of resources such as the Library of Congress, the Smithsonian Institution, or online image banks. These researchers are usually paid per day (approximately $250-$500), although some charge by the hour. As explained in Chapter 3, many picture researchers have specialties, so you may want to contact the American Society of Picture Professionals (listed in the resource section at the end of this chapter) to find someone appropriate for your needs.

Modifying Artwork

Modifications to artwork—for example, colorizing a black-and-white image or digitally removing elements of a picture—require permission under U.S. copyright law. In addition, under European and U.S. laws, artists possess special rights known as moral rights. You may violate these moral rights if you tinker with the artist's aesthetic judgment. When seeking permission, notify the rights holder of your intent to modify the work or seek a release that grants you permission to make your intended alterations. A statement like: "Licensor grants to Licensee the right to modify the artwork as follows: [describe the modification]" should suffice.

Artwork Fees and Agreements

Fees and agreements for using artwork are similar to those for using stock photography—photos and artwork are often licensed from the same source. As with licensing photos, fees and agreements for licensing artwork vary depending on the work and your use, increasing for exclusivity, higher resolution, and advertising and corporate uses. The fee for using a cartoon in a company newsletter may cost as little as $25, while the fee for reproducing fine art within a book may be several hundred dollars. The detailed discussion in Chapter 3 of fee information for rights-protected photos also applies to artwork. Please refer to that section for in-depth fee information.

Below are two sample agreements: a simple all-purpose artwork license agreement and an agreement for using artwork in a film or video. If you want to reproduce artwork on posters, postcards, mugs, or other merchandise, see Chapter 11, "Art and Merchandise Licenses."

Sample Artwork Permission Agreement

Below is a basic all-purpose artwork permission agreement. Note that this agreement lacks some of the provisions (such as dispute resolution and alternative payment systems) that may be included in more complete artwork agreements—omitted here because it is easier to negotiate and obtain permission using short agreements. An explanation of the various provisions follows.

 FORM
You can download this form (and all other forms in this book) from Nolo.com; for details, see the appendix.

Explanation for Artwork Permission Agreement

- In the **introductory paragraph,** insert the names of the licensor (the party who owns the material) and the licensee (you or the person who is seeking permission).

- In the **Licensor Information** and **Licensee Publication Information** sections, complete the blank spaces to describe the artwork you want to use and the work in which you plan to use it.
- In the **Grant of Rights** section, complete the grant to reflect the rights you have negotiated. More information on the rights associated with grants is provided in Chapter 11, "Art and Merchandise Licenses."
- Complete the **Territory** section to reflect the regions in which you are acquiring rights. For more help, review Chapter 11.
- In the **Fees** section, indicate what type of fee has been negotiated by checking the appropriate box(es) and complete the information.
- Complete the **Credit and Samples** section to reflect your agreement with the licensor.
- As explained in Chapter 11, a warranty is a contractual promise made by the licensor. Some licensors do not want to make promises, particularly promises that the work does not infringe any third parties' copyright or other rights. You may have to modify the **Warranty** section or strike it entirely if the licensor objects.
- If you believe you have the bargaining power to get the licensor to agree, you may want to include an indemnity provision in the agreement. Indemnity is a financial punishment if the licensor breaks its promises. Indemnity provisions are not included here. If you wish to add such a provision, samples and explanations are provided in Chapter 11.
- Explanations for the **Miscellaneous** or "boilerplate" provisions are provided in Chapter 11. If you believe you have the bargaining power to get the licensor to agree, you may want to include a provision that covers attorneys' fees or arbitration.

CAUTION

Commercial uses are more complex. If you are seeking permission to use artwork on behalf of an advertising agency or a company selling a product or service (for example, Nike or American Airlines), your use is more likely to be categorized as a commercial endorsement, which will trigger additional legal issues. Review Chapter 12 regarding releases you may be required to obtain.

Artwork Permission Agreement

_____ ("Licensor")
is the owner of rights for the artwork described below (the "Selection"). _____
_____ ("Licensee") wants to acquire
the right to use the Selection as specified in this agreement (the "Agreement").

Licensor Information

Title of work (the "Selection"): _____

Catalog number (if applicable): _____

Artist: _____

Licensee Publication Information

The Selection will appear in the following publication(s) (the "Work"):

(Check if applicable and fill in blanks)

    ☐ book—title: _____

    ☐ website—URL: _____

    ☐ periodical—title: _____

    ☐ event handout—title of event: _____

If to be used on a website, the Selection will appear on:

(Check if applicable)

    ☐ home page

    ☐ internal page

Name of publisher or sponsor (if different from Licensee): _____

Estimated date(s) of publication or posting: _____

If applicable, the estimated number of copies to be printed or produced (if a book, the estimated first print run): _____

If for sale, the price: $ _____

If copies are free to attendees of a program, the cost of program: _____

If a website, the average number of visitors per month: _____

Grant of Rights

Licensor grants to Licensee and Licensee's successors and assigns, the:

(*Select one*)

☐ nonexclusive

☐ exclusive

right to reproduce and distribute the Selection in:

(*Select all that apply*)

☐ the current edition of the Work.

☐ all editions of the Work.

☐ all foreign language versions of the Work.

☐ all derivative versions of the Work.

☐ all media now known or later devised.

☐ promotional materials published and distributed in conjunction with the Work.

☐ other rights _____.

Territory

The rights granted under this Agreement shall be for _____
(the "Territory").

Fees

Licensee shall pay Licensor as follows:

(*Select payment option and fill in appropriate blanks*)

☐ **Flat Fee.** Licensee shall pay Licensor a flat fee of $ _____ as full payment for all rights granted. Payment shall be made:

☐ upon execution of this Agreement.

☐ upon publication.

☐ **Royalties and Advance.** Licensee agrees to pay Licensor a royalty of _____ % of Net Sales. Net Sales are defined as gross sales (the gross invoice amount billed customers) less quantity discounts and returns actually credited. Licensee agrees to pay Licensor an advance against royalties of $ _____ upon execution of this Agreement. Licensee shall pay Licensor within thirty (30) days after the end of each quarter. Licensee shall furnish an accurate statement of sales during that quarter. Licensor shall have the right to inspect Licensee's books upon reasonable notice.

Credit and Samples

(Check if applicable and fill in blanks)

☐ **Credit.** All versions of the Work that include the Selection shall contain the following statement: _____

☐ **Samples.** Upon publication, Licensee shall furnish _____ copies of the Work to Licensor.

Warranty

Licensor warrants that it has the right to grant permission for the uses of the Selection as specified above and that the Selection does not infringe the rights of any third parties.

(Check if applicable)

☐ Licensor warrants that a model release is on file for the Selection.

Miscellaneous

This Agreement may not be amended except in a written document signed by both parties. If a court finds any provision of this Agreement invalid or unenforceable, the remainder of this Agreement shall be interpreted so as best to effect the intent of the parties. This Agreement shall be governed by and interpreted in accordance with the laws of the State of _____ . This Agreement expresses the complete understanding of the parties with respect to the subject matter and supersedes all prior representations and understandings.

Licensor	Licensee
By: _____	By: _____
Name: _____	Name: _____
Title: _____	Title: _____
Address: _____	Address: _____
Date: _____	Date: _____
	Tax ID # _____

Using Artwork in Film and Video

Motion pictures, television programs, and videos often include artwork—for example, a painting, poster, photograph, or sculpture. As a general rule, you should obtain permission if the artwork is recognizable with sufficient detail so that the average viewer can clearly see the work.

For example, in one case, a court ruled that the appearance of a copyrighted poster in a television show for a total of 27 seconds required permission from the copyright owner. (*Ringgold v. Black Entertainment Television*, 126 F.3d 70 (2d Cir. 1997).) On the other hand, in a different case, a court ruled that if the artwork appears fleetingly, or is obscured, out of focus, or virtually unidentifiable, permission is not required because the use is too small (or "de minimis"). (*Sandoval v. New Line Cinema Corp.*, 147 F.3d 215 (2d Cir. 1998).) For more on this subject, see Chapter 9, "Fair Use."

RESOURCE

If you perform clearance on a regular basis for motion pictures, television, or video, review *Clearance and Copyright: Everything the Independent Filmmaker Needs to Know,* by Michael C. Donaldson (Silman-James Press).

Below is a basic permission agreement for using art within a motion picture.

FORM

You can download this form (and all other forms in this book) from Nolo.com; for details, see the appendix.

Explanation for Film and Video License Agreement

- In the **introductory paragraph,** insert the names of the licensor (the person or company who owns the copyright in the artwork) and the licensee (the person producing the motion picture or the authorized representative of the production company).

Agreement to Use Artwork in Motion Picture

_____ ("Licensor")
is the owner of rights for the artwork described below (the "Selection"). _____
_____ ("Licensee")
wants to acquire the right to use the Artwork as specified in this agreement
(the "Agreement").

Use of the Artwork

The Artwork will appear in:

(*Choose one*)

    ☐ motion picture

    ☐ television program

    ☐ music video

    ☐ other:

    ☐ entitled _____ (the "Picture").

Grant of Rights

Licensor grants to Licensee and Licensee's successors and assigns the nonexclusive
worldwide right (but not the obligation) to include the Artwork in the Picture for
the unlimited distribution, advertising, and promotion of the Picture in all languages
and in all forms or devices now known or later devised. This use includes, but is not
limited to, use of the Artwork in foreign language versions of the Picture, advertising,
publicity, or trailers of the Picture, and music videos derived from the Picture.

Limitations on Use

Licensee will use the Artwork in a manner that is consistent with the general
practices of the television and motion picture industry. Licensee will not materially
alter the Artwork or depict it in any manner that conflicts with the restrictions
below, without the consent of Licensor.

Restrictions: _____

Fees

As full payment for all rights granted, Licensee shall pay Licensor a flat fee of
$ _____ . Payment shall be made upon execution of this agreement.

Credit

The Picture shall include the following credit for the Artwork: _____
_____

Warranty and Release

Licensor warrants that it has the right to grant permission for use of the Artwork as specified above and that the Artwork does not infringe upon the rights of any third parties. Licensor waives any claims, known or unknown, arising out of Licensee's use of the Artwork. In the event that Licensee breaches this agreement, Licensor's relief shall be limited to damages and Licensor shall not be entitled to injunctive or equitable relief.

Miscellaneous

This Agreement may not be amended except in a written document signed by both parties. If a court finds any provision of this Agreement invalid or unenforceable, the remainder of this Agreement shall be interpreted so as best to effect the intent of the parties. This Agreement shall be governed by and interpreted in accordance with the laws of the State of _____ . This Agreement expresses the complete understanding of the parties with respect to the subject matter and supersedes all prior representations and understandings.

Licensor   Licensee

By: _____   By: _____

Name: _____   Name: _____

Title: _____   Title: _____

Address: _____   Address: _____

Date: _____   Date: _____

                                     Tax ID # _____

- In the **Use of the Artwork** section, indicate the type of program in which the artwork will appear and the title of the program.
- The first sentence of the **Grant of Rights** section is intended to prevent any problems in the event that the scene with the artwork ends up on the cutting room floor. The agreement grants the filmmaker broad rights—for example, to use the artwork in advertising and promotion. This means that additional permissions will not be required from the copyright owner of the artwork. More information on license grants is provided in Chapter 11.
- If the copyright owner wants to place some limitations on use, they belong in the **Limitations on Use** section. The owner may write in a restriction such as "Artwork shall not be used in any scene depicting nudity or sexual activity."
- In the **Fees** section, indicate the fee amount, if any, that has been negotiated.
- Complete the **Credit** section if it applies.
- As explained in Chapter 11, a warranty is a contractual promise made by the licensor. The **Warranty Release** section promises that licensor does, in fact, have the right to license the artwork and that the licensee won't be liable to a third party (for example, another artist) who claims that the artwork was ripped off. The waiver of claims is intended to prevent the licensor from subsequently claiming that the use violated some undisclosed right—for example, the use violated the artist's moral rights. This section also includes a limitation on the licensor's potential relief. If the filmmaker breaches the agreement—for example, fails to pay for the use—the licensor can sue for payment. However, the licensor cannot seek to prevent the release of the film.
- Explanations for the **Miscellaneous** or "boilerplate" provisions are provided in Chapter 11. Note that you may want to add a provision on attorneys' fees or arbitration (see Chapter 11), not included here.

Artwork Resources

The following resources can help you with various aspects of the permissions process for fine art and graphic art.

Fine Art Resources

- Artists Rights Society (ARS): www.arsny.com
- Getty Images: www.gettyimages.com
- Jacques-Edouard Berger Foundation: www.fondationberger.ch

Graphic Arts Resources

- Graphic Artists Guild: www.graphicartistsguild.org
- Society of Children's Book Writers and Illustrators (SCBWI): www.scbwi.org

Cartoon Resources

- Cartoonbank.com: https://cartoonbank.com
- The National Cartoonists Society: www.nationalcartoonists.com
- The Association of American Editorial Cartoonists: www.editorialcartoonists.com
- The Political Cartoonist's Index: www.cagle.com

Comic Book Resources

- Marvel Comics: www.marvel.com/comics
- DC Comics: www.dccomics.com
- *MAD* Magazine: www.madmagazine.com

Comic Syndicates

- King Features Syndicate: www.kingfeatures.com
- Go Comics: www.gocomics.com
- Creators Syndicate, Inc.: www.creators.com
- The Washington Post Licensing & Syndication: www.washingtonpost.com/licensing-syndication

Medical Image Resources

- Association of Medical Illustrators: www.ami.org
- LifeART: www.fotosearch.com/lifeart

Picture Researchers

- American Society of Picture Professionals: aspp.com

Getting Permission to Use Music

This chapter discusses common music permission situations, describes the options and fees for acquiring music rights, and offers suggestions for locating and dealing with music copyright owners. Acquiring rights for music is often easier than for text or artwork because there are standardized fees and license agreements for most music uses. For example, in some cases, a music owner must permit a use if a fee is paid. It is also easier to track down the copyright owner of music and get permission to use it because clearance services and organizations are available to assist.

Despite the ease with which music can be licensed, the fees are not always predictable, and can escalate beyond what they'd be for similar text or artwork uses. In some cases, owners of music copyright are less receptive to permissions and refuse to negotiate.

With music there's also an additional copyright twist. Every musical recording includes two copyrights: one for the song itself and another for the particular recording of the song. Acquiring permission for music often requires obtaining the permission of both of these copyright owners.

Acquiring Rights to Music

Music rights are generally acquired in one of the following ways:

- **Assignment or work-for-hire agreement.** If a musician or composer is hired to create music for a specific purpose—for example, a computer game—the music rights are transferred to the hiring party by an assignment or work-for-hire agreement. An assignment is a transfer of ownership of the copyright in the music. A work-for-hire arrangement occurs when the hiring party acquires ownership of the music through an employer-employee relationship or an independent contractor agreement. A sample assignment and an explanation regarding works made for hire are provided in Chapter 15. Under an assignment or work-for-hire agreement, the company paying for the work becomes the owner of all music rights.

- **License.** If music already exists and is not created for a specific purpose —for example, a Beyoncé song—the music rights are acquired by a license. This chapter explains how to license music and lyrics. It provides tips on determining the fees and finding the owner of a song or recording, as well as typical license agreements for the use of music or lyrics in books, magazines, movies, videos, commercials, software, live performances, at businesses, and on websites.
- **Production music.** Stock or generic music is available from production music libraries (known as "PMLs"), that provide prerecorded compositions for fixed fees, blanket fees (for multiple uses), or per-use fees. Companies that cannot afford to hire musicians or license popular music commonly use PML music as background or theme music.

RELATED TOPIC

If you seek permission to use music in conjunction with merchandise, be sure to check out Chapter 11, "Art and Merchandise Licenses."

RESOURCE

If you perform music clearance on a regular basis, consult *Kohn on Music Licensing,* by Al Kohn and Bob Kohn (www.bobkohn.com/kohn-on-music-licensing), which provides a complete collection of music licensing agreements.

Song and Sound Recording Copyrights

When a song is recorded, two copyrights are created—a song copyright, usually owned by a music publisher, and a sound recording copyright, usually owned by a record company. The song copyright protects the words and music of the song. The sound recording copyright protects the musical performance and audio sound of the recording of the song. As explained below, if you want to use a recorded song, you must get permission from both the song and sound recording copyright owners.

Song Copyrights and Music Publishers

The songwriter is the initial owner of a song's copyright. The only exception is if the songwriter writes songs as part of a job, in which case the employer owns the songs. Songwriters usually transfer their copyrights to music publishers, who own and manage collections of songs. A music publisher may be a large multinational company or a one-person operation run by the songwriter.

What Do Music Publishers Do?

A music publisher acts like a business agent for the songwriter—promoting songs, administering income from song licensing, and paying the songwriter a royalty. The title "music publisher" refers to the early days of the music business when the primary source of income for songwriters was the publication of sheet music. The concept of using music publishers has become so ingrained in the music business that in order to earn money from their songs, a songwriter must either sell or license their rights to an established music publisher or create their own music publishing business.

When Permission Is Required From a Music Publisher

There are several common situations in which permission is required from a music publisher, including:
- when sheet music is reproduced
- when song lyrics are reproduced, and
- when a song is released on a recording, played publicly, streamed over the Internet, used in an audiovisual work (such as a movie), or downloaded in a digital format (such as an MP3 music file).

Fortunately, for some of these activities, such as releasing a recording, downloading or streaming over the Internet, or playing a song publicly, there are established processes and fixed fees for getting permission. For other activities, such as using music in a movie, there are no fixed fees, and the costs can often be prohibitive.

Reproducing Sheet Music or Lyrics

Permission is required from the music publisher when you reproduce sheet music or song lyrics. The only exceptions to this rule are if the song is in the public domain (see Chapter 8) or if your use qualifies as a fair use (see Chapter 9). Music publishers either grant this permission directly or delegate the responsibility to a broker such as the Hal Leonard Company or Alfred Music.

Songs Released on CD, Vinyl Recording, or as Digital Download

Permission is required from the music publisher when you sell a song on an audio-only recording, such as a compact disc, vinyl recording, or as a digital download (officially referred to as digital phonorecord delivery or DPD). You must also pay a fee to the music publisher for recording and selling a song it owns. This payment is referred to as a "mechanical royalty." Music publishers either collect this money directly or delegate the responsibility to the Harry Fox Agency, an organization that negotiates and collects mechanical royalties.

Songs Played Publicly

Permission is also required from the music publisher when songs are played on the radio, on television, at businesses, in concerts, or at clubs. The fees for these uses are referred to as "performance royalties." Generally, radio stations, clubs, and other places that play music regularly obtain blanket licenses instead of getting permission and paying the fee each time they play a song. The licenses are granted by performing rights societies such as BMI and ASCAP, which execute the agreements, collect the fees, and monitor performances on behalf of music publishers.

Dear Rich: **Can We Sing "Happy Birthday" in Our Movie?**

I'm making a documentary about my aunt who's a well-known accordion player. There is a scene in which people sing "Happy Birthday" to her and she joins in on accordion. Someone told me that I need to get permission to use that song in the film. Can that really be true?

In February 2016, following a lawsuit brought by filmmaker Jennifer Nelson, "Happy Birthday" was determined to be in the public domain. The song's "owner," Warner/Chappell agreed to pay $14 million to filmmakers and others who had previously paid to license the song.

What Is a Public Performance?

Public performances of music require permission from the music publisher; private performances do not. To perform a work publicly means that music is played at a place open to the public or where a substantial number of people outside the normal circle of a family and social acquaintances are gathered. The fact that a performance is not for profit does not affect this determination.

Transmission of music by a radio or television station is also a public performance. It does not matter if the public receives the music at the same time or place as when it was transmitted. For example, if one station transmits a work and another station receives the broadcast and retransmits it later, the retransmission would be a performance. Audio streaming, the process of transmitting music over the Internet in real time, is also considered a public performance.

Examples of public performance include:

- a DJ playing a record in a club
- a band playing music during halftime at a football game
- a singer performing a song in a club
- a business playing music through the office loudspeaker system
- a radio station playing music over the air
- a website streaming music
- a television station broadcasting a television show containing music, and
- a cable company receiving a television station broadcast containing music and rebroadcasting it via cable transmission.

Songs Used in Audiovisual Works

Permission is required from the music publisher when you use music in a movie, television show, commercial, or video. This is referred to as a "synchronization license" or a "videogram license." Depending on the use, this license is negotiated either through the Harry Fox Agency or directly by the music publisher.

Streaming Songs

"Streaming" music refers to a method of playing digital tracks without having to download them. Permission is required from the music publisher when you stream songs. Depending on the use, permission agreements for streaming are negotiated by the Harry Fox Agency, performing rights societies, or directly by the music publisher.

Sound Recording Copyrights and Record Companies

Besides the copyright in the song composition itself, each recorded version of a song (often referred to as a "master") is protected by a sound recording copyright. In other words, a sound recording is a separate and distinct work from the musical composition that is being performed. Since a song can be recorded in many different styles and arrangements, each recording of a performance of the composition is entitled to its own copyright protection. For example, the hundreds of different recorded versions of "White Christmas" are each protected by a separate sound recording copyright, while the song itself is protected by a single song copyright.

Generally speaking, the first owners of a sound recording are the individuals who created it, including the musicians, arrangers, and producer of the recording session. More commonly, however, a musician or band signs a recording agreement, giving the record company that releases its sound recordings the rights to those sound recordings. Even without an official recording agreement, if a company hires the musicians and recording engineers to record the songs, that company—as the employer—would be the initial owner of the sound recordings.

Sound Recording Permission From a Record Company

When using a sound recording, permission is required from the record company in the following situations:

- **Duplicating or sampling a sound recording.** Examples of sound recording duplication include using a sample in another recording, using a pop song in a video or motion picture soundtrack, converting a sound recording into a digital format such as an MP3 file, or copying a compact disc or portion of it to cassette.
- **Digital broadcasting.** Digital broadcasting includes streaming a sound recording over the Internet or over a cable music service. Permission is not required from the record company—but may be required from the music publisher—to reprint music or lyrics, to make a different recording of the same song, or to play or broadcast a recording. (Note, this applies only to performances in the United States. In some countries, permission is required from the record company to broadcast sound recordings.)

When contacting a record company for permission to use its recording, ask for the licensing or special markets department. Most record companies are prepared to issue the licenses described in this chapter and will furnish license agreements, usually known as "master use" licenses. Information on how to locate record companies is included in the resources section at the end of this chapter.

Using Production Music Libraries

Production music libraries (PMLs) provide an inexpensive way to obtain rights for original music and sound effects on a nonexclusive basis. PML music, which is primarily instrumental, is used for films, websites, slide shows, radio and television programming, commercials, software and multimedia, training videos, in-flight services, and similar applications.

Like stock photography, PML music is categorized by genre or mood (for example, old-time rock and roll or outer space music) and is sold on compact disc collections on a royalty-free, blanket fee, or per-use fee basis. A typical PML compact disc may contain ten to 15 original compositions, including a full-length version of each composition as well as shorter "tag" or "cue" version. Larger PMLs have hundreds of compact discs in their collections. You can search through many of these collections online.

Because the PML owns both the music publishing and sound recording rights, obtaining permission to use PML recordings is fairly simple. A typical PML license permits use for most synchronization purposes, such as using the music in a film or software program. However, the PML license does not permit you to use the music in audio recordings sold to the public. For example, while PML music may be used in a film, it cannot be included on a commercial soundtrack album sold to consumers without special permission from the PML. PMLs generally prohibit the use of the music unless it is used in conjunction with other audio or visual elements. These limitations are usually expressed in the PML license as follows:

> The music may be used only in synchronization or mechanical reproduction with other audio and/or visual elements. The licensee must obtain prior written permission and negotiate a separate license if licensee intends to repackage or alter the music and make it available as commercial soundtracks or videos.

There are three methods of acquiring rights for PML music:

- **Blanket agreements** in which the user obtains unlimited use of all PML music on a compact disc or disc library for a specified period of time, such as two years. If continued use is required, the license must be renewed. Blanket licenses may range from several hundred dollars to four or five thousand dollars per year.

- **Per-use agreements** in which the user makes payments when they use compositions in a production. This method of payment is sometimes referred to as a "needle drop," in reference to the days of vinyl recordings when a radio or film producer paid each time the needle was dropped onto a piece of music. Per-use fees depend on the length and type of use and can range from $50 for a five-minute use in a local television show to $500 for the same music in a feature film.

- **Buyout agreements** in which the user acquires unlimited rights by purchasing the PML's compact disc. Fees for buyout rights range from $50 to several thousand dollars.

PMLs offer a variety of fees and payment plans, making it possible to negotiate discounts based on use. Fees are often based on an estimate of per-unit sales. A list of PMLs is provided in the resources section at the end of this chapter.

Researching Song and Sound Recordings in the Copyright Office

Before electronic filing (pre-2008) all song copyrights were registered in the Copyright Office using Form PA (performing arts). Sound recording copyrights were registered in the Copyright Office using Form SR (sound recording). Sound recording copyrights previously existed only for recordings created after 1971, prior to which sound recordings were protected by state laws. However, after passage of the Music Modernization Act (MMA) (signed into law on October 11, 2018), pre-1972 recordings are now covered by copyright, thereby requiring digital music providers to compensate those recording artists and song owners.

Bypassing Sound Recording Rights

It's often more difficult to get permission from a record company than from a music publisher because record companies are obligated to many people— including recording artists and union musicians who receive a reuse fee for certain licensed uses of a sound recording master. Some record companies don't want to bother with master licensing unless there is a return of at least several thousand dollars.

For this reason, many production companies pay for songs to be rerecorded instead of getting permission from a record company to use an existing recording. Going this route requires permission from the music publisher only, not from the record company. Rerecorded sound recording masters may also be available from production music libraries on a one-time flat fee buyout basis.

It is not an infringement of the sound recording copyright to rerecord a song so that it sounds exactly like the original recording. However, there may be other legal limitations. A performer's style cannot be imitated when the recording is used to sell a product or service or to sell recordings that confuse the public into believing they are buying the original recording. (See "Performer Rights," below.)

Performer Rights

Under a legal principle known as the "right of publicity," a performer's permission is required if his or her image, name, or style is used to sell a product or service. Permission is also needed to imitate a performer's style if the imitation is likely to cause the public to believe that the performer is affiliated with or endorses a product. For example, an auto company was found liable for infringing the right of publicity when it imitated, without permission, the singing style of Bette Midler. A snack food company was similarly found liable for using an imitation of Tom Waits. If the performer is deceased, you're not off the hook—in many states, permission is required from the performer's estate. For more information on rights of publicity and performer releases, see Chapter 12, "Releases."

Permission from a performer is also required to make an audio or video recording of a live performance or to distribute recordings of the performance. If the performer has signed an exclusive recording agreement with a record company, permission is required from the record company.

Reprinting Music or Lyrics

You may need permission to reprint music notation or lyrics—for example, to quote lyrics on a website or to reprint music and lyrics in an instructional text. In these cases, you are not actually reproducing the sound of the music, only the words or musical notation. Because of this, you only need permission from the music publisher that owns copyright in the composition, not from any record company that may own a sound recording copyright for the song.

Generally, you need permission from the music publisher to reprint all or part of a song's sheet music or lyrics. The fees for such uses are not fixed, so a music publisher can charge whatever the market will bear. In most cases, the fees are reasonable, such as $50 to reprint lyrics in a book. Two sources for permission to reproduce lyrics are the Hal Leonard Company (www.halleonard.com) and Alfred Music (www.alfred.com).

Music and Lyric Reproduction

Music and lyrics are commonly sold as unbound sheet music, featuring piano notation, guitar chords, and lyrics printed below the corresponding music. Sheet music is also sold or licensed in folios (collections of sheet music bound into a volume), fakebooks (folios with hundreds of songs), or educational editions (sheet music for use in school instruction arranged for school performances). You'll also often find sheet music reproduced in specialty magazines, instructional booklets for musicians, and on websites. Lyrics are often reproduced separately (without musical notation) for use on websites or in books, greeting cards, advertisements, and magazines.

Occasionally, music publishers permit the use of a few lyric lines for free, but more often they will charge a fee, as described below. To reproduce music and lyrics, contact the music publisher. The reproduction of lyrics for a karaoke recording may require a synchronization license.

Also keep in mind that if a music publisher grants permission to record a song, it might not include the right to reprint the lyrics, such as in the liner notes to the compact disc booklet. Permission to print the lyrics must be acquired separately.

CAUTION

Don't assume that because sheet music is out of print it is free to use.
Unless it is in the public domain, sheet music is still protected under copyright law.
See Chapter 8 for an explanation of public domain rules.) If you want to reproduce
out-of-print sheet music, contact the Music Publishers Association (www.mpa.org),
which has a procedure for locating and using out-of-print copyrighted music.

EXAMPLE: I wanted to reproduce four lines from the song "Sneakers on a
Rooster," performed by Bo Diddley. By searching online, I determined that
BMI is the performing rights society that represents the song. BMI provided
contact information for the publisher, including an email address. I emailed the
publisher, who okayed the request without requiring a fee. The publisher did
provide a credit line for me to include with the use.

The clothes I buy for you is what I thought you always wanted
But the ones you buy for me, they feel like they're haunted
Girl I hope your love changes in the future
Cause lovin' you is like putting sneakers on a rooster.

"Sneakers on a Rooster," written by Sam Dees & David Camon. Lyrics
reproduced courtesy of Ginn Music Group, Atlanta, Georgia.

Dear Rich:

Publishing Lyrics at Websites

*I have a question. I am helping to create a website, and one of the
components is to provide some advice about songs and music that might
be appropriate for funerals. I'd really love to include the lyrics so that folks could
peruse them, along with a link to a spot where the piece is being performed. But
I am a wee bit worried about spending sleepless nights in jail for including the
lyrics—even though they're all widely available on many sites. We did not intend
to offer any commentary, just the bald lyrics. Will I run into a legal problem?*

The short answer to your question is that you will be violating the law, but you
probably won't run into problems unless your site becomes a popular destination for people seeking lyrics online. Publishing lyrics without authorization is a
violation of U.S. copyright law. Back in the old days (before the year 2000), music
publishers went after lyrics websites with a vengeance. Then, unauthorized lyric
reproduction became rampant until 2013 when the National Music Publishers
Association (NMPA) began a coordinated effort to stop the biggest sites. Some
smaller and midsized sites also received DMCA takedown notices (a copyright

law mechanism for removing unauthorized content). The NMPA also coordinated a legit alternative—LyricFind.com (www.lyricfind.com)—and set up a licensing process for lyrics via the Harry Fox agency (www.harryfox.com).

Fees

Fees to reproduce music notation or lyrics vary quite widely depending on the use. Below are some general guidelines on what various uses may cost:

- Expect to pay $25 or more for the use of a song's lyrics (or a portion of the lyrics) in a book or magazine.
- Fees for use of lyrics on a website may range from $50 to $1,000, depending on the site and how much traffic it gets. Fees for using lyrics in advertising depend on the type of advertisement, length of use, and territory in which the ad will appear. Fees range from several hundred to several thousand dollars per year.
- For use of lyrics in a greeting card or other merchandise, music publishers seek a royalty of 2% to 5% of the retail price of the merchandise.
- If music and lyrics are reprinted as part of a folio or educational publication, music publishers usually seek a royalty of 10% to 15% of the wholesale price. If the song is one of several within a publication, the royalty is often prorated. Under a pro rata arrangement, a music publisher would, for example, receive 1/10 of the royalty if it provided one of ten songs.
- For those musicians still using CDs, music publishers commonly charge 2 cents per copy to reproduce lyrics on liner notes—for example, the cost to print lyrics on the liner notes of 1,000 copies would be $20.
- Fees for miscellaneous uses typically depend on the length of use, the popularity of the song, and often the publisher's whim.

TIP

Under limited conditions, music instructors are permitted to copy portions of sheet music and recordings without permission. For example, under fair use guidelines, a music instructor can copy excerpts of sheet music, provided that the excerpts do not constitute a "performable unit" such as a whole song, section, movement, or aria. In no case can more than 10% of the whole work be copied, and the number of copies may not exceed one per pupil. See Chapter 7 for more information on educational uses.

Dear Rich:

Public Domain Sheet Music: When Is it Copyrighted?

I have a question. I have an online flute consignment shop. I have created a link where I would like to make a piece of sheet music from the public domain available for free download each month. I could go to the local university Fine Arts library and copy music out of old books (which will look like scans of old music), or I could download the same piece of music from a free online source that is already in existence and have it be clean and pretty because someone took the time to typeset it and make it nice to read (I cannot possibly typeset this music myself ... for many reasons). But I do not know if this is either legal or ethical. In some cases, there are footnotes that say something akin to, "Not to be used for commercial works." In other cases, there is no such notation. Can I take the music from one of these sites and give it away as a download on mine?

You can legally use public domain music provided that the musical notation you mention is obvious, routine, dictated by musical convention, and does not involve any major changes or new arrangements. In other words, if the notation is simply what's typically required to write the music, it's not protected by copyright.

According to Stephen Fishman, an expert on the public domain, it doesn't matter if it takes great skill or musical training to create the musical notation of public domain sheet music; nor does it matter if the end result is digitized. The work can be protected by copyright only if the sheet music contains substantial additional music, is an abridgment, or involves making a new arrangement— for example, creating a suite for several instruments with harmonizations not previously associated with the public domain work.

How then can a music publisher claim copyright in public domain sheet music? According to Fishman, many claims for copyright in public domain music are improper and based on the fact that music publishers have a strong economic incentive to convince the public that its music is copyrighted (even when it is not). Of course, this information won't prevent you from being sued; it just means you're likely to prevail if there is a lawsuit. In addition, it may sometimes be difficult to separate the public domain version from a popular derivative version—as in the case of the folk song "Tom Dooley." (By the way, the rules described here might not be the same outside the United States) As for your question about whether the copying is ethical, the Dear Rich Staff is unable to comment, as they are trained only to wrestle with legal issues.

Lyric Permission Letter Agreement

Most publishers furnish a short license agreement or letter for use of lyrics. Some may okay the use via email or over the phone. If an oral "okay" is granted, follow it up with a letter confirming the arrangement or use the Lyric Permission Letter Agreement below. If you're seeking to use lyrics on merchandise, such as a greeting card or poster, use the agreement provided in Chapter 11, "Art and Merchandise Licenses."

 FORM
You can download this form (and all other forms in this book) from Nolo.com; for details, see the appendix.

Explanation for Lyric Permission Letter Agreement

Use this letter agreement after you have contacted the music publisher and discussed the conditions of the use, number of samples, credit, and fee, if any. Once these details have been agreed upon:

- Insert the names of the music publisher (generally, a company name), the song, the songwriter, and the person who has responsibility for acquiring permission ("Licensee"). The licensee may be you; or, if you're acquiring permission on behalf of someone else, such as a publisher or employer, list that person or entity.
- In the next paragraphs, indicate where the reproduced lyrics will appear (book, magazine, website, or other) and provide information about the fee, number of samples, and any required credit. (For example, "Lyrics by Kevin Teare, reprinted courtesy of Electric Ladybug Music, Copyright 1999.")
- Provide your address and sign the agreement.
- The **Music Publisher's Approval of Request** is an assurance that the music publisher has the legal ability to grant the rights in the agreement. A representative of the music publisher should sign and date this provision and provide his or her name and title.
- It is possible that the music publisher will want to modify this agreement. For example, the publisher may want to limit your use to a specific print run of a book or a specific period of time on a website.

If necessary, modify what the license grants to reflect your agreement with the music publisher.

- You might need more rights than what's provided by the standard language of this agreement—for example, rights for foreign translations, derivative rights, or rights in all media. Either specify the additional rights needed or strike the last sentence of **Music Publisher's Approval of Request** and replace it with the broader grant of rights provided below. Be aware that a music publisher could object to the terms of a broad request, causing a delay in the permissions process.

> I grant Licensee's successors, licensees, and assigns the nonexclusive worldwide right to republish the lyrics in all editions of the Work and in all versions derived from the Work in all media now known or hereafter devised.

Using Lyrics Without Permission

If the music publisher cannot be located, or if permission is denied, the use of small portions of lyrics without permission may qualify as a fair use. Fair use rules for copyrighted materials are based on free speech principles. Permission is not required to use portions of a work if the use is for purposes of education, parody, or disseminating a critical point of view. Unfortunately, there are no quantitative rules as to how many song lyrics can be used as a fair use. However, if all the following factors are present, your reproduction is more likely to be allowed without permission:

- The use is limited—for example, four lines or less.
- The use is to comment upon or parody the song.
- The music publisher is not deprived of income by the use.
- A reasonable effort was made to locate the music publisher and secure permission.

The last factor, seeking permission, is not a necessity to qualify for fair use, but some courts have suggested that it demonstrates good faith. Fair use factors, along with real-life examples, are discussed in greater detail in Chapter 9, "Fair Use."

Lyric Permission Letter Agreement

To _____ ("Music Publisher"):

I am writing to you to obtain permission to reprint portions of the lyrics (the "Lyrics") from the song _____ ,
written by _____ on behalf of
_____ ("Licensee").

The lyrics will appear in the following publication(s) (the "Work"):

(*Check if applicable and fill in blanks*)

☐ Book Use

　Book title: _____

　Name of publisher or sponsor: _____

　Author(s): _____

　ISBN: _____

　Estimated date(s) of publication: _____

　Estimated number of copies to be printed or produced (if a book, the estimated first print run): _____

　Language editions: _____

　Territory of publication: _____

　Estimated price: $ _____

☐ Magazine

　Magazine title: _____

　Volume, issue, ISSN: _____

　Estimated date of publication: _____

　Circulation: _____

☐ Website

　URL: _____

　Name of publisher or sponsor: _____

　Estimated dates of use: _____

　Estimated visitors per day: _____

☐ Other (describe): _____

_____

_____

Fee

Licensee shall pay a fee of $ _____ to Music Publisher at the following

address: _____

_____ upon publication of the Work or

within six months of executing this Agreement, whichever is earlier.

Samples

Upon publication, Licensee shall furnish _____ copies of the Work to Music

Publisher.

Credit

The following credit shall be included with the Work: _____

_____

Signed by Licensee _____

Name: _____

Title: _____

Address: _____

Date: _____

Music Publisher's Approval of Request

Music Publisher warrants that it is the owner of rights for the lyrics and has the right
to grant the permission to republish the lyrics as specified above. This license is for
the nonexclusive worldwide right to republish the lyrics in all editions of the Work.

Signed by Music Publisher _____

Name: _____

Title: _____

Address: _____

Date: _____

Arranging a Copyrighted Musical Composition

Musical arrangements or orchestrations of copyrighted musical compositions are considered to be derivative works and cannot be used without permission. For example, if you intend to write and reproduce an arrangement of the Elvis song "Heartbreak Hotel," you will need permission from the music publisher. An "arrangement" means substantial modifications in the song, such as adding intricate harmonies or reworking rhythm and chord structures. See a sample "Request for Permission to Arrange" form on the Music Publishers Association website at www.mpa.org/wp-content/uploads/2018/06/Permission-to-Arrange.pdf

Dear Rich:

I Want to Publish a Book of Campfire Songs

I am interested in helping publish a songbook of campfire songs for use by traditional campfire groups (Scouts and the like). While some of these songs are in the public domain, others are not. I understand that the performance of the songs by those groups may be a public performance (hat tip to the 1995-96 ASCAP/American Camping Association/Girl Scout flare up), but am more concerned about securing rights to publish the sheet music within the songbook. The book will be sold by a nonprofit entity, but otherwise looks/feels like a commercial use. Is there a clearinghouse through which these sorts of rights may be secured? My review of the ASCAP page indicates that they are more concerned with the public performance (or at least I cannot find a reference to sheet music publication). Is there somewhere else I should be looking?

Yes, you need to contact the music publishers (companies that own or administer the copyrights for songs) and seek permission directly. There may be agents who can acquire these rights for a fee (search for "music licensing agents") but there don't appear to be any clearance houses or licensing organizations that deal specifically with granting sheet music rights.

What good is ASCAP? ASCAP and BMI (ASCAP's main competitor) can't help you with getting the rights for reprinting sheet music. Those organizations are performance rights societies and grant rights for playing music live or broadcasting it over radio or TV. However, BMI and ASCAP, and their sibling organization, the Harry Fox Agency, (which grants rights for so-called mechanical licenses) are good for a related purpose—they can provide you with the name, address, and contact information for the music publisher who owns the rights. You can then contact the music publisher directly. Publishers differ as to their policies for sheet music reproduction. They often grant sheet music rights for a royalty (typically 10% to 15%) or for a flat fee if it is a limited reproduction (for example, 2,000 books). Of course, mention the nonprofit aspect of the effort (in the hopes that you can get a better deal), and be prepared to be flexible in your choice of campfire songs, because in some cases, you may find the publisher nonresponsive, or seeking fees beyond your budget.

Using public domain songs. We're all for the use of public domain campfire songs. In some cases, however, beware that individuals wrongly attempt to claim copyright on PD songs.

Playing Music at a Business or Event

As a general rule, when you perform music publicly at a business or an event, you must obtain permission from the music publisher only. Remember, public performance encompasses more than a musician playing a song live; it also means the playing of recorded music (see "What Is a Public Performance?" above). This means that permission is required for a DJ to play recordings at a club or on the radio. Usually, such permission is not granted directly by the music publisher, but by performing rights societies that handle the process on behalf of the music publishers. This process is described in more detail below.

> EXAMPLE: The Emeryville Hotel wants to play recordings of popular music in its lobby. The hotel needs to get blanket licenses from the performing rights societies for the public performance of the songs.

Performance Rights Blanket Licenses

The two major performance rights organizations that represent music publishers are BMI and ASCAP. There is also a third company, SESAC, that accounts for a smaller share of the performance rights business. These nonprofit organizations collect fees from establishments where music is played (for example, nightclubs, radio and TV stations, concert halls, restaurants, and taverns), and distribute the money to the songwriters and music publishers who own the songs. All three performing rights societies—BMI, ASCAP, and SESAC—issue licenses known as blanket licenses that permit the licensee to play all songs represented by that society. With a blanket license, separate permissions are not required for each play of each song.

Examples of some business uses for which blanket licenses are provided include:

- athletic clubs
- dance classes
- hotels or motels
- restaurants and bars, and
- retail establishments, such as clothing stores.

Blanket licenses for uses other than on radio and TV are sought from BMI and ASCAP. Because of its smaller repertoire, SESAC's blanket licenses are geared more toward gospel and country music users. It's possible that a business could obtain a blanket license from only one performing rights society, but that may prove inefficient because the business would have to make sure that it only played music from that society.

The annual fee for a blanket license is based on the manner in which music is performed and the potential audience for the music. For example, ASCAP computes blanket licenses as follows:

- Restaurant, bar, and club rates are based on whether the music is live or recorded, audio only or audiovisual, the club's seating capacity, the number of nights of music per week, the number of musicians involved, and whether admission is charged.
- Concert event rates are based on the venue's seating capacity and ticket price.
- Corporate rates for playing music at businesses are based on the number of employees.
- Retail store rates depend on the number of speakers in the store and the store's square footage.
- Hotel rates are based on a percentage of entertainment expenses for live music and an additional charge for recorded music.

To obtain a blanket license, contact BMI, ASCAP, or SESAC (contact information is included at the end of this chapter). Ask for the licensing department and explain your business use. The society's representatives will inquire as to the size and type of use and quote you a fee for an annual blanket license.

> ## Permission for Music in Seminars and Training Programs
>
> As explained in Chapter 7, permission is not required if music is played as part of a face-to-face teaching activity at a nonprofit educational institution. Permission is required from BMI and ASCAP when music is used as part of instructional seminars, conventions, or other commercial presentations.

Additional Permissions

Additional permissions are required in the following situations:

- If the business is not just playing the music, but also making a copy of it—for example, compiling songs on a tape or making a new recording—the business should obtain a mechanical license from the Harry Fox Agency. Forms for these licenses are downloadable at the Harry Fox website (www.harryfox.com).

- If the music is transmitted in a digital format—online or via a digital cable music service, for example—the user must obtain permission from the sound recording copyright owner. In some cases, permission for use of a recording on noninteractive digital transmissions, including satellite and Internet radio, can be obtained from the SoundExchange website (www.soundexchange.com).

- If the music is used at a corporate event to promote a product or service, the user must obtain permission from the performer in addition to permission from the music publisher and the record company. For example, if Microsoft debuts a new software product at a convention and plays a song recorded by the Rolling Stones, it must get permission from the music publisher, the record company, and from the Rolling Stones.

How Is Harry Fox Different from BMI, ASCAP, and SESAC?

The performing rights societies, BMI, ASCAP, and SESAC, grant licenses to play songs on the radio and television, at concerts and public events, over the Internet, and in movie theaters. These organizations are concerned with the public performance of the song only—that is, when the public hears the songs. The Harry Fox Agency, a subsidiary of the National Music Publishers Association (NMPA), via its SongFile subsidiary, collects royalties for music publishers whenever a song is copied or reproduced (referred to as "mechanical royalties"), regardless of whether the public hears the song. Harry Fox provides licenses for reproducing songs in movies, videos, TV commercials, online ads, corporate in-house presentations, trade shows, school shows, concerts, cabaret TV programs, products (such as music boxes or other devices that incorporate songs), jukeboxes, and karaoke systems.

There is some overlap between the territory covered by Harry Fox and performing rights societies. Both organizations grant licenses for songs used in film, radio, TV, and online. However, the purposes of the licenses are different. For example, when granting television rights, the performing rights license permits the user to play the song over a television broadcast. The Harry Fox license grants the user the right to copy the song (or synchronize it) onto the television program's soundtrack.

Press 1 for More Music

Music provided for a caller on hold constitutes a public performance because music is being transmitted to the public. The company providing on-hold music must obtain permission from the performing right societies, ASCAP and BMI (and in some cases, SESAC).

Playing the Radio or Television at a Business

Before 1999, businesses using anything larger than a home stereo system had to pay performing rights societies for the right to play the radio or television for customers. However, under new rules, restaurants and bars of less than 3,750 square feet and retail establishments with less than 2,000 square feet don't have to pay any fees to play the radio or television in their establishments. (Note, establishments that play prerecorded music, such as compact discs, are still subject to license requirements.)

In addition, regardless of size, all restaurants, bars, and stores are exempt from paying fees if they have no more than six external speakers (but not more than four per room) or four televisions measuring 55 inches or less (but not more than one per room). These rules only apply to establishments that play radio and television.

Nonprofit and Charitable Business Exemptions

Some nonprofit and charitable uses of music don't require permission. Below is a summary of some of the rules, which are located at 17 U.S.C. Section 110 of the federal copyright laws. Other educational permission rules are discussed in Chapter 7, "Academic and Educational Permissions."

- **Free shows.** No permission is needed if music is performed before a live audience for which no admission is charged and the performers are not paid.
- **Shows with admission fees.** No permission is needed if music is performed before a live paying audience, so long as the performers are not paid, the net proceeds are used exclusively for education, religious, or charitable purposes, and the music publisher is notified and given more than ten days to object. If the publisher objects, the person seeking permission will have to pay for the use and acquire a license from the appropriate performing rights society.
- **Religious services.** No permission is needed to perform music in the course of religious services at a house of worship. However, permission is required to broadcast music performed at a religious service and to copy sheet music for religious services.

- **Agricultural fairs.** Permission is not required for the performance of live music at an annual nonprofit agricultural or horticultural fair. However, see the point below on concessions and for-profit exhibits at fairs.
- **Fraternal and veterans events.** Permission is not required when nonprofit veterans organizations or fraternal groups perform music, provided that the general public is not invited and the net profits are used exclusively for charitable purposes.
- **Fraternity and sorority events.** Permission is not required to perform music at college fraternity and sorority social functions provided that the purpose is solely to raise funds for a charitable cause.
- **Concession stands.** Permission *is* required to play music at concession stands and for-profit exhibits regardless of whether the event at which the stand or exhibit is operating is exempt. For example, permission would be required to play music at a concession stand at a nonprofit agricultural fair.

Releasing Music for Sale

This section explains how to obtain permission to record and release a song as an audio recording—for example, if a singer wants to record and release a version of the Lou Reed song "Walk on the Wild Side" on compact disc. Thanks to federal laws, the process of acquiring permission to record a song is relatively simple and inexpensive (approximately 9.1 cents for each copy you distribute). In addition, the song owner must consent to your use if you follow the procedures described in this section.

RELATED TOPIC
This section is only about using songs on audio recordings distributed to the public. Recording a song for use within a film or video, recording and distributing a song over the Internet, and recording of a song for use in a software program, are all discussed later in this chapter.

To record a song for release to the public, a performer must obtain permission from the music publisher of the song and pay a fee, called a mechanical royalty. A performer must pay a mechanical royalty to reproduce songs on compact discs, vinyl records, and cassettes.

There are two ways to get permission and pay the mechanical royalty:

- Use a compulsory license and pay the preset statutory mechanical royalty rate directly to the music publisher.
- Negotiate permission and the mechanical royalty directly with the music publisher or the Harry Fox Agency.

CAUTION

Beware when proceeding without permission. Some musicians don't obtain compulsory licenses or pay mechanical royalties when producing self-released recordings. For small pressings, this illegal activity usually goes undetected. But if the copyright owner learns of the unauthorized use, the musician may be forced to pay past-due mechanical royalties, plus interest, or to stop distributing the recording entirely. If the music publisher brings a lawsuit, the musician may be subject to additional penalties, including attorneys' fees.

Compulsory Licenses

One way to legally rerecord a song is to use what's known as a "compulsory license." Under this procedure, the user doesn't actually ask for the music publisher's permission to make the recording or negotiate a license fee. Instead, the user merely informs the publisher of the recording (using the compulsory license procedure) and pays a license fee set by law.

Back in the old days (pre-2000), an artist or a record label wrote to the music publisher and provided the compulsory license information and a check for the fee. Nowadays, the whole procedure can be done online. That's much more convenient, but keep in mind that there are often fees that attach to this convenience.

SongFile (www.songfile.com) is a division of Harry Fox (www.harryfox.com) that enables you to license rights for sound recordings.

If you decide to proceed on your own, and not pay a service to obtain the compulsory license, the general rules are that the music publisher cannot prevent the recording of the song so long as all of the following requirements are satisfied:

- The song was previously released on a recording.
- The performer making the new recording does not change the basic melody or fundamental character of the song.
- The performer or record company making the new recording provides a Notice of Intention to Obtain Compulsory License (as described below) at least 30 days prior to distributing the recordings.
- The performer or record company making the new recording pays the statutory mechanical royalty fee.

It's important to note that a compulsory license cannot be used the first time the song is distributed to the public—for example, if the songwriter never released a version of it and your version is the first. Nor can a compulsory license be used if the song was used on television or in a movie, but never released on an audio recording. In these cases, authorization must be acquired directly from the music publisher or songwriter. Since the song has never been recorded, it's possible that the songwriter is still the owner and has not transferred copyright to a music publisher.

Compulsory licenses are usable only when reproducing songs as digital downloads, or on records, compact discs, or cassettes—that is, sound recordings. They do not apply if making copies for use in a music video. In addition, compulsory licenses are not available for use of a song in video or digital movies, or in conjunction with any other media.

Mechanical Royalty Rate

When using the compulsory license procedure, the music publisher must be paid a mechanical royalty rate set by the government (sometimes known as the "statutory rate"). This rate increases every few years, although since 2007 the rate has been locked in at 9.1 cents per song (or 1.75 cents per minute of playing time or fraction of playing time, whichever is greater) per copy.

> **EXAMPLE:** Andrea records Lou Reed's "Walk on the Wild Side." She makes and releases 500 compact discs and 500 digital downloads of the recording. Andrea must pay $91 to the music publisher of the song (9.1 cents times 1,000 copies).

Notice of Intention to Obtain Compulsory License

For uses that meet the criteria described in this section, a Notice of Intention to Obtain Compulsory License should be sent to the copyright owner of the song. An explanation for completing this form is provided below.

Note: A compulsory license to record a song does not grant the right to reprint lyrics on the album artwork. Permission must be acquired separately from the publisher.

FORM

You can download this form (and all other forms in this book) from Nolo.com; for details, see the appendix.

Dear Rich:

Recording a Lindsey Buckingham Song

I have friends in a band in Norway and they want to release a song written by Lindsey Buckingham. They plan on releasing 1,000 CDs and 500 vinyl singles. Does the label ask for permission or should the band?

We think your friends should look at their recording contract (if they have one) to determine who has responsibility for paying for the rights. In the United States, the label typically pays (and then charges it to the band somehow).

Rights organizations. In the United States, the band would have a fairly easy time sorting this out. They could either pay the compulsory license fees and follow the instructions issued by the Copyright Office, or they could take the easier route of charging the fees to their credit card at the Harry Fox site—you just set up an account and tell them how many copies. HFA instructions note, however, that the license is only for recordings distributed in the United States. In Norway, rights are commonly sorted by Kopinor, and your friends might want to check their website for assistance. Other European rights organizations can be found in an online search.

Explanation for Notice to Obtain Compulsory License

- In the first blank of the first paragraph, insert the name of the song owner (usually the music publisher of the song). In the next blank, insert the name of the song and then the songwriters. In the second paragraph, again insert the name of the song.
- In the first row of the table, insert the legal name of the company that owns your recording. If you or your company owns the recording, insert that name.

Notice of Intention to Obtain Compulsory License for Making and Distributing Sound Recordings

To _____ ,

the copyright owner of _____ ,

written by _____ :

Pursuant to the compulsory license provisions of the U.S. Copyright Act (17 U.S.C. § 1115), we apply for a license to make and distribute phonorecords of _____ _____and provide the following information:

Legal name or entity seeking the compulsory license: _____ _____

Fictitious or assumed names used for making and distributing phonorecords: _____ _____

Address:_____

Business organization:

    ☐ corporation   ☐ partnership

    ☐ LLC   ☐ sole proprietor

Names of individuals who own a beneficial interest of 25% or more in the entity: _____ _____ _____

If a corporation, names of the officers and directors: _____ _____ _____

Configuration(s) to be made under the compulsory license (*check all that apply*):

    ☐ 7- or 12-inch vinyl single   ☐ compact disc

    ☐ 12-inch long-playing vinyl record   ☐ minidisc

    ☐ cassette   ☐ digital download

Catalog number(s):_____

Label name(s): _____

Principal recording artists: _____

_____

Anticipated date of initial release: _____

We agree to pay the copyright owner royalties at the statutory rate provided by the Copyright Act.

Date: _____

By: _____

Name/Title: _____

- Under **Fictitious or assumed names,** insert the fictitious business name, if any, that you or your company uses.
- Insert your company's mailing address.
- Indicate the legal business structure of your company (corporation, LLC, partnership, or sole proprietor).
- In the category **Names of individuals who own a beneficial interest,** insert the names of anyone who has a 25% or more interest in the company. For example, if you and your partner own the recording equally (50%–50%), list both your names. If no one owns at least 25% of the company, leave this blank.
- If your company is a corporation, list the officers and directors in the next row.
- Under **Configuration(s),** check all the types of recordings you expect to release.
- List any catalog number you may have created for the recording.
- Insert the name of your record label. If your company is putting out the record, the label name is probably the same as your company name.
- Insert the name of the recording artist.
- Insert the expected release date.
- The final paragraph establishes that the statutory rate will be paid. A company seeking a compulsory license (in this case, you or your company) is supposed to issue an accounting statement and pay statutory royalties every month. You can, however, contact the music publisher and ask if it is okay to make payments on a quarterly basis, rather than monthly.
- The compulsory license is signed by the licensee (you or your company, if you have one). The music publisher does not sign the license because consent from the music publisher is not required. All that is required is that the publisher is notified and paid according to the rules. If you have a partnership, a partner should sign in the space next to the word "By" and indicate his or her partner status below that—for example, "Peggi Fournier, a general partner in the Grosse Pointe Partnership."

Negotiating a License Directly With the Music Publisher

Most major labels and established independent record companies do not use compulsory licenses or pay the statutory rate as described above. Instead, they obtain permission to make the recording directly from the music publisher and negotiate a rate lower than the compulsory license rate, usually three-quarters of the statutory rate. It is not a violation of the law to negotiate a rate lower than that provided in the Copyright Act if both parties consent.

As with performance royalties, many music publishers do not negotiate mechanical licenses directly; instead they delegate that authority to the Harry Fox Agency, via its SongFile system for searching and licensing music. Harry Fox's SongFile system remains the leader in this arena and the organization negotiates and collects mechanical royalties on behalf of approximately 80% of the music publishers.

However, negotiating with the music publisher, either directly or through Harry Fox, might not work for you. Many music publishers won't negotiate a lower rate unless a substantial number of copies of the recording will be distributed or you agree to pay them an advance. If you can't do this, you'll have to use a compulsory license as outlined above.

Dear Rich: *Whale Rider*: **Making a Musical Without Permission**

I am a music and drama director for a tiny K-8 private school in California. Every other year, we put on an all-school musical for parents, friends, and families. I often have trouble finding musicals that work for our age group—most musicals are written for high-school-aged kids or older—so I would like to write my own. Currently, I'm interested in adapting the movie/novel Whale Rider *for our kids. If I don't publish it, and don't charge for tickets to the show, how much material, if any, can I use from the movie and/or book for our play?*

You'll be violating copyright law if you don't obtain permission. It doesn't matter that you are not charging and won't publish the final work. Those may be mitigating factors if you're sued, and they may influence a fair use defense, but they won't prevent your actions from infringing the performance and derivative rights of the copyright owner. Since you'll have to take the major characters, plot, and dialog elements if you wish to conjure up the original, whatever you take will likely amount to an infringement. Asking for permission seems challenging, and you would need to determine who to ask—the novelist, the publisher (who may have acquired those rights), the movie company, or a third party. If the movie differed materially from the book—and you used those movie-specific elements—then you'd likely need more than one permission. So, from a legal point of view, it looks like a lot of hassle (and little chance of success). That said, you could attempt to contact author Witi Ihimaera, explain your situation, and seek his blessings/permission (assuming he still possesses those rights).

So what's a music director in a tiny K-8 school supposed to do? It reminds us of the time our mother called a big music publisher lawyer and asked for permission to perform a song at a nonprofit benefit. The lawyer's response: "As far as I'm concerned, I never got this call." In other words, when a copyrighted tree falls in the forest, sometimes nobody hears it. That appears to be the approach taken by some musical directors.

It would be unwise and unprofessional to advise you to go ahead without permission. However, should you choose to assume the risk—and it does involve some risk—you can lower the odds of seeing lawyers on opening night by doing the following:

- consider using only material from the book (to reduce the chances of the movie company coming after you)
- indicate on promotional material that the program has not been authorized by the author (it won't prevent a lawsuit, but at least you're not misleading consumers)
- follow the steps you mentioned, as those are all mitigating factors—that is, don't charge admission, don't publish the musical, and don't distribute video or audio copies, and
- make sure that the administration at your school is aware of your course of action (CYA).

Unless the author or someone from the movie company reads the Dear Rich blog (Hello!) it's unlikely that your efforts will be the subject of a cease and desist letter. If you do receive one, don't blow it off; respond immediately and halt production until a resolution occurs. Finally, have a backup musical ready, just in case.

Creating a Theatrical Musical: Grand Rights

Grand rights are the rights you need to create theatrical presentations, such as Broadway-style musicals. For example, to create a musical drama using the songs of Bob Dylan, you must secure grand rights from Bob Dylan's publisher or the entity he has designated to handle grand rights. Performance rights organizations such as ASCAP and BMI do not control grand rights. To find the company that controls grand rights for a song, start by contacting the music publisher of the song or the Harry Fox Agency.

Although performing rights societies do not control grand rights, these societies do grant performance permissions for songs from Broadway musicals, provided that the songs are not performed in a dramatic context. For example, playing a song from the musical *Rent* over the radio requires permission from a performing rights society but does not require grand rights clearance.

Using Music in a Podcast

The music industry has made it especially difficult for a podcaster to license music. For that reason, you can often assume that a podcast that uses contemporary music in its intro, as background, or as a featured musical track, is either infringing copyright, or possibly is excused under fair use principles (which I'll discuss later).

Why is it so hard to obtain the right to use pop music in a podcast? As we've discussed, pop music is based on two copyrights: a musical works copyright owned by the songwriter or music publisher that protects the musical composition; and a sound recording copyright owned by the artist or record company that protects the recorded version of the song. In order to play a song on your podcast you need permission from both copyright owners.

Because the song copyright owner is usually a music publisher, you can find the contact information by searching the records at songfile.com, ascap.com, bmi.com, or sesac.com. Then, you can contact the publisher directly and negotiate a podcasting license. Alternatively, you may be able to obtain the license from the Harry Fox Agency (songfile.com), which represents many publishers.

In addition to the song copyright, you would need to obtain the rights for the sound recording copyright. SoundExchange represents the rights of sound recording copyright owners, but alas, it's not empowered to license music to podcasters. So, you'll need to determine the owner of the sound recording copyright—most likely a record label—and then contact the company and negotiate a sound recording license. As you can imagine, the whole experience may prove to be frustrating, expensive, and fruitless. And if you plan to use music with a video podcast, you would also need what is known as a synchronization license from the music publisher and a master use license from the sound recording owner, on top of everything else.

That leaves podcasters with two choices: operate without permission (and hope to be unnoticed, or excused as a fair use) or acquire what's known in the podcasting community as "Podsafe" music, which usually involves public domain, Creative Commons, or additional options we'll cover below.

- **Hope for fair use.** Fair use is a legal defense that permits you to use portions of a copyrighted work for purposes of commentary or criticism. Keep in mind the less you use, the more likely that a fair use defense will succeed, especially if you're using the music to make a point on your show—for example, playing a few bars of R.E.M.'s "It's The End of the World As We Know It (And I Feel Fine)," while discussing global warming.

- **Public domain or Creative Commons music.** Music in the public domain is free for anyone to use … except there's one problem for podcasters. Remember there are two copyrights on music: a song copyright and a sound recording copyright. There are many songs in the public domain (check out pdinfo.com, and pdmusic.org) but because of a quirk in copyright law there are few sound recordings in the public domain. So if you find a public domain song, you'll have to record your own version to make it Podsafe. You'll have better luck finding music under Creative Commons license. Go to search.creativecommons.org and choose a music resource such as SoundCloud, and type in your search—for example, blues, rock, or electronic. Note: This works fine if the musician has created and owns the underlying song, but it's probably a good idea to avoid Creative Commons remixes of popular music. Also note there may be conditions for using Creative Commons music—for example, you may need to credit the musician in order to ensure it's a Podsafe use.

- **Stock or production music (PMLs).** This music is available from production music libraries ("PMLs"). Also, the musical loops that come with GarageBand (as well as loops from other providers) can be used to construct Podsafe intros and backgrounds.
- **Buy or license rights for original music directly from a musician.** You can accomplish this by using the Musician Assignment Agreement in Chapter 15.

Using Music in a Commercial, Radio Show, or as Background Music

Pop music has become a common component of advertising, used extensively in radio and television commercials. Using music in commercials, for syndicated radio shows, or for background music services (such as Muzak) requires permission from the music publisher and record company. The process for obtaining permission for these uses is similar.

If an advertising agency creates a new version of a song, it may only be required to obtain permission from the music publisher. If, however, the agency uses an already-recorded version of the song, it must get permission from both the music publisher and the record company. Using music in a radio or television commercial may also require permission from the artist performing on the recording. The same rule applies if the artist's style is imitated by another performer in a commercial.

Music Publisher Permissions and Fees

Music publishers grant "electrical transcription licenses" for the use of songs in radio commercials or syndicated radio programs. The music publisher may either furnish the electrical transcription license directly to the licensee or use the Harry Fox Agency to manage the licensing process. Electrical transcription licenses permit the radio program to copy the songs for its particular use. When songs are played on the radio, performing rights societies also collect fees from the radio stations for the performance of the songs. In this case, the radio ad or program does not need to get permission from BMI or ASCAP because the radio station that broadcasts the ad or program arranges for performing rights permission.

Fees for using songs in radio ads often start at $1,000 per week for local radio uses and may go as high as $100,000 per year for national radio uses. If a song is used in a syndicated radio show, the fees are often based on the number of copies of the program broadcast by syndicated stations (for example, $100 per station).

Record Company Permissions and Fees

To use an existing recording in a radio commercial or syndicated radio program, sound recording rights should be negotiated directly with the sound recording owner (generally a record company). To use a sound recording this way generally requires a one-time fee for the right to make copies of the sound recording. The amount the sound recording owner will charge varies widely depending on the length and type of use. As noted earlier in this chapter, record companies can be difficult to negotiate with and may charge exorbitant fees for authorizing the use of their recordings. As a result, it's often easier to record a new version of the song—which will only require the music publisher's permission—rather than use the recording itself.

In some countries—but not the United States—you must pay the owner of the sound recording when it is played on the radio. In these countries, two performance payments are required each time a radio station plays a song: one payment to the music publisher and another to the record company.

Using Music in a Film, Television Show, or Video

Music is an essential component of films, television shows, and videos. The businesses that produce these audiovisual works (known as production companies) generally acquire music rights either by hiring musicians to record music or by obtaining the rights to use an existing recording. If the production company hires musicians to record existing songs—for instance, hires musicians to play Beatles songs—the company needs permission from only the music publisher. If a film or video production company wants to use an existing recording—for example, a Dolly Parton recording—it must acquire permission from both the music publisher and the owner of the sound recording (the record company).

TIP

You can also get music for a film, TV show, or other type of program from production music libraries. PMLs, as they're typically called, have broad selections of music to which they own all rights. Licensing music from a PML is generally simple and inexpensive. A list of PMLs appears at the end of this chapter.

In general, when you use a song in a movie—but not a particular recording of that song—you'll need to obtain a synchronization license from the music publisher. The term "synchronization" means simply that the song is being synchronized with the video track of the program. If you're using a recording of the song that you had created for your movie, you'll also need to obtain the rights to the rerecording from the musicians you hired.

> EXAMPLE: Dave is making a movie about Los Angeles and wants to use the song "I Love L.A." by Randy Newman. Dave cannot afford to pay for the Randy Newman master use rights (for the sound recording) so he hires a musician to rerecord the song. He uses a work-for-hire agreement to acquire ownership of the master recording from the musician. To use the song in his movie, Dave needs to obtain permission from only the music publisher of the song.

On the other hand, when you use a specific recording in a movie, you'll also need what's called a master use license from the record company. The term "master use" means you're obtaining permission from the record company to use the master recording of the song.

It's important to understand that to use a particular recording of a song in a movie, television program, or video, you'll generally need both a synchronization license (because you're using a song owned by the music publisher) and a master use license (because you're using the recording owned by the record company). An exception to this is if the song is in the public domain. In that case, you'd only need the master use license from the owner of the sound recording you're using—the protected specific version of the underlying song that is now in the public domain.

This section explains the types of permissions that are required to use music in film, television, or video, and the process for obtaining that permission.

CAUTION

Acquiring permission for the use of music in motion pictures and videos can be complex. Older songs may be subject to copyright rules that resulted in a transfer of rights back to the original songwriter. If clearance is performed improperly, the costs of correcting permission errors can be substantial. For this reason, and to save time and money, many film and video production companies use music clearance services. A list of companies that perform these services is included at the end of this chapter.

RESOURCE

Two helpful resources for clearing music for films are *Clearance & Copyright: Everything the Independent Filmmaker Needs to Know,* by Michael C. Donaldson, and *Kohn on Music Licensing,* by Al Kohn and Bob Kohn.

Synchronization Licenses

As mentioned above, you must obtain permission from the music publisher to use a song in a movie, television show, or video content, whether you use an existing recording or create a new recording. The general term for an agreement to use a song in conjunction with a series of visual images—for example, in a television show or movie—is a "synchronization license." There are more specific names for this agreement depending on the type of program that will include the music. For a movie, the specific type of license is a "theatrical motion picture synchronization license." If a song is used in a television commercial, the license is called a "television commercial synchronization license."

In addition, if you plan to release the program on DVDs or the like for sale to the public, you must also obtain a "videogram license" from the music publisher. In other words, the music publisher's permission to use the song in a movie or other program does not authorize the use of the song on subsequent DVD/video releases of the same program. See below for more information on videogram licenses.

The essential terms of the various types of synchronization agreements are very similar. Synchronization licenses for films can also be tailored to specific purposes—for example, for student films or film festival uses.

Granting of synchronization must be made by the music publisher. You can find contact information for the publisher of a particular song by searching for the song title on the websites of performing rights societies BMI, ASCAP, or SESAC.

Videogram Licenses

If you use a song in a DVD, video cassette, or some other platform that produces a "hard copy" that you plan to sell to the public, you will need an additional permission from the music publisher called a "videogram license." Videogram licenses are required for any programs—such as theatrical films, television shows, exercise videos—that are made available for sale to the public on DVD and the like. This is true whether the program was originally made for video or for cinema or TV and later released on video. The key here is that the video is available for sale to the public. If a music video were made, for instance, only to be shown on BET Jams and not to be sold to the public, a videogram license would not be necessary.

Dear Rich:

Needs License for "Watching the Detectives"

I want to use the melody (we will do the lyrics) of the 1977 Elvis Costello song "Watching the Detectives" in a promotional video. It is for a medical device company. Term is nine months (this year). Do I need a sync license? Who is this sent to? (Costello is within the Universal Music Publishing Group.)

Yes, you need a sync license and you would need permission to modify the lyrics. You should speak with the publisher—yes, it's Universal Music Publishing. Contact them at 2440 Sepulveda Blvd., Suite 100, Los Angeles, CA 90064, 310-235-4700. If you run into a problem—the typical one being that nobody takes your calls—you may need to hire a clearance expert. See "Music Clearance Companies," below. If you create your own version of the song and don't imitate the singing style of Elvis Costello—imitating artists in ads leads to problems— you will only need the permission of the publisher (or administrator).

Music Synchronization and Videogram License Agreement

Music Synchronization and Videogram License Agreement (the "Agreement") is made between: _____ ("Publisher") and _____ ("Producer"). Publisher is the owner of rights for the compositions listed below:

_____

_____

_____ (the "Compositions").

Producer is the owner of rights for the Motion Picture tentatively entitled _____ _____ (the "Motion Picture"). Producer desires to license the Compositions for use in the Motion Picture and in audiovisual devices for home use such as videotapes and DVDs ("Videograms"). The parties agree as follows:

Grant

(Select one or more Grant provisions)

☐ **Grant of Audiovisual License.** Publisher grants to Producer and Producer's successors and assigns the nonexclusive right to record the Compositions solely in synchronization with the Motion Picture (in any medium, now known or later created) within the Territory. Publisher grants to Producer the right to publicly perform the Compositions solely in synchronization with the Motion Picture within the Territory. These public performance rights include public exhibitions of the Motion Picture in theaters and other public places where motion pictures are customarily exhibited, provided that performances outside the United States are cleared by performing rights societies in accordance with customary practice and customary fees. The public performance rights also include television exhibition of the Motion Picture within the Territory, including all methods of television reproduction and transmissions, provided that the entities broadcasting those performances have licenses from the appropriate performing rights societies. Any television performance not licensed by performing rights societies must be cleared directly by the Publisher.

☐ **Grant of Videogram License.** Publisher grants to Producer and his successors and assigns the nonexclusive right to record, copy, and synchronize the Composition, solely as part of the Motion Picture, on audiovisual devices including, but not limited to, videocassettes, DVDs, and similar compact audiovisual devices that reproduce the entire Motion Picture in substantially its original form ("Videogram"). This Videogram license is solely for the distribution of Videograms intended primarily for home use in the Territory.

☐ **Use in Trailers.** Publisher grants to Producer and his successors and assigns the nonexclusive right to record, copy, synchronize, and perform the Composition in connection with trailers used for the advertising and exploitation of the Motion Picture.

Reservation of Rights

Publisher reserves all rights not granted in this Agreement.

Modifications to Composition

Producer shall not make any change in the original lyrics, if any, or in the fundamental character of the music of the Composition or use the title or any portion of the lyrics of the Composition as the title or subtitle of the Motion Picture without written prior authorization from Publisher.

Territory

The rights granted in this Agreement are for the following: _____

_____ (the "Territory").

Audiovisual License Payments

As payment for the rights granted for the Audiovisual License, Producer shall pay Publisher as follows:

(*Select payment option and fill in blanks*)

☐ **One-Time Payment.** Producer shall pay Publisher a one-time payment of $ _____ upon first public performance of the Motion Picture or within nine (9) months of signing this agreement, whichever is earlier.

☐ **Advance and Royalties.** Producer shall pay Publisher a nonrefundable advance ("Motion Picture Advance") in the sum of $ _____ recoupable against royalties derived from the Audiovisual License ("Audiovisual Royalties"). Producer shall pay Publisher Audiovisual Royalties of _____ % of net profits from the public exhibition and public performance of the Motion Picture.

☐ **Royalties.** Producer shall pay Publisher _____ % of the net profits from the public exhibition and public performance of the Motion Picture.

Videogram License Payments

As payment for the rights granted for the Videogram License, Producer shall pay Publisher as follows: (*Select payment option and fill in blanks*)

☐ **One-Time Payment.** Producer shall pay Publisher a one-time payment of $ _____ within nine (9) months of signing this agreement.

☐ **Advance and Royalties.** Producer shall pay Publisher a nonrefundable advance ("Videogram Advance") in the sum of $ _____ recoupable against royalties derived from the Videogram License ("Videogram Royalties"). Videogram Royalties for Videogram copies of the Motion Picture shall be paid as follows:

☐ **Net Profits.** Producer shall pay Publisher _____ % of the Producer's net profits for all Videogram revenues, including all sales, licenses, or other sources of revenue for Videogram distribution (not including shipping charges or taxes).

☐ **Pro Rata Option.** Producer shall pay Publisher _____ % ("Publisher's Pro-Rata Portion") of _____ % of the net revenue for all Videogram income including all sales, licenses, or other sources of revenue for Videogram distribution. Publisher's Pro-Rata Portion represents the proportion the Composition bears to the total number of Royalty-bearing compositions contained in the Motion Picture.

Payments and Statements

Within forty-five (45) days after the end of each calendar quarter (the "Royalty Period"), Producer shall furnish an accurate statement of net revenues derived from the licenses granted in this agreement along with any royalty payments. Producer may withhold a reasonable reserve for anticipated returns, refunds, and exchanges of Videograms, and this reserve shall be liquidated no later than twelve (12) months after the respective accounting statement.

Favorable Rates

If a higher royalty rate than set forth in this Agreement becomes payable by operation of law with respect to Videograms sold in a particular country within the Territory, Producer shall either pay the higher royalty to Publisher with respect to that country or delete the Compositions from the Motion Picture with respect to this country. In the event that a musical composition is licensed for a substantially similar use in connection with the Videogram exploitation of the Motion Picture on a more favorable rate, Producer agrees that such favorable rate shall also be granted to Publisher for the licensing of the Composition.

Audit

Producer shall keep accurate books of account and records covering all transactions relating to the licenses granted in this Agreement, and Publisher or its duly authorized representatives shall have the right upon five (5) days' prior written notice, and during normal business hours, to inspect and audit these accounts and records.

Warranty

Publisher warrants that it has the power and authority to grant the rights in this Agreement and that the Compositions do not infringe any third-party rights. In no event shall Publisher's liability for a breach of this Warranty exceed the amount of payments received under this Agreement.

Credits

Publisher shall receive credit in the following form: _____
_____ .

This credit shall be provided as follows:

(*Select all that apply*)

- ☐ similar to all other musical compositions used in the Motion Picture.
- ☐ a single card in the main titles on all prints of the Motion Picture and Videograms.
- ☐ in all paid advertising similar to all other musical compositions used in the Motion Picture.

Samples

Producer shall promptly furnish Publisher with _____ copies of each format of Videogram release.

Cue Sheets

Producer agrees to furnish Publisher a cue sheet of the Motion Picture within thirty (30) days after the first public exhibition of the Motion Picture.

Term

The term of this Agreement is for the term of United States copyright in the Composition including renewal terms, if any.

Termination and Breach

In the event that Producer (or Producer's assigns or licensees) breaches this Agreement and fails to cure such breach within thirty (30) days after notice by Publisher to Producer, this license will automatically terminate and all rights granted under this Agreement shall revert to Publisher. Failure to make timely payments or to provide credit as provided in this Agreement shall be considered a material breach of this Agreement.

Miscellaneous

This Agreement may not be amended except in a writing signed by both parties. If a court finds any provision of this Agreement invalid or unenforceable, the remainder of this Agreement shall be interpreted so as best to effect the intent of the parties. This Agreement shall be governed by and interpreted in accordance with the laws of the State of _____ . This Agreement expresses the complete understanding of the parties with respect to the subject matter and supersedes all prior representations and understandings. Any controversy or claim arising out of or relating to this Agreement shall be settled by binding arbitration in accordance with the rules of the American Arbitration Association, and judgment upon the award rendered by the arbitrator(s) may be entered in any court having jurisdiction. All notices provided for under this Agreement must be in writing and mailed to the addresses provided in the signature portion of this Agreement.

Publisher's name: _____

Publisher's signature: _____

Publisher's address: _____

Producer's name: _____

Producer's signature: _____

Producer's address: _____

Fees for song rights for a video release of a theatrical motion picture may be several thousand dollars or, on occasion, may be tied to sales of the video. For example, under certain arrangements, an additional payment must be made if video sales pass a certain number. Corporate video uses may be charged a flat fee ($500 to $2,000) or may be tied to the number of units manufactured or distributed.

Synchronization Fees

Fees for using a song in a film depend on the nature of the film (documentary or theatrical; independent or major studio release) and the use in the film—whether the song is used in the background, foreground, or in some special manner (such as when a character sings the song). The fee for use of a song in the background of an independent documentary may start at $500. Fees for nontheatrical corporate video synchronization licenses may range from $500 to $1,500. Fees for using a song in an independent theatrical release may range from $5,000 to $15,000. Fees for use in a major motion picture are generally between $10,000 and $25,000. These synchronization fees do not include separate fees and royalties for videogram licenses, described above.

If you plan to make your program available for sale on DVD or some other media format that results in a "hard copy," you'll have to pay videogram fees as well.

Music Synchronization and Videogram License

Below is an agreement that provides for both synchronization and video-gram rights from a music publisher. It can be used for any film or video that will be released in theaters or on video. This agreement can be used for purposes of comparison, since a music publisher will likely provide its own license agreement.

If the work will only be released on video and not theatrically, you can remove the synchronization language, as described in the explanation following the agreement. Although this agreement is for films and videos, much of the language and principles apply to other audiovisual uses as well.

FORM
You can download this form (and all other forms in this book) from Nolo.com; for details, see the appendix.

Explanation for Music Synchronization and Videogram License

- The **introductory paragraph** identifies the companies entering into the agreement (the "parties"). Insert the name of music publisher ("Publisher") and producer ("Producer") of the film or video. Sometimes, a synchronization license may substitute the terms "Licensee" for Producer and "Licensor" for Publisher. The terms "Television Show" or "Audiovisual Work," if applicable, can be substituted for the term "Motion Picture." In this event, change all references throughout the agreement.

- The **Grant** provisions establish the rights under copyright law (the licenses) that the music publisher is granting to the film producer. The **Grant of Audiovisual License** establishes the right to synchronize—or use—the music in conjunction with public presentations of the film or video—for example, in theaters or on a television broadcast. The **Grant of Videogram License** establishes the right to synchronize—or use—the music with the video version of the motion picture—as well as to make copies for sale for home use. If the licensee is going "direct to video" and the film will not be shown in theaters, he or she does not need the Grant of Videogram License, so do not check the box. If no video rights are sought and the film will only be shown in theaters, the licensee does not need the Grant of Videogram License, so do not check the box. The **Use in Trailers** section permits the use of the Composition in trailers advertising the film.

- The **Reservation of Rights** section establishes that any rights not covered in this agreement are held by the music publisher.

- The **Modifications to Composition** section provides that the producer must acquire written permission from the music publisher to make modifications to the song. Failure to obtain permission may endanger the rights to use the music.

- As for the **Territory,** worldwide rights are preferred if the producer intends to show or distribute the film outside the United States. If the publisher cannot grant worldwide rights, permission will be required from the holder of rights (usually a foreign music publisher) in each country in which the film will be distributed.

- There are separate payment sections for the audiovisual and the videogram licenses. For each one, choose the payment method that reflects the agreement with the publisher. For the **Audiovisual License**

Payments, you can choose either a one-time payment, an advance against royalties, or royalties with no advance. For the **Videogram License Payments,** you can choose a one-time payment or an advance against royalties. You also can choose which type of royalties you will pay—royalties based on net profits or prorated royalties. The pro rata choice provides that you pay a portion of income to the publisher based on the total number of songs being used in the video. For example, if ten songs are used on a video, each publisher would receive 1/10 of the music royalty. If you choose this option, enter the composition's proportional share of the whole video in the first blank and the overall royalty rate in the second blank. If there is no videogram license, do not check any options in the Videogram License Payments section.

- The provision entitled **Favorable Rates** is sometimes referred to as a "Most Favored Nation" clause. It provides that if a country establishes a higher rate of payment for any of the uses described in this agreement, the producer must pay the higher rate. Some film producers may not want to include this provision.

- The **Warranty** is a contractual promise that the publisher is legally capable to grant the rights in this agreement. The last sentence in the Warranty section limits the amount of damages the publisher must pay if it breaches the warranty.

- In the **Credits** section, the publisher will establish the type and size of credit the producer should use. A failure to properly credit the composition may result in a loss of licensing rights. The term "single card" refers to a separate credit on a screen with no other credits.

- If the publisher wants the producer to provide samples, indicate the number agreed upon in the **Samples** section.

- A **Cue Sheet** lists each separate musical use on a film or video. This provision simply provides that you will furnish one to the publisher within 30 days of the program's public premiere.

- For an explanation of the **Term, Termination,** and **Miscellaneous** sections, see Chapter 11, "Art and Merchandise Licenses."

- The agreement must be signed by individuals with the authority to represent the music publisher and the film production company. For information about determining who has authority to sign (also known as "signing capacity"), see the explanation in Chapter 11.

Dear Rich:

Punk Rock Video Rights

My friends and I have some old video footage we took from punk and new wave bands from the early 1990s. Some of these are local Bay Area artists and some are national artists. We never got release forms from the artists, but they knew they were being filmed and didn't demand anything. Could we release these videos for profit? What about releasing them on YouTube? What about making a documentary?

We assume that you have videotaped musical performances, in which case you could have problems with all of the uses you propose. It's true that you (or whoever took the videos) owns the copyright to the video. But the artists (or the artists' publishers) control the rights to reproduce the music. You need what's referred to as a sync right—which is the right to match visuals to a musical performance. (Sample sync rights forms are included above.) As for the nonmusical footage that you shot, you probably are free to use that for documentary and YouTube purposes. The fact that the artists knew they were being filmed does not provide you with any rights, although a lawyer might try to argue that the failure to object implied consent. Based on the Dear Rich Staff's personal observations, individual posting of unauthorized music videos at YouTube doesn't have dire consequences other than disabling of your YouTube account. However, you should assume—as with all infringing uses—that the more you profit, the more likely you will get hassled.

Master Use Licenses

To use a particular recording on a motion picture soundtrack, the record company that owns the recording must grant a master use license. For instance, if a filmmaker wants to use a recording—not a remake—of Johnny Cash's "Ring of Fire" in a film, the filmmaker will need to obtain a master use license from the record company that owns the recording. The license permits the filmmaker to duplicate the recording on the film soundtrack. The cost of the master use license depends on the size and type of production and the prominence of the song's use within the film (for example, in the foreground or in the background). The cost may range from a few hundred dollars for a student film to thousands of dollars for a feature film.

Master Use and Videogram License

This Master Use and Videogram License Agreement (the "Agreement") is made between: _____ ("Owner") and _____ ("Producer").

Owner is the owner of rights for the master recordings: _____
_____
_____ (the "Masters").

Producer is the owner of rights for the Motion Picture tentatively entitled _____
_____ (the "Motion Picture").

Producer desires to license the Masters for use in the Motion Picture and in audiovisual devices for home use such as videotapes and DVDs ("Videograms"). The parties agree as follows:

Grant

(Select one or more Grant provisions if applicable)

☐ **Grant of Audiovisual License.** Owner grants to Producer and Producer's successors and assigns the nonexclusive right to use and reproduce the Masters solely in synchronization with the Motion Picture in any medium, now known or later created within the Territory. Owner grants to Producer the right to publicly perform the Masters solely in synchronization with the Motion Picture within the Territory. These public performance rights include the public exhibitions of the Motion Picture in theaters and other public places where motion pictures are customarily exhibited and for television exhibition of the Motion Picture including all methods of television reproduction and transmissions within the Territory.

☐ **Grant of Videogram License.** Owner grants to Producer and Producer's successors and assigns the nonexclusive right to record, copy, and synchronize the Masters, solely as part of the Motion Picture, on audiovisual devices including, but not limited to video cassettes, DVDs, and similar compact audiovisual devices that reproduce the entire Motion Picture in substantially its original form ("Videogram"). This Videogram license is solely for the distribution of Videograms intended primarily for home use in the Territory.

☐ **Use in Trailers.** Owner grants to Producer and Producer's successors and assigns, the nonexclusive right to record, copy, synchronize, and perform the Masters in connection with trailers used for the advertising and exploitation of the Motion Picture.

Reservation of Rights

Owner reserves all rights not granted in this Agreement.

Modifications to Masters

Producer shall not make any change in the Masters without written prior authorization from Owner.

Territory

The rights granted in this Agreement are for the following: _____
_____ (the "Territory").

Union Reuse Fees

Owner agrees to provide Producer with all information regarding any reuse fees required by unions or guilds as a result of this license. Producer agrees to pay all such reuse payments including related pension or welfare payments and to indemnify Owner from claims arising from such payments.

Musical Works Synchronization Rights

Producer agrees to obtain all appropriate synchronization, performance, and reproduction rights for the musical compositions embodied on the Masters and to indemnify Owner for any claims arising from such rights.

Audiovisual License Payments

As payment for the rights granted for the Audiovisual License, Producer shall pay Owner as follows:

(Select payment option and fill in blanks)

☐ **One-Time Payment.** Producer shall pay Owner a one-time payment of $ _____ upon first public performance of the Motion Picture or within nine (9) months of signing this agreement, whichever is earlier.

☐ **Advance and Royalties.** Producer shall pay Owner a nonrefundable advance ("Motion Picture Advance") in the sum of $ _____ recoupable against royalties derived from the Audiovisual License ("Audiovisual Royalties"). Producer shall pay Owner Audiovisual Royalties of _____ % of net profits from the public exhibition and public performance of the Motion Picture.

☐ **Royalties.** Producer shall pay Owner _____ % of the net profits from the public exhibition and public performance of the Motion Picture.

Videogram License Payments

As payment for the rights granted for the Videogram License, Producer shall pay Owner as follows:

(Select payment option and fill in blanks)

☐ **One-Time Payment.** Producer shall pay Owner a one-time payment of $ _____ within nine (9) months of signing this agreement.

☐ **Advance and Royalties.** Producer shall pay Owner a nonrefundable advance ("Videogram Advance") in the sum of $ _____ recoupable against royalties derived from the Videogram License ("Videogram Royalties"). Videogram Royalties for Videogram copies of the Motion Picture shall be paid as follows:

☐ **Net Profits.** Producer shall pay Owner _____ % of the Producer's net profits for all Videogram revenues including all sales, licenses, or other sources of revenue for Videogram distribution (not including shipping charges or taxes).

☐ **Pro Rata Option.** Producer shall pay Owner _____ % ("Owner's Pro-Rata Portion") of _____ % of the net revenue for all Videogram income including all sales, licenses, or other sources of revenue for Videogram distribution. Owner's Pro-Rata Portion represents the proportion the Composition bears to the total number of Royalty-bearing compositions contained in the Motion Picture.

Payments and Statements

Within forty-five (45) days after the end of each calendar quarter (the "Royalty Period"), Producer shall furnish an accurate statement of net revenues derived from the licenses granted in this agreement along with any royalty payments. Producer may withhold a reasonable reserve for anticipated returns, refunds, and exchanges of Videograms, and this reserve shall be liquidated no later than twelve (12) months after the respective accounting statement.

Audit

Producer shall keep accurate books of account and records covering all transactions relating to the licenses granted in this Agreement, and Owner or its duly authorized representatives shall have the right upon five (5) days' prior written notice, and during normal business hours, to inspect and audit these accounts and records.

Warranty

Owner warrants that it has the power and authority to grant the rights in this Agreement and that the Masters do not infringe any third-party rights. In no event shall Owner's liability for a breach of this warranty exceed the amount of payments received under this Agreement.

Credits

Owner shall receive credit in the following form: _____
_____

This credit shall be provided as follows:

(*Select one or more if appropriate*)

☐ similar to all other Masters used in the Motion Picture.

☐ in all paid advertising similar to all other musical Masters used in the Motion Picture.

Samples

Producer shall promptly furnish Owner with _____ copies of each format of Videogram release.

Cue Sheets

Producer agrees to furnish Owner a cue sheet of the Motion Picture within thirty (30) days after the first public exhibition of the Motion Picture.

Term

The term of this Agreement is for the term of United States copyright in the Masters including renewal terms, if any.

Termination and Breach

In the event that Producer (or Producer's assigns or licensees) breaches this Agreement and fails to cure such breach within thirty (30) days after notice by Owner to Producer, this license will automatically terminate and all rights granted under this Agreement shall revert to Owner. Failure to make timely payments or to provide credit as provided in this Agreement shall be considered a material breach of this Agreement.

Miscellaneous

This Agreement may not be amended except in a writing signed by both parties. If a court finds any provision of this Agreement invalid or unenforceable, the remainder of this Agreement shall be interpreted so as best to effect the intent of the parties. This Agreement shall be governed by and interpreted in accordance with the laws of the State of _____ . This Agreement expresses the complete understanding of the parties with respect to the subject matter and supersedes all prior representations and understandings. Any controversy or claim arising out of or relating to this Agreement shall be settled by binding arbitration in accordance with the rules of the American Arbitration Association, and judgment upon the award rendered by the arbitrator(s) may be entered in any court having jurisdiction. All notices provided for under this Agreement must be in writing and mailed to the addresses provided in the signature portion of this Agreement.

Owner's name: _____

Owner's signature: _____

Owner's address: _____

Producer's name: _____

Producer's signature: _____

Producer's address: _____

If a soundtrack album is released, the record company that owns the original recording will seek a percentage, or "royalty," based upon the sound track album's sales. In some cases, a record company may seek an advance payment plus a "rollover"—a payment made when a certain number of video or soundtrack copies have been sold. Costs are also affected by extra payments (known as "reuse fees") that the record company must make to union and guild members who worked on the recording.

Videogram Licenses

If the program will be released on video, DVD, and the like, you must also obtain a videogram license from the record company. In other words, the record company's permission to use the recording in a movie or other program does not authorize the use of the recording on video or DVD releases of the same program. If your program will be available for sale to the public on video (as opposed to shown on YouTube but not sold), you'll need a videogram license regardless of the original format of the program.

Master Use and Videogram License

Below is an agreement that provides for both master use and videogram rights from the owner of a sound recording (a record company). It can be used for any film or video that will be released in theaters or on video. Although this agreement is for films and videos, much of the language and principles apply to other audiovisual uses as well.

 FORM

You can download this form (and all other forms in this book) from Nolo.com; for details, see the appendix.

CAUTION

If you're obtaining a master use license, you probably need a synchronization license as well. For example, if a producer is obtaining master use rights from a record company to use a specific recording of the song "Stand by Me" in a film, the producer must also obtain synchronization rights from the music publisher of "Stand by Me." However, you won't need synchronization rights from the music publisher if the recorded song you want to use is in the public domain. In that case, you'd only need a master use license from the owner of the specific recording you want to use.

Explanation for Master Use License and Videogram License

- The **introductory paragraph** identifies the companies entering into the agreement (the "parties"). In the Owner blank, insert the name of the owner of the masters (usually the record company), and in the Producer blank enter the name of the producer of the film or video. Sometimes, a synchronization license may substitute the terms "Licensee" for Producer and "Licensor" for Owner. The terms "Television Show" or "Audiovisual Work," if applicable, can be substituted for the term "Motion Picture." In this event, change all references throughout the agreement.

- For explanations of the sections regarding the **Grant, Reservation of Rights, Modifications to Masters, Territory, License Payments, Payments & Statements, Audit, Warranty, Credits, Samples,** and **Cue Sheet** provisions, see the explanation provided to the Music Synchronization and Videogram License Agreement above. For an explanation of the **Term, Termination,** and **Miscellaneous** sections, see Chapter 11, "Art and Merchandise Licenses."

- The **Union Reuse Fees** and **Musical Works Synchronization Rights** sections refer to obligations of the producer. Reuse fees are payments that must be made to the union musicians and engineers who created the masters whenever the masters are used for additional purposes. Musical works synchronization rights are rights that must be obtained from the music publisher to use the song composition. You can acquire synchronization rights from the music publisher by using the Music Synchronization and Videogram License.

Performing a Musical or Play

Let's put on a show! If you and some friends decide to rebuild your community playhouse for a production of *Hamilton* or *Cats*, you'll need to first obtain permission from the rights holder of the musical. The procedure is fairly straightforward: Identify the work, identify the rights holder, and secure permission. (If you intend to produce a dramatic nonmusical such as *Waiting for Godot*, the rules are the same.)

Before printing posters and buying ad space for your show, check to see if your choice is available for production. Some musicals and dramatic plays are not available (referred to as "restricted"). In this case, you'll have to move on to your second choice. Assuming your choice is available, here are the ground rules for putting on a live show.

Payments

Your payment for rights to perform a musical or play is a "royalty" and does not include the cost of acquiring copies of the piano/conductor score, chorus books, or scripts. There are separate fees for permission to make and distribute these copies. In addition, some musicals require payment of a security deposit.

Royalties are charged for all live performances, whether or not admission is charged. Sometimes, a rights holder will provide two royalty quotes, one for the first performance and the second for succeeding performances.

Usually, you can easily and inexpensively get approval online or by phone for live stage productions by amateur groups with maximum seating capacities of 400 or less. The approval process may involve more negotiation and detail if you're a professional group or amateur group with large seating capacity. Most of the time, you'll pay royalties before performing the work.

Rights

Rights owners of musicals and dramatic works commonly put restrictions on performances. They require special permission for performances that include television and radio broadcasting (if you intend to film the performance, you'll probably need prior approval). Some rights holders require special clearance for performances in certain cities, like New York and Los Angeles. Owners typically insist that authorship credit appear on all programs, printing, and advertising for the play.

Other restrictions may include the requirement that the production not deviate from its "published form." One musical publishing house explains it this way:

"The author's intent will be respected in production. No changes, interpolations, or deletions in the text, lyrics, music, title, or gender of the characters shall be made for the purpose of production. This includes changes or updating the time and place/setting of the play. In reference to changing the gender of characters, men will play male roles and women will play female roles."

Acquiring Permission

The easiest way to determine who owns the performance rights to a musical or play is to examine a copy of the script. If a copy is not available, check the publishing houses listed under "Musical and Dramatic Rights Resources" at the end of this chapter.

Once you've located the rights holder, contact them. They will want to know some basic information, such as the work, location of the performance, seating capacity, ticket prices, whether it's a nonprofit performance, the dates for the production, and whether it is a union (Actors' Equity) or nonunion show.

Normally, the rights holder will respond shortly with a price quote. Once you accept the quote and pay any required security deposit (usually refundable), it's showtime!

Using Music in Software, Video Games, or Multimedia Programs

As the sound quality available on computers, smartphones, and gaming systems has improved, so has the quality of music used in conjunction with software programs. Preparing or acquiring music for popular software products has become a major enterprise, sometimes involving specially scored works by Hollywood film composers.

Software companies commonly acquire music rights by hiring musicians or purchasing music from production music libraries. When a software company hires musicians, it acquires ownership rights to the music they create by assignment or under work-for-hire agreements, as explained in Chapter 15.

On some occasions, however, software companies may use preexisting songs or recordings for video games, educational software, multimedia presentations, or MIDI software (a format used for transmitting musical data). This section deals with situations in which a software company wants to use preexisting music in its products.

Music Publisher Permission and Fees

If the software company is rerecording a song, permission is required from the music publisher (usually through the Harry Fox Agency).

> EXAMPLE: Softco creates a software program for guitar students and records a new version of the song "Layla." Softco must obtain permission from the music publisher of the song.

Licenses to incorporate music in software or multimedia programs are usually negotiated directly with the Harry Fox Agency, a company that represents music publishers for certain reproduction rights. A sample copy of the Harry Fox multimedia license (the "MMERL License") can be downloaded from its website.

If music is to be used in connection with audiovisual images, such as in an interactive video game, a multimedia synchronization license is required. If the music is intended for use in a karaoke program, the content of the license depends upon whether the device will display the lyrics, whether film or video imagery will be synchronized with the music, and whether the program is intended for private or public karaoke uses. Some publishers will charge an additional "fixing fee" for the right to synchronize the music with the visual imagery.

Most music publishers will demand an advance payment from you, which you can deduct from any ongoing royalties you owe for use of the music. Advance payments may be several hundred to several thousand dollars depending on the song and use. Royalty rates for multimedia uses also depend on the use. Use of a song in a video game may range from 0.5% to 1% of the retail price, while royalties for use of a song in MIDI software may start at 5% of the retail price. Fees are often prorated based on the total number of songs included on the software. For typical multimedia uses, the royalty is between 5 and 15 cents per unit, and advances starting at $250 are often required. Few publishers will allow multimedia use of a song for a flat fee. (Flat fee payments are common when using music from production music libraries, however.)

Record Company Permission and Fees

If a software company is duplicating a previously released recording, permission is required from the record company that owns the recording in addition to the music publisher that owns the song.

> EXAMPLE: Softco creates a software program for guitar students and incorporates a specific Eric Clapton recording of the song "Layla." Softco must obtain permission from the record company that owns the recording and from the music publisher of the song.

The form you use to obtain permission from the record company is referred to as a multimedia or software master use license and is usually supplied by the record company. This license is similar to the master use license.

A software company should expect to pay a minimum of $500 to $1,000 as an advance fee for use of the master sound recording, plus a continuing royalty. This royalty is separate from the royalty the company must pay the music publisher for use of the song itself. Because of this, software companies often seek to avoid paying two royalties by rerecording songs instead of using existing recordings.

Using Music on a Website

It is possible to preview music online before buying a record, download a song by a pop artist, or copy and send a song from one destination to the other—all with perfect sound clarity. With these capabilities have come a new set of rules for Internet users. There are two common ways that music is transmitted over the Internet:

- The song is made available for **digital downloading**—that is, a copy is delivered from a website to a user's computer, phone, or other device. When downloading, the user obtains a copy. The most popular downloading formats are AAC and MP3.

- The song is broadcast in real time (known as **"webcasting"** or **"audio streaming"**). The listener hears the song as it is played by an Internet website and may or may not have the opportunity to make a digital copy.

Below we discuss both methods of transmitting music and the permissions required for each use.

MP3s and Downloading Music

From a permission standpoint, the process of downloading music files, such as MP3 files, is called "digital phonorecord delivery" or "DPD." MP3 is a computer standard that enables a recording to be compressed so that it can be transmitted faster than uncompressed recordings. (When we refer to MP3 in this book, we are also referring to other digital formats such as AAC and WAV files.) Other downloadable formats are being developed by the music industry.

> EXAMPLE: Kinksology is a website that features music of the rock group The Kinks. Don visits the site, clicks on the song title "You Really Got Me," and an MP3 file with The Kinks' song is downloaded onto Don's computer. Don can play this MP3 file on his computer or on a portable MP3 player. Kinksology is providing digital phonorecord delivery.

Any website providing digital phonorecord delivery must obtain permission from the owner of the song (music publisher) and the owner of the sound recording (record company).

Music Publisher Permission

To provide digital phonorecord delivery, you must get permission from the music publisher. Music publishers used to believe that they were entitled to get paid twice—once for the reproduction of the MP3 file, and again for the transmission of the file over the Internet (supposedly a "performance" of the song). The process was referred to as "double-dipping." But in 2007, a federal court put an end to this "double-dipping" when it ruled that music downloads are not public performances. (*U.S. v. ASCAP*, 485 F.Supp.2d 438 (S.D.N.Y. 2007) and see also the ruling in *In re Cellco Partnership*, 2009 WL 3294861 (S.D.N.Y. 10/14/2009).) The Copyright Office has also issued a similar ruling. All that is required for digital downloads is a compulsory license (or by negotiating a digital delivery agreement directly with the Harry Fox Agency).

MP3 Sound Recording Permission

In addition, digital phonorecord delivery, such as providing MP3 files for downloading, requires permission from the sound recording owner, usually a record company. This can prove to be an expensive and time-consuming procedure because most record companies are wary of licensing rights for making digital copies of their sound recordings.

Webcasting and Audio Streaming

Webcasting and audio streaming are processes by which digital music is broadcast over the Internet, much like a radio station broadcasts music. The user hears the music as it is being played by the website. Both webcasting and audio streaming are referred to as "digital audio transmissions." The music industry characterizes digital audio transmissions as either being interactive or noninteractive.

Interactive Digital Audio Transmissions

An interactive digital audio transmission is one in which a user requests a performance of a particular recording, usually by clicking or tapping on a song title. This type of transmission is popular for purposes of promoting recordings.

> EXAMPLE: Kinksology is a website that features music of the rock group The Kinks. Don visits the site, clicks on the song title, "You Really Got Me," and hears The Kinks' song. Don does not receive a copy of the song on his computer. He can only hear it by clicking on the button. Kinksology is providing interactive digital audio transmissions.

The rules for digital audio transmission are the same as those for downloading MP3s. The website must obtain a mechanical license for the reproduction of the song, usually from the Harry Fox Agency, and the website must also obtain permission from the sound recording owner, usually a record company, to transmit a particular recording of the song. This permission must be negotiated via SoundExchange (www.soundexchange.com) or directly with the record company (or whoever owns the sound recording rights).

What Does SoundExchange Do?

SoundExchange (www.soundexchange.com) is a nonprofit performance rights organization that collects statutory royalties from various providers of digital music, including satellite radio, Internet radio, cable TV music channels, and similar platforms for streaming sound recordings. According to the SoundExchange website, the Copyright Royalty Board, has "entrusted SoundExchange as the sole entity in the United States to collect and distribute these digital performance royalties on behalf of featured and non-featured recording artists, master rights owners (usually record labels), and independent artists who record and own their masters." SoundExchange collects on behalf of:

- Commercial Webcaster/Simulcaster
- Non-Commercial Webcaster/Simulcaster
- Pre-Existing Satellite Digital Radio Service
- Pre-Existing Subscription Service
- New Subscription Service (CABSAT)
- Business Establishment Service, and
- CPB-affiliated, NPR, or similar kind of nonprofit public radio AM/FM broadcaster.

Noninteractive Digital Audio Transmissions

A noninteractive digital audio transmission is one in which a website broadcasts various recordings over the Internet, much like a radio station, typically referred to as webcasting. Listeners can tune in or out at any time to listen to what is being broadcast. Unlike downloading MP3s, a listener does not receive a copy of any music heard on their computer or device. By sending a text message or email, a listener may be able to request to hear a particular song (much like calling into a radio station in the old days), but all listeners to the webcast will hear that requested song.

> EXAMPLE: 60s.com is a website that broadcasts music of the 1960s. Don visits the site and hears various songs. Don does not receive a copy of the songs on his computer. He emails a request and, when it is broadcast, all listeners to 60s.com hear the song on their computers. Thus, 60s.com is providing noninteractive digital audio transmissions.

A website offering noninteractive digital audio transmission (a "webcaster") must obtain permission from the music publisher in the form of a blanket performance license granted by the performing rights societies.

A webcaster must also follow certain rules and pay a fee, fixed by law, to the record company. This permits webcasters to make single copies of recordings necessary in webcasting (known as "ephemeral recordings"). The rules to qualify are lengthy and include requirements such as:

- The digital broadcast cannot be interactive.
- The broadcast cannot activate remote recording devices.
- During a three-hour broadcast period, a site cannot program more than three songs from a single album, nor play two songs in a row from a single album.

More information on these rules can be obtained from SoundExchange (www.soundexchange.com) or from the U.S. Copyright Office website (www.copyright.gov).

The 30-Second Exception

Music publishers and record companies have reached an agreement between themselves to permit the interactive broadcast of a maximum of 30 seconds of a recording for promotional purposes. This agreement is solely between music publishers and record companies and can be used only to promote their own music and recordings. A website owner that does not own rights in either the sound recording or song cannot participate in this 30-second exception. However, as a practical matter, permission is routinely granted for 30-second digital audio segments of recordings used to promote the sale of those recordings.

Simulcasting

Local radio stations sometimes send their broadcast signal through the Internet, a practice known as "simulcasting." Simulcasting radio stations are required to pay a licensing fee but follow a simpler set of rules than for noninteractive digital audio transmissions. To learn more about the rules, check SoundExchange (www.soundexchange.com) or the U.S. Copyright Office website (www.copyright.gov).

Using Music Samples

Sampling is the process of copying a piece of recorded music (usually on a device known as a sampler) and then reproducing it within another recording. Sometimes the sample is used repeatedly, such as a drumbeat or a vocal chorus. Sometimes a sample is used once or twice to accent a composition. Although there are some exceptions for trivial or unrecognizable samples, as a general rule, sampling is illegal without the authorization of the owner of the recording (the record company) and the owner of the song (the music publisher) being sampled.

There are no standardized fees or procedures for obtaining sampling permission, which can prove to be an expensive and time-consuming process. Some artists have had to give up one-third to one-half of their income from a song in order to acquire sampling permissions for the samples it includes.

There are several factors that make getting permission to use a sample a murky subject:

- As discussed throughout this chapter, there are two overlapping copyrights on a record: the song composition copyright and the sound recording copyright. When you take an excerpt of a song recording, you may be infringing both the songwriter's copyright and the copyright for the recording. It may seem that the songwriter's permission wouldn't be necessary—for example, when you want to sample only a few drumbeats—but it's not always clear (see "Vocalizing is Not Composing: The Beastie Boys Case," below). Because of this, most record companies producing a song that contains samples play it safe and obtain permission from both the owner of the song (the music publisher) and the owner of the recorded music (the record company) being sampled.
- To make matters more confusing, a music publisher may not be entitled to a payment for some samples, such as the use of James Brown's voice saying "Get Down," because copyright law does not protect short phrases. However, James Brown may have a separate claim under a legal right known as the right of publicity, which protects a celebrity's right to control the use of his or her image, voice, or persona.

- Also, some samples may be used without permission under "fair use" principles that allow you to use a short sample for purposes of commentary or criticism. Unfortunately, it's not always clear what constitutes fair use, and most users of samples cannot afford the legal costs to find out. For example, in one case, a judge ruled that the use of a sample was so inconsequential that it did not violate copyright law. But by the time the judge made the decision, both sides in the case had spent thousands in legal fees. For more on fair use, see Chapter 9.
- Despite these considerations, a sample may go unnoticed entirely. Because of this, you need to decide whether to bother with obtaining permission for your sample.

Vocalizing Is Not Composing: The Beastie Boys Case

When the Beastie Boys recorded the song "Pass the Mic," they repeated a six-second sample from a song entitled "Choir," off an album by award-winning flautist James Newton, Jr. The sample consisted of a three-note pattern (C, D-flat, C), which Newton simultaneously sang and played in a method known as "vocalization."

The Beastie Boys obtained permission to use the sample from ECM, the label that owned the sound recording copyright, but failed to get permission from Newton, the owner of the musical composition copyright. Newton sued and, in 2002, a federal judge ruled that the three-note pattern from "Choir" was not, by itself, a protectable composition, so permission from Newton was not necessary. In other words, the three-note pattern, even though it included Newton's rare vocalization skills, was not original enough to merit a payment—it was "de minimis" (too small to matter). (*Newton v. Diamond*, 204 F. Supp.2d 1244, (N.D. Cal. 2002).)

If this case is an indication of judicial trends, you may need only one permission—the sound recording owner's—for short samples consisting of generic musical notes or patterns. Unfortunately, the pendulum swung against sampling in a 2005 case when the Sixth Circuit Court of Appeals ruled that the use of a two-second sample was an infringement of the sound recording copyright. The court went even further, stating that when it came to sound recording there was no permissible minimum sanctioned under copyright law. (*Bridgeport Music v. Dimension Films*, 383 F.3d 390 (6th Cir. 2004).)

For an hourly fee, clearance experts often negotiate these issues or review recordings to determine if a sampling problem exists. You can find clearance experts online by typing "Sample Clearance" or "Music Clearance" into a search engine. Some resources are also listed at the end of this chapter. The following section explains the basic rules and provides a model agreement for obtaining permission to use a music sample.

Sampling the Majors

In 1999, when the first edition of this book appeared, only entertainment lawyers could get through the phone lines at the big music companies. Now, many companies are offering online sample clearance. Universal Music (www.umusicpub.com) and BMG Music (www.bmgproductionmusic.com) are among the major players now offering clearance request forms online.

Licenses and Fees for Sampling

While there are no standardized fees for sampling, the music publisher will usually want an advance payment (between $250 and $5,000) plus a percentage of the income derived from the new recording (usually between 15% and 50%). In addition, the owner of the master recording may want an up-front payment (usually at least $1,000) plus a "rollover"—a payment that must be made when a certain number of copies have been sold. Sometimes, instead of a rollover, the owner of the master may want a portion of future record royalties (although sampling consultants advise against this practice).

Record companies and music publishers typically provide sample clearance agreements. You'll also find copies of model sampling agreements in *Music Law: How to Run Your Band's Business* by Richard Stim (Nolo).

Reducing Sample Fees

A portion of sampling clearance fees can usually be avoided by rerecording the sampled section. Instead of sampling the original recording, a company can hire musicians to play the parts, creating a new recording that sounds very similar to the original. In that case, permission is required from the music publisher only. However, this imitation may require additional permissions if it is used to sell a service or product.

Likewise, you can avoid paying fees to a music publisher by using a sample of a song that is in the public domain. Do not assume, however, that sampling fees will be avoided entirely by sampling public domain songs. The sound recording may be protected even though the song is in the public domain, requiring permission from (and payment to) the record company that released the recording you wish to sample.

> **EXAMPLE:** In 2010, the singer Taylor Swift records and releases the public domain song, "I Dream of Jeannie With the Light Brown Hair." George samples the recording and includes the sample on his new album. Although the song is in the public domain, the Taylor Swift sound recording is not. George must obtain permission from Taylor Swift's record company.

Of course, all sampling fees can be avoided by rerecording public domain songs. Companies also save money by using sample discs or downloads available from production music libraries and other sources. These recordings contain short musical parts that are "pre-cleared." These packages grant the user an "unlimited nonexclusive license" to use the samples once they are purchased. Always read the accompanying shrink-wrap or license agreement to verify this right before purchasing.

Operating Without Sample Clearance

Not every use of a sample constitutes an infringement. If an average listener comparing both works (the new composition and the source) can't hear any substantial similarities, there's no violation of the law. It is also possible that the use of a sample may qualify as fair use. The rap group 2 Live Crew's use of the musical tag and opening line lyric from the song "Pretty Woman" was considered to be a fair use because it was limited (the sampled section was used once) and for purposes of parody. *(Campbell v. Acuff-Rose Music,* 510 U.S. 569 (1994).) For more information on fair use, see Chapter 9.

Using Samples to Sell a Product or Service

If a sample is used to sell or endorse a product (for example, using James Brown's voice in a Nike ad), and the sampled performer is identifiable, the sampler must obtain the performer's consent. Without consent, the source artist could sue for violation of the right of publicity (see Chapter 12, "Releases"). The same rule would apply if the performer's voice is imitated by another singer.

Finding Music Publishers

The easiest method to locate the music publisher of a song is to search the online song databases at the three performing rights societies, BMI (www.bmi. com), ASCAP (www.ascap.com), and SESAC (www.sesac.com). Alternatively, you can search all three societies at the website of the Music Publishers' Association (www.mpa.org/directory). These three societies represent all types of music, although SESAC's catalog is primarily gospel and country music.

Performing rights societies do not own songs; they represent music publishers for purposes of negotiating certain types of permissions. A song is usually listed with only one of the performing rights societies, although occasionally, songs written by more than one person may be listed in the catalogs for both societies. Online song databases can be searched by title, writer, performer, or publisher. If you don't have access to the Internet, call the performing rights society and ask for writer/publisher information.

If you cannot locate a song through BMI, ASCAP, or SESAC, check the song database at the Harry Fox Agency (www.harryfox.com), which represents approximately 80% of U.S. music publishers (see "How Is Harry Fox Different from BMI, ASCAP, and SESAC?" above). Harry Fox differs from the performing rights societies in that it deals with permission for copying a song onto a CD or tape (referred to as "mechanical rights") rather than performing a song publicly. Mechanical rights permissions are discussed in more detail throughout this chapter.

> EXAMPLE: I wanted to find the music publisher of "Ring of Fire." I started by searching the BMI and ASCAP databases online. The BMI database provided three different songs entitled "Ring of Fire." Johnny Cash recorded the version I wanted. Searching the BMI database by artist, I discovered numerous songs

recorded by Johnny Cash including "Ring of Fire," for which BMI included the following information:

Writers: June Carter & Merle Kilgore

Publisher: Painted Desert Music Corporation, 640 Fifth Avenue, New York, NY 10019-6102; phone: 212-957-0802, fax: 212-397-4638.

If you're unsure of a song's title, verify it through an online music store such as Amazon.com or iTunes. These sites contain databases searchable by song title, album title, or artist, and usually offer 30-second previews of the music to verify the correct version.

If you can't locate a music publisher using the resources listed in this section, further research may be required. Try using some of the suggestions in Chapter 13, "Copyright Research," or use the services of a music clearance expert.

Finding Record Companies

The record company (the owner of the sound recording) can usually be determined by examining an album's cover artwork or liner notes and reviewing the sound recording copyright notice. The notice consists of the letter P in a circle, followed by the date the recording was published and the name of the recording copyright owner—for example:

" Ⓟ 2019, NBT Records."

If the recording was made before 1972, there will be no sound recording copyright notice because recordings were not protected by copyright before that time. However, even in these cases the name of the record company usually appears prominently on the recording or artwork. Keep in mind that it is common for companies to transfer ownership of sound recordings, so your information may be out of date if you're using an old recording.

If you're having trouble locating a sound recording owner, try the following:

- Check online record stores to determine the record company that is currently releasing the music, and contact that company.
- Find the publisher of a song featured on the recording and ask the publisher for information about the sound recording owner.
- Use the services of a music clearance expert.

When contacting a record company, ask for licensing, clearance, or the special products department. Most large record companies have departments that handle sound recording clearance.

Music Clearance Companies

Music clearance companies help you locate song and sound recording owners and acquire permission to use music for a wide range of purposes (including film, TV, multimedia, and online uses). Many clearance companies also help clear sampling rights. There is a wide variety of services offered and companies often specialize in a particular music clearance niche. A list of music clearance companies is provided in "Music Resources," directly below.

Music Resources

This section lists a variety of resources that may be of help in the process of music licensing.

Production Music Libraries (PMLs)

- KwikSounds.com: www.kwiksounds.com
- LicenseMusic.com: www.licensemusic.com
- Instant Music Now: www.instantmusicnow.com
- Video Helper: www.videohelper.com

Performing Rights Societies

- BMI: www.bmi.com
- ASCAP: www.ascap.com
- SESAC: www.sesac.com

Mechanical Rights Society

- The Harry Fox Agency: www.harryfox.com

Record Company Resources

The Recording Industry Association of America (RIAA): www.riaa.com (a trade organization that may be able to provide contact information for record labels).

Music Clearance Companies

- BZ Rights and Permissions, Inc.: www.bzrights.com
- Jill Meyers Music Consultants: phone 310-576-1387
- License Music: www.licensemusic.com

Musical and Dramatic Rights Resources

- Broadway Play Publishing Co.: www.broadwayplaypub.com
- Dramatic Publishing Co.: www.dramaticpublishing.com
- Dramatists Play Service, Inc.: www.dramatists.com
- Music Theatre International: www.mtishows.com
- Rodgers and Hammerstein Theatre Library: www.rnh.com
- Concord Theatricals: www.concordtheatricals.com

Dear Rich: **Using Music From iTunes at a Website**

Can I use a piece of music that was downloaded from iTunes for a website I have? Is that legal? If not, how do I make it legal without paying an arm and a leg?

The iTunes terms of service do not permit you to use downloaded music at your website (considered a "public performance" under copyright law). You can obtain a website license from ASCAP (around $300 minimum) or from BMI (less than $300, but dependent on traffic and revenue from your site). Of course, you can only license BMI artists from BMI and ASCAP artists from ASCAP. Each site lists their repertoire. Although it is risky (and you would still be subject to legal action) some sites bypass the permissions process. This may succeed if you stay below the legal radar of music publishers—for example, by only playing the music at a low-trafficked noncommercial website, and by not offering downloads or any other tagged references to music that's playing.

Website Permissions

W hile Internet technology has made publishing more accessible to everyone, it's also triggered many novel copyright disputes for the masses. The rules for using text, photos, artwork, and music covered in the previous chapters apply just the same to online uses, so they are not repeated here. Instead, this chapter focuses on two specific problem areas for webmasters, social media users, and others: unauthorized transfers of information to and from online sources, and website linking.

 RELATED TOPIC

Previous chapters cover the basic principles of various unauthorized uses. Readers who turned directly to this chapter may want to cross-reference these discussions:

- Copyrighted material used without authorization. Review Chapters 2 (text), 3 (photographs), 4 (artwork), 5 (music), and 15 (assignments and works for hire).
- Trademarks used without authorization. Review Chapter 10, "Getting Permission to Use Trademarks."
- A person's image used for commercial purposes without authorization. Review Chapter 12, "Releases."
- A person's privacy invaded or character defamed. Review Chapter 12, "Releases."

Five Ways to Stay Out of Trouble Online

This section provides five simple rules for using someone else's work on your website, social media page, and elsewhere online.

Assume It's Protected

As a general rule, it's wise to operate under the assumption that all works are protected by either copyright or trademark law unless conclusive information indicates otherwise. A work is not in the public domain simply because it has been posted on the Internet or because it lacks a copyright notice (both common fallacies). For information on these and other public domain issues, see Chapter 8, "The Public Domain."

Read End-User Agreements (EULAs)

Do not assume that website content such as clip art, shareware, freeware, or materials labeled "royalty free" or "copyright free" can be distributed or copied without authorization. Read the terms and conditions in the end-user license agreements (also referred to as EULAs, "Click to Accept" agreements, click-wrap agreements or browser-wrap agreements) associated with this content. Be certain that your intended use is permitted. One company that failed to honor the terms of a click-wrap agreement was found liable for illegally distributing three volumes of software clip art. (*Marobie-Fl, Inc. v. National Association of Fire Equipment Distributors*, 983 F.Supp. 1167 (E.D. Ill. 1997).)

What is the end-user agreeing to do (or not do)? The provisions of the EULA differ in name (terms and conditions, terms of use, terms of service) and they differ in purpose (for example, disclaiming liability, restricting use of content, setting rules of behavior). Often, they establish dispute resolution procedures. But if the copyright owner fails to obtain assent or provide effective notice of these provisions, a court is unlikely to enforce it. For example, an online gambling app tried to enforce an arbitration provision buried within its terms-of-use agreement. Because the online gambling site failed to acquire user-assent and failed to prove constructive or actual notice of the terms ("the user would need Sherlock Holmes's instincts to discover the Terms," said the court), the Ninth Circuit refused to enforce the provision. (*Wilson v. Huuuge, Inc.*, No. 18-36017, 2019 U.S. App. LEXIS 37952 (9th Cir. 2019).)

Remove Unauthorized Material

If someone complains about an unauthorized use on your website or elsewhere online, remove the offending material immediately. In the case of unauthorized uploads, downloads, or links, you should disable access to the offending material or link. This is not to imply that you should cave in to every complaint. However, you should remove the material for the period during which you investigate the claim and, if necessary, consult with an attorney. Attempts to "contain" the damage will likely help your case should it find its way into court. Continuing to use the offensive material after being notified may aggravate the claim and the chances of your being found liable—and increase the amount of damages you may have to pay.

Removal of infringing material is also an element of the Digital Millennium Copyright Act (DMCA), a 1998 law establishing that an Internet service provider (ISP, a company that provides Internet access to individuals and businesses) that is aware of infringement can avoid liability by following certain rules, including speedy removal of infringing material.

In 2012, a court of appeals clarified one aspect of the DMCA for ISPs—that "awareness" of infringement was not the same as a "duty to police." Viacom sued YouTube, claiming that YouTube failed to police its content even though the company had followed the DMCA by implementing a procedure to respond to takedown notices from copyright owners and removing infringing content of which it was aware. The Second Circuit held that a general awareness of infringement did not trigger a duty to police postings under the DMCA, and that YouTube was responsible only if it knew of specific infringements or deliberately insulated itself from knowledge of such infringement by its users. (*Viacom International Inc. v. YouTube Inc.*, 676 F.3d 19 (2d Cir. 2012).)

You can read a summary of the DMCA on the U.S. Copyright Office website, at www.copyright.gov/legislation/dmca.pdf.

Investigate Claims Promptly

If someone complains about an unauthorized use, investigate the claim quickly and seek evidence of copyright ownership and validity from the complaining person. The webmaster or page owner can verify the facts through copyright research (see Chapter 13, "Copyright Research"), and must also investigate the transfer of the infringing material, if any, to and from the site or page. If copies were downloaded, how many and to whom? If copies were uploaded, by whom?

Below is a sample letter that you can adapt and use in response to a claim of infringement through online use.

Sample Response to Infringement Claim

Dear Ms. Crancastle:

I received your certified letter of May 1, 2022, in which you state that my website, Chihuahua Planet, contains an unauthorized reproduction of a photo entitled "Jimmy the Flying Chihuahua." According to your letter, you are the copyright owner of the photo.

I have not had an opportunity to investigate your claim. However, pending resolution of the dispute, all copies of "Jimmy the Flying Chihuahua" have been removed from the site and access to the file containing the photo was disabled, thereby preventing downloading.

I would like to resolve this matter quickly and to do so will require some evidence of your copyright ownership. At your earliest convenience, please send me a copyright registration or some other evidence that you are the copyright owner of the photo. Once I have that information, I shall complete my investigation and promptly provide you with a response.

Sincerely,

Don Daly

When in Doubt, Seek Permission

Many webmasters manage personal websites or sites for small organizations such as a local tennis team. Do all of the rules on copyright and permissions apply to these intimate or personal uses? For example, is permission needed to reproduce a photo taken by a club member, a friend, or a relative? The short answer is: "Legally, yes, practically, maybe."

Copyright protection extends to any original work regardless of who created it, and permission is required for reproduction, display, or distribution of the work. One of the main reasons for acquiring permission is to avoid a lawsuit. If the webmaster is confident that a friend or family member has consented to the use, the concern over a lawsuit diminishes, as does the need for a formal written permission agreement. Oral consents are valid, although sometimes difficult to prove.

The Likelihood of Getting Caught

As online commerce continues to grow exponentially, so does the likelihood of being caught for unauthorized uses. Many companies such as McDonald's, MTV, Levi's, Mattel, Walt Disney, and Coca-Cola aggressively patrol the Web for infringement. New technology makes it possible for copyright owners to encode music, artwork, photographs, and text with digital tags or marks that allow rapid tracking. If a website is controversial and angers some visitors, they may report perceived violations to copyright or trademark owners. Disgruntled employees are also common sources of infringement reports.

Besides the fact that the Internet abounds with efficient ways of sniffing out copyright violations, the general rule is that the chances of an unauthorized use being discovered will increase as the site becomes more popular. Therefore, if the goal of a site is to increase its traffic, it should avoid unauthorized uses from the start, as they rarely justify the potential aggravation and financial loss they can cause.

But, if you are in doubt about a use, always seek written permission, even if the material comes from a friend or relative. Formal permission agreements are provided online at Nolo.com (see the appendix for the link). However, in cases of cooperative friends and relatives, an informal release can be used, such as the following sentence:

I am the owner of rights to [*title of work*] and I authorize its display and reproduction on the [*name of website*] website located at [*insert URL for site*] for a period of [*insert length of time*].

If you want to include additional items in the agreement, such as a requirement that a credit line for the work appear on the site, you can add them to this brief agreement.

EXAMPLE: Sally is the webmaster for the Jefferson Elementary School and intends to post student paintings. Sally has the parent of each child sign a one-sentence permission agreement stating, "I authorize the display and reproduction of the artwork entitled _____ _____ , credited to my child, _____ on the Jefferson Elementary School website for a period of one year."

Transferring Information to and From Online Sources

Copyright infringement occurs whenever copyrighted material is copied from or posted to a website, social media page, or elsewhere online without authorization from the copyright owner. This section discusses the various ways that information can be transferred between your site and its users and the copyright disputes that may arise with each.

Posting Information Online

Posting involves a user sending information from their computer or other device to a website, social media page, or other online destination ("uploading"). Once posted, others can view or copy the material. If your site or page does not offer users a chance to post material, you can skip this section.

EXAMPLE: A member of a discussion group posts a chapter from a John Grisham book to the group's chat room on the Internet, making it available for others to copy.

While the person who uploaded the material is the actual infringer, whoever maintains the site or page can be held liable for allowing the material to be posted on the site. As with any unauthorized material, the wisest approach to dealing with an unauthorized upload is to remove it quickly or disable access to it pending resolution of the dispute.

A site that permits uploading of material should post an End-User License Agreement (often called a EULA or click-wrap agreement) setting forth similar terms. The EULA appears before the user is allowed to perform a certain function (in this case, an upload) and the user will not be allowed to proceed until they have clicked a box that indicates they have read and accepted the agreement.

Below is an example of a EULA intended to prohibit unauthorized postings.

Uploading Restrictions

User agrees not to post:

- any materials protected under copyright, trademark, or trade secret laws unless with the express authorization of the owner; or
- any material likely to defame or invade the privacy of any individual.

User agrees to indemnify the owners of the site and their affiliates and employees from any liability (including attorneys' fees) related to User's violation of this agreement.

If you agree to the above conditions, click the ACCEPT button.

> [ACCEPT] [CANCEL]

Unfortunately, notices and "Click to Accept" agreements are not uniformly enforced across the states. And, as a practical matter, a notice or an agreement requiring a person who commits an illegal activity to pay your attorneys' fees is worthless if the person has no money. Nevertheless, it's worthwhile to include some form of EULA on your site. It may deter some users from making illegal uploads, and it may help to show your diligence in trying to prevent them.

Dear Rich:

Unauthorized Posting of Master's Thesis

My Master's thesis was posted online (as a PDF document) without my permission. The thesis includes the copyright icon but was not registered with the U.S. Copyright Office. Is the online posting of my thesis an infringement of copyright? If so, how can I have it removed?

The short answer to your question is that yes, the unauthorized reproduction of your thesis is an infringement and yes, you are entitled to have it removed (regardless of whether you have registered the work). However, whether it will be removed depends on a few factors—most notably the site where it is posted.

The key to success. Usually, the most important element in achieving a takedown is locating the agent for service of the DMCA notice. Search online for "DMCA agent for service." In addition to the designated agent (or if you can't find the agent) check the site for other forms of email (or other addresses) for the website owner. Sometimes, you can find it on a "Contact Us" link, and often it is simply "info@nameofsite.com." Many sites that post files or post documents have a special mailbox for dealing with infringements—often that's "abuse@nameofsite.com" or "copyright@nameofsite.com." If there is no designated agent, and no email address for contacting the owners at the site (not a good sign), search for the owner using the database at Whois.net. If your search results in a "proxy" administrator—a company that serves as administrator and hides the name and contact info for the owner, that's also not a good sign. Once you locate an agent, or email or mailing address for the administrator of the site, you should prepare and send a DMCA takedown notice.

What if the site refuses to take it down? The approach described above is usually effective—at least it often works for us. However, if the person who posted the thesis refuses to take it down (or they respond with countermeasures), you will need to proceed with a copyright registration (you can expedite it) and file a lawsuit. Unless you are independently wealthy, that could be cost-prohibitive. If the website owner has deep pockets and you can demonstrate financial damages, perhaps you can find a lawyer who will handle it on a contingency.

Taking Information From a Website or Other Online Source

Just as users can sometimes post information onto a website or page, a user may—in the reverse process—take material from an online source and transfer it to their computer or phone. This is typically done either by downloading or by copying and pasting. Many sites are set up for users to download material. Shareware sites, for example, allow users to download software they want by clicking on a downloadable file, which will then be transferred onto the user's device. Another way of obtaining material online is to select text, copy, and paste it into a word processing document on the user's device. Strictly speaking this is not downloading, but the effect is the same. The user has obtained material from the Internet and copied it onto their own device.

Dear Rich:

Blog Aggregator

I set up a blog aggregator. I don't have ads or anything, it's just for me and a few friends to use. I include excerpts of articles, links to the original articles, and some of the full posts of the original articles. Somebody claimed that I violated their copyright, sent a DMCA complaint to my webhost, who then took my site down without any notification or chance for me to make a correction. My host is now claiming that they have to immediately take the entire website down, without notice, because of the 1998 DMCA. I read about the DMCA at the Copyright Office website. It doesn't say that a website has to come down immediately (or even seem to be very clear on how much written material constitutes "infringement"). I'm a little confused, as most of this is new to me. Could you offer some insight?

As for the content at your site: There is no problem with the links in hypertext form. Reproducing full articles is probably an infringement; providing excerpts is disputable. We presume a copyright owner sent a takedown notice to your online service provider (OSP), who acted "expeditiously" and removed the infringing content. By removing the material, the OSP qualifies for a "safe harbor" from any liability. If you dispute the notice—many are abusive—and you're willing to risk a court battle, consider a counter notice. (You can find samples and more information on the Internet.) If the complaining copyright owner fails to respond to your counter notice by filing a lawsuit (uh-oh!), the OSP may repost your content. These rules and procedures are part of the Digital Millennium Copyright Act.

Unauthorized Copying

If you don't offer material to download at your site, your main concern isn't whether you'll infringe someone else's copyright, but whether users will copy your material without your permission. Particularly if your site contains copyrightable works by outside authors—for instance, if you publish an online magazine—you'll want to do everything you can to prevent users from unauthorized copying of the material. One attempt at deterrence (though not necessarily an effective one) is to display a copyright notice prominently on some or all of your site's pages, clearly stating that the material is protected by copyright.

To deal with the fact that many users may copy information anyway, you can include a prohibition on any commercial use of the material in your copyright notice. Also, you can require that the copyright notice be included with the material, so that anyone who reads it will know who created it. Many webmasters are willing to accept some limited copying by users for personal use, especially if the copies show who originally generated the material.

EXAMPLE: Nolo, the publisher of this book, maintains a website with extensive self-help legal information. Because Nolo's goal is to empower people to take care of their legal affairs, it is willing to accept some copying of the material at its site, with some limitations. Its copyright notice, which can be accessed from nearly every page, reads, in part, as follows:

Nolo.com Copyright Policy

Your Responsibility When Using the Nolo Site

We strive mightily to provide useful and accurate information to help users cope with their own legal needs. But laws and procedures change frequently and are subject to differing interpretations. Nolo makes no claim that all information on this site is up to date. It is your responsibility to make sure that anything you read here is accurate, up-to-date, and applies to your situation. Also, please understand that if you want legal advice backed by a guarantee, you'll need to see a lawyer.

If you use information on this site, before relying on it, it is wise for you to check the information with an authoritative source, for example a lawyer or law books from your state's law libraries. One excellent way to do this is by engaging in your own legal research. To find out how, see our Legal Research area.

Nolo's Copyright Policy for Site Content

Nolo.com provides the information on this site to be read by anyone, but retains the copyright on all text and graphics. To use this information in any other way, you must strictly follow these guidelines.

Use by Individuals

As long as it is for your own personal use only, you may print copies of this information, store the files on your computer, and use hypertext links to reference the information. Any other use or redistribution is strictly prohibited.

Trademark

"Nolo" is a federally registered trademark. All trademarks appearing on nolo.com are the property of their respective owners.

If you take this more liberal approach, make sure that any contributors to your site who may retain copyright in their work understand and accept your policy. Otherwise, if they later discover that their article was copied, they might sue you for allowing their work to be infringed.

Dear Rich:

Publishing Email Posts

I allowed someone to publish one of my emails. The other person asked permission to publish it. He said he wouldn't change the words. I simply said "Yes, but make it anonymous." He published the email in segments and responded to each segment. Later he stopped protecting the anonymity of it. I've asked him to remove my email but he claims that because I gave him permission, he has full right to keep it on his website.

When you give permission to someone to publish your copyrighted work (your email), you're granting a license. We're assuming that the license was made by exchange of email, and these emails form the terms of your license.

The terms of your license. Your license sounds like it had only one condition: anonymity. Since the poster has now breached that condition, you have a right to revoke your license—that is, have the email removed. If the poster is disregarding your request, you have to try a more forceful strategy. One approach may be to contact the other party's service provider and send a DMCA notice. Another possibility is to hire an attorney to threaten the poster with a lawsuit claiming copyright infringement and invasion of privacy.

Is it worth the effort? Keep in mind that hiring a lawyer or sending a DMCA notice should only be used if the posted email is causing you some harm. These are not sure-fire strategies—for example, the poster may assert valid copyright defenses—and they prove expensive.

Unauthorized Downloading

The concept of unauthorized downloading may seem strange, considering that most sites that offer files for download are consenting to the practice. However, even if downloads are specifically allowed from your site, you may still have concerns over unauthorized uses of the downloaded material. For instance, if you offer free clip art for download at your site, you may want to prohibit users from selling the clip art and limit their use to personal use. If the user violates the restriction, you may be able to sue for breach of contract. This approach has been successful in disputes based upon clip art and stock photos. Even if the agreement is not enforceable, its presence may defeat a claim of innocent infringement by the user.

A sample downloading restriction appears below. You can post it as a notice displayed where a downloader would see it or implement it as an end-user license agreement.

Downloading Restrictions

User agrees that the material provided for downloading is to be used solely for personal purposes such as on a personal computer or mobile device and may not be reproduced, displayed, or distributed for any commercial purpose.

If you agree to the above conditions, click the accept button.

ACCEPT   CANCEL

Developer or Site Owner: Who's Responsible for Photo Permissions?

In a 2019 case, a photographer sued the owner of a website who had displayed three of his copyrighted photos without authorization. The website owner had directed his website developer to make his site resemble a Wells Fargo website that had permission to use the photos. The site owner claimed that he believed the developer would take care of obtaining copyright permissions. Absent any proof of the developer's obligation, the site owner was found liable for $450,000 in damage for contributory copyright infringement, which is when a defendant "(1) has knowledge of another's infringement; and (2) either (a) materially contributes to; or (b) induces that infringement." (*Erickson Productions, Inc. v. Kast*, No. 15-16801 (9th Cir. 2019).)

Liability for Other Website Issues

Websites may get into disputes over domain names, obscenity, and fraud. Issues may also arise based upon a website's content. For example, owners of sexually explicit sites may need to post warning notices; commercial sites must meet trade requirements, such as posting refund and return policies; and sites offering stock trading should provide securities disclaimers. Sites providing downloads may want to disclaim liability for any potential viruses. These website issues are beyond the scope of a permissions book. Chapter 16, "Help Beyond This Book," directs you to additional resources to help you with these and other issues.

Connecting to Other Websites

One of the central features of the Internet is the ability for each website or page to connect with other online resources at a click or tap. There are a few ways that sites and pages connect, each with different legal implications for getting permission. This section discusses the issues raised when your site connects to other websites, and it provides a sample linking agreement.

Dear Rich:

Is Permission Needed to List Websites in a Book?

Do I need to get permission to list websites in a published book? All the websites I wish to include are accessible through Google. Do I need to deal with each site for permission or do I need to deal with Google?

You don't need to deal with either; no permission is required when providing the name or publicly accessible URL (Web address) for any website. You may run into problems listing websites only if you are encouraging illegal activity by knowingly listing or linking to sites that promote bad stuff—for example, child porn sites, sources of illegal downloads, or sites that are exposing confidential information or invading privacy.

Linking and Framing

Two common ways websites connect to other sites are linking and framing.

Linking

Most often, one website or page will connect to another in the form of a link (also known as a "hypertext" link), a specially coded word or image that when clicked or tapped, will take a user to another online source. A link can take the user to another page within the same site (an "internal link"), or to another site altogether (an "external link"). You do not need permission for a regular word link to another website.

Deep linking. Despite some inconsistencies in early case law, it is generally agreed that deep linking (a link that bypasses a website's home page) is not copyright infringement—after all, the author of a novel can't prevent readers from skipping to the end first if they so desire, so why should a website owner have the right to determine in what order a user can access a website?

Although many websites—even the listener-friendly National Public Radio— have asserted rights against deep linkers under both copyright and trademark law principles, the cases of *Kelly v. Arriba Soft Corp.*, 336 F.3d 811 (9th Cir. 2003) and *Perfect 10, Inc. v. Amazon.com, Inc.*, 508 F.3d 1146 (9th Cir. 2007), seem to have put the nail in the coffin for deep-linking disputes. Foreign courts general conform to this view, though there have been some anomalies.

Framing

Besides using external links, another way to connect from your website or page to another is by "framing." Framing is a lot like linking in that you code a word or image so that it will connect to another online page when the user clicks/taps it. What makes framing different is that instead of taking the user to the linked resource, the information from that resource is imported into the original page and displayed in a special "frame." Technically, when you're viewing framed information your computer or mobile device is connected to the site doing the framing—not the site whose page appears in the frame.

Framing is generally unpopular with websites whose content is framed on another site (unless they have agreed to it). Websites that frame the content of other sites are often seen as pilfering the other site's content. One court found framing to be a copyright infringement because the process resulted in an unauthorized modification of the linked site. (*Futuredontics Inc. v. Applied Anagramic Inc.*, 45 U.S.P.Q.2d 2005 (C.D. Cal. 1998).) In another case, *The Washington Post*, CNN, and several other news companies sued a website, TotalNews, which framed their news content. Under the terms of a settlement agreement, TotalNews agreed to stop framing and agreed to use text-only links.

A framer is more likely to be found liable for copyright (or trademark) infringement if copyrighted material is modified without authorization or if customers are confused about the association between the two sites or the source of a product or service. For more information on trademark infringement, see Chapter 10, "Getting Permission to Use Trademarks."

Dear Rich: **I Framed a Website; Now PicRights Wants Money!**

I build websites, and one of my clients is a small auto shop. The auto shop's website includes a listing of brands they carry, and includes links. Some of the links steer the user to the brand website. Some of the links allow the user to stay at the auto shop website and to view the brand website within a frame. Several months ago, the auto shop got threatening letters and emails from PicRights.com, a photo rights company, saying that two of the framed brand sites each had a photo that was "copied" from one of their stock photo clients. Naturally, neither the auto shop nor I had any knowledge or control over what one of these brand companies or their Web people used on those sites. I removed the links to those companies, and we told PicRights via email that we took that action. But the auto shop continues to get threatening letters, including one from an attorney.

We can't predict how the auto shop would fare if this matter proceeded to court (and we assume the auto shop doesn't want to litigate), but if we were a betting blog, we'd wager that the auto shop's liability would not exceed $1,500. It's even possible that the shop would owe nothing. Here's why:

Framing and copyright. What makes framing different from typical linking is that instead of taking the user to the linked resource, the information from that resource is displayed in a special "frame." But in reality, the image isn't duplicated because the link is just HTML code pointing to the image or other material. (A similar result occurs when a single photo from one site is embedded in another site—a process called "inlining.")

Conflicting case law. Framing and inlining are often used to deliver search engine results. In two cases where search engines linked to thumbnail images, courts have held that such uses are permitted as fair use. In one of those cases, *Perfect 10*, the Ninth Circuit Court of Appeals devised the "server test" in which the court ruled that if the allegedly infringing work is on your server, you infringed. Under the server test, the auto shop might prevail, assuming no copies of the infringing photos were stored on the auto shop servers. Complicating the analysis, a New York judge in 2018 rejected the server test in a case about an embedded Twitter photo. In other words, your case might achieve a different result in California than in New York. (Hopefully, an appellate court or the Supreme Court will resolve the difference between circuits.)

What should the auto shop do? You were wise to remove the framed links immediately, as that demonstrates your good faith in responding to the claim—it also limits your potential damages. It's also reasonable for the auto shop to request proof that the images have been registered in the Copyright Office. If they haven't been registered before your posting, PicRights or the stock photo company cannot claim statutory damages or attorneys' fees. Also, they can't sue you in federal court without the registration. (Although not conclusive, we found no copyright registrations under either complaining party's name in the Copyright Office database.) If they have registered the copyright before your posting, the minimum for damages would be $750 per photo (or $200 per photo if you were determined to be an "innocent infringer"). Feel free to write to the photo rights company and share our information, but don't expect a reasoned response. (If we analogize to fishing, the company's policy is to use drift nets, not catch-and-release.)

Will you get sued? Oddly, when we searched PACER, we couldn't find any records of copyright lawsuits filed either by PicRights or by the stock photo company claiming to own rights. Perhaps the companies sue under other names, but it's possible that they never file lawsuits, only threaten them. To be prudent, the auto shop should obtain an opinion from an attorney before blowing off the letter.

P.S. Dept. It's possible that you may be threatened with contributory infringement. We believe that under Ninth Circuit standards, you would prevail.

CAUTION

A note about "inlining" content. "Inlining" (sometimes referred to as "embedding") is the process of incorporating a graphic file from one online resource onto another. In the first case involving inlining (*Kelly v. Arriba Soft Corp.*, 336 F.3d 811 (9th Cir. 2003)), an image search engine called ditto.com used inline links to reproduce full-size photographic images from a photographer's website. By clicking on the link, the user got a window containing a full-sized image imported from the photographer's website, surrounded by the search engine's advertising.

The court of appeals in the *Kelly* case ruled that the search engine's practice of creating small reproductions ("thumbnails") of the images and placing them on its own website was permitted as a fair use. The thumbnails were much smaller and of much poorer quality than the original photos and served to index the images, thereby helping the public access them.

A similar result was reached by the Ninth Circuit in a case involving Google. The Court of Appeals determined that Google's use of thumbnails was permitted as a fair use in a case involving reproductions of images from an adult men's magazine website. (*Perfect 10, Inc. v. Amazon.com, Inc.*, 508 F.3d 1146 (9th Cir. 2007).)

Keep in mind that some forms of framing are perfectly legal. For instance, many sites use frames as a way of organizing their content. When framing the content of another site, however, you are entering hazardous territory. Unless you know a site won't object, or you've reached an agreement with the site's owner, you should proceed carefully before framing its content.

Linking Agreements

The purpose of a linking agreement, like all permission agreements, is to avoid a dispute. As the online universe has matured, there is less and less need for these agreements.

However, the following types of links may create disputes:

- image links, particularly where the image that you click on is a trademark from the linked site
- links that result in framing, and
- inlining links that only pull certain elements from a site, such as an image.

The permission may be informal, such as a written statement from the distant site stating, "You have permission to link to our website's home page using the words [*insert the words in the link*]." Or, you can use a longer agreement that covers the terms more specifically.

The agreement provided above can be used to avoid disputes over any of these types of links.

FORM

You can download this form (and all other forms in this book) from Nolo.com; for details, see the appendix.

Explanation for Linking Agreement

- In the **introductory** section, insert the name of the company or person that owns the source site. The source site is the site where the link is located—that is, the starting point for the link. Once the link is clicked the user is taken to the destination site. Insert the URL (Web address—for example, http:// or www.address.com) for each site.
- In the section entitled **The Link,** describe the pages that are linked. For example:

  A link between Source Site's "Other References" page and Destination Site's internal page entitled "Copyright Developments."

  Or,

  A link between Source Site's home page and Destination Site's image entitled "Two Chihuahuas" encapsulated as 2Chihua.JPG.

  Or,

Linking Agreement

This Agreement (the "Agreement") is made between _____ ("Source Site"), with its home page URL of _____ , and _____ ("Destination Site"), with its home page URL of _____ . The parties agree as follows:

The Link

Source Site will provide a link to the Destination Site as follows: _____ _____ (the "Link")

The Link includes Destination Site's URL and:

(*Select if appropriate*)

☐ Hypertext link—the words: _____ .

☐ Image link: _____ .

☐ Framed link: _____ .

Grant

Destination Site grants the right to display the Link at Source Site and the nonexclusive right to display publicly the trademarks or images in the Link. Source Site obtains no trademark rights under this Agreement other than the right to display the marks. Any goodwill associated with Source Site's trademarks automatically vests in Destination Site.

Standards and Notifications

(*Select if appropriate*)

☐ Source Site shall maintain its site in accordance with industry standards and, upon notice from Destination Site, shall promptly remove the Link if required. Source Site shall promptly notify Destination Site of any change to the Link or to Source Site that affects the Link.

By: _____   By: _____

Date: _____   Date: _____

Source Site Title: _____   Destination Site Title: _____

Source Site Mailing Address: _____   Destination Site Mailing Address: _____

_____   _____

Email: _____   Email: _____

A link between Source Site's home page and Destination Site's internal page entitled "Today's News," resulting in a framed page with the frame incorporating Source Site's trademarks and advertisements.

Sometimes, the best way to describe a frame or inlined link is to provide a screen snapshot and attach it to the agreement. In that case, write in: "As attached and incorporated into this agreement" and attach the image to the agreement.

- In the next section, choose a hypertext link or image link (or both if necessary). A hypertext link is a word link (usually viewed as color-highlighted text). An image link should be described. If it is a trademark of the destination site, ask the destination site to supply the image (usually in a GIF or JPG format).

- The **Grant** section permits the use of the link and related trademarks or images. The statement, "Any goodwill associated with Source Site's trademarks automatically vests in Destination Site." is a requirement of trademark law. It guarantees that the destination site preserves its trademark rights.

- The optional section **Standards and Notification** is a further assurance sometimes required by a destination site that the source site won't operate in an unlawful manner or change the link dramatically. It offers the option of instant termination. Even if this section is not included, the destination site can probably force the removal of the link if it desires.

- Both parties should sign the agreement. For information regarding signing authority, see Chapter 11, "Art and Merchandise Licenses." Many of the miscellaneous provisions included in legal agreements, such as dispute resolution, are not included here for brevity and ease. Include any that you wish to apply to your agreement.

Linking Disclaimers

To minimize liability for any activities that occur when a visitor is taken to a linked website, a webmaster may want to include a disclaimer on the home page. A disclaimer is a statement denying an endorsement or waiving liability for a potentially unauthorized activity. A sample disclaimer appears below.

Linking Disclaimer

By providing links to other sites, [*name of site*] does not guarantee, approve, or endorse the information or products available on these sites.

A disclaimer is not a cure-all for infringement, but if a disclaimer is prominently displayed and clearly written a court may take it into consideration as a factor limiting damages (see Chapter 12, "Releases"). For example, in a case involving a dispute between websites for two restaurants, both named Blue Note, one factor that helped the lesser-known restaurant avoid liability was a prominently displayed disclaimer stating that it was not affiliated with the more famous restaurant. (*Benusan Restaurant v. King*, 937 F.Supp. 295 (S.D.N.Y. 1996).)

Dear Rich:

Can I Post Screenshots at My Website?

I have a question. In my book, I'll be using a lot of screenshots from different websites. Do I need to get permission for that or is it a fair use?

Conventional wisdom (and the Electronic Frontier Foundation) says that an unauthorized screenshot is an infringement. That said, the use of screenshots rarely triggers a complaint because either: (1) The copyright owners don't want to complain about something that promotes their company—for example, an online tutorial about using Microsoft Word, or a book about starting an Etsy business, or (2) the copyright owners believe the use is likely to be excused as a fair use. Although issues don't often arise, occasionally copyright owners do complain— for example, Apple complained about prerelease screenshots of the iPhone. Some sites place limits on your use of screenshots in their user agreements.

Keep in mind that if the copyright owners do complain, the results can be unfortunate—it may disrupt publication of a book or another product. Perhaps a more important issue to consider is whether what you are doing is likely to anger or annoy the copyright owner. If it is, proceed with caution and review your use of the company's trademarks so that your use doesn't imply an association or endorsement.

Academic and Educational Permissions

This chapter focuses on getting permission to use copyrighted works for academic purposes, from assembling academic coursepacks to using copyrighted material in the classroom. We also include form agreements you can use to obtain clearances for coursepacks, and details on educational fair use guidelines. This topic has its own chapter because specific legal rules apply to academic uses, and special resources can help educators obtain academic permissions.

The first half of this chapter focuses on the most common need for permission in the academic world—permission to compile a collection of copyrighted materials into a "coursepack" or "reader" used for teaching. The second half of the chapter is devoted to an analysis of academic fair use guidelines, under which permission is not required for educational use of copyrighted materials.

Academic Coursepacks

An academic coursepack is a collection of materials used in the classroom, distributed either in digital file format ("eReserves") or photocopied in book format or as class handouts. Coursepacks are commonly offered for sale in campus bookstores, although professors may arrange to sell them in class. Most publishers grant "clearances" for coursepacks—that is, for a fee, publishers permit their books or articles to be copied and distributed in educational contexts. Such clearances normally last for one semester or school term. After that, the instructor must seek clearance again. In addition to these paper coursepacks, many teaching institutions offer students electronic coursepacks.

Coursepacks and Copyright

Prior to 1991, many instructors and photocopy shops assembled and sold coursepacks without permission and without compensating the authors or publishers. This was based on the assumption that educational copying qualified as a "fair use" under copyright law, which, legally speaking, is a use that is exempt from permissions requirements that normally apply to copyrighted materials. (For a full explanation of fair use principles, see Chapter 9.)

However, in 1991, a federal court ruled that a publisher's copyright was infringed when a Kinko's copy shop reprinted portions of a book in an academic coursepack. (*Basic Books Inc. v. Kinko's Graphics Corp.*, 758 F.Supp. 1522 (S.D.N.Y. 1991).) The court said that reprinting copyrighted materials in academic coursepacks was not fair use, and that permission was required.

The owner of a copy shop in Ann Arbor, Michigan, began a personal crusade to prove that the Kinko's case was wrongly decided, by advertising that he would copy course materials for students and professors. As a result, he was sued by several book publishers. A federal Court of Appeals decided against the copy shop owner, ruling that the copying did not qualify as fair use. This ruling was based on the amount and substantiality of the materials taken, and on the fact that academic publishers were financially harmed—they lost licensing revenues—while the copy shop made money on the coursepacks. (*Princeton Univ. v. Michigan Document Servs.*, 99 F.3d 1381 (6th Cir. 1996).)

Digital Coursepacks. By 2000, digital coursepacks were replacing paper copies, and in 2004 several academic publishers sued an online publisher in Austin, Texas, who offered "netpacks." Faced with the lawsuit, the company settled with the publishers and agreed to become copyright-compliant.

As the digital revolution proceeded, many educational institutions began maintaining digital eReserves of book excerpts. These excerpts were then made available to professors for their students. In 2008, academic publishers sued Georgia State University for maintaining such a system.

Surprisingly, the lower court judge ruled against the publishers, holding that the digital excerpts were fair use. On appeal, the Eleventh Circuit held that the district court erred when it used a mechanical fair use standard (copying less than a chapter or 10% of a book is fair use). The Appeals Court sent the case back for reconsideration, and the result (in 2016) favored GSU again: Digital reproduction of 45 of the 49 excerpts was deemed fair use. (*Cambridge University v. Patton*, 769 F.3d 1232 (11th Cir. 2014).)

This decision may be an anomaly as it seems to set different standards for digital eReserves and paper coursepacks. A conservative approach would be to obtain permission before reproducing copyrighted materials for an academic coursepack. Note, campus copy shops still perform coursepack assembly. However, these copy shops have either affiliated with established clearance services or are prepared to obtain clearance on behalf of instructors.

Obtaining Clearance for Coursepacks

It's the instructor's obligation to obtain clearance for materials used in class, although instructors typically delegate the task to:

- **Clearance services.** These services usually offer the easiest path to clearance and assembly.
- **University bookstores or copy shops.** University policies may require that the instructor delegate the task to the campus bookstore, copy shop, or to a special division of the university that specializes in clearances.
- **Department administration (generally, the instructor's assistant or other administrator).** Below, we offer some suggestions for these administrators on how to assemble a coursepack without a clearance service.

Using a Clearance Service

It can be time-consuming to seek and obtain permission for the 30 or more articles you want to use in a coursepack. Fortunately, private clearance services will, for a fee, acquire permission and assemble coursepacks on your behalf. After the coursepacks are created and sold, the clearance service collects royalties and distributes the payments to the rights holders. Educational institutions may require that the instructor use a specific clearance service. As noted earlier in this chapter, some clearance companies also provide clearance for nonpaper electronic coursepacks used in distance learning.

The largest copyright clearing service is the Copyright Clearance Center (www.copyright.com), which clears millions of works from thousands of publishers and authors. XanEdu Publishing Inc. (www.xanedu.com, formerly known as Campus Custom Publishing) is the leading coursepack provider servicing hundreds of schools. According to XanEdu, it has integrated CCC's rights licensing services within its software to provide 100% copyright-compliant course packs to academic customers.

Clearance Company Fees

The total fees that clearance companies charge for assembling a coursepack are based on the cost of copyright permission for the material copied, plus copying, binding, the clearance service's processing fee, and, if sold in a campus bookstore, the store's markup (usually 20%, sometimes 25%).

Permission fees vary, but most publishers charge approximately 8 to 10 cents per copied page. Ultimately, the cost of the permission is absorbed by the student buying the coursepack. One advantage of using a coursepack service is that fees are often based on the number of copies sold, not printed.

The Copyright Clearance Center (CCC) ordinarily charges customers an annual service fee, regardless of the number of services in which a customer participates.

Clearance companies will sometimes work on a "copyright only" basis. This means the company acquires permission to include the material in the coursepack, but does not assemble the coursepacks itself. This task is usually left to the bookstore, copy shop, or academic support staff. Most clearance services provide free estimates for coursepack permissions and assembly.

ISBNs and ISSNs

When filling out a coursepack permission request, you'll need to provide the ISBN or ISSN for the publications you want to copy. ISBNs and ISSNs are part of a standardized numbering system all publishers use. ISBNs (International Standard Book Numbers) are used for books. ISSNs (International Standard Serial Numbers) are used for magazines, journals, newsletters, and other serialized publications. These numbers can be found on or near the title or copyright page or near the publication's UPC bar code. Since several numbers may be printed on the bar code, look for the number preceded by either "ISSN" or "ISBN."

Coursepack Application Forms

To begin the clearance process, you must complete and submit a coursepack application form to the clearance service. As with all permissions, if you don't make the payment as required under the agreement, the permission may be terminated.

Clearance Company Agreements

You must enter into a written agreement with a clearance company. The agreement establishes that the company will act as your agent to acquire permissions and assemble the coursepack, and details your obligations regarding payment and copyright law.

Assembling Your Own Coursepack

Instead of hiring a clearance company to obtain clearance and assemble a coursepack for you, you can do it yourself. Why take on this extra work? First, a clearance company might be unwilling or unable to obtain permission for certain items. Second, by doing it yourself you can save students money by minimizing your fees.

It's not unusual for a clearance company to be unable or unwilling to acquire permission for certain works. Clearance companies typically enter into affiliations with academic publishers—that is, they get permission in advance to use all the material in the publisher's catalog. This allows them to avoid having to ask for permission to use each individual item. If the material you want to use comes from publishers who have affiliated with the course- pack company, this will work for you. But if the material you want is not from one of these precleared publishers, the clearance company might not even try to get permission, or if they do try, may be unable to get it.

The Association of American Publishers (AAP) also provides sample request forms and information on coursepack requests on its website (www.publishers.org).

What Copyright Notice Should You Use in a Coursepack?

Your coursepack's copyright notice must identify the copyright owners of the materials it includes. A clearance company can help you create the notices. If you are handling clearance on your own, your clearance agreement should require each rightsholder to provide the format for their notice. Below is an example of a notice for a coursepack:

"Dangerous Similarities" by Stan Soocher is excerpted from *They Fought the Law* © Schirmer Books (1998);

"Who Will Own Your Next Good Idea" by Charles C. Mann is excerpted from *Atlantic Monthly* © Atlantic Monthly (Sept. 1998).

Here are some suggestions for preparing your own coursepack:

- Start with the publisher (not the author) of the item you want to use; direct your request to the publisher's permissions, licensing, or clearance department. If the publisher doesn't control the rights you need, they can probably direct you to the rights holder. Information about locating publishers is provided in Chapter 2.
- Obtain permission for works whether or not they are still in print. Even if a work is out of print, you still need permission to use it unless it is in the public domain.
- Fax or mail your request at least three to nine weeks before your class begins (most publishers will not accept email requests for permission).

Sample Coursepack Request Form

Below is a sample coursepack permission request form prepared by the Association of American Publishers.

Forward this to the publisher or other rights holder. If you have already discussed rights with the copyright owner and agreed upon the terms, bypass the request form and send the Coursepack Permission Agreement.

 FORM

You can download this form (and all other forms in this book) from Nolo.com; for details, see the appendix.

Coursepack Permission Request Form

(Association of Academic Publishers)

To:

Publisher Contact: _____

Publisher: _____

Email: _____ Date of Request: _____

From:

Your Name: _____

Department: _____

School name: _____

Address: _____

City: _____

State: _____ Zip code: _____

Phone #: _____ Email: _____

Course name and number: _____

Number of copies needed: _____

Instructor: _____

Semester and year: _____

ISBN/ISSN number: _____

Book or journal title: _____

Author: _____

Translator: _____

Editor: _____

Edition: _____ Volume: _____

Copyright year: _____ Publication year: _____

Chapter/article title: _____

Chapter/article author: _____

Page numbers: _____ Total pages: _____

Is it an out-of-print work? ☐ Yes ☐ No

Have you included a copy of the material with this request? ☐ Yes ☐ No

Are you the author? ☐ Yes ☐ No

Permission is requested for use during one term only. ☐ Yes ☐ No

Coursepack Permission Agreement

_____ ("Licensor")

_____ ("User")

Department: _____

School Name: _____

Course name and number: _____ ("the Course").

Date when Course starts: _____ (the "Course date").

Authorization

Licensor authorizes User to photocopy the Selection, as defined below, for purposes of creating a photocopy anthology (the "Coursepack") for sale or distribution to students and academic customers in the Course.

Number of Copies and Assembly

_____ copies of the Coursepack shall be assembled and distributed for the Course:

☐ by User

☐ by on-campus bookstores or copy centers, or

☐ by off-campus copy shops.

Number of pages (or actual page numbers) to be used _____ .

The permission granted in this Agreement is limited to the Course and institution listed above and to be used for one semester only. Any further rights must be negotiated separately.

Material for Which Permission Is Sought

Title of text or artwork: _____

_____ (the "Selection").

Author: _____ .

Source publication (or product from which it came): _____

_____ .

If from a periodical, the ISSN, volume, issue, and date. If from a book, the ISBN:

_____ .

If from the Internet, the entire URL address: _____ .

Credit

A standard credit line including Licensor's name will appear where the Selection is used. If you have a special credit line you would prefer, indicate it here: _____
_____ .

Fee

User shall pay a fee of $ _____ to Licensor at the following address:
_____
_____ within 30 days of commencement date, listed above.

Warranty

Licensor warrants that it is the owner of rights for the Selection and has the right to grant the permission to republish the materials as specified above.

_____ (User signature)

Name: _____

Title: _____

Address: _____

Date: _____

Permission Granted By: _____ (Licensor signature)

Name: _____

Title: _____

Address: _____

Date: _____

Coursepack Permission Agreement

Ordinarily, when you create your own coursepack you will seek permission to photocopy the materials. You should always obtain written permission from the copyright owners for this. Use the agreement below for this purpose. In the section entitled "Number of Copies & Assembly," indicate the number of copies you will produce for the class and check the box that indicates how the coursepack will be assembled. Coursepack agreements are almost always limited to one semester and to one institution. Unlike the nonnegotiable coursepack agreements provided by clearance companies, you can modify this agreement if you wish to negotiate a multiterm agreement.

FORM

You can download this form (and all other forms in this book) from Nolo.com; for details, see the appendix.

Educational Uses of Noncoursepack Materials

Unlike academic coursepacks, other copyrighted materials can be used without permission in certain educational circumstances under copyright law or as fair use. "Fair use" is the right to use portions of copyrighted materials without permission for purposes of education, commentary, or parody. While Chapter 9 is devoted entirely to explaining fair use principles, special fair use rules for educational purposes are discussed in this chapter. Fair use rules for educational uses are very specific and, if complied with, can generally prevent lawsuits—which is not the case for general fair use principles.

Educational Fair Use Guidelines

Publishers and the academic community have established a set of educational fair use guidelines to provide "greater certainty and protection" for teachers. While the guidelines are not part of the federal Copyright Act, they are recognized by courts and the Copyright Office as minimum standards for fair use in education. A teacher or pupil following the guidelines can feel comfortable that a use falling within these guidelines is a permissible fair use and not an infringement.

In a case filed against Georgia State University (GSU) (discussed earlier in this chapter), the trial court viewed the Copyright Office's 1976 Guidelines for Educational Fair Use as a minimum, not a maximum standard. (*Cambridge University Press v. Georgia State University*, Case 1:08-cv-01425-OD (N.D. Ga., May 11, 2012).)

The educational use guidelines can be found in Circular 21, provided by the Copyright Office.

Keep in mind that none of these guidelines permit creation of coursepacks. They only allow uses that involve much less material than what's included in a coursepack.

The Code of Best Practices in Fair Use for Media Literacy Education

In 2008, the Center for Media & Social Impact, in connection with American University, unveiled a guide of fair use practices for instructors in K–12 education, in higher education, in nonprofit organizations that offer programs for children and youth, and in adult education. The guide identifies five principles that represent acceptable practices for the fair use of copyrighted materials. You can learn more at the center's website, https://cmsimpact.org. Click "Programs," then click "Fair Use Library."

What Is the Difference Between the Guidelines and General Fair Use Principles?

The educational guidelines are similar to a treaty that has been adopted by copyright owners and academics. Under this arrangement, copyright owners will permit uses that are outlined in the guidelines. In other fair use situations, the only way to prove that a use is permitted is to submit the matter to court or arbitration. In other words, in order to avoid lawsuits, the various parties have agreed on what is permissible for educational uses, codified in these guidelines.

What Is an "Educational Use"?

The educational fair use guidelines apply to material used in educational institutions and for educational purposes. Examples of "educational institutions" include K-12 schools, colleges, and universities. Libraries, museums, hospitals, and other nonprofit institutions also are considered educational institutions under most educational fair use guidelines when they engage in nonprofit instructional, research, or scholarly activities for educational purposes.

"Educational purposes" are:

- noncommercial instruction or curriculum-based teaching by educators to students at nonprofit educational institutions
- planned noncommercial study or investigation directed toward making a contribution to a field of knowledge, or
- presentation of research findings at noncommercial peer conferences, workshops, or seminars.

Rules for Reproducing Text Materials for Use in Class

The guidelines permit a teacher to make one copy of any of the following: a chapter from a book; an article from a periodical or newspaper; a short story, short essay, or short poem; or a chart, graph, diagram, drawing, cartoon, or picture from a book, periodical, or newspaper.

Teachers may photocopy articles to hand out in class, but the guidelines impose restrictions. Classroom copying cannot be used to replace texts or workbooks used in the classroom. Pupils cannot be charged more than the actual cost of photocopying. The number of copies cannot exceed more than one copy per pupil. And a notice of copyright must be affixed to each copy.

Examples of what can be copied and distributed in class include:

- a complete poem if less than 250 words or an excerpt of not more than 250 words from a longer poem
- a complete article, story, or essay if less than 2,500 words or an excerpt from any prose work of not more than 1,000 words or 10% of the work, whichever is less; or
- one chart, graph, diagram, drawing, cartoon, or picture per book or per periodical issue.

Not more than one short poem, article, story, essay, or two excerpts may be copied from the same author, nor more than three from the same collective work or periodical volume (for example, a magazine or newspaper) during one class term. As a general rule, a teacher has more freedom to copy from newspapers or other periodicals if the copying is related to current events.

The idea to make the copies must come from the teacher, not from school administrators or other higher authority. Only nine instances of such copying for one course during one school term are permitted. In addition, the idea to make copies and their actual classroom use must be so close together in time that it would be unreasonable to expect a timely reply to a permission request. For example, the instructor finds a magazine article on capital punishment two days before presenting a lecture on the subject.

Teachers may not photocopy workbooks, texts, standardized tests, or other materials that were created for educational use. The guidelines were not intended to allow teachers to usurp the profits of educational publishers. In other words, educational publishers do not consider it fair use if the copying provides replacements or substitutes for the purchase of books, reprints, periodicals, tests, workbooks, anthologies, compilations, or collective works.

Rules for Reproducing Music

A music instructor can make copies of excerpts of sheet music or other printed works, provided that the excerpts do not constitute a "performable unit," such as a whole song, section, movement, or aria. In no case can more than 10% of the whole work be copied, and the number of copies may not exceed one copy per pupil. Printed copies that have been purchased may be edited or simplified provided that the fundamental character of the work is not distorted or the lyrics altered (or added to).

A student may make a single recording of a performance of copyrighted music for evaluation or rehearsal purposes, and the educational institution or individual teacher may keep a copy. In addition, a single copy of a sound recording owned by an educational institution or an individual teacher (such as a CD or cassette) of copyrighted music may be made for the purpose of constructing aural exercises or examinations, and the educational institution or individual teacher can keep a copy.

Instructors may not:

- copy sheet music or recorded music for the purpose of creating anthologies or compilations used in class
- copy from works intended to be "consumable" in the course of study or teaching such as workbooks, exercises, standardized tests and answer sheets, and like material
- copy sheet music or recorded music for the purpose of performance, except for emergency copying to replace purchased copies which are not available for an imminent performance (provided purchased replacement copies are substituted in due course); or
- copy any materials without including the copyright notice which appears on the printed copy.

If copyrighted sheet music is out of print (not available for sale), an educator can request permission to reproduce it from the music publisher. Information about contacting music publishers is provided in Chapter 5. A library that wants to reproduce out-of-print sheet music can use a system established by the Music Publishers Association by downloading and completing a form called the Library Requisition for Out-of-Print Copyrighted Music from the Association's website at www.mpa.org.

Rules for Recording and Showing Television Programs

Nonprofit educational institutions can record television programs transmitted by network television and cable stations. The institution can keep the tape for 45 days, but can only use it for instructional purposes during the first ten of the 45 days. After the first ten days, the video recording can only be used for teacher evaluation purposes, to determine whether or not to include the broadcast program in the teaching curriculum. If the teacher wants to keep it within the curriculum, he or she must obtain permission from the copyright owner. The recording may be played once by each individual teacher in the course of related teaching activities in classrooms and similar places devoted to instruction (including formalized home instruction). The recorded program can be repeated once if necessary, although there are no standards for determining what is and is not necessary. After 45 days, the recording must be erased or destroyed.

A video recording of a broadcast can be made only at the request of and only used by individual teachers. A television show may not be regularly recorded in anticipation of requests—for example, a teacher cannot make a standing request to record each episode of a PBS series. Only enough copies may be reproduced from each recording to meet the needs of teachers, and the recordings may not be combined to create teaching compilations. All copies of a recording must include the copyright notice on the broadcast program as recorded and (as mentioned above) must be erased or destroyed after 45 days.

Proposed (But Not Adopted) Educational Guidelines on Fair Use

The guidelines discussed in the previous section were approved by a consensus of educators, scholars, and publishers (copyright owners). Since these educators and copyright owners have come to an agreement, it is unlikely that a publisher will sue an educator who uses material in a manner that is permitted by the guidelines. Note, however that one federal appeals court has questioned the use of these guidelines when determining fair use. The Eleventh Circuit rejected the "10% standard" discussed below (copying less than 10% is a permissible educational use) and instead emphasized the importance of a flexible case-by-case fair use analysis. (*Cambridge University Press v. Patton*, 769 F.3d 1232 (11th Cir. Ga. 2014).)

Besides these guidelines, other have been discussed and proposed, but not formally approved. These proposed guidelines lack the official consensus of the adopted guidelines. However, the parties created some standards that were included in a report.

The proposed guidelines are provided here to give you a ballpark idea of what may be permissible. For example, these standards may help you formulate a fair use analysis, as described in Chapter 9. You can access the full report from which these proposed guidelines originated at the Patent and Trademark Office's Conference on Fair Use (CONFU) site. See the resources section at the end of this chapter for the website address.

Proposed Guidelines for Digital Copying

Under proposed guidelines, educators can digitize analog images (nondigital photographic prints or paintings). Digitizing is traditionally accomplished by scanning a printed photo. In this process, an analog image (that is, a two-dimensional printed photograph or slide created by a noncomputer photo processing method) is converted into a digital format known as binary code. This digital format is stored in a computer file. Under the proposed guidelines, educators can digitize a lawfully acquired analog image for educational use unless the image is readily available in usable digital form at a fair price. The proposed guidelines for digital imaging are located at the Patent and Trademark Office's CONFU site. See the resources section at the end of this chapter for the website address.

Under the proposed guidelines, an educational institution may include digital thumbnail images created from analog images in a searchable catalog used by the institution. A thumbnail is a small-scale, typically low-resolution, digital reproduction that has no commercial or reproductive value.

An educational institution may display images digitized under the proposed guidelines through its own secure electronic network, provided that it includes a notice stating that the images shall not be downloaded, copied, retained, printed, shared, modified, or otherwise used, except as provided in the educational use guidelines.

Proposed Guidelines for Using Digitized Images in Lectures, Scholarly Presentations, or Publications

Under proposed guidelines, an educator may display a digital image prepared from an analog image if the display is for educational purposes, such as face-to-face teaching or scholarly activities at a nonprofit educational institution. An educational institution may compile digital images for display on the institution's secure electronic network to students enrolled in a course for classroom use, after-class review, or directed study. Educators, scholars, and students may use or display digital images in connection with lectures or presentations in their fields, including uses at noncommercial professional development seminars, workshops, and conferences.

The proposed guidelines do not permit reproducing and publishing images in publications, including scholarly publications in print or digital form, for which permission is generally required.

Proposed Guidelines for Students or Instructors Preparing Multimedia Works

There are extensive proposed guidelines for the creation and use of multimedia works. Multimedia works include music, text, graphics, illustrations, photographs, and/or audiovisual images combined into a presentation using equipment. For example, an instructor in copyright law may use a software program such as Microsoft *PowerPoint* to create a class presentation that includes still and moving images, music, and spoken words. If you are contemplating preparing multimedia works for classroom instruction, you should download and review Appendix J of the CONFU Report (website listed in the resources section at the end of this chapter).

In general, students and instructors may create multimedia works for face-to-face instruction, directed self-study, or remote instruction provided that the multimedia works are used only for educational purposes in systematic learning activities at nonprofit educational institutions. Instructors may use their multimedia works for teaching courses for up to two years after the first use.

There are also certain "portion limitations." An educational multimedia presentation may include:

- Up to 10% or 1,000 words, whichever is less, of a copyrighted text work. For example, you may use an entire poem of less than 250 words but no more than three poems by one poet or five poems by different poets from the same anthology.
- Up to 10%, but not more than 30 seconds, of the music and lyrics from an individual musical work.
- Up to 10% or three minutes, whichever is less, of a copyrighted motion media work—for example, an animation, a video, or a film image.
- A photograph or an illustration in its entirety but no more than five images by the same artist or photographer. When using photographs and illustrations from a published collective work, you may use no more than 10% or 15 images, whichever is less. Or,

- Up to 10% or 2,500 field or cell entries, whichever is less, from a copyrighted database or data table. A "field entry" is defined as a specific item of information, such as a name or Social Security number in a database file record. A "cell entry" is defined as the intersection at which a row and a column meet on a spreadsheet.

Only two copies of an educational multimedia project may be made, only one of which may be placed on reserve. An additional copy may be made for preservation purposes, but may only be used or copied to replace a copy that has been lost, stolen, or damaged. If an educational multimedia project is created by two or more people, each creator may retain one copy for the educational purposes described in the proposed guidelines. Permission is required for uses that are commercial or go beyond the limitations of the proposed guidelines.

Library Photocopying

The Copyright Act at 17 U.S.C. Section 108 provides a set of rules regarding library reproductions. In general, a library or an archive open to the public (or whose collection is available to specialized researchers other than those affiliated with the institution) will not be liable for copyright infringement based upon a library patron's unsupervised use of reproducing equipment located on its premises, provided that the copying equipment displays a notice that the making of a copy may be subject to the copyright law. The notice must appear in a specific form, as shown below.

When patrons ask the library to copy text works, the warning notice must be printed within a box located prominently on the order form, either on the front side of the form or immediately adjacent to the space for the name and signature of the user. The library may make only one copy of such works per patron. Copying a complete work from the library collection is prohibited unless the work is not available at a "fair price." This is generally the case when the work is out of print and used copies are not available at a reasonable price. If a work, located within the library's collection, is available at a reasonable price, the library may reproduce one article or other contribution to a copyrighted collection or periodical issue, or a small part of any other copyrighted work, for example, a chapter from a book. This right to copy does not apply if the library is aware that the copying of a work (available at a fair price) is systematic. For example, if 30 different members of one class are requesting a copy of the same article, the library has reason to believe that the instructor is trying to avoid seeking permission for 30 copies.

The copying, whether performed by the library or whether unsupervised by the library patron, cannot be for a commercial advantage. This means that the library (or a copying service hired by the library) cannot profit from the copying. In addition, the copying for the patron must be done for purposes of private study, scholarship, or research.

If a library or an educational institution makes a copy of a work for a patron, it must include the actual copyright notice from the material being copied, for example, "© 1953, Grove Press." Under 17 U.S.C. § 108(a), if the material contains no copyright notice, the material should be stamped with the notice, "This material may be protected by copyright law (Title 17 U.S. Code)." In addition to limiting the library's liability, the use of the warning notice will defeat an infringer's defense that the copying was an "innocent infringement" and might even support an argument that the infringement was willful, thereby increasing the damages paid to the copyright owner.

NOTICE WARNING CONCERNING COPYRIGHT RESTRICTIONS

The copyright law of the United States (Title 17, United States Code) governs the making of photocopies or other reproductions of copyrighted material. Under certain conditions specified in the law, libraries and archives are authorized to furnish a photocopy or another reproduction. One of these specified conditions is that the photocopy or reproduction is not to be "used for any purpose other than private study, scholarship, or research." If a user makes a request for, or later uses, a photocopy or reproduction for purposes in excess of "fair use," that user may be liable for copyright infringement. This institution reserves the right to refuse to accept a copying order if, in its judgment, fulfillment of the order would involve violation of copyright law.

Library Copying After 75 Years

In 1998, the Sonny Bono Copyright Term Extension Act extended the period of copyright protection for an additional 20 years. As part of the act, Congress provided that during the last 20 years of any term of copyright of a published work, a library or archives may reproduce a copy of the work for purposes of preservation, scholarship, or research provided that: The work was not being distributed commercially; the work cannot be obtained at a reasonable price; or the copyright owner or its agent provides notice that either of the above conditions applies.

Academic Permission Resources

The following resources can help you obtain permission to use materials for academic purposes.

Coursepack Resources

- The Association of Academic Publishers: www.publishers.org
- The Copyright Clearance Center: www.copyright.com
- XanEdu: www.xanedu.com

Educational Fair Use Guidelines

- The established educational guidelines, as well as other rules regarding libraries, are available in Copyright Office Circular 21, "Reproduction of Copyrighted Works by Educators and Librarians," which can be downloaded from www.copyright.gov/circs/circ21.pdf. See Chapter 13 for more information about Copyright Office circulars and contacting the U.S. Copyright Office.
- Copies of proposed guidelines in the report from the Patent and Trademark Office Conference on Fair Use (CONFU) may be downloaded from www.uspto.gov/sites/default/files/documents/confurep_0.pdf or may be obtained, free of charge, by mailing or faxing a written request to: CONFU Report, Office of Public Affairs, U.S. Patent and Trademark Office, Washington, DC 20231; fax: 703-308-5258.

The Public Domain

ABSOLUTELY FREE! MUSIC, TEXT, AND ART!! COPY ALL YOU WANT!! If you saw an advertisement like this, you might wonder, "What's the catch?" When it comes to the public domain, there is no catch. If a book, song, movie, or artwork is in the public domain, then it is not protected by intellectual property laws (copyright, trademark, or patent laws)—which means it's free for you to use without permission.

As a general rule, most works enter the public domain because of old age. As of 2022, this includes any work published in the United States before 1927 or works published before 1964 for which copyrights were not renewed. (Renewal was a requirement for works published before 1978.) A smaller group of works fell into the public domain because they were published without a copyright notice, which was necessary for works published in the United States before March 1, 1989. Some works are in the public domain because the owner has indicated a desire to give them to the public without copyright protection. As discussed throughout this chapter, the rules are different when it comes to establishing public domain status for each of these types of works.

RESOURCE

For a detailed analysis of public domain rules and issues, see *The Public Domain*, by Stephen Fishman (Nolo). You can also find a great deal of public domain information (and inspiration) at The Public Domain Review (https://public domainreview.org).

Welcome to the Public Domain

The term "public domain" refers to creative materials that are not protected by intellectual property laws such as copyright, trademark, or patent laws. The public owns these works, not an individual author or artist. Anyone can use a public domain work without obtaining permission, but no one can ever own it.

An important wrinkle to understand about public domain material is that, while each work belongs to the public, collections of public domain works may be protected by copyright. If, for example, someone has collected public domain images in a book or on a website, the collection as a whole may be protectable even though individual images are not. You are free to copy and use individual images, but copying and distributing the complete collection may infringe what is known as the "collective works" copyright. A collection of public domain material will be protected if the person who created it has used creativity in the choices and organization of the public domain material. This usually involves some unique selection process, for example, a poetry scholar's compiling a book—*The Greatest Poems of e.e. cummings.*

There are four common ways that works arrive in the public domain:

- The copyright has expired.
- The copyright owner failed to follow copyright renewal rules.
- The copyright owner deliberately places the work in the public domain, known as "dedication."
- Copyright law does not protect the particular type of work.

The following section looks more closely at each of these routes into the public domain.

Expired Copyright

As of 2022, copyright has expired for all works published in the United States before 1927. In other words, if the work was published in the United States before January 1, 1927, you are free to use it in the United States without permission. As an example, the graphic illustration of the man with mustache (below) was published sometime in the 19th century and is in the public domain, so no permission was required to include it within this book. These rules and dates apply regardless of whether the work was created by an individual author, a group of authors, or an employee (a work made for hire).

Because of legislation passed in 1998, no new works fell into the public domain between 1998 and 2018 by way of expiration. In 2022, works published in 1926 expired. In 2023, works published in 1927 will expire, and so on.

For works published after 1977, if the work was written by a single author, the copyright will not expire until 70 years after the author's death. If a work was written by several authors and published after 1977, the copyright will not expire until 70 years after the last surviving author dies.

Year-End Expiration of Copyright Terms

Copyright protection always expires at the end of the calendar year of the year it's set to expire. In other words, the last day of copyright protection for any work is always December 31. It's the year that varies. For example, if an author of a work died on June 1, 2000, protection of the works would continue through December 31, 2070.

Dear Rich:

How Can a 100-Year-Old Autobiography Still Be Under Copyright?

I am writing a play about a woman who lived from 1839 to 1930. She wrote an autobiography which was not published in her lifetime. In 1994, it was finally published after some editing by a family member. I am using a lot of the original wording from the woman's autobiography in my play because her voice is really interesting. I'm sure that I'm going far beyond what would be considered fair use, so I would like to get permission from the copyright holder. Unfortunately, the publisher has gone out of business and the editor/relative has a very common name, so I can't find him. He could well have passed on by now. I've tried to track the relatives, but the trail is cold. Would her heirs still hold copyright in her words at this point? Would the relative who edited her autobiography for publication have some copyright? Is there a best way to prove I've shown due diligence in attempting to contact the copyright holders?

Copyright protection typically lasts for the life of the author plus 70 years. So, you would think that copyright for the autobiography would have expired in the year 2000. But the autobiography is still protected because of a quirk in the law that says if an unpublished work created before 1978 was published before January 1, 2003, its copyright would last at least until January 1, 2048, regardless of when the author died. That may have been the reason the relative edited the book and had it published in 1994.

Getting (or not getting) permission. Considering the work is under copyright, you'd need permission from the copyright holder (unless you can demonstrate fair use). We guess that the relative who edited the work (or his heirs) holds the copyright. He apparently instigated the edits and the distribution, so, hard as it might be, you would be tasked with tracking him (or his heirs) down. As you're probably aware "people finder" online searches are available for a fee. (BTW, we don't believe that basic book editing amounts to a separate copyright.)

If for some reason there are no heirs, and after diligently searching you can't find anyone to ask for the autobiography rights (referred to as an "orphan work"), then you have to decide whether to proceed without permission. If you do proceed, keep a record of the steps you took to find the owner. Those records could minimize (but not eliminate) damages in the event the copyright owner steps forward. Finally, if you have success and a company wants to produce your play, you may be required under the contract to clear all rights—in which case you might have to hire a researcher or clearance service.

The Renewal Trapdoor

Thousands of works published in the United States before 1964 fell into the public domain because their copyright was not renewed in time under the law that was then in effect. If a work was first published before 1964, the owner had to file a renewal with the Copyright Office during the 28th year after publication. No renewal meant a loss of copyright.

If you plan on using a work that was published before 1964, you should research the records of the Copyright Office to determine if a renewal was filed. Chapter 13 describes methods of researching copyright status.

Dedicated Works

If, upon viewing a work, you see words such as, "This work is dedicated to the public domain," then it is free for you to use. Sometimes an author deliberately chooses not to protect a work and dedicates it to the public. This type of dedication is rare, and unless there is express authorization placing the work in the public domain, do not assume the work is free to use.

An additional concern is whether the person making the dedication has the right to do so. Only the copyright owner can dedicate a work to the public domain. Sometimes, the creator of the work is not the copyright owner and does not have necessary authority. If in doubt, contact the copyright owner to verify the dedication. Information about locating copyright owners is provided in Chapter 13.

Clip Art Compilations

Generally clip art is sold in books, digital bundles, or from websites, and is often offered as "copyright free." The term "copyright free" is usually a misnomer that actually refers to either royalty-free artwork or work in the public domain. Keep in mind that much of the artwork advertised as copyright free is actually royalty-free artwork, which *is* protected by copyright. Your rights and limitations to use such artwork are expressed in the artwork packaging or in the shrink-wrap agreement or license that accompanies the artwork. These principles are discussed in more detail in Chapter 3.

If the artwork is in the public domain, you are free to copy items without restriction. However, even if the artwork is in the public domain, the complete collection may not be reproduced and sold as a clip art collection if doing so would infringe the unique manner in which the art is collected (known as a compilation or collective work copyright).

Copyright Does Not Protect Certain Works

Copyright law does not protect the titles of books or movies, nor does it protect short phrases such as, "Make my day." Copyright protection also doesn't cover facts, ideas, or theories. These things are free for all to use without authorization.

Short Phrases

Phrases such as, "Show me the money" or, "Beam me up" are not protected under copyright law. Short phrases, names, titles, or small groups of words are considered common idioms of the English language and are free for anyone to use.

However, a short phrase used as an advertising slogan is protectable under trademark law. In that case, you could not use a similar phrase for the purpose of selling products or services. Subsequent chapters explain how this rule applies to specific types of works. For more information on trademarks, see Chapter 10.

Laws, Judicial Opinions, and Model Codes

Neither the opinions of judges, nor the statutes enacted by Congress or state legislatures can be protected by copyright. Although anyone is free to quote or reproduce these statutes and legal opinions, various publishers, legislatures, and reporting systems have claimed proprietary rights to the way these statutes and opinions are annotated or organized. For example, West Publishing unsuccessfully argued that its page numbering system could not be copied onto CD-ROMs by a rival publisher. (*Matthew Bender & Co. v. West Publishing Co.*, 158 F.3d 674 (2d Cir. 1998).)

In 2020, the Supreme Court held that the "government edicts doctrine" —a principle that prevents judges and legislators from claiming authorship in judicial opinions or laws—also applies to annotations prepared and adopted by a state legislature. (*Georgia v. Public.Resource.Org, Inc.*, 140 S. Ct. 1498 (2020).) Model codes—regulations created by a private business that may later be adopted by a public entity—were held to not be protected by copyright once they were adopted as law. (*Veeck v. Southern Building Code Congress International, Inc.*, 293 F.3d 791 (5th Cir. 2002).)

Facts and Theories

A fact or a theory—for example, the fact that a comet will pass by the Earth in 2027—is not protected by copyright. If a scientist discovered this fact, anyone would be free to use it without asking for permission from the scientist. Similarly, if someone creates a theory that the comet can be destroyed by a nuclear device, anyone could use that theory to create a book or movie. However, the unique manner in which a fact is expressed may be protected. Therefore, if a filmmaker created a movie about destroying a comet with a nuclear device, the specific way he presented the ideas in the movie would be protected by copyright.

> EXAMPLE: Neil Young wrote a song, "Ohio," about the shooting of four college students during the Vietnam War. You are free to use the facts surrounding the shooting, but you may not copy Mr. Young's unique expression of these facts without his permission.

In some cases, you are not free to copy a collection of facts because the collection of facts may be protectable as a compilation. For more information on how copyright applies to facts, refer to Chapter 2.

Dear Rich: Chapter Headings and Book Titles

I wrote a nonfiction book and it turns out that one of the chapters has the same title as a book on a similar subject. The person who wrote that book also has seminars and a DVD using the same title. I seem to remember that there's no copyright on titles—but don't know how to make sure. Am I infringing?

The short answer is "No." Copyright law won't protect the book title. Trademark law (with rare exceptions) only protects book titles when used on a series of books. (The author could federally register the title for her seminars but she hasn't done so, yet.) Even if the author could prove trademark rights, she would have to show a likelihood that purchasers would be confused or misled. Proving likelihood of confusion seems difficult since most consumers won't see your chapter heading until after they have purchased your book. All that said, the author or publisher may still fire off a cease and desist letter should they learn of your chapter title (and may even dredge up claims of unfair competition). If you're concerned about getting hassled, the Dear Rich Staff suggests that in the short term, avoid using the chapter heading in promotional materials for your book; and in the long term—assuming you do a second printing of your book— change the heading.

Loss of Copyright Resulting From Omission of Copyright Notice

Under copyright laws that were in effect before 1978, a work that was published without copyright notice fell into the public domain. If the work did not include the word "Copyright" or a © (a "c" in a circle) and the name of the copyright owner, the work would enter the public domain. This rule was repealed; copyright notice is not required for works first published after March 1, 1989 (although works first published prior to that date must still include notice). Just because you find a copy of a book without a copyright notice doesn't mean that the work is in the public domain. It's possible that the copy you are viewing is unauthorized or that the notice has only been removed from a very small number of copies, both of which are excusable. It is also possible that the author followed a copyright law procedure for correcting the error. And, if you're using text from a journal, anthology, newsletter, or magazine published before March 1, 1989, check to see if there is a copyright notice either for the individual article or for the whole publication. Either type of notice will prevent the work from falling into the public domain.

Copyright law does not protect ideas; it only protects the particular way an idea is expressed. What's the difference between an idea and its expression? In the case of a story or movie, the idea is really the plot in its most basic form. For example, the "idea" of the movie *Contact* is that a determined scientist, seeking to improve humankind, communicates with alien life forms. The same idea has been used in many motion pictures, books, and television shows including *The Day the Earth Stood Still*, *The Abyss*, and *Star Trek*. Many paintings, photographs, and songs contain similar ideas. You can always use the underlying idea or theme—such as communicating with aliens for the improvement of the world—but you cannot copy the unique manner in which the author expresses the idea. This unique expression may include literary devices such as dialog, characters, and subplots.

In a 2003 case, the producers of the television show *Survivor* claimed that their show was a "new genre" of television show with a unique format combining the elements of "voyeur verité, hostile environment in the deserted island sense, building of social alliances, challenges arising from the game show element, and serial elimination." They sued to prevent a similar reality-competition show called *Celebrity*.

The court found that this genre of television show was an unprotectable idea, as is any genre. In other words, anyone could produce a show based on the basic idea of contestants in a "reality" situation eliminating each other. *Celebrity* would infringe on *Survivor* only if it copied a substantial amount of the specific details of *Survivor*, which it did not do. There were many differences between the two shows—for example, the way the contestants were eliminated—and *Celebrity* had an audience participation element and a comedic tone, unlike *Survivor*. (*CBS Broadcasting, Inc. v. ABC, Inc.,* 2003 U.S. Dist. LEXIS 20258 (S.D.N.Y. 2003).)

Dear Rich:	**Borrowing a Plot Line**

I was going to write a book that partially borrows the plot of another book. My book will give credit to the original author and will refer to characters in the original book by name. Is this okay or forbidden?

Let's start with a question: Forgetting about copyright for a moment, if you were the author of a book and someone "borrowed" your plot and characters in another book, how would you feel? And not only that, what if the person who copied your stuff credits you—as if you endorsed the whole thing. If you're like most authors, you'd probably be mad. You'd probably talk to a lawyer (or write to the Dear Rich Staff). The lawyer would tell you that it's probably an infringement, but no one can predict with certainty whether it is or isn't (or whether it's fair use). Our guess is that you would be so mad that you would file a lawsuit.

Who will publish your book? Okay, so let's assume that the author files a lawsuit. Your publisher—assuming you were lucky enough to find one these days—(or your publisher's insurer) would likely ask you to pay the costs of the lawsuit based on the indemnity provision in your contract. So even if you win the lawsuit—or you settle—you probably will have given up most of your royalties to pay the attorneys. And if you lose the lawsuit, then you pay the attorneys, and your book goes unpublished.

Can you win the lawsuit? Okay, now for the fine print. Is it legally permissible to borrow? Maybe. Some plots—boy meets girl, boy loses girl, boy gets girl—and some characters—good cop, bad cop—are so stock, that they are considered merely "ideas," not original expressions. In other cases, the author may create something transformative that qualifies as fair use. (Keep in mind these are issues raised at trial, so the attorney is billing as you prove your point.) There are many cases on the subject of borrowing plot and characters, and you may want to peruse a copyright treatise before penning your opus. And of course, as always, disregard all of the legal blather, above, if the book or character you are copying is in the public domain—for example, Sherlock Holmes.

The Merger Doctrine

There is an exception to the principle that you cannot copy the unique expression of a fact or idea. If there are a limited number of ways to express the fact or idea, you are permitted to copy the expression. This is known as the "merger doctrine"—meaning the idea and the expression are merged or inseparable. For example, in the case of a map, there may be very few ways to express the symbol for an airport other than by using a small image of an airplane. In that case, you are free to use the airport symbol. Similarly, there may be a limited way of expressing a rule about the public domain, for example, the statement, "Works published in the United States before 1926 are in the public domain." The fact and the expression are inseparable so you are free to copy the expression. As you can imagine, this is a heavily litigated area, and many companies have butted heads to determine the boundaries of the merger doctrine. For example, Microsoft and Apple litigated over the right to use the trash pail icon as a symbol for deleting computer materials. A federal court of appeals ruled that design constraints made the trash can an unprotectable element of the graphic interface and that Apple could not claim infringement solely based on another company's use of a similar icon. (*Apple Computer, Inc. v. Microsoft Corp.*, 35 F.3d 1435 (9th Cir. 1994).)

U.S. Government Works

In the United States, any work created by a federal government employee or officer is in the public domain, provided that the work was created in that person's official capacity. For example, during the 1980s, a songwriter used words from a speech by then-President Ronald Reagan as the basis for song lyrics. The words from the speech were in the public domain so the songwriter did not need permission from Ronald Reagan. Keep in mind that this rule applies only to works created by federal employees and not to works created by state or local government employees. However, state and local laws and court decisions are in the public domain.

Some federal publications (or portions of them) are protected under copyright law, which is usually indicated on the title page or in the copyright notice. For example, the IRS may acquire permission to use a copyrighted chart in a federal tax booklet. The document may indicate that a certain chart is "Copyright Dr. Matt Polazzo." In that case, you could not copy the chart without permission from Dr. Polazzo.

Publishing Legal Cases and Pagination

As noted above, federal, state, and local laws and court decisions are in the public domain. However, legal publishers have attempted to get around the public domain status by claiming that unique page numbering systems are copyrightable. These publishers argued that you can copy and distribute a court decision, but you cannot copy the page numbering, which is crucial to the official citation system used by the courts. For many years, Lexis and other computerized legal research systems could not cite to the official page numbering system used by West publications. In a 1994 case, West Publishing Company sued when a legal publisher, Matthew Bender, incorporated West's page numbering system on a CD-ROM product. A court of appeals ruled that the use of West's pagination was not protectable and in any case, the page citation copying was permitted as a fair use. As a result of this ruling, you are free to copy a publisher's reproduction of court decisions and page numbering. (*Matthew Bender & Co. v. West Publishing Co.,* 158 F.3d 693 (2d Cir. 1998). But see also *West Publishing Company v. Mead Data,* 799 F.2d 1219 (1986).)

The table below may help you determine public domain status.

Table for Determining Public Domain Status as of 2022*	
Works published in the U.S. before 1927	In the public domain
Works published in the U.S. after 1926 but before 1964	Initial term of 28 years. If not renewed during the 28th year, the work falls into the public domain.
Works published in the U.S. after 1926 but before March 1, 1989	Generally, if a work was published without copyright notice under the authorization of the copyright owner and the law does not provide an exception for the omission, the work is in the public domain

* On January 1 of each subsequent year, new material enters the public domain. For example, in 2023, works published in the United States before 1928 enter the public domain. In 2024, works published before 1929 enter the public domain, and so forth.

Public Domain Trouble Spots

While it's true that no strings are attached to using public domain materials, be aware of certain potholes on the public domain highway, as described below.

Multilayered Works

Works such as movies or sound recordings may contain many underlying works, such as musical sound tracks, painted illustrations, or other works. There has been a disturbing trend by some copyright owners to assert protection in an element of a public domain work. For example, the film *It's a Wonderful Life* fell into the public domain because of a failure to renew copyright. For years, anyone was free to copy and sell the movie on video. However, a production company recently acquired rights to the musical soundtrack that is used in the movie. That soundtrack is not in the public domain. The copyright owner of the soundtrack can now prevent anyone from copying the music, thereby effectively stopping anyone from copying the film (unless the soundtrack is removed). Multilayered works can create confusion when trying to determine public domain status.

Usually you don't have to be concerned with this type of legal maneuver as it is only used in connection with popular and older multilayered works such as classic films. It would be difficult, if not impossible, to apply this procedure to a public domain book or painting.

> **EXAMPLE:** A movie musical containing songs by Cole Porter is in the public domain because of a failure to renew copyright. However, the Cole Porter songs were renewed in time, so they are still protected by copyright and cannot be reproduced without permission. Therefore, you must obtain permission from the copyright owner of the Cole Porter songs in order to copy the public domain film. If you do not want to obtain permission from the owner, you must delete the songs from the film.

Dear Rich:

She Wants to Use Bloch Paintings on TV

I am a television producer who would love to use the work of the Danish painter Carl Bloch within a project of mine. Bloch was born on May 23, 1834 in Copenhagen, Denmark. I'm sure his work is in the public domain and out of copyright but would I have to pay any kind of royalties or fees to anyone to broadcast his paintings on television?

You are correct. Bloch's work is in the public domain. Danish copyright lasts for the life of the author plus 70 years and Bloch died in 1890. You should not have to pay a fee for the right to broadcast the paintings on a television program; however you may have to pay a fee to acquire access to the paintings—for example, some museums require photographic access fees or fees for the right to use photographic reproductions prepared especially for the museum. Note, as we have indicated in previous posts, there is no copyright in a slavish photo reproduction of a public domain painting.

If the work is in the public domain, why is there a copyright notice on Bloch's painting? Possibly because establishments such as the Hope Gallery earn revenue by selling reproductions of public domain works and include the copyright notice with the intention of discouraging competitors and tracking copying online (such as performed here by the Dear Rich Staff). We suppose we could remove the notice (since copyright law prohibits the placement of false copyright notices) but we're too busy packing up personal belongings to mess with *Photoshop* right now. (By the way, copyright law prohibits the fraudulent removal of notices as well.)

Public Domain Works That Are Modified

Modifications to a public domain work may be protected by copyright and cannot be used without permission. A famous example used in many copyright classes is the artist who paints an elaborate hat and mustache on the Mona Lisa. Even though anyone is free to copy the image of the Mona Lisa, the modified image (with mustache and hat) is protected under the artist's copyright.

> EXAMPLE: Color has been added to the black-and-white public domain film *God's Little Acre*. This colorization process is copyrightable. Therefore, the colorized version of *God's Little Acre* cannot be copied without permission.

Plagiarism, Attribution, and the Public Domain

If you copy from a public domain writing, do you have to credit the author? The United States Supreme Court has answered "No," holding that there is no legal requirement to provide any attribution when public domain works are copied and placed into new works. (*Dastar Corp. v. 20th Century Fox Film Corp.*, 123 S.Ct. 2041 (2003).)

However, just because there is no legal requirement to give credit to the creators of public domain works, that doesn't mean you don't have to do it. When copying works from the public domain, be careful to avoid plagiarism. Plagiarism occurs when someone poses as the originator of words they did not write, ideas they did not conceive, or facts they did not discover. Although you cannot be sued for plagiarizing a public domain work, doing so can result in serious professional and personal penalties. For example, in the case of college professors and journalists, it may result in termination; for students, it could lead to expulsion; if done by well-known historians, it can result in public humiliation.

Works Protected by Trademark Law

It is possible that a work that cannot be protected by copyright is still protectable under trademark laws. Chapter 10 provides more information on trademarks.

> EXAMPLE: The gold-colored top of the New York Life building is in the public domain—anyone can photograph it. However, that image also functions as a trademark for the New York Life Insurance Company, and a competing company wouldn't be able to use the image in a way that would be likely to confuse life insurance consumers.

Works Protected in Other Countries

Before 1978, most countries had different periods of copyright protection than the United States. As a result, many works that are public domain in the United States are still protected by copyright in foreign countries, and vice versa. Therefore, you may have to research public domain status in each country in which you plan to publish your work.

Compilations

Often an author creates a work by selecting various public domain components and grouping them together. If the selection, coordination, and arrangement of the material is unique, it will be protected as a copyrightable compilation.

> EXAMPLE: The owners of the book *Bartlett's Familiar Quotations* selected and arranged famous quotes. Anyone may copy a few quotes from *Bartlett's Familiar Quotations*, but no one may copy the selection and arrangement of all the quotes.

Works First Published Outside the United States

The copyrights of some works first published outside the United States have been resurrected, removing them from the public domain. As a result of international treaties signed in the 1990s, public domain works that meet certain qualifications are now protected. (For a detailed discussion, see *The Copyright Handbook*, by Stephen Fishman (Nolo).)

RESOURCE
You may be able to do some public domain detective work yourself (see the research tips offered in Chapter 13) or you can hire private companies or individuals to perform public domain searches for you. Information about such companies is included in Chapter 13.

Fair Use

air use permits the public to use copyrighted materials without permission for purposes of commentary, criticism, and parody.

Millions of dollars in legal fees have been spent attempting to define what qualifies as a fair use. There are no hard-and-fast rules, only guidelines and court decisions. The judges and lawmakers who shaped the fair use doctrine wanted it to have an expansive meaning that adjusts to new technologies and changing cultural mores. To that end, in recent years fair use has been employed to permit copying a portion of the *Java* software code, to scan thousands of books to create a searchable database, and to copy photos when used as thumbnail images for a search engine.

Whether or not a particular instance of copying qualifies as a fair use is decided on a case-by-case basis and ultimately hinges on the four factors, discussed below.

RELATED TOPIC

For educational fair use guidelines, see Chapter 7, which deals with academic permissions.

What Is Fair Use?

Fair use permits the unauthorized copying of copyrighted material for a limited and "transformative" purpose, such as to comment upon, criticize, or parody a copyrighted work. The rationale for fair use is that the public reaps benefits by including the copyrighted material. Another way of looking at fair use is to view it as an affirmative defense against a claim of copyright infringement. That is, if your use qualifies as a fair use, then it would not be an infringement.

Examples of fair use include:

- quoting four lines from a Bob Marley song in a music review
- using five seconds of a children's song in a documentary film
- summarizing and quoting from a medical article on prostate cancer in a news report, or
- copying two paragraphs from a news article for use by a teacher or student in a lesson.

Measuring Fair Use: The Four Factors

Unfortunately, the only way to get a definitive answer on whether a particular use is a fair use is to have it resolved in federal court. Four factors are weighed in each case to determine whether a use qualifies as a fair use. Courts are free to adapt these factors to a particular case, so a judge has a great deal of freedom when making a fair use determination, making the outcome in a given case hard to predict.

The four factors judges consider are:

- the purpose and character of your use
- the nature of the copyrighted work
- the amount and substantiality of the portion taken, and
- the effect of the use upon the potential market.

Educational Fair Use Guidelines

Since the current copyright law was adopted, various organizations and scholars have established guidelines for educational uses. These guidelines are not part of the Copyright Act and are summarized in Chapter 7, which deals with academic and educational permissions.

The Purpose and Character of Your Use (The Transformative Factor)

If you claim fair use, the courts first look at how you are using the copyrighted work. A nonprofit or educational purpose is more likely to be considered fair use than a commercial purpose (although there are many exceptions to this principle). When measuring the first factor, a 1994 Supreme Court decision directed courts to consider whether the use is "transformative." Transformative uses contribute something new, with a further purpose or different character, and do not substitute for the original use of the work.

EXAMPLE: Roger borrows several quotes from the speech given by the CEO of a logging company. Roger prints these quotes under photos of old-growth redwoods in his environmental newsletter. By juxtaposing the quotes with the photos of endangered trees, Roger has transformed the remarks from their original purpose and used them to create a new insight. The copying would probably be permitted as a fair use.

In a parody, for example, the parodist transforms the original by holding it up to ridicule. At the same time, a work does not become a parody simply because the author models characters after those found in a famous work. Purposes such as scholarship, research, or education may also qualify as transformative uses because the work is the subject of review or commentary.

Determining what is transformative—and the degree of transformation—is often challenging. For example, the creation of a *Harry Potter* encyclopedia was determined to be "slightly transformative" (because it made the *Harry Potter* terms and lexicons available in one volume), but this transformative quality was not enough to justify a fair use defense in light of the extensive verbatim use of text from the *Harry Potter* books. (*Warner Bros. Entertainment, Inc. v. RDR Books*, 575 F.Supp.2d 513 (S.D.N.Y. 2008).) Below are three examples of transformative works:

EXAMPLE 1: **Monster Movie Art.** A publisher of monster magazines from the 1950s, '60s, and '70s sued the creator and publisher of a book, *Famous Monster Movie Art of Basil Gogos*. (Gogos created covers for the magazines.) The book publisher had obtained licenses from the artist directly, but not from the magazine publisher, who claimed copyright under work-made-for-hire principles. The district court determined that the use was transformative, since it was for a biography/retrospective of the artist, not simply a series of covers of magazines devoted to movie monsters. In addition, the magazines were no longer in print, and the covers amounted to only one page of the magazine, not the "heart" of the magazine. (*Warren Publishing Co. v. Spurlock d/b/a Vanguard Productions*, 645 F.Supp.2d 402 (E.D. Pa., 2009).)

EXAMPLE 2: **Ed Sullivan Clip.** A seven-second clip from the Ed Sullivan TV show was used in a staged musical history (*The Jersey Boys*) based on the career of the musical group The Four Seasons. The use was transformative. ("Being selected by Ed Sullivan to perform on his show was evidence of the band's enduring prominence in American music," the judge wrote in the ruling.

"By using it as a biographical anchor, [the defendant] put the clip to its own transformative ends.") (*SOFA Entertainment, Inc. v. Dodger Productions, Inc.,* 709 F.3d 1273 (9th Cir. Mar. 11, 2013).)

EXAMPLE 3: **Prince Collages.** The painter Richard Prince created a collage using 35 images from a photographer's book. The artist also used 28 of the photos in 29 additional paintings. In some instances, the full photograph was used, while in others only the main subject of the photo was used. The Second Circuit Court of Appeals held that to qualify as a transformative use, Prince's work did not have to comment on the original photographer's work (or on popular culture). The Court of Appeals concluded that 25 of Prince's artworks qualified as fair use and remanded the case to determine the status of the remaining five artworks. (*Cariou v. Prince,* 714 F.3d 694 (2d Cir. 2012).)

When taking portions of copyrighted work, ask yourself the following questions:

- Has the material taken from the original work been transformed by adding new expression or meaning?
- Was value added to the original by creating new information, new aesthetics, new insights, and understandings?

The Nature of the Copyrighted Work

Because the dissemination of facts or information benefits the public, you have more leeway to copy from factual works such as biographies than you do from fictional works such as plays or novels.

In addition, you will have a stronger case of fair use if you copy the material from a published work than an unpublished work. The scope of fair use is narrower for unpublished works because an author has the right to control the first public appearance of his or her expression.

The Amount and Substantiality of the Portion Taken

The less you take, the more likely that your copying will be excused as a fair use. However, even if you take a small portion of a work, your copying may not be a fair use if the portion taken is the "heart" of the work. In other words, you are more likely to run into problems if you take the most memorable aspect of a work. For example, it would probably not be a fair use to copy the opening guitar riff and the words "I can't get no satisfaction" from the song "Satisfaction."

This rule—less is more—is not necessarily true in parody cases. A parodist is permitted to borrow quite a bit, even the heart of the original work, in order to conjure up the original work. That's because, as the Supreme Court has acknowledged, "the heart is also what most readily conjures up the [original] for parody, and it is the heart at which parody takes aim." (*Campbell v. Acuff-Rose Music*, 510 U.S. 569 (1994).)

Keep in mind that simply using a copyrighted work for humorous purposes is not a parody. For example, it was not a parody when an author sought to use the characterizations, language, and style of Dr. Seuss's *The Cat in the Hat* to rehash the O.J. Simpson murder trial. A parody must focus its commentary and criticism on the original work.

The Effect of the Use Upon the Potential Market

Another important fair use factor is whether your use deprives the copyright owner of income or undermines a new or potential market for the copyrighted work. Depriving a copyright owner of income is very likely to trigger a lawsuit. This is true even if you are not competing directly with the original work.

A judge must consider the effect on the actual and potential market for the copyrighted work. This consideration goes beyond the past intentions of the author or the means by which the author is currently exploiting the work. For example, in one case a photograph was adapted into a wood sculpture without the authorization of the photographer. The fact that the photographer never considered converting the photograph into a sculpture was irrelevant. What mattered was that the potential market existed, as demonstrated by the fact that the defendant earned hundreds of thousands of dollars selling such sculptures.

Some uses are not deemed to undermine the potential market. Copying a magazine cover for purposes of a comparative advertisement is a fair use, because the comparative advertisement does not undermine the sales or need for the magazine. Similarly, a court found that the appearance of a poster in the background of a television series (for less than 30 seconds) did not harm the potential market for the poster.

EXAMPLE: A photographer's picture for a controversial article about dating was not infringed when a writer published an opinion piece that included a screenshot of the article and picture. The district court held that the use was unlikely to harm the market for the picture. (*Yang v. Mic Network, Inc.*, No. 18-7628, 2019 WL 4640263 (S.D.N.Y. 2019).

In another case, a court held that a search engine's practice of creating small reproductions ("thumbnails") of images and placing them on its own website (known as "inlining") did not undermine the potential market for the sale or licensing of those images. One of the reasons was that the thumbnails were much smaller and of much poorer quality than the original photos, and served to index the images and help the public access them. (*Kelly v. Arriba Soft Corp.*, 336 F.3d 811 (9th Cir. 2003).)

A similar result was reached by the Ninth Circuit Court of Appeals in a case involving Google. The court determined that Google's use of thumbnails was permitted as fair use in a case involving reproductions of images from an adult men's magazine website. (*Perfect 10, Inc. v. Amazon. com, Inc.*, 508 F.3d 1146 (9th Cir. 2007).)

What If You Acknowledge the Source Material?

Some people mistakenly believe it's permissible to use a work (or portion of it) if an acknowledgment is provided. For example, they believe it's okay to use a photograph in a magazine as long as the name of the photographer is included. This is not true. Acknowledgment of the source material (such as citing the photographer) may be a consideration in a fair use determination, but it will not protect against a claim of infringement. In some cases, such as advertisements, acknowledgments can backfire and create grounds for additional legal claims, such as a violation of the right of publicity. When in doubt as to the right to use or acknowledge a source, the most prudent course may be to seek the permission of the copyright owner.

The failure to exploit a market may also influence a fair use determination. A group of publishers claimed that Georgia State University (GSU) infringed their rights by using digital excerpts in their coursepacks. On appeal, the Eleventh Circuit held that GSU's use could not have negatively affected the potential market for digital excerpts because the publishers had not fully exploited digital licensing. (*Cambridge University v. Patton*, 769 F.3d 1232 (11th Cir. 2014).)

Again, parody is given a slightly different fair use analysis with regard to the impact on the market. It's possible that a parody may diminish or even destroy the market value of the original work. That is, the parody may be so good that the public can never take the original work seriously again.

The "Fifth" Fair Use Factor: The Objectionable Defendant

You may find that fair use decisions contradict one another or conflict with the rules expressed in this chapter. Fair use involves subjective judgments, often affected by factors such as a judge or jury's personal sense of right or wrong. Even though the Supreme Court has indicated that offensiveness is not a fair use factor, you should be aware that a morally offended judge or jury may rationalize its decision against fair use.

For example, in one case a manufacturer of novelty cards parodied the successful children's dolls the Cabbage Patch Kids. The parody card series was entitled the Garbage Pail Kids and used gruesome and grotesque names and characters to poke fun at the wholesome Cabbage Patch image. Some copyright experts were surprised when a federal court considered the parody an infringement, not a fair use. (*Original Appalachian Artworks, Inc. v. Topps Chewing Gum, Inc.*, 642 F.Supp. 1031 (N.D. Ga. 1986).)

In another case that addressed the "good/bad" conundrum, a festival promoter claimed that its unauthorized use of a photo was fair use partially because the festival had acted in good faith. The Court of Appeals noted that bad faith might preclude a fair use defense, but that good faith should never be a factor when determining fair use. (*Brammer v. Violent Hues*, No. 18-1763 (4th Cir. 2019).)

Too Small for Fair Use: The De Minimis Defense

In some cases, the amount of material copied is so small (or "de minimis") that the court permits it without even conducting a fair use analysis. For example, in the motion picture Seven, several copyrighted photographs appeared in the film, prompting the copyright owner of the photographs to sue the producer of the movie. The court held that the photos "appear fleetingly and are obscured, severely out of focus, and virtually unidentifiable." The court excused the use of the photographs as "de minimis" and didn't require a fair use analysis. (*Sandoval v. New Line Cinema Corp.*, 147 F.3d 215 (2d Cir. 1998).) Twenty years later, a district court issued a similar ruling. In that case, a "fleeting shot of barely visible graffiti" painted on a dumpster, appearing in the HBO series *Vinyl*, was considered de minimis and did not amount to infringement. (*Gayle v. Home Box Office, Inc.*, No. 1:2017cv05867 (S.D.N.Y. May 1, 2018).)

As with fair use, there is no bright line test for determining a de minimis use. For example, in another case, a court determined that the use of a copyrighted poster for a total of 27 seconds in the background of the TV show Roc was not de minimis. What distinguished the use of the poster from the use of the photographs in the Seven case? The court stated that the poster was clearly visible and recognizable with sufficient observable detail for the "average lay observer" to view the artist's imagery and colorful style. (*Ringgold v. Black Entertainment Television, Inc.*, 126 F.3d 70 (2d Cir. 1997).)

Although this may cause a loss of income, it's not the same type of loss as when an infringer merely appropriates the work. As one judge explained, "The economic effect of a parody with which we are concerned is not its potential to destroy or diminish the market for the original—any bad review can have that effect—but whether it fulfills the demand for the original." (*Fisher v. Dees*, 794 F.2d 432 (9th Cir. 1986).)

Dear Rich:

How Do I Word a Copyright Disclaimer for YouTube?

I've seen a lot of different statements posted by YouTube users hoping to avoid a copyright infringement suit. What's the best thing to write to prevent getting sued?

These statements—known in legal parlance as "disclaimers"—are intended to prevent (or at least limit) copyright infringement claims. The most common of the half-million or so disclaimers used at YouTube is apparently "No Copyright Intended" which—despite its ambiguous meaning—is about as effective as going 90 MPH in your car with a sign that says "No Speeding Intended." Other disclaimers state that the user is claiming fair use. Unfortunately, claiming fair use doesn't mean that the work qualifies as a fair use. Only a court can determine that. In truth, we don't believe that there is really any disclaimer that would be effective in preventing a lawsuit if your video infringes someone else's work.

So what do you say? Knowing that disclaimers won't prevent a lawsuit, you might be able to limit damages in a lawsuit by stating something to the effect of:

"No copyright is claimed in [content copied] and to the extent that material may appear to be infringed, I assert that such alleged infringement is permissible under fair use principles in U.S. copyright laws. If you believe material has been used in an unauthorized manner, please contact the poster."

Don't expect this to do much—most copyright owners will bypass this and have it removed under a DMCA notice—but it may set a more sympathetic tone for you as a defendant if you find yourself responding to a lawsuit.

Does It Help to Use a Disclaimer?

A disclaimer is a statement that "disassociates" your work from the work that you have borrowed. For example, if you write an unauthorized biography of Mickey Mouse, you may include a disclaimer such as, "This book is not associated with or endorsed by the Walt Disney Company." Will it help your position if you use a disclaimer? In close cases where the court is having a difficult time making a fair use determination, a prominently placed disclaimer might have a positive effect on the way the court perceives your use, but generally a disclaimer alone won't help if the fair use factors weigh against you. For example, in a case involving a *Seinfeld* trivia book, the publisher included a disclaimer that the book "has not been approved or licensed by any entity involved in creating or producing *Seinfeld*." Despite the disclaimer, the court held that the use of the *Seinfeld* materials was an infringement, not a fair use.

Summaries of Fair Use Cases

The best way to understand the flexible principle of fair use is to review actual cases decided by the courts. Below are summaries of a variety of fair use cases.

Cases Involving Text

- **Fair use.** Publisher Larry Flynt made disparaging statements about the Reverend Jerry Falwell on one page of *Hustler* magazine. Rev. Falwell made several hundred thousand copies of the page and distributed them as part of a fund-raising effort. **Important factors:** Rev. Falwell's copying did not diminish the sales of the magazine (since it was already off the market) and would not adversely affect the marketability of back issues. (*Hustler Magazine, Inc. v. Moral Majority, Inc.*, 606 F.Supp. 1526 (C.D. Cal., 1985).)

- **Fair use.** A biographer of Richard Wright quoted from six unpublished letters and ten unpublished journal entries by Wright. **Important factors:** No more than 1% of Wright's unpublished letters were copied and the purpose was informational. (*Wright v. Warner Books, Inc.*, 953 F.2d 731 (2d Cir. 1991).)

- **Fair use (mostly).** In a case alleging 75 instances of infringement in an educational setting, a district court, proposing a fair use standard based on less than 10% of a book, determined that 70 instances were not infringing. On appeal, the Eleventh Circuit rejected the 10% standard and emphasized the importance of a flexible case-by-case fair use analysis. The case was remanded to the district court which, in 2016, found the majority of instances to be fair use. **Important factors:** On remand, the second factor (the scholarly nature of the work) and the fourth factor (impact of the use on the market value) weighed in favor of fair use. (*Cambridge University Press v. Patton*, 769 F.3d 1232 (11th Cir. Ga. 2014).)

- **Fair use.** A district court ruled that libraries that provided a search engine company (Google) with books to scan were protected by fair use when the libraries later used the resulting digital scans for three purposes: preservation, a full-text search engine, and electronic access for disabled patrons who could not read the print versions. On appeal, the Second Circuit affirmed fair use as to the full-text database ("a quintessentially transformative use") and as to use of text in formats accessible to print-disabled people (although not a transformative use, it is still considered a fair use based on the *Betamax* decision), but remanded the issue of fair use for long-term preservation of books. **Important factors:** As to the full-text database and disabled-access, the Court of Appeals did not find any evidence of financial harm. (*The Author's Guild v. Hathitrust,* 755 F.3d 87 (2d Cir. 2014).)

- **Fair use.** A news organization (Bloomberg) tapped into an earnings report phone call made by executives of a foreign corporation (Swatch) to 132 analysts, and posted a recording and transcript of the phone call. **Important factors:** Bloomberg's publication of the call was analogous to news reporting (publication of such calls is mandatory for American corporations). Because of that newsworthy purpose, a transformative use was not required. Further, the posting of the entire recording was necessary to fulfill this newsworthy purpose. The Second Circuit stated, "Bloomberg's overriding purpose here was not to "scoop" Swatch or "supplant the copyright holder's commercially valuable right of first publication," but rather simply to deliver newsworthy financial information to American investors and analysts." (*Swatch Grp. Mgmt. Servs. Ltd. v. Bloomberg L.P.* 742 F.3d 17 (2d Cir. 2014).)

- **Fair use.** The comedy *Hand to God* features the famed Abbott and Costello routine "Who's on First?" The routine is spoken by a repressed character, whose hand puppet persona mocks him for pretending to be the author of the routine. **Important factors:** Though the use of the routine in the movie and play both elicit laughs, the play's usage is transformative because the audience must be aware of the original in order to "get the joke." (*TCA Television Corp. v. McCollum,* 151 F. Supp. 3d 419 (S.D.N.Y. Dec. 17, 2015).)

- **Not a fair use.** *The Nation* magazine published excerpts from ex-President Gerald Ford's unpublished memoirs. The publication in *The Nation* was made several weeks prior to the date Mr. Ford's book was to be serialized in another magazine. **Important factors:** *The Nation's* copying seriously damaged the marketability of Mr. Ford's serialization rights. (*Harper & Row v. Nation Enters.,* 471 U.S. 539 (1985).)

- **Not a fair use.** A biographer paraphrased large portions of unpublished letters written by the famed author J.D. Salinger. Although people could read these letters at a university library, Salinger had never authorized their reproduction. In other words, the first time that the general public would see these letters was in their paraphrased form in the biography. Salinger successfully sued to prevent publication. **Important factors:** The letters were unpublished and were the "backbone" of the biography—so much so that without the letters the resulting biography was unsuccessful. In other words, the letters may have been taken more as a means of capitalizing on the interest in Salinger than in providing a critical study of the author. (*Salinger v. Random House*, 811 F.2d 90 (2d Cir. 1987).)

- **Not a fair use.** An author copied more than half of an unpublished manuscript to prove that someone was involved in the overthrow of the Iranian government. **Important factors:** A substantial portion was taken (half of the work) and the work had not been published yet. (*Love v. Kwitny*, 772 F.Supp. 1367 (S.D.N.Y. 1989).)

- **Not a fair use.** A company published a book entitled *Welcome to Twin Peaks: A Complete Guide to Who's Who and What's What*, containing direct quotations and paraphrases from the television show *Twin Peaks*, as well as detailed descriptions of plots, characters, and setting. **Important factors:** The amount of the material taken was substantial and the publication adversely affected the potential market for authorized books about the program. (*Twin Peaks v. Publications Int'l, Ltd.*, 996 F.2d 1366 (2d Cir. 1993).)

- **Not a fair use.** A company published a book of trivia questions about the events and characters of the *Seinfeld* television series. The book included questions based upon events and characters in 84 *Seinfeld* episodes and used actual dialog from the show in 41 of the book's questions. **Important factors:** As in the *Twin Peaks* case, the book affected the owner's right to make derivative *Seinfeld* works such as trivia books. (*Castle Rock Entertainment, Inc. v. Carol Publ. Group*, 150 F.3d 132 (2d Cir. 1998).)

- **Not a fair use.** In a case involving the author J.D. Salinger, an author wrote a book in which a character known as Mr. C was allegedly modeled after the character of Holden Caulfield, from Salinger's *The Catcher in the Rye*. After Salinger sued, the sequel's author claimed that his work was a parody, an argument rejected by the district court. The court determined that fair use would not succeed as a defense and granted Salinger's request for a preliminary injunction. (The Second Circuit Court of Appeals agreed with the fair use analysis but reversed the case regarding the standard used for the preliminary injunction.) **Important factors:** Aging the character and placing him in the present day does not add something new, particularly since the character's personality remains intact as derived from the original work. (*Salinger v. Colting*, 641 F.Supp.2d 250 (S.D.N.Y. 2009).)
- **Not a fair use.** Although the creation of a *Harry Potter* encyclopedia was determined to be "slightly transformative" (because it made the *Harry Potter* terms and lexicons available in one volume), this transformative quality was not enough to justify a fair use defense. **Important factors:** An important factor in the court's decision was the extensive verbatim use of text from the *Harry Potter* books. (*Warner Bros. Entertainment, Inc. v. RDR Books*, 575 F.Supp.2d 513 (S.D.N.Y. 2008).)

Artwork, Visual Arts, and Audiovisual Cases

- **Fair use.** After completing a film, an actress incorporated clips from the movie in her acting reel (an actor's video resume). The film's director sued the actress for infringement. **Important factors:** A district court ruled that the acting reels wouldn't interfere with the film's market or profitability. (*Bain v. Film Indep., Inc.* No. 18-4126 (C.D. Cal. 2020).)
- **Fair use.** In a lawsuit commonly known as the *Betamax* case, the Supreme Court determined that the home videotaping of a television broadcast was a fair use. This was one of the few occasions when copying a complete work (for example, a complete episode of the *Kojak* television show) was accepted as a fair use. Evidence indicated that most viewers were "time-shifting" (taping in order to watch later) and not "library building" (collecting the videos in order to build a video library). **Important factors:** The Supreme Court reasoned that the

"delayed" system of viewing did not deprive the copyright owners of revenue. (*Universal City Studios v. Sony Corp.*, 464 U.S. 417 (1984).)

- **Fair use.** The makers of a movie biography of Muhammad Ali used 41 seconds from a boxing match film in their biography. **Important factors:** A small portion of film was taken and the purpose was informational. (*Monster Communications, Inc. v. Turner Broadcasting Sys. Inc.*, 935 F.Supp. 490 (S.D.N.Y., 1996).)

- **Fair use.** A search engine's practice of creating small reproductions ("thumbnails") of images and placing them on its own website (known as "inlining") did not undermine the potential market for the sale or licensing of those images. **Important factors:** The thumbnails were much smaller and of much poorer quality than the original photos and served to help the public access the images by indexing them. (*Kelly v. Arriba-Soft*, 336 F.3d. 811 (9th Cir. 2003).)

- **Fair use.** It was a fair use, not an infringement, to reproduce Grateful Dead concert posters within a book. **Important factors:** The Second Circuit focused on the fact that the posters were reduced to thumbnail size and reproduced within the context of a timeline. (*Bill Graham Archives v. Dorling Kindersley Ltd.*, 448 F.3d 605 (2d Cir. 2006).)

- **Fair use.** A Google search engine did not infringe a subscription-only website (featuring nude models) by reproducing thumbnails. **Important factors:** The court of appeals aligned this case with *Kelly v. Arriba-Soft* (above), which also permitted thumbnails under fair use principles. (*Perfect 10, Inc. v. Amazon.com, Inc.*, 508 F.3d 1146 (9th Cir. 2007).)

- **Fair use.** A publisher of monster magazines from the 1950s, '60s, and '70s sued the creator and publisher of a book, *Famous Monster Movie Art of Basil Gogos*. (Gogos created covers for the magazines.) The book publisher had obtained licenses from the artist directly, but not from the magazine publisher who claimed copyright under work-made-for-hire principles. The district court determined that the use was transformative. **Important factors:** The use was for a biography/retrospective of the artist, not simply a series of covers of magazines devoted to movie monsters. In addition, the magazines were no longer in print, and the covers amounted to only one page of the magazine, not the "heart" of the magazine. (*Warren Publishing Co. v. Spurlock d/b/a Vanguard Productions*, 645 F.Supp.2d 402, (E.D. Pa., 2009).)

- **Fair use.** A seven-second clip from the Ed Sullivan TV show was used in a staged musical history (*The Jersey Boys*) based on the career of the musical group, The Four Seasons. **Important factors:** The use was transformative. ("Being selected by Ed Sullivan to perform on his show was evidence of the band's enduring prominence in American music," the judge wrote in the ruling. "By using it as a biographical anchor, [the defendant] put the clip to its own transformative ends.") Further, the use caused no financial harm to the copyright owners of the show. (*SOFA Entertainment, Inc. v. Dodger Productions, Inc.,* No. 2:08-cv-02616 (9th Cir. Mar. 11, 2013).)

- **Fair use.** The painter, Richard Prince, created a collage using—in one collage—35 images from a photographer's book. The artist also used 28 of the photos in 29 additional paintings. In some instances the full photograph was used while in others, only the main subject of the photo was used. **Important factors:** The Second Circuit Court of Appeals held that to qualify as a transformative use, Prince's work did not have to comment on the original photographer's work (or on popular culture). The court of appeals concluded that 25 of Prince's artworks qualified as fair use and remanded the case to determine the status of the remaining five artworks. (*Cariou v. Prince,* 714 F. 3d 694 (2nd Circuit, 2013).)

- **Fair use.** The re-creation of three scenes from the film *Deep Throat* was a fair use when made for a biographical film about actress Linda Lovelace. **Important factors:** The re-created scenes were used in a non-pornographic film biography (with no nudity) about an actress who ultimately railed against pornography. This use illustrated a strong transformative purpose and demonstrated that the copyright owner of *Deep Throat* would be unlikely to lose revenue from this non-pornographic use. (*Arrow Productions, LTD v. The Weinstein Company LLC,* 44 F. Supp. 3d 359 (S.D.N.Y. Aug. 25, 2014).)

- **Fair use.** A modified photo of a Wisconsin mayor was reproduced on a T-shirt and used to raise money for an event opposed by the mayor. **Important factors:** The Seventh Circuit was primarily persuaded by the level of alteration—the photo was posterized, background removed, text added, and a lime green outline featuring the mayor's smile remained. The resulting image of the mayor, the court stated, "can't be copyrighted." (*Kienitz v. Sconnie Nation LLC,* 766 F.3d 756 (7th Cir. 2014).)

- **Fair use.** A disgruntled former commercial tenant (Chevaldina) used an unflattering photo of her former landlord (Katz) in 25 critical blog posts. Katz purchased the copyright in the photo and sued Chevaldina for infringement. **Important factors:** The use was considered noncommercial, and transformative because, "in the context of the blog post's surrounding commentary, Chevaldina used Katz's purportedly 'ugly' and 'compromising' appearance to ridicule and satirize his character." (*Katz v. Chevaldina*, No. 14-14525 (11th Cir. 2015).)
- **Fair use.** In a battle over the use of viral videos, a humor program, *Equals Three*, reproduced viral videos from another source, Jukin Video, and commented on them, often reproducing the clips in their entirety. **Important factors:** The court determined that in the case of 18 of the 19 videos, *Equals Three* used no more than necessary of each video for purposes of its commentary; and that the jokes and commentary added something new to the viral videos. (*Equals Three, LLC v. Jukin Media, Inc.*, 139 F. Supp. 3d 1094 (C.D. Cal. 2015).)
- **Fair use.** An author created a parody of the surfer-thriller *Point Break*. The court found the work to be sufficiently transformative to justify fair use of the underlying movie materials. At issue in this case was the more novel question of whether the resulting parody could itself be protected under copyright. **Important factors:** The Second Circuit held that if the author of the unauthorized work provides sufficient original material and is otherwise qualified under fair use rules, the resulting work will be protected under copyright. (*Keeling v. Hars*, 809 F. 3d 43 (2d Cir. 2015).)
- **Not a fair use.** Andy Warhol used a photograph of the musician Prince as the basis for a series of silkscreens. Important factors: The Second Circuit determined that silkscreens were derivative, not transformative, reversing a fair use decision by the district court. (*Andy Warhol Foundation for the Visual Arts, Inc. v. Goldsmith*, __ F.3d __ (2d Cir. Aug. 24, 2021).) [Note: The Supreme Court will hear this case on its 2022 docket.]
- **Not a fair use.** A television news program copied one minute and 15 seconds from a 72-minute Charlie Chaplin film and used it in a news report about Chaplin's death. **Important factors:** The court felt that the portions taken were substantial and part of the "heart" of the film. (*Roy Export Co. Estab. of Vaduz v. Columbia Broadcasting Sys., Inc.*, 672 F.2d 1095, 1100 (2d Cir. 1982).)

- **Not a fair use.** A television station's news broadcast used 30 seconds from a four-minute copyrighted videotape of the 1992 Los Angeles beating of Reginald Denny. **Important factors:** The use was commercial, took the heart of the work, and affected the copyright owner's ability to market the video. (*Los Angeles News Service v. KCAL-TV Channel 9*, 108 F.3d 1119 (9th Cir. 1997).)

- **Not a fair use.** A poster of a "church quilt" was used in the background of a television series for 27 seconds. **Important factors:** The court was influenced by the prominence of the poster, its thematic importance for the set decoration of a church, and the fact that it was a conventional practice to license such works for use in television programs. (*Ringgold v. Black Entertainment Television, Inc.*, 126 F.3d 70 (2d Cir. 1997).)

- **Not a fair use.** The U.S. Postal Service (USPS) licensed the use of a photograph of the Korean War veterans' memorial sculpture for a postage stamp, but failed to obtain permission from the sculptor who held copyright in the underlying three-dimensional work. The U.S. Court of Appeals for the Federal Circuit held that the use of the underlying sculpture depicted in the photograph was not permitted under fair use principles. **Important factors:** It was not enough to transfer the work from three dimensions to two dimensions (despite the creative use of photography and snow in conjunction with the photos). (*Gaylord v. United States*, 595 F.3d 1364 (Fed. Cir. 2010).)

- **Not a fair use.** A wedding guest photographed President Trump as he "crashed" a wedding at Trump's golf course in New Jersey. The photo appeared on Instagram and was subsequently reproduced by CNN, TMZ, and several other media companies. **Important factors:** The court rejected the theory that the use was transformative simply because the photographer took the photo for personal use, not news use. (*Otto v. Hearst Comm.*, 1:17-cv-04712-GHW-JLC (S.D.N.Y. 2018).)

- **Not a fair use.** A photographer created a portrait of a bond-trader for *Forbes* magazine. Subsequently, *Barron's*, a competitor of *Forbes*, reproduced the photo without permission. **Important factors:** The court did not consider the use by a competitor to be transformative: "[U]sing a photo for the precise reason it was created does not support a finding that the nature and purpose of the use were fair." (*Michael Grecco Productions, Inc. v. Valuewalk, LLC*, 345 F. Supp. 3d 482 (S.D.N.Y. 2018).)

- **Not a fair use.** A group of artists created *Oh, the Places You'll Boldly Go!* — a "remix" of the Dr. Seuss classic *Oh, the Places You'll Go!* and *Star Trek.* The estate of Dr. Seuss sued the artists, and a district court refused to dismiss the case, finding no fair use. **Important factors:** In a 1997 ruling *Dr. Seuss Enterprises v. Penguin Books*—by the Ninth Circuit Court of Appeals, the court found that a publisher could not simply use the vehicle of *The Cat in the Hat* to rehash the O.J. Simpson murder trial. (*Dr. Seuss Enterprises v. ComicMix LLC*, 256 F. Supp. 3d 1099 (Cal S.D. 2017).)

- **Not a fair use.** VHT, who licensed real estate photos to Zillow, claimed Zillow exceeded its license by displaying the images after the sale, and at a second website for home renovations. Zillow argued unsuccessfully that tagging the photos and making them searchable qualified as fair use. **Important factors:** The Court of Appeals ruled that making the images searchable did not fundamentally transform their original purpose—displaying the property. (*VHT, Inc. v. Zillow Group, Inc.*, No. 17-35587, -35588 (9th Cir. Mar. 15, 2019).)

- **Not a fair use.** A film festival reproduced a cityscape photo without authorization at its website. The photographer sued, and a lower court ruled that it was fair use, partially because of the good-faith actions of the film festival. The Fourth Circuit reversed the lower court and found no fair use. **Important factors:** The Fourth Circuit held that there was no precedent for the proposition that "good faith" helped a fair use argument. Because infringement is a strict liability defense, the state of the defendant's mind makes no difference to the issue of liability. (*Brammer v. Violent Hues*, No. 18-1763 (4th Cir. 2019).)

- **Not a fair use.** An online company, TVEyes, offered a video news clipping service that allowed professional subscribers to monitor news programs. After Fox News sued, a lower court ruled that the TV searching service was fair use, not unlike Google's book searching feature. On appeal, the Second Circuit reversed the fair use ruling. **Important factors:** The Second Circuit did not agree that the TVEyes searching system was analogous to Google book search, pointing out that the book search only provided snippets of text. Also, the court ruled that the fourth fair use factor—effect on the market—weighed heavily in favor of Fox. (*Fox News Network, LLC v. TVEyes, Inc.*, 883 F. 3d 169 (2nd Circuit, 2018).)

Internet/Software Cases

- **Fair use.** Oracle's *JAVA* SE program contains coding tools (Application Programming Interfaces or APIs) that allow the program to connect to, or be accessed by, various platforms. Google incorporated parts of the APIs into its code without permission. **Important factors:** Google's copying of the *JAVA* SE API included only those lines of code that were needed to allow programmers to work in a new and transformative program. (*GOOGLE LLC v. Oracle America, Inc.*, 141 S. Ct. 1183 (2021).)

- **Fair Use.** A writer published an opinion piece that included a screenshot of a controversial dating article and picture. **Important factors:** The use was transformative and unlikely to harm the market for the picture. (*Yang v. Mic Network, Inc.*, No. 18-7628, 2019 WL 4640263 (S.D.N.Y. 2019)

- **Fair use.** *The Washington Post* used three brief quotations from Church of Scientology texts posted on the Internet. **Important factors:** Only a small portion of the work was excerpted and the purpose was for news commentary. (*Religious Technology Center v. Pagliarina*, 908 F.Supp. 1353 (E.D. Va., 1995).)

- **Fair use.** Displaying a cached website in search engine results is a fair use and not an infringement. A "cache" refers to the temporary storage of an archival copy—often a copy of an image of part or all of a website. With cached technology it is possible to search webpages that the website owner has permanently removed from display. An attorney/author sued Google when the company's cached search results provided end users with copies of copyrighted works. The court held that Google did not infringe. **Important factors:** Google was considered passive in the activity—users chose whether to view the cached link. In addition, Google had an implied license to cache webpages since owners of websites have the ability to turn on or turn off the caching of their sites using tags and code. In this case, the attorney/author knew of this ability and failed to turn off caching, making his claim against Google appear to be manufactured. (*Field v. Google Inc.*, 412 F.Supp.2d 1106 (D. Nev., 2006).)

- **Fair use.** A real estate blog copied the first eight sentences from a newspaper article. **Important factors:** The blogger had copied only eight sentences and had not copied the "valuable" section (the commentary included with the article), and the court did not believe that the copying would affect the market for the article (the third and fourth fair use factors). (*Righthaven LLC v. Realty One Group, Inc.,* No. 2:10-cv-LRH-PAL, 2010 WL 4115413 (D. Nev., October 19, 2010).)

- **Fair use.** A nonprofit organization posted a newspaper article about police discrimination on its website. The newspaper assigned its right in the article to a third party, Righthaven, which filed the lawsuit. **Important factors:** The court's reasoning was influenced by the fact that Righthaven had acquired the copyright and was not in the newspaper business (it appeared to be in the "litigation business"). For that reason, the court reasoned that the nonprofit's use was transformative because its purpose was to educate the public about immigration issues, whereas Righthaven had no such purpose for the article (because it was not in the news business). And also, because Righthaven was not in the news business, it could show no harm from the defendant's dissemination of the article. (*Righthaven LLC v. JAMA,* No. 2:2010-cv-01322, 2011 WL 1541613 (D. Nev., April 22, 2011).)

- **Fair use.** A user of an online political forum posted a five-sentence excerpt from a newspaper article with a link back to the newspaper's website. **Important factors:** The use was quantitatively small and did not cause the newspaper financial harm. In addition, the online political forum was permitted to use the safe harbor provisions of the Digital Millennium Copyright Act. (*Righthaven LLC v. Democratic Underground,* 791 F. Supp. 2d 968 (D. Nev., 2011).)

- **Fair use.** Google made digital copies of millions of books submitted to it by libraries, scanned them and made them available to search through its Google Books service, so that users could—for free—identify relevant words, terms, or snippets from the scanned text. Google also allowed participating libraries to retain the copies they submitted. **Important factors:** Google's digitization was deemed a transformative use because it provided limited information about the books without allowing users more complete access to the works. (*Authors Guild v. Google, Inc.,* 804 F. 3d 202 (2d Cir. 2015).)

- **Not a fair use.** Several individuals without church permission posted entire publications of the Church of Scientology on the Internet. **Important factors:** Fair use is intended to permit the borrowing of portions of a work, not complete works. (*Religious Technology Center v. Lerma,* 40 U.S.P.Q.2d 1569 (E.D. Va., 1996).)

Consider Fair Use Before Requesting DMCA Takedown

In 2008, a district court ruled that prior to requesting a takedown notice, a copyright owner must consider the likelihood of a claim of fair use. In that case, Universal Music issued a takedown notice for a video of a child dancing to the song, "Let's Go Crazy," by Prince. The owner of the video claimed that since Universal didn't consider the issue of fair use, Universal could have not had a "good-faith belief" they were entitled to a takedown. Faced with this novel issue a district court agreed that the failure to consider fair use when sending a DMCA notice could give rise to a claim of failing to act in good faith. (*Lenz v. Universal Music Corp.*, 572 F.Supp.2d 1150 (N.D. Cal., 2008).)

Music Cases

- **Fair use.** A documentary about burlesque used eight seconds of a 190-second children's song. **Important factors:** The use was transformative and the amount used (though the heart of the composition) was not more than required. The court held that fair use does not obligate a defendant to use the shortest possible snippet to convey its message. (*Brown, et al. v. Netflix, Inc., et al.*, No. 20-2007 (2d Cir. 2020).)
- **Fair use.** A person running for political office used 15 seconds of his opponent's campaign song in a political ad. **Important factors:** A small portion of the song was used and the use was for purposes of political debate. (*Keep Thomson Governor Comm. v. Citizens for Gallen Comm.*, 457 F.Supp. 957 (D. N.H., 1978).)
- **Fair use.** A television film crew, covering an Italian festival in Manhattan, recorded a band playing a portion of a copyrighted song "Dove sta Zaza." The music was replayed during a news broadcast. **Important factors:** Only a portion of the song was used, it was incidental to the news event, and it did not result in any actual damage to the composer or to the market for the work. (*Italian Book Corp., v. American Broadcasting Co.*, 458 F.Supp. 65 (S.D.N.Y., 1978).)
- **Fair use.** The musician Drake sampled a 1982 jazz recording on which Jimmy Smith stated, "Jazz is the only real music that's gonna last/All that other bullshit is here today and gone tomorrow. But jazz was, is and always will be." Drake edited the sample so that on his recording,

it states, "Only real music's gonna last. All that other bullshit is here today and gone tomorrow." **Important factors:** In Smith's recording, his words spoke of the supremacy of jazz; Drake converted their meaning for a broader class of "real music." The court held that the use was transformative and therefore amounted to fair use. (*Estate of James Oscar Smith v. Cash Money Records, Inc.*, 253 F. Supp. 3d 737 (S.D.N.Y., 2017).)

- **Not a fair use.** Downloading songs is not a fair use. A woman was sued for copyright infringement for downloading 30 songs using peer-to-peer file sharing software. She argued that her activity was a fair use because she was downloading the songs to determine if she wanted to later buy them. **Important factors:** Since numerous sites, such as iTunes, permit listeners to sample and examine portions of songs without downloading, the court rejected this "sampling" defense. (*BMG Music v. Gonzalez*, 430 F.3d 888 (7th Cir. 2005).)

- **Not a fair use.** A defendant in a music file sharing case could not claim a fair use defense since he had failed to provide evidence that his copying of music files involved any transformative use (an essential element in proving fair use). **Important factors:** The court held that the defendant was confusing "'fairness' and 'fair use'—in the end, fair use is not a referendum on fairness in the abstract. ..." (*Capitol Records Inc. v. Alaujan*, 593 F. Supp. 2d 319 (D. Mass., 2009).)

Parody Cases

- **Fair use.** Comedians on the late-night television show *Saturday Night Live* parodied the song "I Love New York" using the words "I Love Sodom." Only the words "I Love" and four musical notes were taken from the original work. **Important factors:** The *Saturday Night Live* version of the jingle did not compete with or detract from the original song. (*Elsmere Music, Inc. v. National Broadcasting Co.*, 482 F.Supp. 741 (S.D.N.Y.), aff'd 632 F.2d 252 (2d Cir. 1980).)

- **Fair use.** The composers of the song "When Sunny Gets Blue" claimed that their song was infringed by "When Sonny Sniffs Glue," a 29-second parody that altered the original lyric line and borrowed six bars of the song. A court determined this parody was excused as a fair use. **Important factors:** Only 29 seconds of music were borrowed (not the complete song). (*Fisher v. Dees*, 794 F.2d 432 (9th Cir. 1986).) (Note: As a general rule, parodying more than a few lines of a song lyric is unlikely to be excused as a fair use. Performers such as Weird Al Yankovic, who earn a living by humorously modifying hit songs, seek permission of the songwriters before recording their parodies.)

- **Fair use.** The rap group 2 Live Crew borrowed the opening musical tag and the words (but not the melody) from the first line of the song "Pretty Woman" ("Oh, pretty woman, walking down the street"). The rest of the lyrics and the music were different. **Important factors:** The group's use was transformative and borrowed only a small portion of the original song. The 2 Live Crew version was essentially a different piece of music; the only similarity was a brief musical opening part and the opening line. (Note: The rap group had initially sought to pay for the right to use portions of the song but were rebuffed by the publisher, who did not want "Pretty Woman" used in a rap song.) (*Campbell v. Acuff-Rose Music*, 510 U.S. 569 (1994).)

- **Fair use.** A movie company used a photo of a naked pregnant woman onto which it superimposed the head of actor Leslie Nielsen. The photo was a parody using similar lighting and body positioning of a famous photograph taken by Annie Leibovitz of the actress Demi Moore for the cover of *Vanity Fair* magazine. **Important factors:** The movie company's use was transformative because it imitated the photographer's style for comic effect or ridicule. (*Leibovitz v. Paramount Pictures Corp.*, 137 F.3d 109 (2d Cir. N.Y. 1998).)

- **Fair use.** A pro-life video organization created two antiabortion videos by borrowing video clips from a pro-choice video and juxtaposing them with actual abortion footage. **Important factors:** The court characterized the pro-life videos as parodies despite the fact they did not meet the classic definition of a parody—something that humorously mimics or ridicules another's work. In a unique holding, the court held that a parody need not be humorous, but may merely comment on, or criticize the original. (*Northland Family Planning Clinic v. Center for Bio-Ethical Reform*, 868 F. Supp. 2d 962 (C.D. Cal., June 15, 2012).)

- **Not a fair use.** A proposed project—"Oh, the Places You'll Boldly Go!" —was intended as a mash-up of TV's *Star Trek* and a Dr. Seuss book, "Oh, the Places You'll Go!" **Important factors:** The proposed work was not a parody because it did not critique or comment on the Dr. Seuss work. Instead, the authors simply intended to make a humorous book by combining characters from *Star Trek* with layouts and illustrations lifted directly from the Dr. Seuss book. (*Dr. Seuss Enterprises v. ComicMix, LLC*, No. 19-55348 (9th Cir. 2020).)

- **Not a fair use.** An artist created a cover for a *New Yorker* magazine that presented a humorous view of geography through the eyes of a New York City resident. A movie company later advertised their film *Moscow on the Hudson* using a similar piece of artwork with similar elements. The artist sued and a court ruled that the movie company's poster was not a fair use. **Important factors:** Why is this case different from the previous case involving the Leslie Nielsen/Annie Leibovitz parody? In the *Leibovitz* case, the use was a true parody, characterized by a juxtaposition of imagery that actually commented on or criticized the original. The *Moscow on the Hudson* movie poster did not create a parody; it simply borrowed the *New Yorker*'s parody (the typical New York City resident's geographical viewpoint that New York City is the center of the world). (*Steinberg v. Columbia Pictures Industries, Inc.*, 663 F.Supp. 706 (S.D.N.Y., 1987).)

- **Not a fair use.** An author mimicked the style of a Dr. Seuss book while retelling the facts of the O.J. Simpson murder trial in *The Cat NOT in the Hat! A Parody by Dr. Juice*. The Ninth Circuit Court of Appeals determined that the book was a satire, not a parody, because the book did not poke fun at or ridicule Dr. Seuss. Instead, it merely used the Dr. Seuss characters and style to tell the story of the murder. **Important factors:** The author's work was nontransformative and commercial. (*Dr. Seuss Enterprises, L.P. v. Penguin Books USA, Inc.*, 109 F.3d 1394 (9th Cir. 1997).)

Disagreements Over Fair Use: When Are You Likely to Get Sued?

The difficulty in claiming fair use is that there is no way to guarantee that your use will qualify as fair. You may believe that your use qualifies—but, if the copyright owner disagrees, you may have to resolve the dispute in a courtroom. Even if you ultimately persuade the court that your use was in fact a fair use, the expense and time involved in litigation may well outweigh any benefit of using the material in the first place.

EXAMPLE: Sam quotes from four pages of a biography in his documentary film about poet Allen Ginsberg. He believes that his use qualifies as a fair use and he does not seek permission from Barbi, the author of the biography. Barbi does not think that Sam's copying is a fair use and wants to be paid for having her work used in his film. She sues Sam for copyright infringement, and Sam is forced to hire a lawyer to defend him in the lawsuit. Even though the court ultimately rules that Sam's use was a fair use, Sam's lawyer fees exceed $20,000, which far exceeds any profits he earned from the film.

Because there is a sizable gray area in which fair use may or may not apply, there is never a guarantee that your use will qualify as a fair use. The fair use doctrine has been described as a murky concept in which it is often difficult to separate the lawful from the unlawful. Two types of situations are especially likely to cause legal problems:

- Your work causes the owner of the original work to lose money. For example, you borrow portions of a biology text for use in a competing biology text.
- The copyright owner is offended by your use. For example, you satirize the original work and your satire contains sexually explicit references or other offensive material.

Remember, these criteria do not determine whether you will prevail in a fair use lawsuit—they simply indicate whether you are likely to trigger a lawsuit. When you use someone's work and deprive them of money or offend them, the chances of being sued increase.

Just as there are situations that are more likely to cause lawsuits, there are some situations that may lower the risk:

- You use a very small excerpt of a factual work, for example, one or two lines from a news report, for purposes of commentary, criticism, scholarship, research, or news reporting.
- You diligently tried to locate the copyright owner but were unsuccessful, and after analyzing the fair use factors, you became convinced that your use would qualify as a fair use.

If in doubt about your fair use assessment, consult with a copyright attorney. For information on dealing with attorneys, see Chapter 16, "Help Beyond This Book."

Getting Permission to Use Trademarks

T his chapter is about obtaining permission to use trademarks—words, symbols, or devices that identify specific products and services. It includes an explanation of when trademark permission is necessary, how to find a trademark owner, and how to license a trademark for commercial purposes.

Trademark rights can overlap with copyright. For example, a fictional character such as Superman can be protected by both trademark and copyright laws. This chapter provides some guidance in sorting out the differences.

At the end of the chapter, you'll find an agreement for licensing a trademark for merchandise purposes. Although there are a few minor differences, you will notice that this agreement is similar to the merchandise agreement in Chapter 11.

CAUTION

Even if your use is legally permissible, an aggressive trademark owner might file a lawsuit to intimidate you and get you to stop using the mark. Sometimes you may be legally entitled to use a trademark without permission on the grounds of free speech. But defending your right to free speech can be expensive, easily costing tens of thousands of dollars. The chances of a legal confrontation increase when you use a famous trademark without permission. Review the rules in this chapter carefully and weigh the benefits against the potential risks before making unauthorized uses of famous trademarks. Keep in mind that trademark owners are notoriously protective of their business interests and often use trademark law as a means to bully competitors and critics.

Trademark 101

This section provides an overview of trademark basics.

RESOURCE

For more trademark information, consult *Trademark: Legal Care for Your Business & Product Name,* by Stephen Fishman (Nolo).

What Is a Trademark?

A trademark is any word, symbol, or device that identifies and distinguishes a product or service. For example, the word "McDonalds," the distinctive yellow arches, and the Ronald McDonald character are all trademarks of the McDonald's company.

Trademarks used to identify services are also known as service marks. For example, the service mark "UPS" represents a company that provides package delivery services; the mark "U2" identifies a band that provides music services. Service marks have the same legal rights and follow the same rules as trademarks. For this reason, the term "trademark," or sometimes simply "mark," is often used when discussing either trademarks or service marks.

Most trademarks, such as brand names, slogans, and logos, are easy to spot because the trademark owner displays them in a distinct manner, often using stylized lettering. A trademark may also be explicitly identified with the symbols ®, TM, or SM. While most trademarks are easily identifiable, some are more difficult to discern, particularly trade dress, product configurations, colors, and other nontraditional trademarks. The next section discusses the different kinds of trademarks in more depth.

Types of Trademarks

There are many different types of trademarks, including:

- **Brand names.** The most common form of trademark is a brand name—for example, Sweet 'N Low or FedEx. Brand names are usually words, although they can be a combination of words, letters, and numbers, such as 7-Up.
- **Slogans.** A combination of words used as a slogan qualifies as a trademark—for example, "Just do it." for Nike products.
- **Logos.** A graphic image or symbol may serve as a trademark—for example, the open-banded cross used by Chevrolet.
- **Sounds.** A sound can function as a trademark—for example, the roaring lion sound used by MGM.
- **Trade dress.** Any distinctive combination of elements may serve as a trademark—for example, the pale blue shade that signifies goods from Tiffany's.

> ### Websites and Trade Dress
>
> A website using a distinctive combination of colors, graphic borders, and functionality can stop a competitor from imitating this combination of trade dress elements under trademark law. Although website designers are free to incorporate animations, *Java* applets, and other eye-catching features, the chances of litigation increase if you copy a competitor's distinctive combination of website elements such that consumers confuse the two websites.

- **Product configurations.** Distinctive product packaging that is primarily nonfunctional is protected as a trademark—for example, the shape of the Mrs. Butterworth's syrup bottle (resembling a female cook).
- **Fictional characters.** Trademark law protects a fictional character used to sell a product or service.

EXAMPLE 1: The Pebble Beach Company incorporated a distinctive Cypress tree growing on its golf course into an abstract design. This graphic image became a logo distinguishing the Pebble Beach Company's golf services and products from other golf courses. The public is free to photograph the tree, and other golf courses can grow cypress trees, but only the Pebble Beach Company can use this distinctive tree image to identify its golfing services and goods.

EXAMPLE 2: A restaurant owner named his seafood eatery The Krusty Krab, a name borrowed from the fictitious establishment on the TV show *Spongebob SquarePants*. Viacom, the owner of the TV show, claimed that the fictitious restaurant was a central element of its show and that it was conceivable that the company could someday license the name for food establishments. The Court of Appeals agreed that the restaurant's use would infringe Viacom's trademarks.

Trademark Rights

Trademark protection is granted to the first company to use a particular trademark in the marketplace. Trademark rights are created only when the mark is actually used in commerce—that is, in an effort to sell a product or service. Trademark protection lasts for as long as a business continuously uses a trademark to help sell goods or services. Many trademarks have been protected for over a century.

On rare occasions, however, trademark rights end if the public believes that the trademark is a generic term. For example, the terms "aspirin" and "escalator" were trademarks that lost protection once the public used the term to describe all versions of these products, not one manufacturer's version. Nowadays, companies such as Kimberly-Clark (manufacturer of Kleenex) and Dow Chemical (manufacturer of Styrofoam) oppose this loss of trademark rights (known as "genericide") by educating the public. For example, a journalist who mistakenly writes "styrofoam cup" may receive an email from Dow indicating that its trademarked Styrofoam products are not used in drinking cups (they are used primarily in boat and house insulation). Until 2017, it was also assumed that using a trademark as a verb (known as "brandverbing") was also a decisive indicator of genericide. But in a case involving Google, a federal appeals court ruled that it was a mistaken assumption that verb use ("I Googled that") by a majority of the public automatically converted the mark to generic. What matters is whether, to the relevant public, the primary significance of the word "google" was as a mark that identifies the Google search engine in particular.

Trademark Registration

A trademark owner can register the mark with the federal or state government. Registration is not required to obtain trademark protection, but it strengthens and broadens your rights, which is especially important if someone infringes your trademark.

The United States Patent and Trademark Office (PTO) administers federal registrations. The PTO can be accessed on the Web at www.uspto.gov. State registrations are handled by the secretary of state offices of the 50 states. For state-by-state information, see www.uspto.gov/trademarks/basics/state-trademark-information-links.

Trademark Symbols

Typically, the symbols ®, TM, or SM are used along with trademarks—for example, "NIKE®." The symbol ® indicates that a trademark has been registered at the PTO. It is illegal to use the ® symbol if the trademark in question has not been registered with the PTO. There is no legal requirement that the ® be used, but the failure to use it may limit the amount of damages that the trademark owner can recover in an infringement lawsuit. If the trademark hasn't been registered, the owner can use the TM symbol. Similarly, the owner can use the SM symbol for service marks that have not been registered. The TM and SM have no legal significance other than to indicate that the owner is claiming trademark rights.

Violations of Trademark Owners' Rights

Trademark owners' rights can be violated in two ways: by direct infringement and by dilution.

Direct Infringement

Infringement occurs when one company uses another company's trademark (or a substantially similar mark) in a manner that is likely to confuse consumers into believing that there is some connection, affiliation, or sponsorship between the two companies. Usually this occurs when a trademark is used on similar goods—for example a counterfeit Rolex watch. The counterfeiter is relying on the unauthorized Rolex trademark to confuse consumers into believing that the watch came from the Rolex company. Subtler forms of consumer confusion occur when companies use similar but nonidentical marks or use similar marks on related but nonidentical products or services.

> EXAMPLE: A comic book store uses the name "The Batcave" without authorization. Because "Batcave" is a trademark of DC Comics, consumers may believe that DC Comics endorses or is connected with the store. On this basis, the owners of the "Batcave" trademark can bring a trademark infringement lawsuit against the comic book store to stop the unauthorized use.

Trademark Dilution

Trademark dilution occurs when the integrity of a trademark is "muddied" by an unwanted commercial association, either by a vulgar or insulting affiliation (tarnishment) or by a connection with a lesser product (blurring):

- **Tarnishment.** A company may tarnish the image of a famous trademark if it uses the trademark to promote a product or service that may be considered offensive. For example, if an adult website named itself "Candyland," its use might tarnish the image of the trademark "Candyland" used on the children's game.
- **Blurring.** Normally, the rules of trademark prohibit someone from using a trademark commercially that's owned by someone else if the use is likely to cause customer confusion. However, sometimes even if there's little likelihood of customer confusion, one company can stop another company that uses its famous trademark commercially in a manner that blurs the two companies in the customers' minds. For example, say a toilet paper maker named its product "Rolls-Royce Toilet Paper." Even though most people wouldn't think that Rolls-Royce toilet paper was produced by the famous luxury car maker, the Rolls-Royce car company might pursue the toilet paper maker for diluting its trademark.

When Congress passed the Trademark Dilution Revision Act of 2006, it did so in response to a Supreme Court ruling involving Victoria's Secret. (*Moseley v. Secret Catalogue, Inc.*, 537 U.S. 418 (2003).) The federal act enabled the owner of a famous trademark to obtain an injunction for dilution without having to demonstrate actual economic harm (as the Supreme Court had previously ruled).

The act also redefines famous marks, tarnishment, and blurring. Most important for our purposes is that it makes it official that certain activities are *not* dilution including: (1) any fair use of a famous mark by another person other than as a designation of source for the person's own goods or services, including for advertising or promotion that permits consumers to compare goods or services, or identifying and parodying, criticizing, or commenting upon the famous mark owner or the owner's goods or services; (2) all forms of news reporting and news commentary; and (3) any noncommercial use of a trademark.

Altering a Trademark

In addition to blurring and dilution, altering a trademark in a comparative advertisement has also been found to violate a trademark owner's rights. In a television advertisement, a competitor of the farm equipment company John Deere animated the John Deere "deer" logo and appeared to make it run from the competition. The competitor was found liable for trademark dilution. (*Deere & Company v. MTD Prods. Inc.*, 34 U.S.P.Q. 1706 (S.D.N.Y. 1995).) Based on this ruling, it would be unwise to modify another company's trademark unless it can be justified under free speech or parody rules.

Disparagement and Defamation

Other practices for which you can be sued by a trademark owner are disparagement and defamation. Disparagement is making false statements that interfere with a company's business relations. Defamation is making false statements that injure a business's reputation. Disparagement affects a company's ability to do business; defamation affects the manner in which the public perceives the company's trademarked products.

Unlike infringement and dilution, defamation and disparagement do not have to occur in a commercial context. For example, using a trademark in a newspaper article, if based on false statements, can result in a claim of disparagement or defamation. Disparagement and defamation are not claims under trademark law; they fall into a broad category of laws known as "business torts." For more information on basic defamation principles, see Chapter 12.

When You Need Permission to Use a Trademark

This section describes when permission is required for various types of trademark uses. In certain situations, you can use a trademark without obtaining the owner's permission. In others, you'll need to do a bit more analysis before using a trademark without an okay from the owner. Whether a given use is legally okay depends on a number of factual issues that can be tricky to figure out.

Below we discuss the various ways that trademarks are typically used and whether permission is required for each type of use. Keep in mind, however, that even if you're legally entitled to use a trademark, that doesn't mean that the trademark owner will always be agreeable. If you're forced into court to prove that your use is allowed by law, in a sense you've already lost the battle. Make sure your use is, in fact, within the bounds of the law, and be aware of the trademark owner's likely response. You'll need to carefully weigh the benefits of using the trademark if you suspect the owner will fight you with legal action.

Also remember that what might be permitted under trademark law might not be permitted under copyright law. Therefore, if the trademark contains some copyrightable elements, analyze your use under both trademark and copyright rules.

Informational Uses

Informational (or "editorial") uses of a trademark do not require permission. These are uses that inform, educate, or express opinions protected under the First Amendment of the United States Constitution—freedom of speech and of the press. For example, permission is not required to use the Chevrolet logo in an article describing Chevrolet trucks, even if the article is critical of the company. Similarly, if you are making a documentary film on the history of American trucks, you do not need permission to include the Chevrolet logo. However, the use of the logo must have some relevance to the work. For example, it would not be wise to publish an article critical of overseas auto manufacturing practices and include the Chevrolet logo unless Chevrolet were mentioned in the article.

Dear Rich: **You Can See Trademarks in My Film: Is That Okay?**

I just got done shooting the major portion of my new short film Quick Shop, *which takes place in a convenience store/meat market. There are several shots where logos and brand names are fairly apparent, and I'm wondering if I should be worried. Take this shot for instance. You can distinctly see most of the Marlboro name and logo in the back. Other shots include images of Shurfine, Martin's Potato Chips, and possibly a Pepsi logo. I did my best to cover up really obvious brand names and logos, but I guess I missed a couple. So am I going to run into any problems when I go to submit to film festivals, or is something like this okay? I mean, it's not like I was going out of my way to include this stuff. I'm pretty sure I can fuzz out these images, but I'd rather not.*

We'd rather you didn't fuzz them out either. As a general rule, there's nothing wrong with including trademarks in a documentary or fictional film. In both cases, your free speech rights should trump someone else's trademark rights. That was the case when Caterpillar sued Walt Disney over use of the tractors and trademarks in the movie *George of the Jungle 2*. (Alas, no Brendan Fraser in this direct-to-video sequel!) A district court ruled there was no trademark confusion or trademark dilution (Caterpillar might have been displeased by the fact that the bad guys in the film used Caterpillar tractors). By the way, the amazing 2010 Academy Award short, *Logorama*, used over 3,000 trademarks without permission. We should also mention, there's a case in which the makers of a film could not use the title *Dairy Queen* under various trademark theories (though we wonder about the logic of that case).

Even though the law is likely to be on your side, that doesn't mean you won't run into problems. Distributors may require trademark clearance regardless of our legal explanation, and the same may be true for networks, festivals, or if the film is purchased. (Hopefully, if the film is sold, you'll be able to afford a clearance expert to help you.) At the same time, a company may feel that its trademark is being exploited for an improper association and fire off a cease and desist letter. Even though chances are good that you would eventually prevail in court, you may not be capable of overcoming the bullying tactics (and be forced into fuzzing your signage). By the way, you can further lower your risks of getting a "cease and desist" (C&D) letter by avoiding any implication that the other company endorses or is associated with your film—that is, by not using any other company's trademarks in your film's advertising, posters, and possibly even the trailers.

Dear Rich:

Can We Name Our Non-*Superman* Movie After the *Superman* Villain?

I'm stumped here. I'm doing a title search for a client and their film is the name of a superhero villain in the Superman *series and has nothing to do with this superhero. Is this kosher?*

We can't tell you whether you will violate Jewish dietary laws, but we can tell you that you may trigger a battle over intellectual property and free speech laws. Most likely your use will be permitted under First Amendment grounds—assuming that consumers are not likely to associate your film with the *Superman* franchise. If *Superman*'s owners believe consumers will be confused or that their trademark will be diluted—in other words, you're causing their franchise to lose value—they'll sue. (*Superman*'s legal posse is not shy about litigating; they have gone after everything from reversionary rights to kryptonite.) These battles between First Amendment and trademark rights can be expensive. Mattel fought to keep Barbie's name out of a pop song (and lost) and Dairy Queen battled to keep the name out of the title of a movie about beauty queens (and won). Even though the law might favor your right to use the name, your film's insurers and backers may not want to risk the distraction of a legal battle.

Whether to Use Trademark Symbols

When using a trademark in text for informational purposes, it is not necessary to include the ®, TM, or SM symbols. However, it is good trademark etiquette to distinguish a trademark by capitalizing or italicizing it—for example, "The house was constructed with Styrofoam insulation," or "He used a NordicTrak exercise machine."

Comparative Advertising

It's permissible to use a trademark when making accurate comparative product statements in advertisements. However, since comparative advertisements tend to provoke trademark owners into legal action, an attorney knowledgeable in trademark or business law should review the advertisement before publication. Modification of another company's trademark may result in a claim of dilution.

Commercial Uses

Commercial uses of a trademark include advertising, promotion, or marketing, and require permission (except for cases of comparative advertising as explained in the previous section). Commercial uses include business-sponsored promotional activities (such as public presentations), informational advertisements (known as "advertorials"), and merchandise.

> EXAMPLE: A sportswear company distributes a catalog which includes models drinking Perrier water. The use of the Perrier logo would be considered a commercial use, so the sportswear company should obtain permission.

Include Trademark Symbols for Commercial Uses

When using a trademark in a commercial context, such as an advertisement, product manual, or in connection with the sale of a product or service, include the ®, TM, or SM symbols adjacent to the trademark—for example, "Adobe®" or "InDesign®." Remember, the ® symbol should only be used if the trademark is federally registered. This may be evident from the trademark owner's use, or you can determine registration status by researching the federal trademark database. Also, include a statement such as, "Adobe and *InDesign* are registered trademarks of the Adobe Corporation." Place the statement on the index page of a website, the copyright page of a publication, or at the end of a movie.

Dear Rich: No Soup: Using *Seinfeld* in Ads

I work for a law firm that advertises on BART (Bay Area Rapid Transit). We're preparing some new ads and we want to use the phrase NO SOUP FOR YOU (which you may recognize from a series of Seinfeld episodes). Our research shows that there are no live registrations at the USPTO for the phrase. We found a domain name using the phrase, "Nosoupforyou.com," which appears to be a Gainesville, Florida, local restaurant Web-guide. And according to the Dear Rich blog, copyright laws disfavor protection for short phrases. Are we correct to conclude that we're safe to use this phrase in our ads as long as we don't use it in connection with Seinfeld images?

Yes, absent any other *Seinfeld* connection in the ad, you should be good to go. Nobody appears to be exploiting "No Soup for You," as a trademark for legal services (and it's hard to imagine that anyone would). As you indicated, applications were made for restaurant services but both applicants never filed a statement of use indicating that they were actually using the mark. You are correct as to short phrase protection as well. It's possible that the *Seinfeld* creators could object under principles of unfair competition, arguing that your use confuses consumers as to *Seinfeld*'s association with the law firm—a long shot that seems extremely unlikely. P.S. A few months after this question was posted at our blog, the Dear Rich Staff saw the advertisement on a BART train.

Parodies: Laughing All the Way to Court

A trademark parody occurs when someone imitates a trademark in a manner that pokes fun at the mark. A newspaper called *The San Francisco Chomical*, meant to poke fun at *The San Francisco Chronicle*, is an example of a parody. Chapter 9, on dealing with fair use of copyrighted materials, provided some general rules as to when parodies are permissible and when they infringe copyright. Below are some specific rules for trademark parodies.

Keep in mind the general rule that applies to both types of parodies: Offensive parodies often trigger lawsuits. Therefore, weigh the legal consequences carefully before proceeding.

Generally speaking, a trademark parody is less likely to run into problems if it:

- **Doesn't compete.** The use of the parody product does not directly compete with the trademark product.
- **Doesn't confuse.** The parody does not confuse consumers; they get the joke and do not believe the parody product comes from the same source as the trademarked goods.
- **Does parody.** Not all humorous uses are parodies. To avoid trouble, the use should specifically poke fun at the trademark.

Below are some court cases that may provide some context:

- **Allowable trademark parody.** A company sold tote bags that read "My other bag is a Louis Vuitton" (and references to other high-end fashion designers). Louis Vuitton sued, claiming the tote bags diluted the

Vuitton mark. The Second Circuit upheld the summary judgment against Louis Vuitton because the tote bags, though they mimicked LV, were clearly "a joke on LV's luxury image." (*Louis Vuitton Malletier, S.A v. My Other Bag, Inc.* 674 F. App'x 16, 2016 WL 7436489 (2d Cir. 2016).)

- **Allowable trademark parody.** A college student sold T-shirts at Myrtle Beach depicting a red, white, and blue beer can with the phrase, "This Beach is for You." Anheuser-Busch, the owners of the Budweiser trademark, filed a lawsuit, seized all of the T-shirts, and raided the college student's home and his mother's business. A jury determined that the T-shirts were a parody, but the lower court judge overturned the jury verdict and ruled for Anheuser-Busch. An appeals court reversed the ruling again and ruled that the use was a parody. Seven years and several lawsuits later, the parties reached a settlement in which Anheuser-Busch granted a license for sales of the T-shirt. (*Anheuser-Busch, Inc. v. L & L Wings, Inc.*, 962 F.2d 316 (4th Cir.), cert. denied, 113 S.Ct. 206 (1992).)

- **Allowable trademark parody.** During a half-time show, the San Diego Chicken mascot initiated a fistfight with Barney, the once-popular purple dinosaur. A court held that the use of the Barney trademark was a permissible parody because the aggressive manner in which Barney behaved once engaged in battle was not likely to cause consumer confusion. (*Lyons Partnership L.P. v. Giannoulas*, 14 F.Supp.2d 947 (N.D. Texas).)

- **Allowable trademark parody.** The video game, "Grand Theft Auto: San Andreas" included a parody of the East Los Angeles strip club, "The Play Pen," (referred to as the "Pig Pen" in the game). The court permitted the parody under First Amendment principles, noting that artistic use of a mark is permitted when (1) the use has artistic relevance to the work at issue (the video game) and (2) it doesn't explicitly mislead consumers as to the source of the mark or the work—a test adopted by the Ninth Circuit in *Mattel v. Walking Mountain*. (Note: the Ninth Circuit rejected the defense of nominative trademark fair use—when someone uses a mark to describe the product for purposes of comparison and criticism—because the video game did not describe or comment on the "Play Pen" mark.) (*E.S.S. Entertainment 2000, Inc. v. Rock Star Videos, Inc.*, 547 F.3d 1095 (9th Cir. 2008).)

- **Not allowable as trademark parody.** Nike successfully opposed registration of the phrase, "Just Jesu It" for athletic apparel. The Trademark Trial and Appeal Board (TTAB) found the mark both likely to confuse consumers and likely to dilute Nike's "Just Do It." trademark. A parody defense was rejected: A parody defense is unavailable when the goods are the same and the marks are confusingly similar. (*Nike, Inc. v. Maher,* 100 U.S.P.Q.2d 1018 (TTAB 2011).)

- **Not an allowable trademark parody.** A gaudy, '60s-style nightclub in Houston used the trademark "The Velvet Elvis" and, after being sued by the owner of the Elvis trademark, claimed that the club's name was an Elvis parody. A court disagreed, pointing out that the intent of the club's name and decor was to parody the Las Vegas lounge scene and the velvet painting craze, not to parody Elvis. (*Elvis Presley Enterprises v. Capece,* 141 F.3d 188 (5th Cir. 1998).)

Conflicting case law and the discretionary power of judges make it difficult to predict the outcome of a lawsuit based on trademark parody. It is also difficult to predict when a company will take action against a parodist. Some companies, like Anheuser-Busch, prefer to fight to the end, while others believe that chasing parodists generates negative publicity and prefer to let the parody run its course.

Dear Rich:

Terrible Towel Satire? Uh... Not Really

We would like to spoof the Pittsburgh Steelers' "Terrible Towel" with a "We ARE Terrible Towel" for the Detroit Lions. It would be white with no logos. Satires can't infringe copyright, can they? Thoughts?

If you're making one towel to hold up for the TV cameras, you're probably okay. But if you're thinking of making more than one, the Dear Rich Staff would advise against it. First of all—it's not a copyright issue, as copyright doesn't protect short phrases or individual words.

It's a trademark issue. The term "Terrible Towel" was created by Pittsburgh sportscaster Myron Cope, who acquired trademark rights and then assigned the registered trademark to a charity, the Allegheny Valley School, an institution for the disabled. Considering that licensing revenues from the towel have earned the school over $3 million, the school and the Steelers (who acknowledge that the towel is one of the most popular merchandise concepts in football history) both have a vested interest in preventing others from making and selling Terrible

Towels. It could infringe and dilute a world-famous mark (and one that is carried to the far corners of the earth).

Does satire matter? We must clarify one thing: You stated that satires can't infringe copyrights. That's not correct. A parody may be excused as a fair use under some circumstances. The same is not always true for satires. In any case, your use does not seem to qualify as either a satire or a parody, does it? Bottom line: Sales and distribution of your towel will likely trigger a cease and desist letter.

Using a Trademark Containing Copyrightable Elements

Use of a trademark containing a copyrightable image such as a character, photograph, or illustration may be prohibited under copyright law even if permitted under trademark law. Examples of copyrightable trademarks include:

- animated logos such as the "Look Inside" Intel logo
- logos containing artwork or photos, such as the floral image in the Herbal Essences logo, and
- characters such as Mr. Peanut or Betty Crocker.

Characters are discussed in the next section.

Before proceeding with the unauthorized use of a trademark containing copyrightable elements, compare trademark and copyright rules to minimize potential liability. Certain elements such as fonts, simple geometric shapes, individual words, and short phrases are not protected under copyright law (see Chapter 8).

Using Characters

As discussed in previous chapters on artwork and photographs, literary and pictorial characters such as Katniss Everdeen and Fred Flintstone are protected under copyright law. In addition, these characters may be protected under trademark law, which protects a wide range of text and images that are used to sell products or services. Trademarked characters can be either graphic (for example, Snoopy or Spiderman) or human (for example, Holly Golightly or James Bond). Characters may have an association with a specific product or service, such as Mr. Clean and home cleaning products. Or, a character may be used to sell a variety of merchandise—such as the Teenage Mutant Ninja Turtle characters that were used to sell breakfast cereal, T-shirts, and other assorted merchandise.

Because characters often tell stories and sell products simultaneously, the difference between the two forms of legal protection is often indistinct. If this overlap seems confusing, take solace in the fact that it has often confounded attorneys and the courts. In the real world, this overlap is sometimes an academic issue, since the owner of the fictional character usually controls both copyright and trademark rights. Therefore, the company will tailor your license to permit all appropriate uses. If there are a number of owners involved, however, obtaining permission to use the character may become somewhat trickier.

The section below offers guidance on how to deal with using various types of characters, particularly when trademark and copyright rules may overlap.

Graphic Character; Informational Use

Trademark permission is not required to reproduce a graphic character, such as Woody Woodpecker, for informational purposes. Copyright authorization, on the other hand, is required. Chapter 4, "Getting Permission to Use Artwork," provides information on getting permission to use cartoon and comic characters. Keep in mind that copyright permission is not required if the character is in the public domain or if the reproduction qualifies as a fair use. For example, the use of Mickey Mouse (a character owned by the Disney Corporation) in a news story qualifies as a fair use, but the use of Mickey Mouse in a trivia book about Disney characters requires permission. See Chapter 9 for detailed information on whether a use of copyrighted material qualifies as fair use.

Human Character; Informational Use

Using a photograph of a human character, such as Captain Kirk, for an informational use, such as in a news story, does not require trademark permission. However, it does require copyright authorization from the owner of the photograph (usually an entertainment production company). Chapter 3, "Getting Permission to Use Photographs," explains how to locate production companies. Permission is not required from the actor portraying the character.

Graphic Character; Commercial Use

Trademark permission is required for the commercial use of a graphic character in an advertisement or on merchandise. For example, reproducing the Road Runner character in an advertisement for an auto race would require permission from the owners of Road Runner. Follow the rules in this chapter. As we mentioned earlier, the trademark owner almost always controls the copyright as well and will tailor the license to permit both uses.

Human Character; Commercial Use

Trademark permission is required to reproduce an image of a human character, such as James Bond, for commercial uses. Permission must also be obtained from the person portraying the character. Chapter 12, "Releases," provides model releases that you can use to obtain permission from actors who portray fictional characters. Failure to obtain permission from the human who portrays the character may prove expensive. For example, a federal court permitted two actors from the TV show *Cheers* to sue a company that sold robots based on their characters without obtaining their permission. The case eventually settled. (*Wendt v. Host Int'l, Inc.*, 125 F.3d 806 (9th Cir. 1997).) Based on the *Cheers* litigation, a company that uses fictional characters personified by human actors for a commercial purpose should obtain permission from the actors or risk a lawsuit.

Using a Trademark in a Title

You should also obtain permission to use a trademark on the cover of a book, in the title of a film or song, or in advertising for an informational work. The following cases illustrate that failure to obtain such permission can easily result in a lawsuit:

- The owner of the Godzilla trademark successfully stopped a book publisher from selling a film-study book entitled *Godzilla*. The court ruled that the use of the name without a prominent disclaimer amounted to a trademark infringement. (*Toho Inc. v. William Morrow and Co.*, 33 F.Supp.2d 1206 (C.D. Cal., 1998).)

- A film company producing a movie satirizing Minnesota beauty queens was prohibited from using the title *Dairy Queen* even though no Dairy Queens or Dairy Queen trademarks were seen in the film. The court ruled that consumers would be confused as to the source of the film and would believe that the owner of the Dairy Queen trademark had permitted the use. (*American Dairy Queen Corp. v. New Line Productions Inc.*, 35 F.Supp.2d 727 (Minn. 1998).)
- The makers of Tron fuses sued the makers of the film *Tron,* not over the use of the name in the film, but over use of the name on merchandise related to the film—video games and telephones, two products that might cause confusion among consumers of Tron fuses. The case was ultimately settled. (*McGraw-Edison Co. v. Walt Disney Productions*, 787 F.2d 1163 (7th Cir. 1985).)

Using a Trademark as a Character Name

You don't need permission to name a fictional character in a story or movie after a trademark—for example, naming a character Nerf or Advil. However, this practice is likely to provoke the trademark owner if the character is unsavory or is used to sell merchandise. In one case, Hormel, the makers of Spam, sued the makers of a Muppet movie because a pig character was named Sp'am. The court ruled against Hormel, noting that it did not tarnish Spam's trademark to be associated with a pig, and that Spam had been so maligned in popular culture that the association with the film character, a helpful boar who befriends Muppet characters, could not possibly tarnish the trademark. (*Hormel Foods Corp. v. Jim Henson Productions Inc.*, 73 F.3d 497 (2d Cir. 1996).)

Trademark Practices: Books, Movies, Songs, and Websites

How to acquire trademark permissions differs within various media industries. Some of these rules are provided below. Often, permission is not required by law, so a court will permit an unauthorized use. However, since book publishers, software companies, Internet providers, and movie companies do not want to risk a lawsuit, they often seek permission anyway. Some short model permission forms are provided.

Book Publishing

Although publishers are not usually required to obtain permission for informational uses of trademarks, many seek authorization anyway. Note that authorization is required to use a trademark in a book published as a means of promoting a product or service. For example, a computer company producing a manual on desktop publishing should obtain permission to reproduce trademarks from software companies whose products are mentioned in the manual.

An example of a simple permission statement is provided below.

FORM
You can download this form (and all other forms in this book) from Nolo.com; for details, see the appendix.

Basic Permission to Use a Trademark in a Book or Magazine

_____ ("Owner") is the owner of rights in the trademark _____ (the "Trademark"). Owner grants permission to reproduce the Trademark in the format indicated below in the publication _____ and in any subsequent editions or derivative versions in any media. Any goodwill associated with the Trademark vests in Owner.

Owner Name: _____

Signature: _____

Date: _____

[Insert sample of Trademark]

The Film Industry

Most film, video, and television production companies obtain permission for the use of trademarks that appear in their movies and videos. This includes trademarks on signs in public locations. Below is a sample permission agreement for use of a trademark in a film, television show, or video.

Companies with trademarks that are eager to see their products in films will enter into special permission agreements known as "product placement agreements." Under these agreements, the companies that own the trademarks may provide free products, services, or cross-promotions. For example, America Online allowed use of its trademarks, including the phrase "You've Got Mail," in the film of the same name. Clearance companies in Los Angeles and New York review scripts and prepare clearance reports. For further information regarding film clearance, see *Clearance & Copyright*, by Michael C. Donaldson (Silman-James Press).

FORM
You can download this form (and all other forms in this book) from Nolo.com; for details, see the appendix.

Basic Permission to Use a Trademark in a Movie

_____ ("Owner") is the owner of rights in the trademark _____ (the "Trademark"). Owner grants permission to reproduce the Trademark in the format indicated below in all versions of the film _____
(the "Film") and any derivative versions in any media. Any goodwill associated with the Trademark vests in Owner.

Owner Name: _____

Signature: _____

Date: _____

[Insert sample of Trademark]

Artwork and Photography

Artwork and photographs sometimes include trademarks. Permission from the trademark owner is required if the art or photograph is created and reproduced for commercial purposes, such as in advertising or on merchandise. For example, a company that sold trading cards of collectible cars was prohibited from reproducing Chrysler trademarks and trade dress because Chrysler licensed similar collectible products. (*Chrysler Corp. v. Newfield Publications Inc.*, 880 F.Supp. 504 (E.D. Mich., 1995).)

A photograph that portrays a trademark in a morally offensive manner is liable to trigger a trademark dispute. For example, lawsuits were filed over lewd photos of the Pillsbury Doughboy and of photos showing the Barbie and Ken dolls in compromising positions. Below is a sample permission form for use of a trademark in artwork.

FORM

You can download this form (and all other forms in this book) from Nolo.com; for details, see the appendix.

Basic Permission to Use a Trademark in a Photograph or Artwork

_____ ("Owner") is the owner of rights in the trademark _____ (the "Trademark"). Owner grants permission to reproduce the Trademark in the format indicated below in all versions of the artwork _____ (the "Artwork") and any derivative versions in any media. Any goodwill associated with the Trademark vests in Owner.

Owner Name: _____

Signature: _____

Date: _____

[*Insert sample of Trademark*]

The Internet

Using a word trademark as a link on a website is permitted without authorization. For example, no authorization is needed to link to the General Motors website by using the text link "General Motors." However, use of another company's trademark as a graphic or visual link requires authorization. Chapter 6, "Website Permissions," provides a linking agreement and discusses additional website issues. Chapter 12, "Releases," explains how to figure out whether a site is primarily informational or commercial. For information about domain name and related trademark uses, review Chapter 16, "Help Beyond This Book."

The Music Industry

The unauthorized use of a trademark in a song title or album title may be permitted under First Amendment principles, provided that the title does not confuse or dilute the mark. Regardless of the law, however, this type of use may provoke a trademark dispute. For example, toymaker Mattel Inc. sued MCA Records over a song entitled "Barbie Girl" by the Danish pop group Aqua. A federal court ruled in favor of the record company based upon First Amendment issues and refused to halt the sale of the song. (*Mattel, Inc. v. MCA Records, Inc.*, 28 F.Supp.2d 1120 (C.D. Cal., 1998).) The owner of the Dr. Feelgood trademark, used primarily on hospital scrubs, sued the band Mötley Crüe over its song by the same name. In that case, the band prevailed by demonstrating there was no customer confusion. (*Reeves v. Mötley Crüe Inc.*, 21 U.S.P.Q.2d (BNA) 1587, (N.D. Ala., 1991).)

Using a Trademark in Connection With an Award

A business receiving an award or a favorable review from an organization needs authorization to use the organization's trademark. For example, if a software company received an award from a computer magazine called *MegaSoft*, the software company could state it received an award from *MegaSoft*, but would have to obtain permission in order to use the magazine's graphic awards trademark in an advertisement.

Generally, companies that provide ratings or create awards have guidelines for how their trademarks can be used in advertising. For example, one computer magazine requires that a company using the magazine's trademarks in stating its award include the date it issued the award and the version of the software to which it gave the award. Some consumer companies do not permit the use of their trademarks for other companies' products regardless of the rating, review, or award.

The person at a publication who grants trademark permission is usually in the company's business department. Larger companies have departments for managing trademark rights and permission.

Using a Certification Mark

Certain trademarks certify that a product or service meets a certain standard. For example, the "CCOF" logo guarantees that produce is from a California Certified Organic Farm. These certification marks may also establish standards for the materials used in, the accuracy of, source of labor for, or region of origin of a product.

If your company or business wants to qualify to use a certification mark, you must contact the certification mark owner and obtain the standards. For example, if you were a potato farmer in Idaho who wanted to use the "Idaho Potatoes" certification mark, you would contact the mark owner to learn the standards you must meet.

Trademark Disclaimers

A disclaimer is a statement intended to minimize confusion in consumers' minds or deflect liability. A disclaimer is only effective if it is placed prominently, affixed permanently, readable and understandable, and really minimizes confusion. A disclaimer, by itself, will not provide a shield against litigation but, when done properly, can minimize confusion and prevent dilution.

> EXAMPLE: An individual publishes a parody of the newspaper *Newsday*, entitled *Snoozeday*. A prominently displayed disclaimer, such as, "This newspaper is intended as a parody of *Newsday* and makes no claim to *Newsday*'s trademarks or related proprietary rights," may minimize potential liability.

Locating a Trademark Owner

You can usually locate a trademark owner through business directories, by contacting the trademark owner's website, or by searching trademark records to locate the name and address of the trademark owner. Many large companies, such as Coca-Cola, General Motors, and FedEx, have departments that handle licensing and permission arrangements.

Business Directories

There are several general business directories online. For example, Superpages (www.superpages.com), enables the user to search via localized yellow pages.

Federally Registered Marks

You can research ownership of federally registered trademarks at the PTO website, which provides free access to records of marks that are registered or pending (meaning an application is undergoing examination at the PTO). Searching tips and techniques are provided at the site. You can search the trademark database by going to the trademark home page (www.uspto.gov/ trademarks) and clicking "Search Trademarks."

> EXAMPLE: A movie company wants permission to include an In-N-Out Burger sign in a film. Accessing the PTO Trademark database and typing in "In N Out Burger" uncovers the following information:
>
> Word Mark: IN-N-OUT BURGER
> Serial Number: 73724432
> Owner name (REGISTRANT):
> IN-N-OUT BURGERS CORPORATION CALIFORNIA
> 4199 CAMPUS DRIVE, NINTH FLOOR
> IRVINE CALIFORNIA 92612
> Attorney of Record: ARNOLD M WENSINGER

CAUTION
The PTO trademark database has limitations. It might not include applications filed during the last two to four months, nor does it contain information on state, foreign, or common law trademarks or inactive applications and registrations (that is, abandoned applications or canceled or expired registrations). The database may be as much as four months out of sequence with the PTO's internal trademark database, so it might not be possible to locate the owner of a mark for which an application was filed recently. For more up-to-date federal registration trademark information, consider using one of the private databases described below.

Common Law Marks

Trademark owners do not have to register their trademarks to obtain trademark rights. These unregistered trademarks are sometimes referred to as "common law marks." The owners of these marks are harder to locate than registered mark owners because they don't appear in government databases. It may be possible to locate common law marks using Internet search engines (type the mark in as the keyword) or in online business directories.

Private Trademark Databases

Private (fee-based) databases offer more extensive and current trademark searching capability than the PTO trademark database. Below are some of the more popular services:
- **Clarivate** (www.clarivate.com)
- **Trademarkia** (www.trademarkia.com)
- **LexisNexis** (www.lexis.com), and
- **Trademark Express** (www.tmexpress.com).

Owners of Characters

You can locate the owner of a character by contacting the business owner directly, searching trademark databases (see example below), or searching journals that specialize in character and trademark licensing.

> **EXAMPLE:** A nonprofit children's organization wants permission to use Daffy Duck on fundraising posters. Accessing the PTO trademark database and typing in Daffy Duck produces the following information:
>
> Word Mark: DAFFY DUCK
> Serial Number: 75011036
> Owner Name (REGISTRANT):
> TIME WARNER ENTERTAINMENT COMPANY, L.P.
> Owner Address: 75 ROCKEFELLER PLAZA
> NEW YORK NEW YORK 10019
> Limited Partnership Delaware
> Attorney of Record: Christopher Jackson

Dear Rich:

Free to Use Dead or Canceled Trademarks?

Am I free to use a trademark that is listed as "Dead" at the USPTO?

That depends ... When the U.S. Patent and Trademark Office (USPTO) indicates that a trademark is dead, it means that the registration for the mark (or application for registration) was abandoned by the owner or canceled by the USPTO. The live/dead classifications refer to the USPTO's jurisdiction over the mark.

How do marks get "dead"? There are various reasons why an applicant may abandon an application—for example, the applicant may believe that registration is unlikely, or perhaps the applicant decides to discontinue the product or service because of the marketplace. If a mark shows up as being abandoned during the application process, it often pays to dig deeper in the application file (use the USPTO's Trademark Status and Document Retrieval (TSDR) database to read documents; you'll find it at tsdr.uspto.gov) to find out if the reason was due to an examiner objection. That may foretell what's in store for your application. There is a different type of abandonment if a mark has been registered but then later abandoned or canceled. For example, a mark may be canceled because the owner failed to file a Section 8 affidavit.

Dead doesn't mean "not in use." When a mark shows up as "dead," it's possible that the mark is still being used, albeit in an unregistered status. As long as the mark is still in use, no one else can use it (in a way that would create the likelihood of customer confusion) without infringing it. (And keep in mind, many trademarks also "arise from the dead.") There are many ways to determine if a trademark is no longer being used. The simplest method is to call the company and ask if the product can be purchased. If the response is something like, "No, we haven't sold that product in years," then there is a chance that the trademark is truly abandoned. A presumption of abandonment arises after three years. If you can afford additional expenses, professional investigators can help you determine the extent of the company's use. If you believe that a mark has been abandoned, even if it is showing up as live on the search report, you may file a Petition for Cancellation based upon abandonment with the Patent and Trademark Office.

Trademark Licensing

This section deals with trademark licensing, primarily the use of a trademark on merchandise in return for periodic payments known as royalties. The underlying principle of trademark licensing is that consumers are more likely to buy merchandise if it includes a familiar trademark. Trademarks are often licensed in the following situations:

- Characters such as Peppa Pig or Thomas the Tank Engine are often licensed to merchandise producers, providing lucrative licensing income for the trademark owners.
- Licensing collegiate trademarks to merchandise producers provides an important revenue source for universities. (In 1999, Ohio University and Ohio State settled a bitter dispute over which university could license the word "Ohio.")
- Companies such as Harley-Davidson and Jack Daniel's earn income by licensing their corporate trademarks.
- Designers such as Calvin Klein have created billion-dollar enterprises placing their names on a wide array of products.
- Entertainment trademarks such as "Marvel" or "The Late Show" provide additional earnings for entertainment companies.

- Annual festivals and activities such as the Gilroy Garlic Festival license their trademarks to augment income for the event.
- State and municipal tourism offices license trademarks such as "Ski Colorado."
- Trademark licensing earns revenue for nonprofit causes—for example, the Audubon Society licenses its name for a clock that provides birdcalls.
- Licensing of league and sports team trademarks for teams like the Chicago Bulls or the San Francisco Forty-Niners is probably the greatest single generator of trademark licensing revenue.

The rest of this section describes the trademark licensing process in more detail and provides a sample licensing agreement.

Overview of the Licensing Process

The trademark licensing process is usually more challenging than the process for licensing copyrighted works. The trademark owner often has a strong interest in controlling the quality and consistency of affiliated merchandise and is concerned about misuse of the mark or that shoddy goods bearing the mark will diminish the trademark's goodwill.

The trademark licensing process is initiated in one of three ways: A licensee locates a trademark owner, the trademark owner contacts a licensee, or a third-party agency facilitates the licensing arrangement. Many famous trademarks, such as "Harley-Davidson," are represented by agencies that seek out suitable merchandise partners. After the parties make contact, they sort out the basic terms of the agreement. Chapter 11 provides a worksheet for organizing the various aspects of a merchandise license agreement.

It is quite common for owners of well-known trademarks to dictate the terms and furnish the agreements for merchandise licensing. Often these terms are on a "take it or leave it" basis—if the licensee does not agree, the trademark owner will go elsewhere. In other cases, a licensee will furnish the trademark license agreement. Usually, prior to furnishing the agreement, the licensee and the licensor have worked out all of the business terms. Even after the terms are agreed upon and the license is furnished, the parties can make additional changes.

Royalty Payments

Payment of royalties depends on industry trends. To use a trademark on merchandise such as clothing or ceramic goods, a licensee must pay royalties ranging from 2% to 10% of net sales. A trademark owner may accept a lump sum payment for a one-time license—for example, the use of the image on 10,000 T-shirts at a sporting event.

RESOURCE

For more information on trademark licensing, review *A Primer on Licensing,* by Jack Revoyr (Kent Press).

Sample Trademark License Agreement

Below is a sample trademark license agreement, followed by an explanation of selected provisions. This trademark license is very similar to the merchandise license provided in Chapter 11, "Art and Merchandise Licenses." The primary distinctions are in quality control standards and ownership rights related to the trademarks.

FORM

You can download this form (and all other forms in this book) from Nolo.com; for details, see the appendix.

Trademark License Agreement

Introduction

This Trademark License Agreement (the "Agreement") is made between _____ _____ (referred to as "Licensor") and _____ (referred to as "Licensee").

The Parties agree as follows:

The Trademarks

The "Trademarks" refer to any trademark, service mark, trade name, logo, or other device and its associated goodwill used to identify and distinguish Licensor's products and services as included in Exhibit A. Licensor is the owner of all rights to the Trademarks, and Licensee shall not claim any right to use the Trademarks except under the terms of this Agreement.

Licensed Products

Licensed Products are defined as Licensee's products incorporating the Trademarks specifically described in Exhibit A (the "Licensed Products").

Grant of Rights

Licensor grants to Licensee:

(*Select one*)

☐ an exclusive license

☐ a nonexclusive license

to reproduce and distribute the Trademarks on the Licensed Products.

Sublicense

(*Select one*)

☐ **Consent required.** Licensee may sublicense the rights granted pursuant to this Agreement provided: Licensee obtains Licensor's prior written consent to such sublicense; and Licensor receives such revenue or royalty payment as provided in the Payment section below. Any sublicense granted in violation of this provision shall be void.

☐ **No sublicensing permitted.** Licensee may not sublicense the rights granted under this Agreement.

Reservation of Rights and Assignment of Goodwill

Licensor reserves all rights other than those being conveyed or granted in this Agreement. Licensee assigns to Licensor any goodwill from the Trademarks that may accrue under this Agreement or from the distribution of the Licensed Products. Licensee's rights to the Trademarks are only in connection with the Licensed Products and Licensee shall not assert any other association with Licensor or the Trademarks. Licensee acknowledges the validity of the Trademarks and agrees not to challenge Licensor's ownership of the Trademarks or their validity.

Territory

The rights granted to Licensee are limited to _____ (the "Territory").

Term

The "Effective Date" of this Agreement is defined as the date when the agreement commences and is established by the latest signature date.

(*Select one*)

☐ **Specified term with renewal rights.** This Agreement shall commence upon the Effective Date and shall extend for a period of _____ years (the "Initial Term"). Following the Initial Term, Licensee may renew this Agreement under the same terms and conditions for _____ consecutive _____ year periods (the "Renewal Terms"), provided that Licensee provides written notice of its intention to renew this Agreement within thirty (30) days before the expiration of the current term.

☐ **Term with renewal based upon sales.** This Agreement shall commence upon the Effective Date and shall extend for a period of _____ years (the "Initial Term") and may be renewed by Licensee under the same terms and conditions for consecutive _____ year periods (the "Renewal Terms"), provided that:

(a) Licensee provides written notice of its intention to renew this Agreement within thirty days before the expiration of the current term; and

(b) Licensee has met the sales requirements as established in Exhibit A.

☐ **Indefinite term.** This Agreement shall commence upon the Effective Date and shall continue until terminated pursuant to a provision of this Agreement.

☐ **Fixed term.** This Agreement shall commence upon the Effective Date and shall continue for _____ unless sooner terminated pursuant to a provision of this Agreement.

☐ **Term for as long as Licensee sells Licensed Products.** This Agreement shall commence upon the Effective Date as specified in Exhibit A and shall continue for as long as Licensee continues to offer the Licensed Products in commercially reasonable quantities or unless sooner terminated pursuant to a provision of this Agreement.

Approval of Samples and Quality Control

Preproduction. Licensee shall submit to Licensor a reasonable number of preproduction designs and prototypes at no cost prior to production, as well as production samples of every Licensed Product to assure that the product meets Licensor's quality standards. Licensee agrees not to distribute any Licensed Product until receipt of Licensor's written approval of such Licensed Product.

Production and Promotion. At least once every six (6) months, Licensee shall submit to Licensor two (2) production samples of each Licensed Product for review. Licensee shall pay all costs for delivery of these materials. In the event that any production sample does not meet Licensor's quality standards, Licensee agrees to immediately correct such deficiencies. Licensor shall have the right to inspect Licensee's premises upon reasonable notice for purposes of observing the manufacturing process. Licensee shall submit all advertising and promotional materials to Licensor and shall not distribute such materials until receipt of written approval from Licensor.

Royalties

All royalties ("Royalties") provided for under this Agreement shall accrue when the respective Licensed Products are sold, shipped, distributed, billed, or paid for, whichever occurs first.

Net Sales

"Net Sales" are defined as Licensee's gross sales (the gross invoice amount billed to customers) less quantity discounts or rebates and returns actually credited.

A quantity discount or rebate is a discount made at the time of shipment. No deductions shall be made for cash or other discounts, commissions, manufacturing costs, uncollectible accounts, or for fees or expenses of any kind that the Licensee may incur in connection with the Royalty payments.

Fees

(Select one or more provisions)

☐ **Advance Against Royalties.** As a nonrefundable advance against royalties (the "Advance"), Licensee agrees to pay to Licensor upon execution of this Agreement the sum of $ _____ .

☐ **Licensed Product Royalty.** Licensee agrees to pay a Royalty of _____ % of all Net Sales revenue of the Licensed Products ("Licensed Product Royalty").

☐ **Per-Unit Royalty.** Licensee agrees to pay a Royalty of $ _____ for each unit of the Licensed Product that is ☐ manufactured ☐ sold *[select one]*.

☐ **Guaranteed Minimum Annual Royalty Payment.** In addition to any other advances or fees, Licensee shall pay an annual guaranteed Royalty (the "GMAR") as follows: $ _____ . The GMAR shall be paid to Licensor annually on _____ . The GMAR is an advance against Royalties for the twelve-month (12-month) period commencing upon payment. Royalty payments based on Net Sales made during any year of this Agreement shall be credited against the GMAR due for the year in which such Net Sales were made. In the event that annual Royalties exceed the GMAR, Licensee shall pay the difference to Licensor. Any annual Royalty payments in excess of the GMAR shall not be carried forward from previous years or applied against the GMAR.

☐ **License Fee.** As a nonrefundable, nonrecoupable fee for executing this license, Licensee agrees to pay to Licensor upon execution of this Agreement the sum of $ _____ .

☐ **Sublicensing Revenues.** In the event of any sublicense of the rights granted pursuant to this Agreement, Licensee shall pay to Licensor _____% of all sublicensing revenues.

Payments and Statements to Licensor

Within thirty (30) days after the end of each calendar quarter (the "Royalty Period"), an accurate statement of Net Sales of Licensed Products along with any Royalty payments or sublicensing revenues due to Licensor shall be provided to Licensor, regardless of whether any Licensed Products were sold during the Royalty Period. All payments shall be paid in United States currency drawn on a United States bank. The acceptance by Licensor of any of the statements furnished or Royalties paid shall not preclude Licensor questioning the correctness at any time of any payments or statements.

Audit

Licensee shall keep accurate books of account and records covering all transactions relating to the license granted in this Agreement, and Licensor or its duly authorized representatives shall have the right upon five days prior written notice, and during normal business hours, to inspect and audit Licensee's records relating to the Licensed Products under this Agreement. Licensor shall bear the cost of such inspection and audit, unless the results indicate an underpayment greater than $ _____ for any six-month (6-month) period. In that case, Licensee shall promptly reimburse Licensor for all costs of the audit along with the amount due with interest on such sums. Interest shall accrue from the date the payment was originally due and the interest rate shall be 1.5% per month, or the maximum rate permitted by law, whichever is less. All books of account and records shall be made available in the United States and kept available for at least two years after the termination of this Agreement.

Late Payment

Time is of the essence with respect to all payments to be made by Licensee under this Agreement. If Licensee is late in any payment provided for in this Agreement, Licensee shall pay interest on the payment from the date due until paid at a rate of 1.5% per month, or the maximum rate permitted by law, whichever is less.

Licensor Warranties

Licensor warrants that it has the power and authority to enter into this Agreement and has no knowledge as to any third-party claims regarding the proprietary rights in the Trademarks that would interfere with the rights granted under this Agreement.

Indemnification by Licensor

(*Select one if appropriate*)

☐ **Licensor indemnification without limitations.** Licensor shall indemnify Licensee and hold Licensee harmless from any damages and liabilities (including reasonable attorneys' fees and costs) arising from any breach of Licensor's warranties as defined in Licensor's Warranties, above.

☐ **Licensor indemnification limited to amounts paid.** Licensor shall indemnify Licensee and hold Licensee harmless from any damages and liabilities (including reasonable attorneys' fees and costs) arising from any breach of Licensor's warranties as defined in Licensor's Warranties, above. Licensor's maximum liability under this provision shall in no event exceed the total amount earned by Licensor under this Agreement.

Licensee Warranties

Licensee warrants that it will use its best commercial efforts to market the Licensed Products and that sale and marketing of the Licensed Products shall be in conformance with all applicable laws and regulations, including but not limited to all intellectual property laws.

Indemnification by Licensee

Licensee shall indemnify Licensor and hold Licensor harmless from any damages and liabilities (including reasonable attorneys' fees and costs) arising from any breach of Licensee's warranties and representation as defined in the Licensee Warranties above or arising out of any alleged defects of the Licensed Products, any product liability claims, or any claims arising out of advertising, distribution, or marketing of the Licensed Products.

Intellectual Property Rights

The license granted in this Agreement is conditioned on Licensee's compliance with the provisions of the intellectual property laws of the United States and any foreign country in the Territory.

Proprietary Notices

Licensee shall identify Licensor as the owner of rights to the Trademarks and shall include the notices provided in Exhibit A on all copies of the Licensed Products.

Infringement Against Third Parties

In the event that either Party learns of imitations or infringements of the Trademarks or Licensed Products, that Party shall notify the other in writing of the infringements or imitations. Licensor shall have the right to commence lawsuits against third persons arising from infringement of the Trademarks or Licensed Products. In the event that Licensor does not commence a lawsuit against an alleged infringer within sixty (60) days of notification by Licensee, Licensee may commence a lawsuit against the third party. Before filing suit, Licensee shall obtain the written consent of Licensor to do so, and such consent shall not be unreasonably withheld. Licensor will cooperate fully and in good faith with Licensee for the purpose of securing and preserving Licensee's rights to the Trademarks. Any recovery (including, but not limited to, a judgment, settlement, or licensing agreement included as resolution of an infringement dispute) shall be divided equally between the Parties after deduction and payment of reasonable attorneys' fees to the Party bringing the lawsuit.

Exploitation Date

Licensee agrees to manufacture, distribute, and sell the Licensed Products in commercially reasonable quantities during the term of this Agreement and to commence such manufacture, distribution, and sale by _____ . This is a material provision of this Agreement.

Advertising Budget

(*Select if appropriate*)

☐ Licensee agrees to spend at least _____ % of estimated annual gross sales for promotional efforts and advertising of the Licensed Products.

Licensor Copies and Right to Purchase

Licensee shall provide Licensor with _____ copies of each Licensed Product. Licensor has the right to purchase from Licensee, at Licensee's manufacturing cost, at least _____ copies of any Licensed Product, and such payments shall be deducted from royalties due to Licensor.

Confidentiality

The Parties acknowledge that each may have access to confidential information that relates to each other's business (the "Information"). The Parties agree to protect the confidentiality of the Information and maintain it with the strictest confidence, and no Party shall disclose such Information to third parties without the prior written consent of the other.

Insurance

(Select if appropriate)

☐ Licensee shall, throughout the Term, obtain and maintain, at its own expense, standard product liability insurance coverage, naming Licensor as an additional named insured. Such policy shall provide protection against any claims, demands, and causes of action arising out of any alleged defects or failure to perform of the Licensed Products or any use of the Licensed Products. The amount of coverage shall be a minimum of $ _____ , with no deductible amount for each single occurrence for bodily injury or property damage. The policy shall provide for notice to the Licensor from the insurer by Registered or Certified Mail in the event of any modification or termination of insurance. The provisions of this section shall survive termination for three (3) years.

Right to Terminate

Licensor shall have the right to terminate this Agreement in the following situations:

(Select one or more provisions)

☐ **Failure to Make Timely Payment.** Licensee fails to pay Royalties when due or fails to accurately report Net Sales, as defined in the Payment Section of this Agreement, and such failure is not cured within thirty days after written notice from the Licensor.

☐ **Failure to Introduce Product.** Licensee fails to introduce the product to market by the date set in the Exploitation section of this Agreement or to offer the Licensed Products in commercially reasonable quantities during any subsequent year.

☐ **Assignment or Sublicensing.** Licensee assigns or sublicenses in violation of the Agreement.

☐ **Failure to Maintain Insurance.** Licensee fails to maintain or obtain product liability insurance as required by the provisions of this Agreement.

☐ **Failure to Meet Quality Standards or Submit Samples.** Licensee fails to provide Licensor with samples for approval or fails to meet the quality standards established by Licensor.

Licensor shall have the right to terminate the grant of license under this Agreement with respect to any country or region included in the Territory in which Licensee fails to offer the Licensed Products for sale or distribution or to secure a sublicensing agreement for the marketing, distribution, and sale of the product within two years of the Effective Date.

Effect of Termination

Upon termination of this Agreement, all Royalty obligations as established in the Payments Section shall immediately become due. After the termination of this license, all rights granted to Licensee under this Agreement shall terminate and revert to Licensor, and Licensee will refrain from further manufacturing, copying, marketing, distribution, or use of any Licensed Product or other product that incorporates the Trademarks. Within thirty (30) days after termination, Licensee shall deliver to Licensor a statement indicating the number and description of the Licensed Products that it had on hand or is in the process of manufacturing as of the termination date.

Sell-Off Period

Licensee may dispose of the Licensed Products covered by this Agreement for a period of ninety (90) days after termination or expiration, except that Licensee shall have no such right in the event this agreement is terminated according to the Licensor's Right to Terminate, above. At the end of the post-termination sale period, Licensee shall furnish a Royalty payment and statement as required under the Payment Section. Upon termination, Licensee shall deliver to Licensor all original designs or reproductions of Trademarks used in the manufacture of the Licensed Products. Licensor shall bear the costs of shipping for these materials.

Attorneys' Fees and Expenses

The prevailing Party shall have the right to collect from the other Party its reasonable costs and necessary disbursements and attorneys' fees incurred in enforcing this Agreement.

Dispute Resolution

(Select one if appropriate)

☐ **Mediation and Arbitration.** The Parties agree that every dispute or difference between them, arising under this Agreement, shall be settled first by a meeting of the Parties attempting to confer and resolve the dispute in a good faith manner. If the Parties cannot resolve their dispute after conferring, any Party may require the other Party to submit the matter to nonbinding mediation, utilizing the services of an impartial professional mediator approved by all Parties. If the Parties cannot come to an agreement following mediation, the Parties agree to submit the matter to binding arbitration at a location mutually agreeable to the Parties. The arbitration shall be conducted on a confidential basis pursuant to the Commercial Arbitration Rules of the American Arbitration Association. Any decision or award as a result of any such arbitration proceeding shall include the assessment of costs, expenses, and reasonable attorneys' fees and shall include a written record of the proceedings and a written determination of the arbitrators. An arbitrator experienced in trademark and merchandising law shall conduct any such arbitration. An award of arbitration shall be final and binding on the Parties and may be confirmed in a court of competent jurisdiction.

☐ **Arbitration.** If a dispute arises under or relating to this Agreement, the Parties agree to submit such dispute to binding arbitration in the State of ____ _____ or another location mutually agreeable to the Parties. The arbitration shall be conducted on a confidential basis pursuant to the Commercial Arbitration Rules of the American Arbitration Association. Any decision or award as a result of any such arbitration proceeding shall be in writing and shall provide an explanation for all conclusions of law and fact and shall include the assessment of costs, expenses, and reasonable attorneys' fees. An arbitrator experienced in trademark and merchandising law shall conduct any such arbitration. An award of arbitration may be confirmed in a court of competent jurisdiction.

Governing Law

This Agreement shall be governed in accordance with the laws of the State of

_____ .

Jurisdiction

The Parties consent to the exclusive jurisdiction and venue of the federal and state courts located in _____ in any action arising out of or relating to this Agreement. The Parties waive any other venue to which either Party might be entitled by domicile or otherwise.

Waiver

The failure to exercise any right provided in this Agreement shall not be a waiver of prior or subsequent rights.

Invalidity

If any provision of this Agreement is invalid under applicable statute or rule of law, it is to be considered omitted, and the remaining provisions of this Agreement shall in no way be affected.

Entire Understanding

This Agreement expresses the complete understanding of the Parties and supersedes all prior representations, agreements, and understandings, whether written or oral. This Agreement may not be altered except by a written document signed by both Parties.

Attachments and Exhibits

The Parties agree and acknowledge that all attachments, exhibits, and schedules referred to in this Agreement are incorporated in this Agreement by reference.

No Special Damages

Licensor shall not be liable to Licensee for any incidental, consequential, punitive, or special damages.

Notices

Any notice or communication required or permitted to be given under this Agreement shall be sufficiently given when received by certified mail or sent by facsimile transmission or overnight courier.

No Joint Venture

Nothing contained in this Agreement shall be construed to place one of the Parties in the relationship of agent, employee, franchisee, officer, partner, or joint venturer to the other Party. Neither Party may create or assume any obligation on behalf of the other.

Assignability

(*Select one*)

☐ **Assignment Requires Licensor Consent.** Licensee may not assign or transfer its rights or obligations pursuant to this Agreement without the prior written consent of Licensor. Any assignment or transfer in violation of this section shall be void.

☐ **Licensor Consent Not Required for Assignment to Parent or Acquiring Company.** Licensee may not assign or transfer its rights or obligations pursuant to this Agreement without the prior written consent of Licensor. However, no consent is required for an assignment or transfer that occurs: (a) to an entity in which Licensee owns more than 50% of the assets; or (b) as part of a transfer of all or substantially all of the assets of Licensee to any party. Any assignment or transfer in violation of this Section shall be void.

Each Party has signed this Agreement through its authorized representative. The Parties, having read this Agreement, indicate their consent to the terms and conditions by their signature below.

By: _____

Date: _____

Licensor Name: _____

By: _____

Date: _____

Licensee Name/Title: _____

EXHIBIT A

The Property _____

_____

Licensed Products _____

_____

Sales Requirements

$ _____ in Gross Sales per year.

Proprietary Notices

All licensed products shall bear the following proprietary notice: _____

_____

_____

Explanation for Trademark License Agreement

The Trademark License Agreement is similar to the Merchandise License Agreement provided in Chapter 11. For explanations of most of the terms, see Chapter 11. Explanations of three items—goodwill, quality control, and proprietary notices—are not covered in Chapter 11, so they are provided below.

Reservation of Rights: Assignment of Goodwill

This section of the license provision establishes that the trademark owner is only delivering a narrow group of rights and is retaining everything else. This section also provides that the trademark owner always owns the goodwill associated with the mark. Goodwill is an intangible item—a measurement of the consumer's attitude toward the trademark. The stronger the goodwill, the more momentum the trademark maintains. For example, Coca-Cola trademarks have extraordinary goodwill, demonstrated by the fact that consumers insist on Coca-Cola products over other products that may claim to have similar ingredients.

This license provision guarantees that only the trademark owner earns the goodwill. If the licensee accumulates any goodwill, it is automatically transferred to the trademark owner. In the real world, this simply means that the licensee can't make any claims to the trademark.

This license provision also provides that the licensee won't attack the licensor's ownership of the trademarks. This is to avoid the possibility of a successful licensee attempting to destroy the trademark owner's rights.

Approval of Samples and Quality Control

Failure of a trademark owner to maintain quality standards over the trademark uses can result in the loss of trademark rights (known as "abandonment"). For this reason, every trademark license agreement includes reasonable quality control standards. The important issue for trademark owners is not simply that the agreement provides for quality control, but that the control is actually exercised.

The license provision provides for written approval both prior to production and during production. The termination section of the agreement permits the licensor to end the agreement if the licensee does not meet these quality control standards.

Proprietary Notices

The Proprietary Notices provision, included in Exhibit A, establishes what notices must be included on the licensed products. For example, if the licensor wants the products to include a registered trademark notice such as "™ Meathead Designs," this should be indicated here.

Art and Merchandise Licenses

T his chapter is about merchandising: the business of affixing an image or text to products you plan to sell, such as T-shirts, buttons, caps, and posters. Getting permission for merchandising is similar to establishing other permission arrangements in that a copyright owner must consent to a specific use. The primary difference between merchandising and other permission situations is the payment system. In merchandising, the copyright owner usually negotiates an arrangement for continuing periodic payments known as "royalties."

In this chapter, we examine the principles of merchandise licensing and analyze two merchandise agreements: a long-form merchandise agreement and an abbreviated version.

Overview of Merchandise Licensing

Under the terms of a merchandise license, the owner of the image or text being used (the licensor) is usually paid an advance plus a royalty based on a percentage of income from sales. The company selling the merchandise (the licensee) must meet certain obligations including payments, quality control, and enforcement of rights. If the licensee fails to do so, the license can be terminated. Termination can be very expensive for both parties, since it means loss of income for the licensor and the loss of a substantial investment for the licensee.

"Copyright-Free" Artwork and Merchandise Agreements

Some artwork is labeled "copyright free" or "royalty free" to indicate that it can be used without permission after a one-time payment is made. Can this type of artwork be used freely on merchandise? Not necessarily. Despite the name, copyright-free artworks are often protected under copyright laws, so there are limitations on their use. (This book tries to avoid such confusion by using the term "royalty-free artwork" to refer to a work that does have copyright protection, but can be used in a wide range of ways once a fee is paid.) Only public domain artworks are truly free to use with no strings attached. In order to determine if permission is required, read the shrink-wrap, click-wrap, or other license agreement supplied with the royalty-free artwork.

There are alternatives to licensing rights under a merchandise agreement. One alternative is to purchase the copyright in the artwork (known as an assignment). The other choice is to hire an artist, photographer, or musician to create the material and acquire ownership under a work-for-hire agreement. These options are explained in Chapter 15.

What Is Merchandise?

Licensable merchandise is any consumer product on which an image or text can be affixed. In general, merchandise has some utility or function, such as clothing, jewelry, or stationery. However, merchandise has no limitations; artwork can be placed on anything that can be reproduced. Products that are commonly the subject of merchandise licenses include: auto sunshades, auto tire covers, backpacks, badges, bank checks, beach mats, bed sheets, belt buckles, belts, blankets, bumper stickers, caps, casual shoes, calendars, ceramic cups, children's wear, clocks, cuff links, decals, desk sets, dress shirts, drink holders, fabric, flags, gift wrap, golf bags, golf club covers, greeting cards, handkerchiefs, hats, heat transfer patches, jackets, jerseys, jewelry, key rings, knit shirts, lamps, letter openers, license plate frames, loose-leaf binders, magnets, mittens, napkins, neckties, notebooks, pennants, pens, phone cases, pins, polo shirts, postcards, posters, pot holders, rain jackets, rings, running shorts, running shoes, scarves, shower curtains, sleepwear, snack trays, socks, stationery, stuffed animals, sunglasses, sweatpants, sweatshirts, sweaters, swimwear, tablecloths, tank tops, tie clips, tote bags, towels, toys, training suits, T-shirts, umbrellas, underwear, wallpaper, watches, and water bottles.

RELATED TOPIC

Information about locating copyright owners of text, photos, art, and music is provided in Chapters 2 through 5.

Different Types of Materials Used on Merchandise

Most merchandise licenses are for artwork or photographs. However, text and music are also licensed in connection with merchandise. In general, the rules are the same. But when it comes to licensing music, additional issues arise depending on whether you are licensing an already-recorded composition or will be rerecording a composition for your specific use.

Using Art on Merchandise

Using art on merchandise generally consists of using an artistic image such as a drawing or painting on items you plan to sell. Examples include reproducing a Keith Haring painting on a T-shirt or using images from Georgia O'Keeffe paintings on notecards. Of course, if the image is in the public domain, such as the *Mona Lisa*, no permission is required. If the artwork is labeled "royalty free," you will need to review the license or agreement that accompanies the purchase of the artwork to determine if your merchandise use is permitted.

Agreements for the use of art on merchandise are sometimes called "art licenses" or "design licenses." Whatever such an agreement is called, it is essentially a merchandise license as described in this chapter. You may occasionally find unique provisions in some art licenses for the use of fine artworks—for example, a clause permitting the artist to enter and inspect a poster-making facility to ensure a quality production process. While special provisions such as these are sometimes included to protect the artist, they don't change the basic character of the agreement as a merchandise license.

Dear Rich:

T-Shirt License Needed

I am an artist and was recently approached by a woman who wants to use one of my images on T-shirts. She has proposed a simple arrangement doing 24 shirts at a time. As she sells out of one batch, she will make another 24. This is not a million-dollar transaction but I have no idea how to respond to it. How do I know what the going rate is?

The short answer is that artists get anywhere between 5% to 20% (or more) of the revenue generated by the shirt. It depends on the demand, the size of the print run, and your bargaining power. Sometimes the royalty is paid only after costs are deducted; sometimes it is straight off the top. Some online T-shirt merchants even let the artist set the royalty.

Beyond the royalty. You should also ask yourself a few questions. Is the amount of money coming in worth your time and energy? What if you're not satisfied with the quality of the reproduction? Will the arrangement preclude you from other more lucrative deals? Do you have any reason to believe the T-shirt maker is not a trustworthy businessperson? If you have any doubts, it's probably a good idea to make the initial term of the agreement short, perhaps six months to a year (you can always renew). And it's best to keep it nonexclusive as well (you can always amend it later). And as they say in the music business, don't do a handshake deal, get some paper. You'll find a license agreement on the following pages. And of course, make sure your artwork doesn't cross over into personality rights, trademarks, or otherwise illegal content.

Using Music on Merchandise

The ability to digitize music has made it possible to include songs and other compositions in merchandise such as greeting cards, watches, toys, musical equipment, music boxes, and even clothing.

Many songs used on merchandise are not copied directly from an existing recording; instead, they are rerecorded in order to be embedded on a computer chip. Since an existing recording of the song isn't being used, permission is required from the music publisher (who owns a song composition) but not from the record company (which owns a specific sound recording). Similarly, if lyrics will be reprinted on merchandise but no recording will be reproduced, permission is required from the music publisher, not the record company.

The merchandise license agreements provided in this chapter can be used for licensing music or for reprinting lyrics on merchandise. However, the licensor (the music publisher) may want to incorporate additional requirements—for example, that the music cannot be used in advertisements for the merchandise. The music publisher usually provides the language for such provisions.

An example of a music merchandise license is also available at the Harry Fox Agency website (www.harryfox.com). (Harry Fox is an organization that represents music publishers.) Although the license agreement provided by Harry Fox is intended for use with agency-affiliated publishers, it establishes basic music licensing standards and can be adopted for your purposes. Chapter 5 explains how to locate copyright owners of songs and sound recordings.

Using Trademarks, Fictional Characters, or Celebrities on Merchandise

A trademark is any word, photograph, or symbol that is used to identify a business's products or services. Trademarks are commonly licensed for merchandise—for example, the licensing of a university's trademark (the school name or the name of its mascot) on sports equipment or apparel.

Fictional characters include characters from books, television, or movies, such as Harry Potter, Lara Croft, or Don Draper. A fictional character may be animated (Homer Simpson), literary (Lisbeth Salander), or cinematic (James Bond). The rules for licensing characters may change if a real person has portrayed the character (Christian Bale as Batman), in which case, additional permission may be required, as explained in Chapter 10.

Most of the provisions contained in a merchandise agreement are also used in trademark, character, and celebrity licenses. However, there are some unique aspects to these agreements, some of which require knowledge of trademark law or the right of publicity. For example, character licensing involves overlapping trademark, copyright, and design patent laws. These types of licenses are often handled by special licensing agencies that represent trademark owners, fictional characters, and celebrities. A sample trademark license and additional trademark licensing information is provided in Chapter 10, "Getting Permission to Use Trademarks."

Using Short Phrases on Merchandise

Merchandise, by its nature, can generally only accommodate small amounts of text. Since copyright law does not protect short phrases (see Chapter 8), most of the text used on merchandise—for example, "Honk if you like Prune Tacos"—can be used without permission.

However, in the following situations, you should obtain permission to use a short phrase:

- **The phrase is associated with a fictional character.** For example, the unauthorized use of the phrase "E.T., Phone Home" on a ceramic cup was found to be a copyright infringement. (*Universal City Studios, Inc. v. Kamar Indus.*, 217 U.S.P.Q. (BNA) 1162, (S.D. Texas, 1982).) In this case, the outcome was directly related to use of "E.T." in the phrase. The use of "Phone Home" without "E.T." would not require authorization.
- **The phrase is a trademark.** You should always obtain permission to use a phrase on merchandise if it is used as a trademark or is taken from an advertising campaign, such as Coke's "It's the Real Thing."
- **The phrase is extremely inventive.** An extremely clever phrase such as Ashleigh Brilliant's epigram, "I may not be perfect but parts of me are excellent," or Lewis Carroll's phrase, "Twas brillig and the slithy toves," are protectable. There is no hard and fast rule for how inventive the phrase must be, but it's best to avoid phrases that appear highly unique.

Royalty Rates for Merchandise Licensing

When you license text, art, graphics, or music for use on merchandise, you are ordinarily required to pay the owner of the licensed material a royalty—that is, a continuing payment based upon a percentage of the income you earn from the sale of the merchandise.

Royalty rates for merchandise licensing vary depending on the merchandise involved. Below are some royalty estimates:

- Greeting cards and gift wrap: 2% to 5%
- Household (cups, sheets, towels): 3% to 8%
- Fabrics, apparel (T-shirts, caps, etc.), decals, bumper stickers: 5% to 10%, and
- Posters and prints: 10% or more.

Additional Information About Merchandise Licensing

Many libraries contain general business directories, such as the multivolume publication *Thomas Register of American Manufacturers* (Thomas Register Publishing) (searchable online at www.thomasnet.com) or the *Directory of Corporate Affiliations* (*DCA*) (Reed Reference Publishing Company). The *Thomas Register* lists manufacturers by subject, including profiles and phone numbers. The *DCA* lists companies by name, brand name, product or service, geographic location, or SIC code—a four-digit number created by the Department of Commerce to classify a business by service or product types.

A good place to search for information about merchandise licensing, brands, and related news is Apparel Search (www.apparelsearch.com/licensing.htm), which provides a comprehensive contact listing of licensing agents, brands, and licensees.

General business directories on the Internet can also identify merchandise manufacturers; you should be able to find them using a search engine. One website that may be helpful is SuperPages, the business directory located at www.superpages.com. Most online services have general business directories that perform the same functions.

If you're pursuing merchandise licensing on a regular basis, consider a subscription to *The Licensing Journal* (Walters Kluwer). Although pricey (about a $1000 a year), the journal contains thorough information on current trends in art, merchandise, trademark, and toy licensing.

Dear Rich:

Sports Licensing: Is the System Rigged?

I have a great idea for a sports-team-related product and have started looking into a patent. I looked into licensing and can't even believe that it's legal to put the restrictions on that these teams do. I don't want to cheat these universities and professional teams out of their money on these things, but they make it impossible to make a new product, not similar to anything they are offering, without going through one of their existing suppliers or having an exemplary record of mass producing similar products. Why is it so hard to license products to a university or professional sports franchise?

The short answer is that as a general rule, the bigger the enterprise, the less that the enterprise wants to hear from outsiders, a principle sometimes referred to as "NIH (not invented here)."

There is, however, a logic behind the closed-door approach of the sports licensing industry. Like the toy licensing business, sports licensing execs don't want to deal with strangers or companies that can't meet manufacturing numbers, accept legal requirements, or provide quality assurance. This is especially true in a depressed business climate when risk aversion is the name of the game. (Although that doesn't stop sports licensing of some crazy concepts—including MLB-licensed "fan" coffins.) As you may be aware, the road you are seeking—attempting to patent your invention, get investors, and manufacture the product yourself (can you deal with foreign manufacturers?)—is littered with unhappiness and bankruptcies. The Dear Rich Staff advises that you reconsider the idea of pitching your invention (hopefully, patented) to an existing manufacturer or agent—that is, a middle entity who already has cachet with the teams. That's the way many "little guys" get started in the sports licensing world—by slowly building trust with existing companies.

Merchandise License Agreement

Occasionally, a seasoned copyright owner who has licensed many copyrighted items may furnish the merchandise license agreement. However, most of the time, the licensee—the company that is manufacturing and selling the merchandise—furnishes the merchandise license agreement. Usually, prior to furnishing the agreement, the licensee and the licensor have worked out all of the business terms. For example, they have already determined the royalty rate, the rights being transferred, the length of time for the agreement, and other financial terms.

To help you prepare this information, a Merchandise License Worksheet is included. In addition to helping you determine the essential elements of the license agreement, the worksheet is also helpful for monitoring the license agreement after it is signed. Sometimes essential elements from the worksheet are included on an "exhibit" sheet that is attached to the agreement and incorporated into its provisions. Our model agreement includes such an exhibit.

Even after the terms are agreed upon and the license is furnished, the parties can make additional changes. For example, the licensor may want to modify provisions about sublicensing or dispute resolution. Be prepared to make modifications, to cut and paste provisions, or to restructure the agreement so that the sections are in a different order. These types of changes are common.

Below is a long-form merchandise license agreement for licensing artwork, text, or music for use in merchandise.

What If the Licensor Furnishes the Agreement?

If the licensor (the copyright or trademark owner) furnishes the merchandise license agreement, the licensee (merchandise seller) will need to review its provisions. Deciphering a license agreement can be a challenge, even for experienced attorneys. Unfortunately, there are no rules for how to order or arrange provisions in a license agreement. Many agreements seem to be organized haphazardly. In order to analyze a new agreement, use the following strategies:

- Be prepared to spend several hours making an analysis.
- Make a photocopy of the agreement.
- Locate the major provisions (as discussed below) and label them in the margin.
- Compare each provision with the language suggested in this book.
- Underline everything you don't like or don't understand.
- Prepare a chart, listing the number of the provision and your concerns about that section.
- Convert the chart into a response letter detailing your requested changes.

FORM

You can download this form (and all other forms in this book) from Nolo.com; for details, see the appendix.

Merchandise License Agreement

Introduction

This License Agreement (the "Agreement") is made between _____
_____ (referred to as "Licensor")
and _____ (referred to as "Licensee").

The Parties agree as follows:

The Work

The Work refers to the work described in Exhibit A. Licensor is the owner of all rights to the Work and Licensee shall not claim any right to use the Work except under the terms of this Agreement.

Licensed Products

Licensed Products are defined as Licensee's products incorporating the Work specifically described in Exhibit A (the "Licensed Products").

Grant of Rights

Licensor grants to Licensee:

(*Select one*)

☐ an exclusive license

☐ a nonexclusive license

to reproduce and distribute the Work in or on the Licensed Products.

Licensor grants to Licensee:

(*Select if appropriate*)

☐ the right to modify the Work to incorporate it in or on the Licensed Products provided that Licensee agrees to assign to Licensor its rights, if any, in any derivative works resulting from Licensee's modification of the Work. Licensee agrees to execute any documents required to evidence this assignment of copyright and to waive any moral rights and rights of attribution provided in 17 U.S.C. § 106A of the Copyright Act.

☐ the right to publicly display the Work as incorporated in or on the Licensed Products.

☐ the right to publicly perform the Work as incorporated in or on the Licensed Products.

Sublicense

(Select one)

☐ **Consent required.** Licensee may sublicense the rights granted pursuant to this agreement provided: Licensee obtains Licensor's prior written consent to such sublicense; and Licensor receives such revenue or royalty payment as provided in the Payment section below. Any sublicense granted in violation of this provision shall be void.

☐ **Consent to sublicense not unreasonably withheld.** Licensee may sublicense the rights granted pursuant to this agreement provided: Licensee obtains Licensor's prior written consent to such sublicense. Licensor's consent to any sublicense shall not be unreasonably withheld, and Licensor receives such revenue or royalty payment as provided in the Payment section below. Any sublicense granted in violation of this provision shall be void.

☐ **No sublicensing permitted.** Licensee may not sublicense the rights granted under this agreement.

Reservation of Rights

Licensor reserves all rights other than those being conveyed or granted in this Agreement.

Territory

The rights granted to Licensee are limited to _____ (the "Territory").

Term

The "Effective Date" of this Agreement is defined as the date when the agreement commences and is established by the latest signature date.

(Select one)

☐ **Specified term with renewal rights.** This Agreement shall commence upon the Effective Date and shall extend for a period of _____ years (the "Initial Term"). Following the Initial Term, Licensee may renew this agreement under the same terms and conditions for _____ consecutive _____ year periods (the "Renewal Terms"), provided that Licensee provides written notice of its intention to renew this agreement within thirty (30) days before the expiration of the current term. In no event shall the Term extend beyond the period of United States copyright protection for the Work.

☐ **Term with renewal based upon sales.** This Agreement shall commence upon the Effective Date and shall extend for a period of _____ years (the "Initial Term") and may be renewed by Licensee under the same terms and conditions for consecutive _____ year periods (the "Renewal Terms"), provided that:

(a) Licensee provides written notice of its intention to renew this agreement within thirty days before the expiration of the current term; and

(b) Licensee has met the sales requirements as established in Exhibit A.

☐ **Indefinite term.** This Agreement shall commence upon the Effective Date and shall continue until terminated pursuant to a provision of this Agreement.

☐ **Fixed term.** This Agreement shall commence upon the Effective Date and shall continue for _____ unless sooner terminated pursuant to a provision of this Agreement.

☐ **Term for as long as Licensee sells Licensed Products.** This Agreement shall commence upon the Effective Date as specified in Exhibit A and shall continue for as long as Licensee continues to offer the Licensed Products in commercially reasonable quantities or unless sooner terminated pursuant to a provision of this Agreement. In no event shall the Term extend beyond the period of U.S. copyright protection for the Work.

Payments

All royalties ("Royalties") provided for under this Agreement shall accrue when the respective Licensed Products are sold, shipped, distributed, billed, or paid for, whichever occurs first.

Net Sales

Net Sales are defined as Licensee's gross sales (the gross invoice amount billed to customers) less quantity discounts or rebates and returns actually credited. A quantity discount or rebate is a discount made at the time of shipment. No deductions shall be made for cash or other discounts, commissions, manufacturing costs, uncollectible accounts, or for fees or expenses of any kind that the Licensee may incur in connection with the Royalty payments.

Fees

(Select one or more provisions)

☐ **Advance Against Royalties.** As a nonrefundable advance against Royalties (the "Advance"), Licensee agrees to pay to Licensor upon execution of this Agreement the sum of $ _____ .

☐ **Licensed Product Royalty.** Licensee agrees to pay a Royalty of _____ % of all Net Sales revenue of the Licensed Products ("Licensed Product Royalty").

☐ **Per-Unit Royalty.** Licensee agrees to pay a Royalty of $ _____ for each unit of the Licensed Product that is: (*Select one*)

  ☐ manufactured.

  ☐ sold.

☐ **Guaranteed Minimum Annual Royalty Payment.** In addition to any other advances or fees, Licensee shall pay an annual guaranteed Royalty (the "GMAR") as follows: $ _____ . The GMAR shall be paid to Licensor annually on _____ . The GMAR is an advance against Royalties for the twelve-month period commencing upon payment. Royalty payments based on Net Sales made during any year of this Agreement shall be credited against the GMAR due for the year in which such Net Sales were made. In the event that annual Royalties exceed the GMAR, Licensee shall pay the difference to Licensor. Any annual Royalty payments in excess of the GMAR shall not be carried forward from previous years or applied against the GMAR.

☐ **License Fee.** As a nonrefundable, nonrecoupable fee for executing this license, Licensee agrees to pay to Licensor upon execution of this Agreement the sum of $ _____ .

☐ **Sublicensing Revenues.** In the event of any sublicense of the rights granted pursuant to this Agreement, Licensee shall pay to Licensor _____ % of all sublicensing revenues.

Payments and Statements to Licensor

Within thirty (30) days after the end of each calendar quarter (the "Royalty Period"), an accurate statement of Net Sales of Licensed Products, along with any Royalty payments or sublicensing revenues due to Licensor, shall be provided to Licensor, regardless of whether any Licensed Products were sold during the Royalty Period. All payments shall be paid in United States currency drawn on a United States bank. The acceptance by Licensor of any of the statements furnished or Royalties paid shall not preclude Licensor questioning the correctness at any time of any payments or statements.

Audit

Licensee shall keep accurate books of account and records covering all transactions relating to the license granted in this Agreement, and Licensor or its duly authorized representatives shall have the right upon five days prior written notice, and during normal business hours, to inspect and audit Licensee's records relating to the Work licensed under this Agreement. Licensor shall bear the cost of such inspection and audit, unless the results indicate an underpayment greater than $ _____ for any six-month (6-month) period. In that case, Licensee shall promptly reimburse Licensor for all costs of the audit along with the amount due with interest on such sums. Interest shall accrue from the date the payment was originally due and the interest rate shall be 1.5% per month, or the maximum rate permitted by law, whichever is less. All books of account and records shall be made available in the United States and kept available for at least two years after the termination of this Agreement.

Late Payment

Time is of the essence with respect to all payments to be made by Licensee under this Agreement. If Licensee is late in any payment provided for in this Agreement, Licensee shall pay interest on the payment from the date due until paid at a rate of 1.5% per month, or the maximum rate permitted by law, whichever is less.

Licensor Warranties

Licensor warrants that it has the power and authority to enter into this Agreement and has no knowledge as to any third-party claims regarding the proprietary rights in the Work that would interfere with the rights granted under this Agreement.

Indemnification by Licensor

(Select one if appropriate)

☐ **Licensor indemnification without limitations.** Licensor shall indemnify Licensee and hold Licensee harmless from any damages and liabilities (including reasonable attorneys' fees and costs) arising from any breach of Licensor's warranties as defined in Licensor's Warranties, above.

☐ **Licensor indemnification limited to amounts paid.** Licensor shall indemnify Licensee and hold Licensee harmless from any damages and liabilities (including reasonable attorneys' fees and costs), arising from any breach of Licensor's warranties as defined in Licensor's Warranties, above. Licensor's maximum liability under this provision shall in no event exceed the total amount earned by Licensor under this Agreement.

☐ **Licensor indemnification with limitations.** Licensor shall indemnify Licensee and hold Licensee harmless from any damages and liabilities (including reasonable attorneys' fees and costs) arising from any breach of Licensor's warranties as defined in Licensor's Warranties, above, provided that:

(a) such claim, if sustained, would prevent Licensee from marketing the Licensed Products or the Work;

(b) such claim arises solely out of the Work as disclosed to the Licensee and not out of any change in the Work made by Licensee or a vendor;

(c) Licensee gives Licensor prompt written notice of any such claim;

(d) such indemnity shall only be applicable in the event of a final decision by a court of competent jurisdiction from which no right to appeal exists; and

(e) the maximum amount due from Licensor to Licensee under this paragraph shall not exceed the amounts due to Licensor under the Payment Section from the date that Licensor notifies Licensee of the existence of such a claim.

Licensee Warranties

Licensee warrants that it will use its best commercial efforts to market the Licensed Products and that sale and marketing of the Licensed Products shall be in conformance with all applicable laws and regulations, including but not limited to all intellectual property laws.

Indemnification by Licensee

Licensee shall indemnify Licensor and hold Licensor harmless from any damages and liabilities (including reasonable attorneys' fees and costs):

(a) arising from any breach of Licensee's warranties and representation as defined in the Licensee Warranties, above;

(b) arising out of any alleged defects or failures to perform of the Licensed Products or any product liability claims or use of the Licensed Products; and

(c) any claims arising out of advertising, distribution, or marketing of the Licensed Products.

Intellectual Property Registration

Licensor may, but is not obligated to, seek in its own name and at its own expense, appropriate copyright registrations for the Work. Licensor makes no warranty with respect to the validity of any copyright that may be granted. Licensor grants to Licensee the right to apply for registration of the Work or Licensed Products provided that such registrations shall be applied for in the name of Licensor and licensed to Licensee during the Term and according to the conditions of this Agreement. Licensee shall have the right to deduct its reasonable out-of-pocket expenses for the preparation and filing of any such registrations from future Royalties due to Licensor under this Agreement. Licensee shall obtain Licensor's prior written consent before incurring expenses for any foreign copyright applications.

Compliance With Intellectual Property Laws

The license granted in this Agreement is conditioned on Licensee's compliance with the provisions of the intellectual property laws of the United States and any foreign country in the Territory. All copies of the Licensed Product as well as all promotional material shall bear appropriate proprietary notices.

Licensor Credits

Licensee shall identify Licensor as the owner of rights to the Work and shall include the following notice on all copies of the Licensed Products: "_____ . All rights reserved."

Licensee may, with Licensor's consent, use Licensor's name, image, or trademark in advertising or promotional materials associated with the sale of the Licensed Products.

Infringement Against Third Parties

In the event that either Party learns of imitations or infringements of the Work or Licensed Products, that Party shall notify the other in writing of the infringements or imitations. Licensor shall have the right to commence lawsuits against third persons arising from infringement of the Work or Licensed Products. In the event that Licensor does not commence a lawsuit against an alleged infringer within sixty days of notification by Licensee, Licensee may commence a lawsuit against the third party. Before filing suit, Licensee shall obtain the written consent of Licensor to do so, and such consent shall not be unreasonably withheld. Licensor will cooperate fully and in good faith with Licensee for the purpose of securing and preserving Licensee's rights to the Work. Any recovery (including, but not limited to, a judgment, settlement, or licensing agreement included as resolution of an infringement dispute) shall be divided equally between the Parties after deduction and payment of reasonable attorneys' fees to the Party bringing the lawsuit.

Exploitation Date

Licensee agrees to manufacture, distribute, and sell the Licensed Products in commercially reasonable quantities during the term of this Agreement and to commence such manufacture, distribution, and sale by _____ . This is a material provision of this Agreement.

Advertising Budget

(*Select if appropriate*)

☐ Licensee agrees to spend at least _____ % of estimated annual gross sales for promotional efforts and advertising of the Licensed Products.

Approval of Samples and Quality Control

Licensee shall submit a reasonable number of preproduction designs, prototypes, and camera-ready artwork prior to production as well as preproduction samples of the Licensed Product to Licensor to assure that the product meets Licensor's quality standards. In the event that Licensor fails to object in writing within ten (10) business days after the date of receipt of any such materials, such materials shall be deemed to be acceptable. At least once during each calendar year, Licensee shall submit two (2) production samples of each Licensed Product for review. Licensee shall pay all costs for delivery of these approval materials. The quality standards applied by Licensor shall be no more rigorous than the quality standards applied by Licensor to similar products.

Licensor Copies and Right to Purchase

Licensee shall provide Licensor with _____ copies of each Licensed Product. Licensor has the right to purchase from Licensee, at Licensee's manufacturing cost, at least _____ copies of any Licensed Product, and such payments shall be deducted from Royalties due to Licensor.

Confidentiality

The Parties acknowledge that each may have access to confidential information that relates to each other's business (the "Information"). The Parties agree to protect the confidentiality of the Information and maintain it with the strictest confidence, and no Party shall disclose such Information to third parties without the prior written consent of the other.

Insurance

Licensee shall, throughout the Term, obtain and maintain, at its own expense, standard product liability insurance coverage, naming Licensor as an additional named insured. Such policy shall provide protection against any claims, demands, and causes of action arising out of any alleged defects or failure to perform of the Licensed Products or any use of the Licensed Products. The amount of coverage shall be a minimum of $ _____ , with no deductible amount for each single occurrence for bodily injury or property damage. The policy shall provide for notice to the Licensor from the insurer by Registered or Certified Mail in the event of any modification or termination of insurance. The provisions of this section shall survive termination for three years.

Licensor's Right to Terminate

Licensor shall have the right to terminate this Agreement for the following reasons:

(*Select one or more provisions*)

☐ **Failure to Make Timely Payment.** Licensee fails to pay Royalties when due or fails to accurately report Net Sales, as defined in the Payment Section of this Agreement, and such failure is not cured within thirty (30) days after written notice from the Licensor.

☐ **Failure to Introduce Product.** Licensee fails to introduce the product to market by the date set in the Exploitation section of this Agreement or to offer the Licensed Products in commercially reasonable quantities during any subsequent year.

☐ **Assignment or Sublicensing.** Licensee assigns or sublicenses in violation of this Agreement.

☐ **Failure to Maintain Insurance.** Licensee fails to maintain or obtain product liability insurance as required by the provisions of this Agreement.

☐ **Failure to Submit Samples.** Licensee fails to provide Licensor with preproduction samples for approval.

☐ **Termination as to Unexploited Portion of Territory.** Licensor shall have the right to terminate the grant of license under this Agreement with respect to any country or region included in the Territory in which Licensee fails to offer the Licensed Products for sale or distribution or to secure a sublicensing agreement for the marketing, distribution, and sale of the product within two (2) years of the Effective Date.

Effect of Termination

Upon termination of this Agreement ("Termination"), all Royalty obligations as established in the Payments Section shall immediately become due. After the Termination of this license, all rights granted to Licensee under this Agreement shall terminate and revert to Licensor, and Licensee will refrain from further manufacturing, copying, marketing, distribution, or use of any Licensed Product or other product that incorporates the Work. Within thirty (30) days after Termination, Licensee shall deliver to Licensor a statement indicating the number and description of the Licensed Products that it had on hand or is in the process of manufacturing as of the Termination date.

Sell-Off Period

Licensee may dispose of the Licensed Products covered by this Agreement for a period of 90 days after Termination or expiration except that Licensee shall have no such right in the event this agreement is terminated according to the Licensor's Right to Terminate, above. At the end of the post-Termination sale period, Licensee shall furnish a Royalty payment and statement as required under the Payment Section. Upon Termination, Licensee shall deliver to Licensor all original artwork and camera-ready reproductions used in the manufacture of the Licensed Products. Licensor shall bear the costs of shipping for the artwork and reproductions.

Attorneys' Fees and Expenses

The prevailing Party shall have the right to collect from the other Party its reasonable costs and necessary disbursements and attorneys' fees incurred in enforcing this Agreement.

Dispute Resolution

(Select one if appropriate)

☐ **Mediation and Arbitration.** The Parties agree that every dispute or difference between them, arising under this Agreement, shall be settled first by a meeting of the Parties attempting to confer and resolve the dispute in a good faith manner. If the Parties cannot resolve their dispute after conferring, any Party may require the other Party to submit the matter to nonbinding mediation, utilizing the services of an impartial professional mediator approved by all Parties. If the Parties cannot come to an agreement following mediation, the Parties agree to submit the matter to binding arbitration at a location mutually agreeable to the Parties. The arbitration shall be conducted on a confidential basis pursuant to the Commercial Arbitration Rules of the American Arbitration Association. Any decision or award as a result of any such arbitration proceeding shall include the assessment of costs, expenses, and reasonable attorneys' fees, and shall include a written record of the proceedings and a written determination of the arbitrators. An arbitrator experienced in copyright and merchandising law shall conduct any such arbitration. An award of arbitration shall be final and binding on the Parties and may be confirmed in a court of competent jurisdiction.

☐ **Arbitration.** If a dispute arises under or relating to this Agreement, the Parties agree to submit such dispute to binding arbitration in the State of
_____ or another location mutually agreeable to the Parties. The arbitration shall be conducted on a confidential basis pursuant to the Commercial Arbitration Rules of the American Arbitration Association. Any decision or award as a result of any such arbitration proceeding shall be in writing and shall provide an explanation for all conclusions of law and fact and shall include the assessment of costs, expenses, and reasonable attorneys' fees. An arbitrator experienced in copyright and merchandising law shall conduct any such arbitration. An award of arbitration may be confirmed in a court of competent jurisdiction.

Governing Law

This Agreement shall be governed in accordance with the laws of the State of
_____ .

Jurisdiction

The Parties consent to the exclusive jurisdiction and venue of the federal and state courts located in _____ in any action arising out of or relating to this Agreement. The Parties waive any other venue to which either Party might be entitled by domicile or otherwise.

Waiver

The failure to exercise any right provided in this Agreement shall not be a waiver of prior or subsequent rights.

Invalidity

If any provision of this Agreement is invalid under applicable statute or rule of law, it is to be considered omitted, and the remaining provisions of this Agreement shall in no way be affected.

Entire Understanding

This Agreement expresses the complete understanding of the Parties and supersedes all prior representations, agreements, and understandings, whether written or oral. This Agreement may not be altered except by a written document signed by both Parties.

Attachments and Exhibits

The Parties agree and acknowledge that all attachments, exhibits, and schedules referred to in this Agreement are incorporated in this Agreement by reference.

No Special Damages

Licensor shall not be liable to Licensee for any incidental, consequential, punitive, or special damages.

Notices

Any notice or communication required or permitted to be given under this Agreement shall be sufficiently given when received by certified mail or sent by facsimile transmission or overnight courier.

No Joint Venture

Nothing contained in this Agreement shall be construed to place one of the Parties in the relationship of agent, employee, franchisee, officer, partner, or joint venturer to the other Party. Neither Party may create or assume any obligation on behalf of the other.

Assignability

(Select one)

☐ **Assignment Requires Licensor Consent.** Licensee may not assign or transfer its rights or obligations pursuant to this Agreement without the prior written consent of Licensor. Any assignment or transfer in violation of this section shall be void.

☐ **Licensor Consent Not Unreasonably Withheld.** Licensee may not assign or transfer its rights or obligations pursuant to this Agreement without the prior written consent of Licensor. Such consent shall not be unreasonably withheld. Any assignment or transfer in violation of this section shall be void.

☐ **Licensor Consent Not Required for Assignment to Parent or Acquiring Company.** Licensee may not assign or transfer its rights or obligations pursuant to this Agreement without the prior written consent of Licensor. However, no consent is required for an assignment or transfer that occurs: (a) to an entity in which Licensee owns more than 50% of the assets; or (b) as part of a transfer of all or substantially all of the assets of Licensee to any party. Any assignment or transfer in violation of this Section shall be void.

Each Party has signed this Agreement through its authorized representative. The Parties, having read this Agreement, indicate their consent to the terms and conditions by their signature below.

By: _____

Date: _____

Licensor Name: _____

By: _____

Date: _____

Licensee Name/Title: _____

EXHIBIT A

The Property _____

_____

Licensed Products _____

_____

Sales Requirements

$ _____ in Gross Sales per year.

Explanation of Merchandise License Agreement

Every merchandise license agreement contains essential elements, including a grant of rights, territory, term, and identification of the parties. Most, like the model merchandise license agreements in this chapter, contain additional provisions such as warranties, indemnity, termination, and miscellaneous clauses.

The Introductory Paragraph: Identifying the Parties

The introductory paragraph identifies the people or companies entering into the agreement, known as the "parties." The licensor (the copyright or trademark owner) grants permission. The licensee is the person or company seeking permission. The introductory paragraph may also include the parties' business form (for example, corporation or sole proprietorship) and business address. Insert that information, if desired, following the name of each party—for example, "Artco Printing, a California corporation located at 434 W. Oakdale Avenue, Los Angeles, California, 90015."

"Whereas" Provisions

In some license agreements, the introductory information is referred to as the "Whereas" provisions, for example: "Whereas DTK publishing (the licensee) desires to acquire rights ...." The use of the term "whereas" has no particular legal significance and it is not included in this book's model agreements.

Instead of licensee and licensor, the agreement can be drafted to use the names of the parties throughout the agreement or terms such as "Artist" for the licensor and "Manufacturer" for the licensee, as long as this terminology is used consistently within the agreement.

The Work

The licensor's material (the art, text, or music licensed) is referred to as the "Work." Any term can be substituted instead of "Work"—for example, the "Photograph" or the "Book"—as long as this terminology is used consistently within the agreement. If more than one work is being licensed from the licensor, each work can be identified separately, such as "Work #1," "Work #2," and so on. In Exhibit A, each work should be described or, if possible, a photocopy of the artwork or text should be attached to the agreement and referenced in Exhibit A.

The Licensed Product

A licensed product is any merchandise that incorporates the work. If the definition of the product is too narrow, the licensee may be precluded from certain markets. For example, if the licensed product is described as "T-shirts," the licensee cannot sell other shirts like tank tops. Similarly, the term "ceramic cups" precludes the sale of plastic cups. If you don't want to exclude large categories of items from the merchandise you can sell, be sure to define your licensed product broadly enough. For instance, instead of "T-shirts," you could define your licensed product as "upper-body apparel." Any plain-language definition is suitable. Insert your definitions in Exhibit A.

The Grant of Rights

The grant of rights (also known as simply the "grant") officially permits use of the work, describes the rights under copyright law that the copyright owner is licensing, and establishes whether the rights are exclusive or nonexclusive. In a merchandise license agreement, the grant must include the following rights:

- **The right to reproduce.** This refers to the right to make copies of the art or other work on merchandise. This is similar to the grant of rights for a regular license agreement that gives the right to make copies on various media, such as print or film. This right is essential for the merchandise agreement—without it, the material cannot be duplicated. Note that the right to reproduce is not unlimited. The agreement specifically limits it to the use of the material on "Licensed Products." In other words, the artwork can only be used on specific products as defined in the attached exhibit.

- **The right to distribute copies.** This refers to the right to sell or give away the work as reproduced on the merchandise.

Reproduction and distribution are closely related, and every merchandise license agreement requires both rights.

Other rights, however, are optional. The section below discusses what optional rights may be granted and the difference between exclusive and nonexclusive rights.

Optional Rights

The following rights may be included in a merchandise agreement:

- **The right to adapt or create derivatives.** This refers to the right to modify the work—for example, to alter a photograph so that only a portion is used. The result of the modification is referred to as a "derivative work." If you plan to create a derivative work, the grant of rights must include permission to modify the original work. For example, if the licensee plans on creating a series of T-shirts based upon a character, each modification of the character would be a derivative. The language in the model agreement allows the licensor to own any modifications or contributions the licensee makes to the work. This is standard contract language, and you have little choice but to accept it. If this language is not included, the licensee and licensor may become coauthors of any jointly created derivative work.

- **The right to display publicly.** This refers to the right to exhibit or display a licensed product publicly. As a general rule, the licensee should always acquire this right, as it permits activities like displaying the work—for example, selling posters of artwork over the Internet.

However, even without this right, the licensee can display the artwork as it appears on the merchandise in connection with advertisements. The U.S. Copyright Act (17 U.S.C. § 113) permits the reproduction of artwork or photographs on "useful articles" in advertisements. A useful article includes clothing, tote bags, or most other merchandise that has a utilitarian function.

- **The right to perform publicly.** This refers to the right to perform the work publicly—for example, if you license music for use in a toy and the toy is demonstrated in a television or radio commercial. Note that if you are obtaining a license to use music in merchandise, you will always need this right. For more information on public performance of music, see Chapter 5, "Getting Permission to Use Music."

Exclusive Versus Nonexclusive Rights

Every merchandise license agreement is either exclusive or nonexclusive. Exclusive means that only the licensee will have the rights granted in the agreement—no one else can be given the same rights during the term of the agreement. Nonexclusive means that the licensor (the copyright owner) can give the same rights to someone else. The primary reason for seeking exclusive rights is to prevent a competitor from using the same material in the same way.

An exclusive license is usually more expensive than a nonexclusive license, but not always. For example, the fee for an exclusive license to use an image on auto seat covers may be the same as a nonexclusive license simply because the seat cover market is limited and has few manufacturers. However, an exclusive license for T-shirts or calendars may be two or three times the cost of a nonexclusive license.

Note that if you're seeking exclusive rights, you must obtain the consent of all owners of the work, not just one. Sometimes more than one person or entity owns a copyrighted work. For nonexclusive rights, you need only the consent of one owner. But all owners must agree to grant exclusive rights.

Sublicenses

A sublicense allows the licensee to license its rights to another company. Often, a licensee will sublicense rights to foreign companies. Retaining or granting sublicensing rights depends on each situation. For example, if a licensee has experience in foreign markets and can handle the licensing abroad, then the licensee would want to prohibit foreign sublicensing and retain those rights. If the licensor was unsure of whether it could license rights abroad, then the licensor may want a provision requiring written consent. That way, the licensor could review each sublicensing arrangement to determine its relative advantages and disadvantages.

Our model agreement provides that sublicensing is permitted with written consent of licensor, but the consent cannot be withheld unreasonably. This is the preferred option for most licensees because it means that the licensor can only withhold consent for a valid business reason.

Reservation of Rights

If a licensor does not grant a specific right, the licensor has retained or "reserved" that right. Although it is not essential to state this fact, most licensors prefer to include this statement.

Territory

Geographic limits ("territory") determine where the licensee can exercise rights. The territory can be as small or as large as desired. Worldwide rights are always desirable because they allow the licensee to sell his or her merchandise in any country. If the territory is the world, insert the word "worldwide" into this section. If the territory is a specific region or country, insert that information. Many merchandise licenses are only for the United States and Canada. Since the cost of a worldwide license is usually greater than for a license for an individual country, review your sales potential in any country before you include it in the territory.

Term

Term refers to the length of the merchandise license. As a general rule, the licensee wants permission for as long as possible while the licensor prefers to give permission for a shorter period of time. The date that an agreement commences is usually referred to as the "effective date." If the agreement has a fixed date of termination, say ten years, the agreement would end ten years from the effective date.

The agreement prohibits a term that is longer than United States copyright protection because after copyright expires, the licensee should not have to pay to use the once copyrighted materials. Even if no time limit is expressed, under some circumstances the law allows the copyright owner to terminate the merchandise license after 35 years. This is true even if the agreement contains a statement that the license is "forever" or "in perpetuity."

Payments

Most merchandise licenses are based on a payment system of royalties. A "royalty" is a continuing payment based on a percentage of the income from the licensed product. The advantage of a royalty system is that the licensee only has to pay if the licensed product earns money. The disadvantages are that royalty obligations often include advance or guaranteed annual payments and continuing accounting responsibility. Below are the definitions of some royalty terms:

- "Gross sales" are the total amount billed to customers. "Net sales" are the licensee's gross sales minus certain deductions. In other words, the licensee calculates the total amount billed to customers and then deducts certain items before paying the royalty. It is generally acceptable to deduct from gross sales any amounts paid for shipping, freight, taxes, credits, returns, and discounts made at the time of sale.
- An "advance against royalties" is an up-front payment to the licensor, usually made at the time the license agreement is signed. An advance is almost always credited or "recouped" against future royalties unless the

agreement provides otherwise. It's as if the licensee is saying, "I expect you will earn at least $1,000 in royalties so I am going to advance you that sum at the time we sign the agreement." When the licensor starts earning royalties, the licensee keeps the first $1,000 as repayment for the licensor's advance. If the licensor doesn't earn the $1,000 in royalties, the licensee takes a loss. Generally, a licensor does not have to return the advance unless he or she breaches the agreement.

- The "licensed product royalty" is the most common form of royalty payment—a percentage of net sales. Net sales royalty payments are computed by multiplying the royalty rate against net sales. For example, a royalty rate of 5% multiplied by net sales of $1,000 equals a net sales royalty of $50.

- A "per-unit royalty" is tied to the number of units sold or manufactured, not the total money earned by sales. For example, under a per-unit royalty, a licensor might receive 50 cents for each licensed product sold or manufactured. (Note that the licensee cannot choose both per-unit and net sales royalties.) If the licensor is using the merchandise as part of a free distribution, for example, giving out hundreds of the products at a promotion for a restaurant, check the "manufactured" box. If the merchandise will be offered for sale, check the "sold" box. Generally, net sales royalties are used instead of per-unit royalties because revenue may come from sources such as sublicensing, in which case the total net sales will be easier to track.

- The guaranteed minimum annual royalty payment (GMAR) is an annual payment that guarantees that the licensor receives a specific payment, regardless of how well the merchandise sells in any year. At the end of each year, the earned royalties are totaled and, if they are more than the GMAR, the licensor is paid the difference. If the earned royalties are less than the GMAR, the licensee takes a loss. In some cases, a licensee may not want to take the loss and will insist that this difference be carried forward and deducted against the next year's royalties. If a license agreement includes a GMAR, the licensee may want to limit the initial term of the agreement. Otherwise, the licensee risks being locked into paying GMARs when the merchandise no longer sells.

- A license fee is a one-time fee usually paid at the time the agreement is signed. The licensee may arrange to make the payment when the licensed product is first distributed. That way, if the licensed product is not produced, the licensee does not have to pay.
- Include the provision for sublicensing revenue in the agreement if the licensor permits sublicensing.

Audits

The audit provision describes when the licensor (or the licensor's representative) can have access to the licensee's records. If the licensee has failed to pay the licensor properly, the audit will detect that information. The licensee will have to pay for the audit if the audit detects an error of a certain magnitude, usually anywhere from $500 to $2,000. Insert an amount in the blank space.

Warranties and Indemnity

Warranties are contractual promises. If the licensor breaches a warranty, under an indemnity provision, the licensee will have to pay for certain costs that result from the breach. In this way, warranties and indemnity work together. They are each discussed in more detail below.

Keep in mind that the merchandise license can be executed without including warranties or an indemnity provision. They are recommended but not essential for the agreement.

Warranties

In some agreements, warranties are labeled "covenants" or "representations." Regardless of the title, they are essentially the same things: promises and assurances made between the parties regarding certain aspects of the contract. A common warranty, for instance, is that the licensor owns the rights to the work and has the power to grant them to the licensee. In addition, the licensee should seek a promise that the work doesn't infringe third-party rights (rights of people who are not part of the agreement). Since licensors are often wary of making this type of assurance, the model agreement provides a more palatable warranty that the licensor "has no knowledge as to any third-party claims." This means that a reasonable person in the licensor's position would know whether the work is infringing someone else's rights.

A licensor may ask that the licensee provide a warranty that sales and marketing of the licensed product will conform to applicable laws. A sample provision is included in the model merchandise agreement.

If an agreement includes a warranty but no indemnity provision, the parties can still sue for "breach of warranty." However, a judge or jury will decide whether the breaching party must pay the costs or attorneys' fees associated with the breach.

Indemnity

A licensor who provides indemnity is agreeing to pay for the licensee's damages for certain situations. For example, if the licensor indemnifies the licensee against infringement, the licensor will have to pay damages (and legal fees) if the licensee is sued for infringement for his or her use of the work. Indemnity acts like a shield: the licensee can deflect a lawsuit from him or herself, and the licensor pays for the damages. Indemnity provisions are also sometimes referred to as "hold harmless" provisions because the provision often states that the "Licensor shall hold the Licensee harmless from any losses, etc."

Licensors are often unwilling to provide indemnity because they don't want to be legally obligated to pay legal costs. Since indemnification involves a financial risk, many licensors will avoid it completely or will only agree to it with further limitations. For example, a licensor may agree to pay indemnity but only if the amount is not larger than any amounts they received under the agreement. The licensor may request that the licensee provide indemnification as well. For example, if the licensee promises to market and distribute the licensed product in a legal manner, the licensee may indemnify the licensor from any liability arising out of the licensee's marketing and distribution.

It is also important to remember that indemnity is only worthwhile if the party who agrees to pay has money or insurance to cover the costs. An indemnity provision is useless if the indemnifier (the person who is supposed to indemnify) is broke.

Intellectual Property Rights

If the licensor has not filed a copyright registration and does not plan to do so, the licensee may register for protection under this provision. It is common for the licensee to deduct the reasonable costs of registration from future royalties.

Credits

The licensor should insert any credit he or she wants to appear on the merchandise. For instance, a photographer who wanted to be credited for a photograph he's licensing could insert the desired credit line: "Tom Bamberger Photo Studios."

If the licensee does not display the credit on the merchandise, it could provide a basis for the licensor to terminate the agreement.

The credit section also provides the licensee with the right to use the licensor's name and trademark in advertising for the merchandised product. This is essential if the licensor is an established artist or writer whose name or image the licensee intends to use in promotional materials.

Infringement Against Third Parties

If the licensed product is successful, unethical competitors may create imitations. If the licensor does not have the financial resources to fight the infringer, this provision allows the licensee to deal with infringers. It provides for funding of a lawsuit and for dividing any money that is recovered from the infringer. The provision in the model agreement establishes a 50/50 division of any award money after payment of attorneys' fees.

Exploitation Date

This provision establishes the date by which the licensee must release the licensed product. Without this assurance, a licensor may be worried that the licensee will simply sit on the work and not exploit it. Sometimes the release date coincides with a specific trade show or a seasonal catalog. If the licensee fails to meet this date, the licensor can claim that there has been a "material breach," which is a basis for termination of the license agreement.

Approval of Samples and Quality Control

The licensor needs to guarantee that the work is being reproduced properly and that the licensed product is not inferior to competing products. This provision permits the licensor to review the preproduction artwork and prototypes before providing approval (within a ten-day period).

Licensor Copies and Right to Purchase

The licensor will want free copies of the licensed product and the right to purchase more at wholesale cost. If the licensee is concerned that the copies will be sold or transferred to a competitor, he or she can add a statement to this provision that prevents the licensor from selling the copies.

Confidentiality

It's possible that the licensee or licensor may be disclosing confidential information in the course of the merchandise license. Confidential information includes any information that gives the business an advantage and is maintained in confidence. This clause requires that each party to the agreement preserve confidential information. For example, if the licensor has a secret marketing plan and the licensee discloses that information in an interview, that would be a breach of the agreement.

Insurance

If a consumer is injured using the licensed product and claims it's defective, the licensee and licensor may be sued for product liability. It is for this reason that the sellers of merchandise (licensees) acquire product liability insurance. By naming the licensor in the policy, the licensee shields the licensor from claims of product injuries as well. The minimum amount of coverage inserted for the policy should be $1,000,000. A separate business policy is required for protection against claims of infringement.

Termination

Even without a termination provision, either party can terminate a merchandise license agreement if there is a material breach. A "material breach" is a substantial abuse of the agreement—for example, if the licensee used the work for purposes that were not described in the agreement. Most licensors will insist upon including a termination provision, including some or all of the clauses listed in the sample agreement (for example, the right to terminate as to a specific portion of the territory if the work is not exploited there).

Effect of Termination

At the time of termination, the licensee may have boxes of licensed products left in the warehouse. If the agreement has ended amicably, it is reasonable to allow the licensee a period of time to sell off the remaining inventory. Naturally, the licensor is entitled to royalties for these products. A period between three and six months is probably sufficient for sell-off. In addition, the licensor should obtain an accounting of the remaining inventory. If the licensee is not paying royalties or has breached the agreement, the licensee is not permitted to sell off the remaining inventory.

Miscellaneous Provisions

Many agreements contain a section of provisions entitled "Miscellaneous" or "General." These provisions actually have little in common except that they don't fit anywhere else in the agreement, so they are grouped together at the end. Lawyers often refer to them as "boilerplate."

Don't be misled by the fact that these provisions are buried in the back of the agreement. They can affect important issues like how disputes are resolved and how a court should enforce the agreement. However, even though they are important, they are not mandatory—they can be removed without affecting the validity of the agreement. Below is a summary of some common boilerplate provisions.

Attorneys' Fees

In the event of a legal dispute between the licensee and licensor, the attorneys' fees provision establishes that the winner of the dispute will receive payment for legal fees. Without this provision, neither party will be reimbursed for attorneys' fees unless the lawsuit is for copyright infringement. Even in that case, the award is not mandatory; it is at the judge's discretion.

Dispute Resolution

Arbitration is like going to court with less formality. Instead of filing a lawsuit, the parties hire one or more arbitrators to evaluate the dispute and make a determination. Arbitrators are trained to evaluate disputes; many of them are retired judges.

Mediation is similar to arbitration except that instead of making a determination, a neutral evaluator attempts to help the parties settle their dispute themselves. That is, the mediator offers advice so that the parties reach a solution together. Mediation and arbitration are often referred to as "alternative dispute resolution" or "ADR."

The model agreement includes two alternative dispute resolution provisions. The first provides for mediation first, then arbitration if mediation fails. The second provides for arbitration only.

Governing Law

In the event of a dispute, this provision (sometimes called "Choice of Law") determines which state's law will govern the lawsuit. Every state has laws regarding contract interpretation. The licensor usually favors the state in which its headquarters are located, often New York or California. Does it matter which state is chosen? Some states have a reputation as being favorable for certain kinds of disputes, but generally, the differences in state law are not great enough to make this a major negotiating issue.

Jurisdiction

In the event of a dispute, this provision establishes in which state (and, if you want to specify, which county) the lawsuit or arbitration must be filed. Each party will prefer having jurisdiction in its home location, so this section is sometimes a matter of negotiation.

Pros and Cons of Arbitration

Arbitration has both good and not-so-good aspects when compared to litigating a dispute in court. Here is an overview of the pros and cons of arbitration:

- **Pros:** Arbitration is usually more expedient than litigation. Also, the parties can select an arbitrator who has knowledge in the merchandising field.
- **Cons:** Unlike in a lawsuit, there is no right to discovery—the process by which parties must disclose documents and information about their cases. However, the licensee can include a requirement for discovery in the arbitration provision. Also, unlike a court ruling, a binding arbitration ruling is not appealable. It can only be set aside if the arbitrator was biased or the ruling violated public policy. Arbitrators must be paid (unlike state and federal judges), and fees can run to $10,000 or more. And, most participants in arbitrations hire attorneys, so the licensee will still have to pay attorneys' fees (although probably less than in a lawsuit).

Private arbitration is offered by a number of organizations, the best known of which is the American Arbitration Association (AAA). For information on arbitration and the AAA, check its website at www.adr.org.

If the section creates contention, remove it. If there is no reference to jurisdiction, the location is usually determined by whoever files a lawsuit. If you use a jurisdiction clause, it should conform to the governing law section (as discussed above) and designate the same state.

In Some States, Jurisdiction Clauses Are Invalid

In the past, many courts believed that citizens should not be able to bargain for jurisdiction (sometimes referred to as "forum shopping") and refused to enforce jurisdiction provisions. Today, only two states—Idaho and Montana— refuse to honor these provisions. In other states (Florida, for example), courts have required that the parties have some contacts with the state designated by this provision beyond the existence of the contract provision itself. (*McRae v. J.D./M.D., Inc.*, 511 So.2d 540 (1987).)

Waiver

This provision permits the parties to waive (forgo or give up claim to) a portion of the agreement without establishing a precedent—that is, without giving up future claims under the same portion of the agreement.

Invalidity

This provision (sometimes referred to as "severability") permits a court to remove an invalid provision and keep the rest of the agreement intact. Otherwise, if one portion of the agreement is invalid, a court may rule that the whole agreement is invalid.

Entire Understanding

This provision (sometimes referred to as "integration") establishes that the agreement is the final version and that any further modification of the agreement must be in writing.

Attachments

This provision guarantees that any attachments or "exhibits" attached to the agreement will be included as part of the agreement.

No Special Damages

If either party breaches the agreement, state laws provide that the non-breaching party can recover the amount of the loss resulting from the breach. For example, if the licensee fails to pay royalties accurately, the licensor can sue to recover the unpaid amount and attorneys' fees, if the agreement provides for such fees. Under some state laws, a party can make claims for additional damages—for example, special or punitive damages that are awarded to punish the breaching party. This provision prevents either party from claiming any damages other than those actually suffered directly from the breach.

Notices

If a dispute arises, each party is entitled to be notified of the problem; the purpose of the notice provision is to establish the method of notification. If the notice procedures are not followed, claims against either party may be delayed until proper notification is provided.

No Joint Venture

The relationship between the parties is defined by the agreement. But to an outsider, it may appear that a licensee and licensor have a different relationship, such as a partnership or joint venture. It's possible that an unscrupulous licensor will try to capitalize on this appearance and make a third-party deal. That is, a licensor may claim to be a partner of the licensee to obtain a benefit from a distributor or sublicensee. In order to avoid liability for such a situation, most agreements include a provision disclaiming any relationship other than licensee/licensor.

Assignability

It is possible that the licensee may, at some point, want to transfer the rights under this agreement to another company. For example, say the licensee has two agreements with a licensor, one for shirts and another for hats. The licensee later decides it only wants to concentrate on shirts, so it wants to assign its rights in the hat agreement to a company that specializes in hat merchandising. Since agreements are only binding between the parties who sign them, the hat company can only acquire the licensee's rights in the contract if the licensee assigns those rights. The licensor may not be happy with the change. For example, the new company may have a bad reputation when it comes to paying royalties. Since assignability can be a sensitive issue, three choices are provided in the model agreement.

The first option requires that the licensor's written consent be given for an assignment. In that case, the licensor can review the deal and decide, for any reason, whether or not it wants to participate with the new licensee.

The second choice also requires written consent, but requires that the licensor cannot withhold consent unreasonably. In that situation, the licensor can review the prospective arrangement and, if there is a valid business reason for refusing to consent, the licensor can refuse. A valid business reason usually relates to some financial quality of the new licensee.

The third provision permits the transfer of rights without the licensor's consent provided that the transfer is made to a company that is purchasing the licensee's company. In this arrangement, another company is acquiring all of the licensee's interests. Some licensees insist on this because they want the freedom to sell their whole company (and its licenses).

Signatures

Each party must sign the agreement. The people who sign on each party's behalf must have the authority to do so. Use the following rules to determine how the agreement should be signed:

- **Sole Proprietorship.** If either party is a sole proprietorship, that party signs using his or her own name. If either party is using a fictitious business name (sometimes known as a "d.b.a."), list the name of the business above the signature line.

  EXAMPLE: Tom Lennon is a sole proprietor who calls his business "Lennonism." He would sign as follows:

  Lennonism
  By: _____
  Tom Lennon, sole proprietor

- **Partnership.** If either party is a general or limited partnership, the only person authorized to sign the agreement is a general partner or someone who has written authority from a general partner (usually in the form a partnership resolution). The name of the partnership must be mentioned above the signature line or the partnership will not be bound—only the person who signed the agreement.

  EXAMPLE: Cindy Peacock is a general partner in Speculative Ventures Partnership. She would sign as follows:

  Speculative Ventures Partnership
  By: _____
  Cindy Peacock, general partner

- **Corporation or LLC.** If either party is a corporation or limited liability company (LLC), only a person authorized by the corporation can sign the agreement. The president or chief operating officer (CEO) usually has such power, but not every officer of a corporation has the authority to bind the corporation. If in doubt, ask for written proof of the authority. This proof is usually in the form of a corporate resolution.

The name of the corporation should be mentioned above the signature line or the corporation may not be bound—only the person who signed the agreement.

EXAMPLE: Matthew LaNotta is CEO of Sunday Marketing. He would sign as follows:

Sunday Marketing, Inc., a New York corporation

By: _____

Matthew LaNotta, CEO

If either party has doubts about any person's authority to sign the agreement, don't proceed until satisfied that the person has full authority to represent the company.

Exhibit A

Agreements often have attachments known as "exhibits," which are separate documents stapled or joined to the agreement. In license agreements, the exhibit summarizes some of the essential business elements. For example, in the model agreement, Exhibit A includes a description of the work, the licensed product, and, if applicable, the sales minimum required to renew the agreement.

Merchandise License Worksheet

The Merchandise License Worksheet below is provided to help you (the licensee, presumably) keep track of the merchandise license agreement elements discussed throughout this chapter. It can function in two ways: as a record of the elements upon which the parties agreed, or to help decipher an agreement furnished by the licensor.

 FORM

You can download this form (and all other forms in this book) from Nolo.com; for details, see the appendix.

Merchandise License Worksheet

Licensor

Name of licensor business: _____

Licensor address: _____

Licensor business form:

☐ sole proprietorship

☐ general partnership

☐ limited partnership

☐ corporation (state of incorporation: _____)

☐ limited liability company (state of organization: _____)

Name and position of person signing for licensor: _____

_____

The Work(s)

Source: _____

Description: _____

Page number: _____

Relevant data (e.g., ISBN, copyright notice): _____

Licensed Product(s)

Tentative title: _____

Format: _____

Grant of Rights (*Check those rights needed*)

☐ reproduce _____

☐ distribute _____

☐ modify, adapt _____

☐ display _____

☐ perform _____

Market and Format Limitations

☐ specific market: _____

☐ specific format: _____

Territory

☐ worldwide

☐ countries or states (name which): _____

Exclusivity

☐ exclusive

☐ nonexclusive

Term

☐ no time limits

☐ fixed term (how long: _____)

☐ unlimited term until one party terminates

☐ an initial term with renewals (see below)

☐ other _____

Renewals

If the parties have agreed upon an initial term with renewals:

How many renewal periods? _____

How long is each renewal period? _____

What triggers renewal? _____

Fee

☐ one time fee $ _____

☐ date due: _____

☐ recurring fee $ _____

☐ date due/trigger _____

☐ advance against royalties $ _____

☐ date due: _____

☐ royalty rate(s): _____ % of

   ☐ net sales

   ☐ gross sales

☐ If royalty payments, are there any:

☐ deductions: _____

☐ audits (how many per year: _____)

Warranties

☐ licensor warranty conditions: _____

☐ licensee warranty conditions: _____

Indemnity

☐ licensor indemnity conditions: _____

_____

☐ licensee indemnity conditions: _____

Credit

☐ licensor credit: _____

Furnished Samples

☐ licensor samples required (how many: _____)

☐ (when: _____)

Miscellaneous

☐ jurisdiction state: _____

☐ governing law state: _____

☐ arbitration

Termination

☐ conditions: _____

_____

Right of First Refusal and Most Favored Nation Provisions

Some merchandise agreements include a provision known as a right of first refusal. The purpose of this provision is to give the licensee the first shot at licensing any new works from the licensor. For example, if the licensor creates new illustrations, the licensee will have the first opportunity to license those new works. If another company makes a better offer than the licensee, the licensee has a period of time to match the offer. A sample right of first refusal provision reads as follows:

> **Right of First Refusal.** Licensor may identify and develop new works suitable to be used as Licensed Products ("New Works"). Licensee shall have the first right to license such New Works, and the parties shall negotiate in good faith to reach agreement as to the terms and conditions for such license. In the event that the parties fail to reach agreement and Licensor receives an offer from a third party for the New Works, licensee shall have 30 days to notify Licensor whether Licensee desires to execute a license on similar terms and conditions. In the event that Licensee matches any third-party terms and conditions, Licensor shall enter into a License Agreement with Licensee and terminate negotiations with any third parties.

A right of first refusal is occasionally confused with a "most favored nations" provision. A most favored nations provision is common in a nonexclusive arrangement and guarantees that a licensee won't be charged any more for new works than any other licensee. For example, say your film company has a nonexclusive license agreement (that includes a most favored nations clause) to use a song. You pay $10,000 for the rights. The owner/licensor subsequently licenses the same song under a nonexclusive license with another film company for $9,000. Under the most favored nation provision, the licensor must lower your rate to $9,000.

Short-Form Merchandise License Agreement

Below is a short-form merchandise license agreement. It is intended primarily for licensing an image on merchandise such as a T-shirt. The short-form agreement eliminates many of the choices in the longer agreement and, instead, includes the most commonly used provisions. You should consider using this agreement if your arrangement is limited to one or two years or to a specific number of copies (for example, 2,000 T-shirts). This agreement is suitable if the relationship and trust between the parties is such that you do not need the increased formality of a full-length agreement.

FORM

You can download this form (and all other forms in this book) from Nolo.com; for details, see the appendix.

Short-Form Merchandise License Agreement

Introduction

This License Agreement (the "Agreement") is made between _____
_____(referred to as "Licensor")
and _____ (referred to as "Licensee").

The parties agree as follows:

Grant of Rights

The "Work" is defined as follows: _____.

Licensed Products are Licensee's products incorporating the Work, specifically

_____

(the "Licensed Products").

Licensor is the owner of all rights to the Work, and Licensee shall not claim any right to use the Work except under the terms of this Agreement. Licensor grants to Licensee:

(Select one)

    ☐ an exclusive license

    ☐ a nonexclusive license

to reproduce and distribute the Work in or on the Licensed Products.

Sublicense

Licensee may sublicense the rights granted pursuant to this agreement provided: Licensee obtains Licensor's prior written consent to such sublicense, and Licensor receives such revenue or Royalty payment as provided in the Payment section below. Licensor's consent to any sublicense shall not be unreasonably withheld. Any sublicense granted in violation of this provision shall be void. Licensor reserves all rights other than those being conveyed or granted in this Agreement.

Territory

The rights granted to Licensee are limited to _____
(the "Territory").

Term

This Agreement shall commence upon the "Effective Date," established by the latest signature date, and shall extend for a period of _____ years (the "Initial Term"). Following the Initial Term, Licensee may renew this agreement under the same terms and conditions for _____ consecutive _____ periods (the "Renewal Terms"), provided that Licensee provides written notice of its intention to renew this agreement within thirty (30) days before the expiration of the current term.

Royalties

All royalties ("Royalties") provided for under this Agreement shall accrue when the respective Licensed Products are sold, shipped, distributed, billed, or paid for, whichever occurs first.

Net Sales

Net Sales are defined as Licensee's gross sales (the gross invoice amount billed to customers) less quantity discounts or rebates and returns actually credited. A quantity discount or rebate is a discount made at the time of shipment. No deductions shall be made for cash or other discounts, commissions, manufacturing costs, uncollectible accounts, or for fees or expenses of any kind that the Licensee may incur in connection with the Royalty payments.

Advance Against Royalties

As a nonrefundable advance against Royalties (the "Advance"), Licensee agrees to pay to Licensor upon execution of this Agreement the sum of $ _____ .

Licensed Product Royalty

Licensee agrees to pay a Royalty of _____ % of all Net Sales revenue of the Licensed Products ("Licensed Product Royalty").

Sublicensing Revenues

In the event of any sublicense of the rights granted pursuant to this Agreement, Licensee shall pay to Licensor _____ % of all sublicensing revenues.

Payments and Statements

Within thirty (30) days after the end of each calendar quarter (the "Royalty Period"), an accurate statement of Net Sales of Licensed Products along with any Royalty payments or sublicensing revenues shall be due to Licensor. The acceptance by Licensor of any of the statements furnished or Royalties paid shall not preclude Licensor from questioning the correctness at any time of any payments or statements.

Audit

Licensee shall keep accurate books of account and records covering all transactions relating to the license granted in this Agreement, and Licensor or its duly authorized representatives shall have the right upon five (5) days' prior written notice, and during normal business hours, to inspect Licensee's records relating to the Work licensed under this Agreement.

Late Payment

If Licensee is late in any payment provided for in this Agreement, Licensee shall pay interest on the payment from the date due until paid at a rate of 1.5% per month, or the maximum rate permitted by law, whichever is less.

Warranties

Licensor warrants that it has the power and authority to enter into this Agreement and has no knowledge as to any third-party claims regarding the proprietary rights in the Work that would interfere with the rights granted under this Agreement.

Licensee warrants that it will use its best commercial efforts to market the Licensed Products and that sale and marketing of the Licensed Products shall be in conformance with all applicable laws and regulations, including but not limited to all intellectual property laws.

Licensor Credits

Licensee shall identify Licensor as the owner of rights to the Work and shall include the following notice on all copies of the Licensed Products:

"_____ . All rights reserved."

Licensee may, with Licensor's consent, use Licensor's name, image, or trademark in advertising or promotional materials associated with the sale of the Licensed Products.

Exploitation

Licensee agrees to manufacture, distribute, and sell the Licensed Products in commercially reasonable quantities during the term of this Agreement and to commence such manufacture, distribution, and sale by _____ . This is a material provision of this Agreement.

Approval of Samples and Quality Control

Licensee shall submit a reasonable number of preproduction samples of the Licensed Product to Licensor to assure that the product meets Licensor's quality standards. In the event that Licensor fails to object in writing within ten (10) business days after the date of receipt of any such materials, such materials shall be deemed to be acceptable.

Licensor Copies and Right to Purchase

Licensee shall provide Licensor with _____ copies of each Licensed Product. Licensor has the right to purchase from Licensee, at Licensee's manufacturing cost, at least _____ copies of any Licensed Product, and such payments shall be deducted from Royalties due to Licensor.

Licensor's Right to Terminate

Licensor shall have the right to terminate this Agreement for the following reasons:

(*Select one or more provisions*)

☐ **Failure to Make Timely Payment.** Licensee fails to pay Royalties when due or fails to accurately report Net Sales, as defined in the Payments and Statements section of this Agreement, and such failure is not cured within thirty (30) days after written notice from the Licensor.

☐ **Failure to Introduce Product.** Licensee fails to introduce the product to market by the date set in the Exploitation section of this Agreement or to offer the Licensed Products in commercially reasonable quantities during any subsequent year.

Effect of Termination

After the termination of this license, all rights granted to Licensee under this Agreement shall terminate and revert to Licensor, and Licensee will refrain from further manufacturing, copying, marketing, distribution, or use of any Licensed Product or other product that incorporates the Work. Licensee may dispose of the Licensed Products covered by this Agreement for a period of 90 days after termination or expiration, except that Licensee shall have no such right in the event this agreement is terminated according to the Licensor's Right to Terminate, above.

Miscellaneous

The prevailing Party shall have the right to collect from the other Party its reasonable costs and attorneys' fees incurred in enforcing this Agreement. This Agreement expresses the full, complete, and exclusive understanding of the Parties with respect to the subject matter and supersedes all prior proposals, representations, and understandings. If a dispute arises between the Parties arising under or relating to this Agreement, the Parties agree to submit such dispute to arbitration conducted under the rules of the American Arbitration Association. An arbitration award may be confirmed in a court of competent jurisdiction. The waiver or failure of any Party to exercise in any respect any right provided for in this Agreement shall not be deemed a waiver of any further right under this Agreement. No Party shall represent themselves to be the employee, franchisee, franchiser, joint venturer, officer, or partner of the other Party, and nothing in this Agreement shall be construed to place the Parties in the relationship of partners or joint venturers. If any provision of this Agreement is invalid under any applicable statute or rule of law, it is to that extent to be deemed omitted and the remaining provisions of this Agreement shall in no way be affected or impaired. Licensee may not assign or sublicense the rights granted under this Agreement without the written consent of Licensor. Such consent shall not be unreasonably withheld. Each Party has signed this Agreement through its authorized representative. The Parties, having read this Agreement, indicate their consent to the terms and conditions by their signature below.

By: _____

Date: _____

Licensor Name: _____

By: _____

Date: _____

Licensee Name/Title: _____

Releases

A "release" is an agreement by which someone waives (gives up) any rights to sue in connection with a certain activity. A release is usually needed when a publication (or broadcast) of a person's name or image could trigger legal claims such as defamation, invasion of privacy, or violation of the right of publicity. These types of legal claims are personal and relate to false statements, intrusions into personal affairs, or commercial uses of a personality. The person signing the release usually forgoes any right to bring these kinds of claims.

Traditionally, releases (sometimes known as "model releases") are needed when a person's name or image is used for commercial purposes. This chapter covers that situation, and describes other instances where it may be prudent to obtain a signed release. We'll also provide samples and explanations of two types of personal releases: a release to use interview statements, and a release to use images of property (such as photos of a building) in an advertisement.

Legal Risks of Failing to Obtain a Release

Without a written release, if you reproduce photos, video, or other representations of an individual, that person might be able to bring you into court to face various personal rights-based claims. These include defamation and invasion of the right to privacy or the right of publicity. Each of these legal claims is discussed in more detail below.

> **TIP**
> **Keep releases as short and simple as possible,** because people are often asked to sign them with short notice and may balk if the agreement is complex or intimidating.

As a general rule you will not need a release for the use of a person's name or image if your use is not defamatory, does not invade privacy, and is not for a commercial purpose. For example, a celebrity's photo can be used in a news story without a release. However, you often will need to obtain copyright permission from the owner of the photograph. See Chapter 3 for more information on obtaining permission from the copyright owners of a photograph.

Dear Rich: **I Didn't Get a Model Release**

A long time ago, I took a picture of two girls after asking permission from their parents (the two girls were minors). Sometime in 2016, I displayed this picture in an art gallery. I realized that I don't have a model release. What can I do?

If all you've done is display the girls' photo at a gallery, a release probably isn't required.

When you need a release. A properly drafted release protects you from two types of lawsuits: (1) if you use the girls' image to sell or endorse something; or (2) if you use the image in a way that defames, or invades the subjects' privacy. By signing the release, the subject promises not to sue over these uses. A release is usually not required for informational or artistic uses (that is, those uses considered an expression of free speech).

Going forward. If you plan on making other uses of the image, it's not too late to get a model release. If the women have reached the age of majority, they can sign the release. If they're still minors, a parent/guardian should affirm the contract.

Invasion of Privacy

Every person has a right to be left alone—this is called the right of privacy. You need a release to use a living person's name or image in a manner that constitutes an invasion of the person's right to privacy. Releases are vital because the person whose privacy you invade can sue you for monetary damages. Generally, invasion of privacy isn't an issue if an individual is deceased.

There are several different ways a person's right to privacy can be invaded, including:

- **False Light.** This type of invasion of privacy occurs when an individual is falsely portrayed in a highly offensive manner—for example, posting a photograph of a man at the "America's Most Wanted" website, even though he has never committed a crime.
- **Disclosure of Private Facts.** This invasion of privacy occurs when private or embarrassing facts are disclosed about an individual without relation to a legitimate public concern.

EXAMPLE: A man who served time for a robbery 20 years ago has rehabil-
itated himself and is now a pastor. Publication of the facts of the 20-year-old
robbery would be an invasion of privacy unless there was a related public
interest—for example, the pastor was again arrested for a crime.

- **Intrusion.** Intruding upon situations in which people have a reasonable
expectation of privacy—for example, spying on a person at home,
secretly eavesdropping on conversations, or opening mail—can give
rise to an invasion of privacy claim. However, it is not an invasion of
privacy to photograph someone in a public place or at any event where
the public is invited. Such photos can be used freely for informational
purposes, provided that the use does not defame or hold the individual
up to a false light.

  EXAMPLE: Mary is photographed sleeping on a bench in a public park.
  The photo appears in the newspaper under the caption, "A Sunny Day
  in the Park." No release is required. However, if the caption were "Opioid
  Addicts Seek Refuge in Park," Mary would have a claim for invasion of
  privacy and defamation (provided she was not an opioid addict).

Right of Publicity

The right of publicity is the right to control the commercial exploitation of a
person's name, image, or persona. This right is traditionally associated with
celebrities, because the name or image of a famous person is often used to
sell products or services. For example, it is much easier to sell a T-shirt if
there is a picture of Beyoncé or Adele on it. However, the unauthorized use
of the image of Beyoncé or Adele for such purposes would infringe their
right of publicity. This right extends only to commercial exploitation, that
is, it prohibits any implication that a person endorses a product (without the
person's permission).

The use of the name, likeness, or persona for news, information, or
public interest purposes is not a violation of the right of publicity. For this
reason, Taylor Swift cannot prevent the use of a photo of her in the *National
Enquirer*. Similarly, fictionalized stories about real people are protected by
the First Amendment and are not a violation of the right. For example,

actress Olivia de Havilland could not prevent the use of her name or her portrayal in the miniseries, *Feud*.

The right of publicity is not only for celebrities. Any person whose name or image is used to sell products may claim a misappropriation of this right. For example, if a child's photograph is taken and used to sell toys, that child could claim a misappropriation of the right of publicity. It is for this reason that all models or persons used in advertisements or endorsements sign consent or release agreements.

The right of publicity extends to a performer's identifiable voice. For example, in two separate cases, advertisements that used vocal performances that sounded like singers Tom Waits and Bette Midler were found to violate the singers' rights of publicity. In both of these cases, the advertising agency had sought permission from the performer and, when it was not granted, hired someone to deliberately imitate the singer's voice—a good example of what not to do. As a general rule, if your performer's voice mimics a well-known performer, either accidentally or intentionally, don't use it.

In many states, the right of publicity survives death and can be asserted by a person's estate.

Defamation

Defamation occurs when information is published about a person that creates a false impression and injures the person's reputation. Defamation is often divided into two categories: slander, which is an oral comment made to others, and libel, which is a fixed statement printed, broadcast, or published electronically. The rules for both types of defamation are similar. A deceased person cannot be defamed, but a false statement about a deceased person can be defamation if it reflects badly on a living relative. In addition to personal defamation, a corporation or partnership can also be defamed if a false statement affects the business's integrity, credit, or solvency.

The key to a defamation claim is determining the injury caused to the victim's reputation in the community. The term "community" can be interpreted as narrowly as a small group of persons acquainted with the injured person. Courts have permitted claims for statements that ridicule, humiliate, or subject the victim to contempt.

If the information that is published is true, there is no defamation. Or, as some courts have stated, the truth is an absolute defense to defamation. Literal truth in every element is not required, provided that the statement is substantially true.

There are exceptions to defamation rules for politicians and celebrities and, to a limited extent, for people who have become the subjects of a public controversy. Because they are in the public eye, already subject to public attention, these people are expected to have tougher skins. They can only be defamed if it is proven that the false statements were made with actual malice and a reckless disregard for the truth—for example, a website owner posting what he knows to be false information about a celebrity's sex life.

Dear Rich:

Opera Composer Seeks Rights to Deaf Poet's Life Story

I am a composer looking to write an opera celebrating the life and work of British Sign Language poet Dorothy Miles. I am struggling to find out how I may gain access to the rights to her life story, to compose a 20-minute work. Dorothy passed in 1993, and according to my preliminary research, she has no living descendants or relatives. Would you be able to advise me as to the best course of action in order to set aspects of her life story to music?

If you want to avoid lawyers and limit lawsuits, the best course of action is to base your opera on public records, existing news articles, and other public facts.

Facts are free. The facts of Dorothy's life are free for all to use under U.S. and UK law. This use of public facts often provides the springboard for life-story dramatizations, as in the Dorothy Miles documentary, *Dot*.

Using Dorothy Miles's poetry and writings. If you want to use material taken from Dorothy Miles's books or poetry, you will need to investigate its copyright status. Under U.S. and UK law, permission is required from whoever acquired rights from Miles after her death, perhaps Miles's niece.

Living people. If you plan to identify and portray living people you don't need their permission under U.S. law unless you are trying to prevent three types of legal claims: right of publicity, defamation, or invasion of privacy. We don't imagine this will be an issue for you unless you are casting a living individual in a negative light or unearthing secret information about a private citizen. (We're not knowledgeable about British law but it's our understanding that the UK has no right of publicity.)

Adopting source material. If you're adopting source material, for example working from a biography and taking more than facts, you'll need a derivative rights agreement from the copyright owner. If you are using source material obtained directly from an individual portrayed in your opera, you may need either a release, a consulting agreement, or in some cases life-story rights. The latter agreement prevents lawsuits over fictionalization and releases the producers from any claimed injuries resulting from how the character is depicted.

When to Use a Release

Whether you need to obtain a release depends on why you want to use a person's name or image. If your use is for commercial purposes—for example, using a person's photo in an advertisement—you need to obtain a release. If your use is for informational purposes such as a documentary film or news article, you may not need a release. However, even if a release is not required, you should be careful that your use does not defame or invade the privacy of the individual. If there's any potential that your use might violate these laws, a release will provide legal protection. Sorting out these differences can be confusing; examples are provided below. When in doubt, however, obtain a signed release.

Informational Uses

You do not need a release to use a person's name or image for informational purposes. An informational (or "editorial") purpose is anything that informs, educates, or expresses opinions protected under the First Amendment of the United States Constitution—freedom of speech and of the press. An informational use would include using a person's name or photograph in a newspaper or magazine article, an educational program, a film, or a nonfiction book, or an informational website.

If you use a person's name or image in an informational publication, you may also use that name or image in incidental advertising for the publication. For example, in an advertisement for a publication that includes an interview, you may state "Featuring an interview with Robert Pattinson." However, to use a person's name in an advertisement posing as an informational publication, you need a release.

Even if your use is informational, a release may be required if the person's name or image is used in a defamatory manner or invades the person's privacy. It may seem odd to seek a release for a use that may defame a person or invade privacy. After all, why would anyone sign a release for a use that would create a false impression? Such releases are usually used in cases in which a model or actor is posing to illustrate an article, such as "The Horror of Date Rape."

Commercial Uses

You need a release for the commercial use of a person's name or image. A "commercial use" occurs when a name or image appears while a product or service is being sold or endorsed. For example, if your website offers hair products and features photographs of people using the products, you would need a release from the people in the photos. You do not need a release if the person cannot be recognized in the photo: for example, if the photo only includes the person's hands.

Several decades ago, the failure to obtain such a release would have led to an invasion of privacy lawsuit. However, the "right of publicity" has now become the more popular claim for those whose names or images are used for commercial purposes without their permission.

Is Your Use Commercial or Informational?

Unfortunately, there is no definitive test that tells you whether your intended use is informational or commercial. Below are summaries of cases that straddle the border between informational and commercial uses. Cases with similar facts may seem to have different results because judges have broad discretion in making these determinations.

- **Informational use.** Singer Bobby Brown sued the makers of a Whitney Huston documentary claiming that the filmmakers violated his right of publicity under California law by using his name and image without his permission. The district court held that Brown's right-of-publicity claim was barred under the First Amendment since the film was an expressive work and a matter of public interest. (Brown also claimed he never signed a release, to which the judge stated that no such agreement was necessary under the First Amendment.) (*Brown v. Showtime Networks, Inc.*, 394 F. Supp. 3d 418 (S.D.N.Y. 2019).)

- **Informational use.** A Facebook page was critical of a country-rap singer. The singer asked to have the page removed, and Facebook declined. Because Facebook ran ads on the page, the singer claimed a violation of his right of publicity. A Court of Appeal held that there was insufficient evidence to conclude that third-party advertisers profited from the singer's name or persona. (*Cross v. Facebook*, 2017 WL 3404767 (Cal. App. Ct. Aug. 9, 2017).)

- **Informational use.** A photo of football player Joe Namath was featured on the cover of *Sports Illustrated* and later used in advertisements to sell subscriptions to *Sports Illustrated*. No permission was required because the initial use of the photo was editorial and the subscription ads were "merely incidental" to indicate the nature of the magazine contents. (*Namath v. Sports Illustrated*, 371 N.Y.S.2d 10 (1975).)

- **Informational use.** *The National Enquirer* and *USA Today* conducted telephone polls about the musical group New Kids on the Block. Use of the names and images of the members of the group to publicize the newspapers' profit-making telephone numbers did not require permission because it was primarily for purposes of "news gathering and dissemination." (*New Kids on the Block v. News America Publishing Inc.*, 971 F.2d 302 (9th Cir. 1992).)

- **Informational use.** Public domain film clips of Fred Astaire were used as a prologue to an instructional dance video. The use of Mr. Astaire's name was permitted in the prologue based on the informational content of the video. (*Astaire v. Best Film & Video Corp.*, 136 F.3d 1208 (9th Cir. 1998).)

- **Informational use.** A film company that acquired the rights to rerelease two 1950s films featuring actress Betty Page commissioned drawings of Ms. Page to promote the films. Ms. Page sued to prevent the use of her image and name to promote the films. A court permitted the use because the advertising was incidental to the rerelease and was "newsworthy" due to the reemergence of the two 1950s movies. (*Page v. Something Weird Video*, 960 F.Supp. 1438 (C.D. Cal., 1996).)

- **Informational use.** Following a Superbowl victory, a San Jose newspaper sold posters of quarterback Joe Montana. Mr. Montana sued but, in a surprising ruling, a court permitted the use, claiming it was newsworthy because of the "relatively contemporaneous" publication of the posters with the news event. (*Montana v. San Jose Mercury News*, 34 Cal.App.4th 790 (1995).)

- **Informational use.** *Los Angeles Magazine* printed a fashion article that featured a digitally modified photograph combining Dustin Hoffman's head with a male model's body in a gown and woman's shoes. The text stated: "Dustin Hoffman isn't a drag in a butter-colored silk gown by Richard Tyler and Ralph Lauren heels." Although one effect of the use was commercial—promoting the specific designers—the Ninth Circuit held that the use of Hoffman's head on another model's body did not violate the right of publicity and was permitted under free speech standards. (*Hoffman v. Capital Cities/ABC Inc.*, 255 F.3d 1180 (2001).)

- **Informational use.** The TV miniseries *Feud*, about the relationship of Bette Davis and Joan Crawford, featured a portrayal of actress Olivia de Havilland. De Havilland sued but could not prevent the use of her name or her portrayal in the miniseries, because the court determined *Feud* was a form of storytelling protected by the First Amendment. (*De Havilland v. FX Networks, LLC*, B285629, Cal. Court of Appeals (2018).)

- **Commercial use.** During the NCAA tournament broadcast, an ad for Oldsmobile featured a voice asking who held the record for being voted the most outstanding player of the tournament. The answer printed onscreen "Lew Alcindor, UCLA, '67, '68, '69." (The basketball player Kareem Abdul-Jabbar was previously known as Lew Alcindor.) The ad stated that Oldsmobile was the winner of a *Consumer's Digest* award three years in a row and ended with the statement, "A Definite

First Round Pick." Abdul-Jabbar sued, claiming that his name was used without permission. The court decided in his favor, ruling that although the advertisement provided information, the overall effect was commercial and required permission. (*Abdul-Jabbar v. General Motors Corp.*, 85 F.3d 407 (9th Cir. 1996).)

- **Commercial use.** A photo of Cher was featured in *Forum Magazine* and was later used in advertisements for subscriptions to the magazine. Beneath Cher's photo in the advertisements was a caption implying Cher's endorsement of the magazine. The implied endorsement created a commercial use of Cher's name that distinguished it from the *Sports Illustrated* case involving Joe Namath, above. (*Cher v. Forum Inter. Ltd.*, 692 F.2d 634 (9th Cir. 1982).)

- **Commercial use.** The Bulova watch company gave astronaut David Scott a watch to take with him on a moon landing. Bulova then issued a special Moon edition of the watch referencing Scott's expedition. Scott sued and the district court determined the use of Scott's name was a commercial use requiring Scott's permission. (*Scott v. Citizen Watch Company American, Inc,*. 17-cv-00436-NC (N.D. Cal. 2018).)

Are Websites or Social Media Pages Commercial or Informational?

Can a website, social media page, or other online presence be informational if its primary purpose is to promote a business? Online uses raise many of the issues highlighted in the cases described in the previous section. Several factors determine whether the online use of a name or an image is commercial or informational:

- If the online use of the name or image relates to a newsworthy event, the use is more likely to be informational.
- The more online space devoted to selling, the less likely the use is informational.
- The longer the person's name or image remains on the site or page, the less likely the use is informational.
- The more separation between informational content and the sponsorship of the site and related advertisements, the more likely the use is informational.

Dear Rich:

Quasi-Celebrity in Title of Movie

I have a question. If one uses the name of a quasi-celebrity in the title of a movie that parodies subject matter (organized crime, for example), is one protected under the fair use doctrine?

The fair use doctrine has nothing to do with the use of a name in a movie title. (Copyright does not protect titles.) The fair use defense can only be used when one is accused of stealing copyrighted expression—for example, taking text from a book, or a photo from a magazine.

The use of the name may trigger a claim under the right of publicity under which anyone (celebrity, quasi-celebrity, or noncelebrity) can sue if their name or image is used to imply endorsement of a product or service. If it's clearly a parody (or obvious that the title doesn't imply the quasi-celebrity's endorsement) you would likely prevail in a lawsuit under free speech principles. For example, John Gotti's name was used in the title of parodies, biopics, and documentaries without any apparent repercussions. All of this information may prove academic, however, as the Dear Rich staff wonders whether a member of an organized crime family will bother pursuing intellectual property rights, when they have other methods of enforcement.

What Good Are Disclaimers?

"Disclaimers" are statements advising readers about potential confusion or danger and disavowing legal responsibility. When using a person's name or image, some businesses attempt to avoid liability for breaching a person's publicity or privacy rights by providing a disclaimer, such as "Woody's One-Liners is not associated with or endorsed by Woody Allen."

A disclaimer by itself will never shield a business from liability. In many cases, disclaimers have been found to create rather than reduce confusion in the minds of customers or readers as to whether or not a celebrity is endorsing a product or service. Moreover, a disclaimer is an acknowledgment that the business admits the potential for confusion, a fact that may be used against the business in a lawsuit.

To have any legal effect, a disclaimer must be in close proximity to the person's image or name and as prominent as the name or image. It must also disclaim any sponsorship, endorsement, or association with the product or service involved. Because of the legally tenuous value of disclaimers, it is not wise to rely on them for protection.

Releases and Free Speech

You can use a person's name or image for commercial purposes without permission if the commercial use qualifies as free speech. Generally, this occurs when the use is categorized as a parody. (For more information on trademark parodies see Chapter 10. For more information on copyright parodies, see Chapter 9).

For example, a company sold trading cards featuring caricatures of major league baseball players. Text on the cards ridiculing player salaries and egos included a statement: "Cardtoons baseball is a parody and is NOT licensed by Major League Baseball Properties or Major League Baseball Players Association." A federal court permitted the use of player's names and caricatured images as free speech. (*Cardtoons v. Major League Baseball Players Assn.*, 838 F.Supp. 1501 (N.D. Okla., 1993).)

However, individuals wary of litigation should weigh the consequences and costs of a lawsuit before claiming a free speech right to use an individual's name or image.

Personal Release Agreements

This section provides and discusses personal release agreements that permit the use of a person's name and image. Personal releases are often referred to as "model releases," although the term "model" can be used for anyone, not just professional models. There are two classes of personal releases: blanket releases and limited releases:

- A **blanket release** permits any use of the photographic image of the person signing the release and is suitable if the company or photographer needs an unlimited right to use the image. Stock photographers who sell their photos for unlimited purposes commonly use blanket releases.
- Celebrities and professional models usually sign **limited releases** that specify the particular ways their image and name may be used. If a use exceeds what's permitted under the limited release, the person can sue for breach of the agreement. For example, a model that signed a release limiting use of her image for a museum brochure sued when the photo appeared on a Miami transit card.

General Rules for Releases

In addition to the specific legal rules for releases discussed throughout this chapter, some general advice is helpful when dealing with release situations.

Get It in Writing

Although oral releases are generally valid, you should always try to get a release in writing. This way, the model can't claim he or she never agreed to the release. In addition, the terms of an oral release can be hard to remember and even harder to prove in court if a dispute arises.

Make It Clear

When a release is sought for a specific purpose, do not hide or misrepresent facts to get the signature. A fraudulently obtained release is invalid. For example, a model who was told that his image would be used by an insurance company signed a blanket release based on that statement. However, a company that pays cash for life insurance policies owned by AIDS patients used the photo. A Florida court permitted the model to sue.

Keep It Simple

Release agreements do not include many of the legal provisions found in other agreements in this book. Instead, releases are usually "stripped down" to pose less likelihood of triggering a discussion or negotiation. Keep your release short and simple (see tip below).

 TIP
You may find it easier to obtain a signed release if you shrink the release information to the size of a 3x5 or 5x7 card. Photographers have found that photo subjects find the smaller documents less intimidating. Some photographers reduce the material to a font size that fits on the back of a business card. However, if the contract is difficult to read, it will be less likely to be enforceable.

Get the Right Signatures

There are two requirements for the signature on a release: it must be "informed consent," which means that the person signing the release understood it; and the person signing the release must have the authority to grant the release.

In the majority of states, a minor is any person under 18 years of age, although in some states, the age may be 19 or 21. Since a minor may not understand the terms of a release, the signature of a parent or guardian is required before using a minor's name or image.

> EXAMPLE: A 16-year-old boy who was photographed on the beach at Cape Canaveral signed a release; his parents did not. The photo was later used on the cover of a novel about a gay adolescent. His father sued the publisher and settled out of court.

In some cases, an agent representing the person may have the authority to sign a release. For example, an agent signed a release granting an unlimited time period for use of a model's image in a Nintendo advertisement. The model had intended that the image only be used for one year. A court held that the agent had the authority to sign the release on behalf of the model and the release was binding.

It is always preferable to have a release signed by the subject, not an agent. When dealing with an agent, seek an assurance that the agent has the legal authority to sign. This can be done by including the statement, "I am the authorized agent for [name of model]" above the agent's signature line.

TIP

Get a release signed ASAP. It is sometimes difficult to track down a subject after a photo has been taken and there is less incentive for the subject to sign a release. Therefore, most photographers obtain releases prior to or directly after a photo session or when the model is paid.

Dear Rich: **Stopped Taking Photos Because of Photo Releases**

I work for a nonprofit and my board members are obsessed with getting photo releases—but as they don't have a good one and they often want to photograph events with LOTS of people—they refrain from taking photos at all. I was under the impression that unless a photo was going to be sold, no release was needed. Is there a guideline that will enlighten both myself and my board about when photos and video that will be used for things like social media and newsletters require releases from their subjects? I am afraid this question is going to lead to an "it varies from state to state" answer.

Actually, the answer doesn't vary from state to state (and in any case the Dear Rich Staff would never do you like that!).

You need a release if ... A properly drafted release basically shields you from lawsuits over two things: (1) You're using someone's image to sell or endorse something; or (2) using the image in a way that harms the person—it invades the person's privacy or defames the person or otherwise gets them so upset that they call a lawyer and go after the publisher of the photo and sometimes the photographer.

You do not need a release if ... You do not need a release to use a person's name or image for informational purposes. An informational (or "editorial") purpose is anything that informs, educates, or expresses opinions protected as freedom of speech. So if you have a section of your website such as "About Our Members" or you include the images in your nonprofit newsletter—for example, "Members Protest Disney World Mouse Exploitation"—then you wouldn't need a release.

Finally ... although it doesn't have the full legal punch of a release, you can always prominently post your photo policy at group gatherings—a statement such as "We'll be taking photos at our event and posting them at our website. If you don't wish to be included, please inform the photographer."

Consideration: Paying for a Release

A contract is legally binding only if each party obtains something of value (referred to as "consideration") in return for performance of the contract obligations. For this reason, releases traditionally stipulated payment of a nominal amount such as one dollar. However, most courts now take a modern approach to contract law and accept the fact that consideration can be implied and an actual payment is not mandatory. Each release in this chapter establishes that the contract has met the consideration requirement by beginning with the statement, "For consideration that I acknowledge..." However, to fortify this position, you may wish to make a payment—even if nominal—to the person signing the release and indicate the amount of the payment somewhere in the release.

Dear Rich: **Can I Sell Golf Paintings and Prints?**

I'm a graphic artist with over 30 years' professional experience. Now, I am creating a series of original golf images, in my personal style, to sell as limited-edition prints. Some of these images depict famous players but they are not depicted in recognizable events (derived partially from my visual memory abilities and also from sketches made from the TV). I am concerned about being sued by the golfer(s) for rights to publicity ... even despite the fact I am aware that a while ago a very famous golfer's agents sued a sports artist for selling prints of the artist's painting depicting that famous golfer, and lost ... essentially due to the ruling determining the athlete's right to publicity did not trump the artist's First Amendment rights. Is this good news? Or for every ruling like this, are there just as many that have gone against the artist? Does it matter that, in part, I am painting a known golfer's image based on my sketches from the TV, which is a "publicly viewable" situation? I know the famous golfer believes that people are buying the art print solely because of his image, but what if the person is buying it primarily because of the quality of the artwork? Also, famous golf courses like the Pebble Beach Golf Links (Monterey Peninsula in California) have trademarks on their property/business names. If I create a painting that is merely suggestive of that course's famous holes, but is not actually a factual view ... and if their trademark encompasses the phrase "PEBBLE BEACH," can I use the term "PEBBLE"? In other words, are there infringement issues for implying an actual place?

We hope we can answer all your questions before our Stash green tea high wears off. Yes, you are correct—a painter created images of famous golfers including Eldrick "Tiger" Woods, and then sold the prints. Woods's licensing people sued and lost.

Why did Tiger lose? The Sixth Circuit believed that the First Amendment trumped the right of publicity. A similar ruling happened in a case involving a painting of a famous sports scene from Alabama football history. These are great cases for painters, and we want all artists to exploit their First Amendment rights (no matter how dopey that can sometimes be). But our takeaway points should also include the fact that both cases took almost four years from filing to final gavel. So, like Clint says, you have to ask yourself, "Do you feel lucky?" We know that's not the answer you were hoping for, but like the fair use defense, that's the reality. Any celebrity or trademark owner can drag you through litigation until a court agrees with you that the balance is tipped in favor of free speech. So, please proceed with caution.

Does it matter whether they're buying the work for my artwork or for the celebrity? That's not the way to frame the question exactly (and in any case it's usually a little of both). In these kinds of lawsuits, the inquiry isn't why people are buying the work, it's more about what the artist has done with the work. Or as one California court put it, "Another way of stating the inquiry is whether the celebrity likeness is one of the 'raw materials' from which an original work is synthesized, or whether the depiction or imitation of the celebrity is the very sum and substance of the work in question." Like fair use analyses, courts seem to be looking for something transformative in the work. The same California court looked at Andy Warhol's celebrity imagery and wrote:

"Through distortion and the careful manipulation of context, Warhol was able to convey a message that went beyond the commercial exploitation of celebrity images and became a form of ironic social comment on the dehumanization of celebrity itself .... Although the distinction between protected and unprotected expression will sometimes be subtle, it is no more so than other distinctions triers of fact are called on to make in First Amendment jurisprudence."

Gee, we're getting a little winded with all this jurisprudential verbiage. Is it okay if we answer one more question and go lie down?

Can I use publicly viewable images from TV? The Dear Rich Staff thinks you're mixing a couple of concepts, here. Generally you don't need a release for a person (or property) that is viewable in the public. An image on TV may be viewable by the TV-viewing public, but it's not the same as "being in public." We know it's hard to separate the two these days and we have problems with it as well. Eventually they'll all be one thing and we won't have to wrestle with it anymore.

Unlimited Personal Release Agreement

The following form is an unlimited or blanket release agreement. It permits you to use the model's image and name in all forms of media throughout the world forever.

FORM
You can download this form (and all other forms in this book) from Nolo.com; for details, see the appendix.

Unlimited Personal Release Agreement

Grant

For consideration that I acknowledge, I irrevocably grant to _____
_____ ("Company") and Company's
assigns, licensees, and successors the right to use my image and name in all forms
and media including composite or modified representations for all purposes,
including advertising, trade, or any commercial purpose throughout the world and
in perpetuity. I waive the right to inspect or approve versions of my image used for
publication or the written copy that may be used in connection with the images.

Release

I release Company and Company's assigns, licensees, and successors from any claims
that may arise regarding the use of my image, including any claims of defamation,
invasion of privacy, or infringement of moral rights, rights of publicity, or copyright.
Company is permitted, although not obligated, to include my name as a credit in
connection with the image.

Company is not obligated to utilize any of the rights granted in this Agreement.

I have read and understood this agreement and I am over the age of 18. This
Agreement expresses the complete understanding of the parties.

Name: _____ Date: _____

Signature: _____

Address: _____

Witness Signature: _____

Parent/Guardian Consent (include if the person is under 18)

I am the parent or guardian of the minor named above. I have the legal right to
consent to and do consent to the terms and conditions of this release.

Parent/Guardian Name: _____ Date: _____

Parent/Guardian Signature: _____

Parent/Guardian Address: _____

Witness Signature: _____

Limited Personal Release Agreement

The following form is a limited personal release agreement. It allows you to use the model's name or image only for the purposes specified in the agreement.

 FORM
You can download this form (and all other forms in this book) from Nolo.com; for details, see the appendix.

Explanation for Limited and Unlimited Personal Releases

- The **Grant** section establishes the rights granted by the person. In the unlimited agreement, a "blanket" grant is used. This grant is broad and intended to encompass all potential uses, whether informational, commercial, or other. In the limited agreement, the uses must be listed—for example, "For use on the cover of trade book and for related advertisements." This release also has limitations regarding territory and term. Insert the appropriate geographic region and term—for example, "North America for a period of two years."
- The **Release** section is the person's promise not to sue the company for legal claims such as libel and invasion of privacy.
- If the person is a minor, the parent or guardian should sign where it is marked **Parent/Guardian Consent**. Since issues about release authenticity often crop up many years after a photo was made, a witness should sign the agreement to verify the person's signature or the signature of the parent. The witness should be an adult. An employee or assistant is suitable.

Limited Personal Release Agreement

Grant

For consideration that I acknowledge, I grant to _____ ("Company") and Company's assigns, licensees, and successors, the right to use my image for the following purposes: _____

_____

_____

in the following territory _____
for a period of _____ year(s) (the "Term").

I grant the right to use my name and image for the purposes listed above in all forms and media, including composite or modified representations, and waive the right to inspect or approve versions of my image used for publication or the written copy that may be used in connection with the images.

Payment

(Select if appropriate)

☐ For the rights granted during the Term, Company shall pay $_____ upon execution of this release.

Renewal

(Select if appropriate)

☐ Company may renew this agreement under the same terms and conditions for _____ year(s) provided that Company makes payment of $_____ at the time of renewal.

Release

I release Company and Company's assigns, licensees, and successors from any claims that may arise regarding the use of my image including any claims of defamation, invasion of privacy, or infringement of moral rights, rights of publicity, or copyright. Company is permitted, although not obligated, to include my name as a credit in connection with the image.

Name: _____

Date: _____

Signature: _____

Address: _____

_____

Witness Signature: _____

Parent/Guardian Consent (*include if the person is under 18*)

I am the parent or guardian of the minor named above. I have the legal right to consent to and do consent to the terms and conditions of this release.

Parent/Guardian Name: _____

Date: _____

Parent/Guardian Signature: _____

Parent/Guardian Address: _____

_____

Witness Signature: _____

Interview and Property Releases

There are occasions when a release is required for a purpose other than using someone's name or image. Below are two other forms of release: a release to use statements from an interview; and a release permitting use of photos of a building.

Interview Releases

Most reporters and writers do not obtain signed interview releases because they presume that by giving the interview, the subject has consented to the interview and, therefore, cannot claim invasion of privacy. In addition, many interview subjects don't have the ability or inclination to execute a written release—for example, a person interviewed by telephone for a newspaper story on a deadline.

Nevertheless, a written interview release can be useful. It can help avoid lawsuits for libel, invasion of privacy, or even copyright infringement (since the speaker's words may be copyrightable). It's wise to obtain a signed release if the interview is lengthy, will be reprinted verbatim (for example, in a question and answer format), or if the subject matter of the interview is controversial.

It is common for an interview subject to ask to read or edit the interview or to have some comments removed or kept "off the record." Any agreement that is made with the interview subject (including an agreement for anonymity) should be documented. Failure to honor the arrangement may give rise to a lawsuit for monetary damages.

If the interview subject is willing to proceed with the interview but does not want to sign a release, ask if he or she will make an oral consent on audio- or videotape. Although not as reliable as a written release, a statement such as, "I consent to the use of my statements in the *Musician's Gazette*," will provide some assurance of your right to use the statement.

Interview Release Agreement

An interview release is a hybrid agreement, part release and part license. The release above is suitable if you are seeking permission to use an existing interview or to conduct a new interview.

Interview Release Agreement

Grant

For consideration that I acknowledge, I consent to the recording of my statements and grant to _____ ("Company") and Company's assigns, licensees, and successors the right to copy, reproduce, and use all or a portion of the statements (the "Interview") for incorporation in the following work _____ (the "Work").

I permit the use of all or a portion of the Interview in the Work in all forms and media including advertising and related promotion throughout the world and in perpetuity. I grant the right to use my image and name in connection with all uses of the Interview and waive the right to inspect or approve use of my Interview as incorporated in the Work.

Release

I release Company and Company's assigns, licensees, and successors from any claims that may arise regarding the use of the Interview including any claims of defamation, invasion of privacy, or infringement of moral rights, rights of publicity, or copyright. I acknowledge that I have no ownership rights in the Work.

Company is not obligated to utilize the rights granted in this Agreement.

I have read and understood this agreement and I am over the age of 18. This Agreement expresses the complete understanding of the parties.

Name: _____

Date: _____

Signature: _____

Address: _____

_____

Witness Signature: _____

Parent/Guardian Consent (*include if the person is under 18*)

I am the parent or guardian of the minor named above. I have the legal right to consent to and do consent to the terms and conditions of this release.

Parent/Guardian Name: _____

Date: _____

Parent/Guardian Signature: _____

Parent/Guardian Address: _____

_____

Witness Signature: _____

FORM

You can download this form (and all other forms in this book) from Nolo.com; for details, see the appendix.

Explanation for Interview Release Agreement

- It's possible that the interview may already have been recorded, in which case the language "consent to the recording of my statements and" can be stricken from the **Grant** section. If the interview will be included in more than one work, list all works and change the term "Work" to "Works" throughout the agreement. Unlimited or blanket releases for interviews are not common, partly because subjects usually are not prepared to relinquish unlimited rights.
- If seeking unlimited rights (the interview can be used for any purpose) substitute the following **Grant** section:

Grant

For consideration that I acknowledge, I consent to the recording of my statements and grant to _____

_____ ("Company") and Company's assigns, licensees, and successors the right to copy, reproduce, and use all or a portion of the statements (the "Interview") for all purposes, including advertising, trade, or any commercial purpose throughout the world and in perpetuity.

I grant the right to use my image and name in connection with all uses of the Interview and waive the right to inspect or approve any use of my Interview.

- If the interview subject does not wish to waive the right to inspect the final work, strike that sentence and arrange for the interview subject to provide approval.
- If the release is executed after the interview has been transcribed, it is helpful to attach a transcription of the interview to the release agreement. This provides an assurance that the interview subject has notice of what was said in the interview. Add a sentence to the

Grant section such as, "A complete transcription of the interview is attached and incorporated in this Agreement." The **Release** section provides protection against subsequent legal claims.

- If the interview subject is under 18, a parent or guardian's consent is required.

Dear Rich: Does Home Sale Imply Permission to Use Photo?

So, is an agent who is helping a buyer, who is not trespassing, who is invited into a home for sale (via a Realtor's ad), allowed to snap photos and publish them online for all to see, without specific expressed permission? Or is the permission implied with allowing 100+ buyers into the vacant home? Or is it a conditional invitation with limitations on rights to photograph?

Just because you were invited onto someone's property, vacant or not, does not imply the right to take photos. The best argument you could make would be that the seller or the seller's agent was aware of you taking photos and didn't complain. (For example, the Dear Rich Staff was recently at the Google offices in San Francisco, taking a video of the free lunch—it was pretty impressive stuff, gourmet pizza, fresh broccoli, incredible salads, and free wheat grass juice in these little shot glasses—until a Google rep explained that no photos were permitted. Okay, we got the point, even though we still like looking at the video when we're hungry.) The next question is whether permission is required. After all, permission is only needed if you are violating someone else's rights. Someone may claim your posted photos violate copyright law—a long shot—assuming there's something copyrightable in the photos (artwork on the walls?); or someone may possibly claim invasion of privacy (although if the house is vacant and hundreds of people are walking through it, that's a tough argument to make). It may be a violation of contract if ads for the home state "No Photos." It may violate someone's right of publicity if you photo them in the house and you use that photo to sell the home, blah, blah, blah. The real issue is why are you asking this? Are you being hassled because you're an agent who showed up at a home for sale, took pictures, and posted them without permission? If that's the case—and since agents need to work together cooperatively in most communities (especially in a tough real estate market)—don't you want to work this out with the people you are dealing with on a day-to-day basis? It's always more satisfying to "get to yes" without bringing in the legal blowhards.

Property Releases

In some cases, you'll need to obtain a release for using pictures of places. You may find this odd—after all, if a building can be viewed publicly, why is permission required to use an image of it? Over the last few decades some buildings have earned protection under both trademark or copyright laws, or both. Trademark law will protect a building's appearance under very limited circumstances. If a distinctive-looking building is used to signify a business's services, you cannot use an image of that building in a manner that will confuse consumers. For example, the Sears Tower in Chicago functions as a trademark; if you intend to use it in the foreground of an advertisement, you must obtain permission from the Sears Company. Use of the building's image for informational purposes, such as in magazine article, does not require permission.

Is permission needed to use the image of a trademarked building on a postcard or poster? That issue arose when a photographer sold images of the Rock and Roll Hall of Fame. A federal court of appeals permitted the use of the trademarked building on posters and did not consider it to be a trademark infringement. (*Rock and Roll Hall of Fame v. Gentile*, 134 F.3d 749 (6th Cir. 1998).)

Copyright protection also extends to architectural works, specifically for architectural works created after March 1, 1989. However copyright protection also has limitations. You do not need a release to photograph a building or property visible from a public place, but you do need permission to photograph and reproduce images of a building protected by copyright and not visible from a public place. Entering private property to photograph a building or property may also trigger a claim of trespass. To avoid such claims, photographers, publishers, and filmmakers use a property release, sometimes known as a "location release."

Property Release Agreement

This form may be used as a property release.

 FORM
You can download this form (and all other forms in this book) from Nolo.com; for details, see the appendix.

Property Release Agreement

The Property: _____

Grant

For consideration that I acknowledge, I irrevocably grant to _____
_____ ("Company") and Company's assigns,
licensees, and successors the right to enter onto the property listed above and to
photograph, copy, publish, display, and use images of the property in all forms and
media, including composite or modified representations, throughout the world and
in perpetuity for the following purposes: _____

_____

I waive the right to inspect or approve the manner in which the images of the
property are used and waive the right to inspect any text that is used in connection
with the images of the property.

Dates of Use

Company shall enter onto the property on the following dates and times: _____

_____ .

In consideration for the rights granted under this Agreement, Company shall pay me
$_____ upon execution of this Agreement.

Company is not obligated to utilize any of the rights granted in this Agreement.

Warranty, Indemnity, and Release

I warrant that I am the owner of the property and have the authority to grant the
rights under this agreement and agree to indemnify Company from any claims
regarding my ownership of the property. I release Company and Company's assigns,
licensees, and successors from any claims that may arise regarding the use of the
images of the property.

I have read and understood this agreement. This Agreement expresses the complete
understanding of the parties.

Owner's Signature: _____

Owner's Name: _____

Owner's Address: _____

Date: _____

Explanation for Property Release

- The **Grant** section allows access to photograph the property (on the dates provided in the **Dates of Use** section) and the right to use the photographs for the purposes listed in the agreement.
- If payment is required for the release, indicate the amount in the paragraph after the **Dates of Use** section.
- The owner provides an assurance of ownership in the **Warranty, Indemnity, & Release** section and agrees to defend the Company from anyone else with a property ownership claim.

Copyright Research

This chapter explains how to conduct a very specific type of research: finding information about copyright ownership and validity. This information is usually contained in U.S. Copyright Office and Library of Congress records on copyright registrations, assignments, renewals, and related documents. We'll explain how to search these documents, including how to gather information to prepare for your searches.

It's possible you may not have to perform copyright research. You might be able to locate all the copyright information you need through other sources. However, if you seek permissions on a regular basis, there may come a time when you will have to trace copyright ownership (known as "the chain of title"), determine the first date of publication, or find out if copyright for a work has been renewed.

Before walking you through the basics of copyright research and approaches, this chapter begins with answers to some common questions regarding copyright ownership and transfers.

> **CAUTION**
>
> **This chapter does not cover other types of research, such as locating stock photos or private databases of art or music.** For more media-specific research, review the relevant chapter that covers the type of media you seek (see Table of Contents).

> **CAUTION**
>
> **Copyright Office records are not always conclusive.** Records of the Copyright Office and Library of Congress are helpful for locating ownership information and determining copyright status. Unfortunately, these records don't always show the whole picture because filing copyright registration and assignment (transfer of copyright ownership) documents is not mandatory. Because you don't have to file these documents to own a copyright, there may not be a Copyright Office record regarding a particular work.

Despite this fact, it is still worth your while to search the Copyright Office and the Library of Congress—the largest repositories of copyrighted materials in the United States. In addition, even if you can't find records of ownership, your research will demonstrate that you acted in good faith and are an "innocent infringer" if you're later sued for an unauthorized use, which will limit any damages you may have to pay.

Copyright Ownership and Transfers FAQs

When performing copyright research, you may have questions about copyright rules or terminology. For example, you might uncover a registration indicating the work is "made for hire," or you could find a document indicating that the copyright has been "reclaimed" by the author. Below are some answers to frequently asked questions (FAQs) about copyright ownership and transfers.

RESOURCE

For a more detailed discussion of these copyright issues, refer to *The Copyright Handbook,* by Stephen Fishman (Nolo).

What Is a Work Made for Hire?

Usually, the person who creates a work is also the initial owner of the copyright in the work. But this isn't always the case. Under some circumstances, a person who pays another to create a work becomes the initial copyright owner, not the person who actually created it. The resulting works are called "works made for hire" (or sometimes simply "works for hire"). There are two distinct types of work that will be classified as made for hire:

- a work created by an employee within the scope of employment, or
- a commissioned work that falls within a certain category of works and that is the subject of a written agreement. (The types of works that qualify and other relevant requirements are explained in more detail in Chapter 15.)

If the work qualifies under one of these two methods, the person paying for the work (the hiring party) is the author and copyright owner. If you want to use the work, you should seek permission from the employer or hiring party, not the person who created the work. If in doubt, you may be able to determine work-for-hire status by examining the copyright registration.

What Is a Transfer of Title?

The person who owns a copyright is sometimes referred to as having "title" to the copyright. A "title" is the document that establishes ownership to property, like the title to your car or house. But even in the absence of an official document, the owner of a copyright is often said to have title to it.

Just like title to your car or house, title to a copyright can be sold or otherwise transferred. A person or company can have ownership (title) of a copyright transferred to it by means of an assignment (a sale in which all or part of a copyright is transferred) or through a will or bankruptcy proceedings. Since title to a copyright can be transferred, you may have to search copyright records to determine the current owner of a work you want to use.

There are two ways to determine if copyright ownership has been transferred: by reviewing the copyright registration certificate issued by the Copyright Office, or by locating an assignment or transfer agreement. By reviewing the copyright registration certificate, you can find out who currently claims copyright and on what basis. For example, if a publisher has been assigned copyright to a work, it will file a copyright registration in its own name and indicate on the registration that it acquired copyright through a legal transfer. Also, many companies file the agreement that establishes the assignment, license, or transfer with the Copyright Office. For example, if an artist assigned his work to a company, the company could file the assignment document with the Copyright Office.

What Is a Termination of a Transfer?

Sometimes an author transfers copyright to someone and then later the author reacquires it through a process known as "terminating a transfer." Copyright laws provide a method by which authors can reclaim rights after a number of years. This termination and reclamation process is complex, and the rules differ depending on when the work was first published. As a very general rule, transfer terminations occur between 28 and 56 years after the first publication. Terminations are filed with the Copyright Office and can be located by researching Copyright Office records.

EXAMPLE: In June of 1996, the author J.D. Salinger terminated his transfer to the publisher Little, Brown, and Company and reacquired ownership rights to the story, "A Perfect Day for Bananafish." Below is the information from the termination notice as displayed in the Copyright Office's online records.
RECORDED: 11 Jun96
PARTY 1: Phyllis Westberg, as agent for J. D. Salinger.
PARTY 2: Little, Brown, and Company.
NOTE: A perfect day for bananafish & 5 other titles; stories.

From Nine stories. By J. D. Salinger. Notice of termination of grant under 17 U.S.C. sec. 304; date & manner of service of the notice: 6Jun96, by certified mail, return receipt requested.

For more information on terminations of transfers, see Chapter 9 of *The Copyright Handbook* by attorney Stephen Fishman (Nolo).

What If More Than One Person Owns a Copyright?

A common question is whom to ask for permission if several people jointly own a copyright. Co-ownership of copyright can occur in various ways. For example:

- Two people jointly create a work.
- The author transfers portions of the rights to different people (for example, giving half to each child).
- The author sells a portion of the copyright to someone and keeps the remainder.

Co-owners of copyright have a legal status known as "tenants in common." When a co-owner dies, his or her share goes to his or her beneficiaries or heirs, not to the other co-owner. Each co-owner has an independent right to use or nonexclusively license the work—provided that he or she accounts to the other co-owners for any profits. What this means for our purposes is that if you obtain the permission of any one co-owner, you can use the work. However, there are a few exceptions to this rule, as explained in the next section.

You can determine whether there is co-ownership of a certain work by reviewing Copyright Office documents. For example, a registration for a song might indicate that a composer and a lyricist co-own a song.

When Must You Get Multiple Permissions?

There are several situations in which you must obtain permission from all the co-owners of a work instead of just one. All co-owners must consent to an assignment of the work (a transfer of copyright ownership) or to an exclusive license (an agreement granting rights solely to one person).

> EXAMPLE: Two programmers create a software program. Company A wants an exclusive license to distribute the program, which means that Company A is the only company that can distribute the program. Since the desired license is an exclusive one, Company A must obtain the consent of both programmers.

In addition, you must obtain the consent of all co-owners if any of the following are true:

- The co-owners have an agreement amongst themselves prohibiting any individual owner from granting a license and you are aware of this agreement.
- You want to use the text on a worldwide nonexclusive basis (and some countries require consent of all co-owners even for nonexclusive uses).
- You want to use the text for a commercial purpose, such as to sell a service or product.
- The desired license is for the first public release of a song.

Is There a Difference Between an Author and a Copyright Owner?

The author is the first owner of copyright. The author is either the creator of the work or the person who employs someone to create the work (see work-for-hire rules discussed above). Many authors do not retain their copyright ownership; they sell or transfer it to someone else in return for a lump sum payment or periodic payment known as a royalty. In this way, the author and copyright owner (sometimes referred to as "copyright claimant") may be two different people. Even if you do not know the name of the current copyright owner, knowing the name of the author will help you find the owner in the Copyright Office records.

What If a Work Does Not Contain a Copyright Notice?

It's common to start copyright research by examining the copyright notice. However, in some cases, the notice may be missing from the work. One reason you may not find a notice is because notice is not required on works first published after March 1, 1989. In addition, for works published prior to that date, notice is required only on visually perceptible copies—that is, copies that can be seen directly or with the aid of a device such as a film projector. Printed books, paintings, drawings, films, architecture, and computer programs are all visually perceptible. However, some works are not visually perceptible, such as a song on a compact disc. But copyright notice would be required if the song lyrics were printed on the album cover.

Another reason that a work may not include notice is that the owner failed to affix it, which may result in the loss of copyright. For works first published before 1978, for example, the absence of a copyright notice from a published copy generally indicates that the work is not protected by copyright. The absence of notice on works published between January 1, 1978 and March 1, 1989 may or may not result in the loss of copyright, depending on whether the owner corrected the error within five years of the publication and met other copyright law requirements.

What If There Is a Copyright Notice for an Entire Magazine but Not for the Specific Article You Want to Use?

If a story or a photograph is used in a magazine, there may be a copyright notice for the magazine but not for the specific story or photo that you want to use. That's because the owners of magazines, anthologies, or greatest hits collections in which many different copyrighted works are collected (referred to as "collective works") can use one copyright notice to protect all the works in the collection. This does not necessarily mean that the magazine owns the copyright in all of the works. It may or may not, depending on the contract with the author or photographer. Copyright Office research may not necessarily help you locate copyright information for these works because they may not be listed separately by title in the records. You may be better off contacting the owner of the collective work directly. The principles for contacting copyright owners are explained in the chapters dealing with specific media (text, artwork, photographs, and so on).

Starting Your Copyright Research

There are three parts to copyright research. First, you must isolate elements that are necessary to perform your research. For example, you must examine the work for clues such as copyright notice or publication date that will help your research. Second, you must define a method for searching copyright records. You may choose to have the Copyright Office perform the research or you may attempt to search copyright records on the Internet. Finally, you must initiate the search and examine the documents it retrieves. This section discusses the first step—examining the work for clues.

Your first step is to physically examine the work you want to use for information that will help you locate copyright documents in the Copyright Office records. Check the work for the following information:

- **Copyright notice.** The copyright notice is usually on or near the title page of a book; visible at the end of a movie; printed on a compact disc cover or video box; or stamped on the back of a photograph or artwork. For computer programs, it may be located in the Help File under "About this Program." The copyright notice has three parts: the "c" in a circle (©) or the word "copyright," the date of first publication (or, in rare cases, the date of registration), and the name of the copyright owner.

- **Title of the work.** Because Copyright Office records are indexed by title, the title of the work is one of the most important elements in copyright research. Alternative titles may also be helpful (both main and alternative titles are usually listed on the copyright registration).

- **Name(s) of author(s).** Like the title, the name of the author(s) is helpful when searching Copyright Office records because it is usually listed on every copyright document pertaining to that work. Pseudonyms are also traceable in the Copyright Office. Even "Anonymous," as a listing for an author, when cross-referenced with the title, can be helpful in locating a work.

- **The name of the copyright owner.** This may be the author, publisher, or producer of a work. The likely name of the owner is listed in the copyright notice—"likely" because you can never rely solely on the copyright notice for determining the current copyright owner. If you're dealing with an older work, for example, it's possible that ownership may have been transferred or reclaimed since publication. However, the name of the owner listed in the copyright notice is a helpful starting point for your research.

- **Year of publication or registration.** The date of publication is ordinarily listed in the copyright notice. This date usually indicates when copyright protection began, though it may be the year that particular version of the work was first published.

EXAMPLE: Bruce first publishes a book on guitar repair in 1980. He updates it in 2016. The copyright notice on the new version states 2016, so the notice refers only to the new material in the update. The publication date for the earlier material is still 1980.

What If the Copyright Notice Does Not Include the Date?

Because certain industries successfully lobbied Congress for the right to omit the year on copyright notices, the copyright notice may not include the date of first publication. The date can be omitted on greeting cards, stationery, jewelry, toys, or useful articles on which a photograph, graphic, or sculptural work (and accompanying text) appears. For example a greeting card may include the notice "© Hallmark Greetings," with no date. Where no date is provided, you may need to research Copyright Office records to verify the date of first publication.

- **Title, volume, or issue of serialized publication.** If the work you want to use was originally published as a part of a periodical or collection, the title of the publication and other information, such as the volume or issue number, may be useful in searching the Copyright Office records.
- **Underlying works and works contained within works.** Many works, referred to as "derivatives," are based upon other works. For example, motion pictures are often based on books or plays. The work upon which another is based is referred to as the "source" or "underlying" work. For instance, the movie *Gone Girl* is based on the novel of the same name. Copyright information about a source work, such as its title or author, can often be found within the derivative work. For example, the motion picture *Gone Girl* indicates in its opening credits, "Based upon the novel *Gone Girl,* by Gillian Flynn."

- **Identifying numbers.** Identifying numbers, particularly the registration number or other indexing data, may help in your copyright search. Many media industries have a system of cataloging works. For example, publishers use ISBNs (International Standard Book Numbers) for books or ISSNs (International Standard Serial Numbers) for serial publications. The Library of Congress has its own catalog system known as the LCCN (Library of Congress Catalog Number). These numbers, which are usually located on the same page as the copyright notice, may prove helpful in identifying works when performing copyright research.

Searching the Copyright Office and Library of Congress Records

Now that you have isolated the information necessary for searching, you can begin examining the records at the Copyright Office and at the Library of Congress. Each of these databases has valuable information about public domain status and copyright ownership:

- Think of the Copyright Office as the source for copyright records. Search this database if you want specific information about copyright ownership, publication, transfers, and derivative works.
- Consider the Library of Congress as a 200-year-old library catalog. Search the catalogs if you want general information about a work such as the author, date of publication, subject matter, and publisher.

One common search strategy is to use Library of Congress files to identify an author, title, or publisher and then use that information to search the Copyright Office records online, as described below. If you are uncomfortable searching online, consider hiring the Copyright Office to perform the search on your behalf.

Defining Your Search

Your search of Copyright Office records will vary depending on your goal. Most likely, you have one of two goals: You want to find the current owner of a copyright or you want to know whether the work has fallen into the public domain. Methods for achieving each goal are described below.

Ownership Searching

When trying to determine the owner of copyright, review:

- certificates of registration, and
- assignments or other transfer documents.

Both of these documents are issued by and recorded with the Copyright Office. The registration will indicate who initially acquired ownership. The assignment will indicate if the registration has been transferred to another party.

The certificate of registration is issued by the Copyright Office and is the basic copyright document establishing date of publication, author, source of underlying material, contact person, and initial owner of copyright. The owner's name is listed in the space in Section 4 entitled "Copyright Claimant." If the owner is a different person than the author, the method of acquiring ownership (for example, "by written contract") is indicated in the space in Section 4 entitled "Transfer."

Assignments are transfers of copyright ownership. For example, an author may transfer rights to a publisher by signing an assignment of copyright, often included as part of a publishing agreement. Filing an assignment with the Copyright Office is not mandatory, but many copyright owners do so. When searching online at the Copyright Office, the person acquiring rights (the assignee) is usually listed as PARTY2 or PTY2 and the person transferring rights (the assignor) is usually listed as PARTY1 or PTY1.

Public Domain Searching

When researching whether a work is in the public domain, review:

- copyright registrations or other records containing the date of first publication, and
- renewal notices.

Both registrations and renewal notices are issued by and recorded with the Copyright Office. The registration is the initial statement of copyright information about a work and indicates the author, date of registration, copyright claimant (at the time of filing the registration), and date of first publication. A renewal must be filed in order to extend the length of protection for works published or registered before 1964. Although a renewal is no longer required for works published or registered after 1963, many copyright owners still file it.

Works published in the years 1927 through 1963 receive 95 years of protection if they were renewed during their 28th year. If not, they are in the public domain. Works published in the years 1964 through 1977 receive 95 years of protection. Works created after 1977 and all unpublished works are protected for the life of the author plus 70 years.

You may be able to determine if a work was published before 1927 (and is in the public domain) by examining the date in the work's copyright notice. For example, James Joyce's *Dubliners* is in the public domain because the Library of Congress database indicated that *Dubliners* was first published in the United States before 1927.

Note that copyright notice dates included in a book are not always accurate, because many public domain works are often republished with new dates in their copyright notices. For example, current editions of James Joyce's *Dubliners* have copyright notices with dates after 1980. These "new" dates reflect the fact that the work contains some new material such as a preface, notes, or previously unpublished material. Only this new material is protected under the copyright claim. The public domain part of the work remains in the public domain.

> **EXAMPLE:** To determine if the James Joyce short story collection *Dubliners* is in the public domain, I reviewed the Library of Congress records. The Library of Congress record, below, indicates that the work was first published in 1916.
>
> Title Search For: Dubliners /
> ITEM 1.CALL NUMBER: Microfilm 76492 PZ
> AUTHOR: Joyce, James, 1882-1941
> TITLE: Dubliners,
> PUBLISHED: New York, B. W. Huebsch, 1916.
> DESCRIPTION:2 p.l., 7-278 p. 20 cm.
> LCCN NUMBER:17-24698

Works published in the United States after 1926 and before 1964 are also in the public domain if the owner failed to file a renewal during the 28th year after first publication. Unlike copyright registrations or assignments, renewal notices for works published before 1964 had to be filed with the Copyright Office. If a work published after 1926 and before 1964 was not renewed, it fell into the public domain. According to Copyright Office surveys, the great majority of pre-1964 works were never renewed and, therefore, are in the public domain. Unfortunately, the Copyright Office does not maintain lists of public domain materials. You must search Copyright Office records to determine whether a renewal was filed on time for each work.

Searching Copyright Office Records

Once you have all the available information about your work and know what you're searching for, you need to choose the search method that best suits your purposes. You can either hire a search firm or work directly with the Copyright Office, which will do your search for a fee. Another option is searching the Copyright Office online, discussed in the next section.

What Else Can You Get From the Copyright Office?

Besides copyright research, the Copyright Office offers the following:
- information circulars
- answers to common questions
- announcements of changes in federal regulations
- compulsory licensing guidelines, and
- information on pending legislation.

These materials can be obtained by writing to the Copyright Office or by visiting the Copyright Office website at www.copyright.gov. You can also order circulars and publications by calling the Copyright Office's Forms and Publications Hot Line (202-707-9100).

Hire a Private Search Company

For a fee, you can hire a private company to search Copyright Office records for you. These companies provide additional services such as tracing the copyright history of a fictional character or locating similarly titled works. These companies may be able to determine if a work is in the public domain or whether you can obtain the rights to use the work. The advantage of using these companies is their speed and thoroughness. Search companies compile comprehensive reports using Copyright Office and other database records and can deliver the materials within two to ten days. The disadvantage is the cost, ranging from $75 to $300 per search. The largest and best known copyright search company is Clarivate CompuMark (https://clarivate.com/compumark).

Title #1	
Type of Work*	All works under the name or names ⬍
Requested Information*	☐ Registration ☐ Renewal ☐ Assignment ☐ Address What search information do you require? Indicate as much information as needed.
Title	
Author	If not known, please indicate N/A. Leaving this out will limit the search and the results may be inconclusive.
Copyright Claimant	If not known, please indicate N/A.
Year of Publication or Creation*	2014 ⬍ If approximate, provide earliest date to begin search.
Registration Number	If known
Other Info:	Any other identifying information for your request.

Figure 1

If You Only Need a Certificate of Registration

It's possible that all you need is the certificate of registration—the document recorded at the Copyright Office indicating who owns the work. You can use the search form above (Figure 1) to obtain a copy or simply furnish a letter to the Copyright Office with the following information:

- title of the work
- type of work involved (for example, novel, lyrics)
- registration number, including the preceding letters (for example, TX000-000)
- year of registration or publication
- author(s), including any pseudonym by which the author may be known, and
- any other information needed to identify the registration.

If you do not have all this information, you can furnish what you have. If the information furnished is insufficient for locating the certificate, you may need to pay for a copyright search.

There is a $40 fee for the certificate. The Copyright Office charges a fee for locating or retrieving records, providing additional certificates of registration, or certifying copyright records. The hourly fee to locate or retrieve nonelectronic records is $200 per hour with a one-hour minimum. The fee to retrieve electronic records is $200 per hour with a half-hour minimum; billing occurs thereafter in quarter-hour increments. Additional certificates of registration are $40 each.

Pay the Copyright Office to Perform the Search

Upon request, the Copyright Office will estimate the total cost of a search. The fee for a search estimate is $200, which is applicable to the search fee. The hourly search fee, including the preparation of an official search report, is $200, with a two-hour minimum. An online search request form (see Figure 1, above) is available from the Copyright Office website (www.copyright.gov/forms/search_estimate.html). The Copyright Office will respond with an estimate within two to five days.

Although the cost of a Copyright Office search is lower than a private search company, the disadvantage is that it may take longer to receive a response. The Copyright Office will conduct an expedited search if you pay a higher fee. For more information, see Copyright Circular 22. Also, note that the search fee does not include the cost of additional certificates or photocopies of deposits or other Copyright Office records. For information concerning these services, request Copyright Office Circular 6. (See Chapter 16 for information on how to obtain Copyright Office publications.)

All requests for copies of Copyright Office records should be submitted to: Certifications and Documents Section, LM-402, Copyright Office, Library of Congress, Washington, DC 20559; 202-707-6787. It is also possible to go to the office and request records in person (see "Searching in Person," just below).

Searching in Person

It's possible to inspect Copyright Office records by visiting the Library of Congress in Washington DC, at 101 Independence Avenue, SE, on the 4th floor of the James Madison Memorial Building. The building is open on weekdays from 8:30 a.m. to 5 p.m. There is a card catalog available to the public in Room 459. You can use the catalog to obtain essential facts about registrations, such as copyright ownership and whether a work was renewed. Alternatively, you may ask the Reference and Bibliography Section in Room 450 to conduct a search for you for an hourly fee. You can get extensive information on the Copyright Office Card Catalog by visiting the Copyright Office website (www.copyright.gov) and downloading Circular 23 or using Fax-on-Demand.

Another important research tool you can access in person is *The Catalog of Copyright Entries* (CCE). The CCE contains the same information as the Card Catalog, but is in book form (and is actually more complete than the Card Catalog). The CCE is not only available at the Copyright Office but in many libraries throughout the country—typically large university research libraries and city libraries such as the New York Public Library. Portions of the CCE are available only in microfiche form (a photographic format requiring a special viewer). The CCE contains essential facts about registrations, such as copyright ownership and whether a work was renewed, but does not include verbatim reproductions of the registration record. In addition, there is a time lag, so more recent registrations may not be included. Finally, the CCE cannot be used for researching the transfer of rights, because it does not include entries for assignments or other recorded documents.

Searching Copyright Office Records Online

Searching the online Copyright Office records is free and easy. You can search through copyright files by visiting the Copyright Office at www.copyright.gov (see Figure 2, below). Click "Search Copyright Records," and then click "Official Public Catalog" (it's within the box marked "Online Records Collection"). This contains information about works registered since January 1978. Included are published and unpublished text works, maps, motion pictures, music, sound recordings, works of the performing and visual arts, graphic artworks, and games. Also included are renewals of previous registrations.

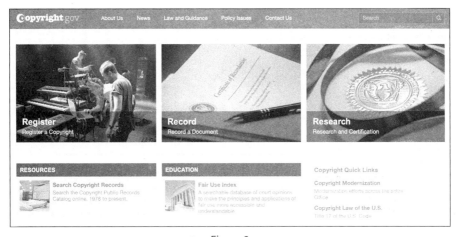

Figure 2

Once you access the post-1978 records (see Figure 3), you can search either by "Basic Search" or by using the Boolean "Other Search Options" feature (see Figure 4). You can search by author, claimant, title, or registration number. The search files are updated weekly. Note that renewal information is only available for works published after 1949.

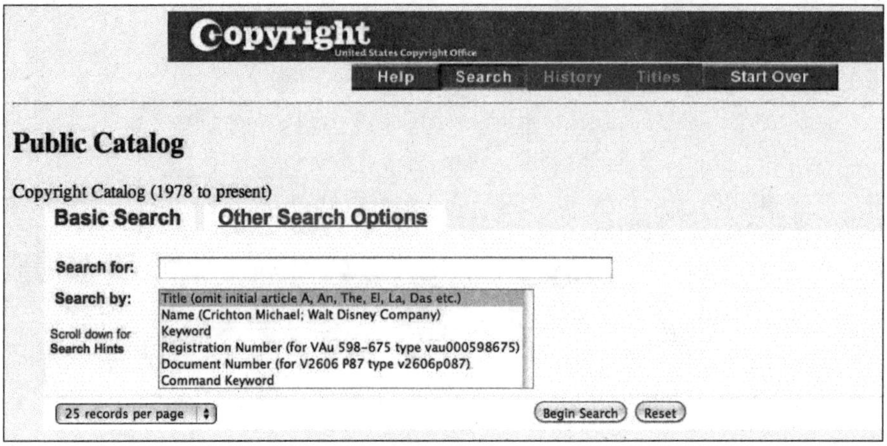

Figure 3

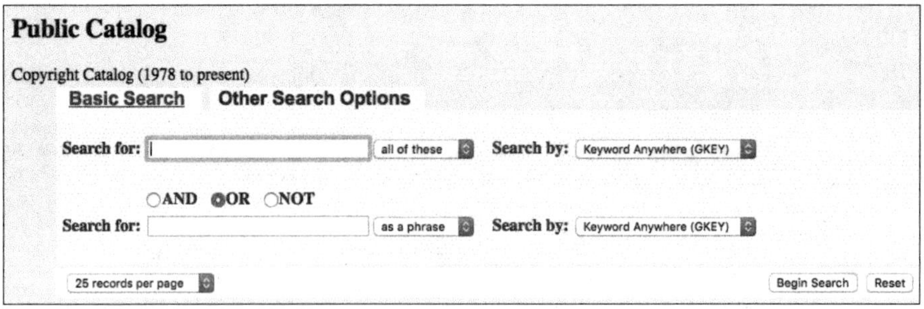

Figure 4

We tested the Basic Search feature by typing in the title of the book, *Franny and Zooey*, and found the resulting records (see Figure 5). Clicking on the second record (Figure 6), we learn that the owner of copyright is the late J.D. Salinger, and that the work, although first published in 1961, has been renewed (indicated by the letters "RE" by the registration number). The original registration number is A591015. Based on this information we can conclude that this work is not in the public domain because the owner filed a timely renewal of copyright after 28 years. (For more information on renewal requirements, see Chapter 8.)

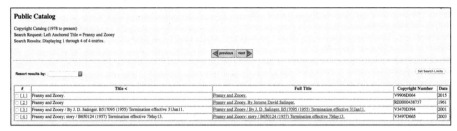

Figure 5

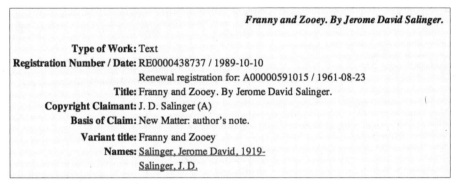

Figure 6

Searching Library of Congress Records

In addition to Copyright Office records, there is another catalog of helpful information at the Library of Congress in Washington, DC. The Library of Congress is the largest library in the world and has been collecting and cataloging materials for over 200 years. However, contrary to popular belief, the Library of Congress does not contain copies of every work ever published in the United States. The Library of Congress Online Catalog (http://catalog.loc.gov) includes data for books, serials (magazines and periodicals), music and sound recordings, maps, visual materials (such as photos and graphics), computer files from 1975, and an index of names and subjects. It also includes an incomplete, unedited listing of books cataloged between 1898 and 1975.

Because of the ease of searching and the vast catalog of materials, use the LOC Catalog for basic research, such as locating the publisher or owner of a work and researching public domain information. Unlike Copyright Office files, the LOC Catalog is searchable by subject matter. Or, you can search by ISBN, ISSN, or LCCN (Library of Congress Catalog Number). You can even limit or define your search by language. For example, you can search for books that are not in English. You may be able to use Library of Congress files to identify an author, title, or publisher and then use that information to search the Copyright Office records.

After Permission Is Granted

Your work doesn't end once you have tracked down a copyright owner and obtained permission to use their work. To avoid disputes you should keep careful records and manage your permissions process efficiently. Common disputes stem from unauthorized uses or failure to honor the terms of a permission agreement. This chapter addresses potential conflicts and suggests means of minimizing your liability, including the use of business insurance.

Permissions Tracking Sheet

The permissions process creates responsibilities. For example, if you fail to make a payment on time or to send a sample for approval, you can lose the right to reproduce the work. If you are managing multiple permissions—for example, reproducing several photographs in a book—you will need to track all the details properly.

A tracking sheet listing information such as ownership, the rights acquired, and payment arrangements enables the user to keep a running total of fees paid and due, and to keep track of who must receive samples or complimentary copies.

Below is a sample tracking sheet to help you manage the details of multiple permissions. An explanation for each section of the tracking sheet is also provided. This sheet is geared primarily toward copyright permissions, though it can be modified for use with trademark permissions as well. Since the tracking sheet is a modified spreadsheet, you could also prepare it using a computer program such as *Excel* or *Google Sheets*.

FORM

You can download this form (and all other forms in this book) from Nolo.com; for details, see the appendix.

Permissions Tracking Sheet

PTN	Type of Work, Title, Source, and ID Numbers	Author	Owner, Contact Person, Phone, Address, and Email	Payment	Payment Due Date	Date Paid and Form of Payment	Credit	Sample Approval of Comp Copies	Rights Acquired	How the Work Is Used

PTN (Permission Tracking Number)

Create a number for each permission use, adopting a coding system that reflects the project name. For example, if preparing a text on how to prevent hand injuries, each permission could be consecutively titled as HAND1, HAND2, and so on. The tracking numbers do not have to reflect the order in which the works are used or acquired; what's important is that each permission use has its own PTN.

Type of Work

Insert the type of work for which you have acquired permission—for example, photograph, graphic work, text, or trademark.

Title

Insert the title of the work—for example, the title of the article, novel, photograph, or graphic image for which you have acquired permission. If there is no title or if the title is not available, create a title that helps to identify the work—for example, "Boy with dog." If the work is a trademark, insert the name or a description of the mark.

Source

If you're using a work originally printed in another work—for example, a photograph within a book—insert the title of the source work. For works from serial publications, such as a magazine or journal, insert the title and volume or issue number. If the work is from a website, insert the URL.

Identifying Numbers

Many works are identified by code numbers, such as the ISBN, ISSN, LCCN, or Dewey Decimal numbers for textual works. Sound recordings also have catalog numbers. If the copyright registration number or trademark registration number is available, list it here.

Author(s)

Insert the name of the author (the person who created the work). The author may not be the same as the copyright owner. If no author is listed—for example, you're using a newspaper article without a byline or the author is "anonymous" or uses a pseudonym—include that information.

Owner and Contact Information

Insert all contact information for the copyright or trademark owner, including the right person to contact (such as a manager or an agent, if the owner has one), address, phone number, and email. As indicated in Chapter 15, the author of a copyrighted work is the original owner, but he or she may have transferred rights to a company or another individual.

Payments Due

If a payment is required, insert the terms of payment here—for example, "$50 per year"—and indicate when payment is due.

Payments Made

When payment is made, insert the date and the method of payment, such as credit card, online payment app, or check. If paid by check, include the check number.

Credit Required

If the copyright owner requires that a credit line be included, insert the type of credit here—for example, "Photograph copyright Prudence O'Neal."

Sample Approval/Complimentary Copies

In some cases, the owner has a right to approve samples prior to production or the owner is entitled to complimentary copies. If either samples or complimentary copies are required per your agreement, insert that information and the name of the person who should receive the samples or copies.

Rights Acquired

List the rights you acquired under the permission agreement. In general, your primary concerns are exclusivity, territory, language, and term (or length of use). For example, the rights acquired might be stated as: "Nonexclusive English language rights for four years."

How the Work Is Used

Indicate where and how the work will be used in your work. For example, if you're creating a book, insert the page number of your book on which you use the work; if the work will be used on a website, insert the URL.

Permissions Calendar

If you're performing a lot of permission work, use a calendaring system to keep track of any renewals, payments, or dates samples must be furnished for approval. If possible, use a software program or app that can provide timely reminders (known as a "tickler" system).

Good Permissions Gone Bad

Regardless of the degree of care the user exercises, not all disputes can be prevented. Two common categories of permission disputes are contract disputes and intellectual property infringements. Quite often these types of claims overlap. For example, a use that exceeds the written permission agreement may end up as a contract dispute or a copyright dispute. Each type of claim has different remedies and may be brought in different courts. The section below discusses how to approach such disputes.

Cease and Desist Letters

The opening salvo in breach of contract or infringement situations is usually a letter from an attorney asking that the user "cease and desist" from using the work further. To minimize any potential damages, you should:
- respond immediately to the owner, indicating that you have received the letter and are investigating the claims
- investigate the claims and, if necessary, request further information from the copyright owner, such as proof of ownership
- if possible, stop using or distributing the work (for example, remove the photo from a website or stop selling a book) until the claim has been fully investigated, and
- contact an attorney knowledgeable in copyright law. Information about finding and evaluating an attorney is provided in Chapter 16, "Help Beyond This Book."

Not all legal threats are valid. An attorney's opinion will help you evaluate the claim. As part of the evaluation, seek an estimate of the legal expenses for fighting the dispute.

Contract Disputes

A contract dispute can arise if the terms of the permission agreement are broken (or "breached"). The two most common disputes that arise under a license agreement are claims that the use exceeds the grant of permission, or that a payment was not made:

- **The use exceeds the grant.** A dispute might arise if the work is being used in a manner that the copyright owner believes exceeds the rights granted under the agreement. To avoid this type of dispute, monitor the work in all stages of production and review the final product to make sure the use of the work is within the rights granted by the permissions agreement.
- **Payment was not made.** If payment is a condition of permission and payment is not made, the agreement may be terminated by the copyright owner. A prudent approach to avoid this problem is to calendar any dates payments are due and mark payments, you make immediately and clearly. (Note, many companies demand payment before production.)

The permission agreement may provide specific remedies for disputes—for example, arbitration or mediation. In cases of breach, the owner can sue for monetary damages and, if provided under the agreement, attorneys' fees. Breach of contract claims are usually brought in state courts, but can also be brought in federal court—for instance, as part of a copyright infringement claim.

Intellectual Property Infringement

The owner of a work you're using can sue in federal court and seek monetary damages (and in some cases attorneys' fees) if you infringe on his or her copyright, trademark, or publicity rights.

Infringement claims are typically brought because of unauthorized uses. If the use is not addressed at all in the license agreement (for example, the grant is for use of a photo in a book and you use it on T-shirts), the copyright owner will usually bring the lawsuit under copyright law (although it's possible to bring the claim under contract law in some cases). If the use simply exceeds the dimensions of the grant (for example, you are permitted to reproduce a photograph in a 5,000-print run of a book and you use it in 7,000 copies), a court will probably consider the claim to be a breach of the license (a contract claim as discussed in the previous section) rather than an infringement of copyright. The determinations in these cases—whether copyright law or contract law controls—vary depending on the facts of the case and the judicial district in which the case is filed.

Sometimes a copyright owner files an infringement suit because the user obtained permission from the wrong person, and the correct owner now seeks to assert his or her rights. For example, a magazine claims to own a photograph but, after publication, the photographer claims ownership and sues for infringement. This type of dispute is difficult to predict and equally difficult to prevent. One approach to minimizing liability in this situation is to require that the person signing the permission agreement promise that he or she has authority to grant the permission, and if possible, provide indemnity. (Sample indemnity provisions are provided in many of the permission agreements throughout this book.)

Libel, Invasion of Privacy, and Other Claims

Unauthorized uses of work may give rise to additional claims such as defamation or invasion of privacy. These claims are discussed in Chapter 12, "Releases." If confronted by a claim of libel or defamation, seek the advice of an attorney knowledgeable in media law.

Insurance

Insurance may shield a user from some potential damages. The protection will vary depending on the terms of the insurance policy. Some general business insurance policies contain a provision entitled "advertising injuries" that protect against trademark, copyright, or libel claims. The extent of protection depends upon the wording of the policy and the manner in which insurance policies are interpreted in the state. The model form language used by the insurance industry to define advertising injuries has changed repeatedly over the past two decades as insurers seek ways to avoid paying for claims.

If you are threatened with a claim, examine your business insurance immediately. An attorney should be able to advise you as to whether the insurance company must assume coverage. Publishers and media companies sometimes acquire more comprehensive insurance known as "media perils" policies. Check with your insurance agent for more information.

It is quite common for insurance carriers to attempt to deny coverage to copyright owners. That means that if you assert a claim, the company will look for a way out. One of the most common methods an insurance company uses to avoid payment is to argue that the type of claim raised is not listed explicitly in the policy—for example, the policy does not cover claims from a certain time period or claims involving certain works.

In other situations, the carrier will seek to deny coverage if the insurance company is not informed of the claim promptly. For example, in 1994, the Andy Warhol estate was sued by Time-Life, Inc., and a photographer over Warhol's use of a photograph of Jacqueline Kennedy. The Warhol estate waited until 1996 to notify its insurance company and, on the basis of this late reporting, the insurance company refused to provide coverage. This refusal was upheld by a federal court. (*The Andy Warhol Foundation for the Visual Arts Inc. v. Federal Insurance Co.*, 97 Civ. 2716 (TPG), 1998 U.S. Dist. LEXIS 8094, June 2, 1998 (S.D.N.Y., June 2, 1998).) Therefore, if a claim is made against your company, investigate coverage immediately and report the claim promptly to your carrier.

Assignments and Works Made for Hire

This chapter is not about getting permission—it's about acquiring ownership. Once you become the owner of a copyrighted work, you don't need permission from anyone to use it. Instead, others must obtain permission from you.

Acquiring ownership may be your best option in a number of situations—for example, when you want an illustration for permanent use on your website. This chapter discusses the two methods of acquiring ownership: by assignment and by commissioning a work for hire.

An assignment is a permanent transfer of ownership, such as acquiring copyright ownership of a photograph from the photographer. A work-for-hire agreement on the other hand, makes the person who pays for the work the owner and author of the work. For example, the Disney Company employs animators who create a cartoon; the Disney Company is the author and owner of the cartoon. The advantages and disadvantages to both approaches are discussed in this chapter. We'll also provide several model assignments and work-for-hire agreements that can be used with copyright owners, artists, and musicians.

Copyright Assignments

When someone who owns a copyrighted work sells all rights in it to another party, the transaction is called an "assignment." Unlike a license agreement in which the licensee obtains only a temporary, conditional right to use a work that is still owned by the licensor, in an assignment, the buyer (assignee) purchases the copyright and the person selling the copyright (the assignor) retains no rights. There are some exceptions, and it is possible to acquire an assignment of a part interest in a copyright, for example, from a co-owner of copyright. In that case, only a part ownership is purchased and the purchaser becomes a co-owner. However, this chapter focuses on acquiring full ownership of a copyrighted work only.

Depending on the terms of the assignment, the assignor might be paid by the assignee with a lump sum or with periodic royalty payments. In addition, an assignment may provide that the rights are assigned back to the assignor in the event of a certain condition—for example, if the assignee stops selling the work.

An assignment is a transfer of ownership, but it might not last for the full term of copyright protection. This is because copyright law permits creators of work transferred after 1977 to recapture all the copyrights that were assigned 35 years from the date of the assignment. (Terminations of transfers for works transferred in or before 1977 are subject to fairly complex rules that are beyond the scope of this book. See *The Copyright Handbook,* by attorney Stephen Fishman (Nolo), for more information.) For example, an author that assigned rights to a book publisher in 2000 can reclaim the rights in 2035. This recapture right is usually not important because few works have a useful economic life of more than 35 years. And this recapture right does not apply to the creator of a work made for hire, as discussed below.

You can use an assignment to acquire a work that already exists, or an artist can agree to assign a work that will be created in the future. An assignment must be in writing. Notarization is not required but is recommended, especially if the assignee is concerned about the assignment's validity. Notarization creates a legal presumption that the signature on the transfer is valid. If there are multiple owners of a copyright, the signature of all owners must be obtained to make the assignment valid.

An assignment can be recorded (made into public records) by filing it with the Copyright Office. Recordation isn't a legal requirement, but it provides public notice of the transfer. For information on recording assignments, call the Copyright Office's Public Information Office at 202-679-0700 or the Certification and Documents office at 202-707-6850. The assignment and fee should be mailed to: Documents Unit LM-462, Cataloging Office, Library of Congress, Washington, DC 20559.

An Heir Cannot Terminate Assignment If a New Arrangement Has Been Reached

Superman had two creators: Joe Schuster and Jerry Siegel. Under copyright law, an estate can cancel an assignment of a pre-1978 copyright assignment or grant after 35 years. Siegel's estate was able to terminate its grant to Warner Brothers but Schuster's estate was not. That's because Schuster's sister had negotiated a new agreement in 1992 and therefore, this new agreement superseded and replaced the pre-1978 grant. (*Larson v. Warner Bros.,* CV-08400-ODW (January, 2013).)

Basic Copyright Assignment

The agreement below is a basic copyright assignment that can be used for any type of work.

 FORM
You can download this form (and all other forms in this book) from Nolo.com; for details, see the appendix.

Basic Copyright Assignment

I, _____ ("Assignor"),
am owner of the work entitled _____ (the "Work")
and described as follows: _____
_____ .

In consideration of $ _____ and other valuable consideration, paid
by _____ ("Assignee"),
I assign to Assignee and Assignee's heirs and assigns all my right, title, and
interest in the copyright to the Work and all renewals and extensions of the
copyright that may be secured under the laws of the United States of America
and any other countries, as such may now or later be in effect. I agree to
cooperate with Assignee and to execute and deliver all papers as may be
necessary to vest all rights to the Work.

Signature of assignor(s) _____

Explanation of Basic Copyright Assignment

- In the first two blanks of the first paragraph, insert the assignor's name (usually the author) and the title of the work. In the next blank space, either describe the work or enter "See attached Exhibit A" and attach a copy of the work to the assignment. If you attach a copy, be sure to label it "Exhibit A."

- In the next paragraph, insert the amount of the payment and the name of the assignee.
- The assignor must sign the agreement. To have the agreement notarized, the assignor should wait to sign the agreement until in the presence of a notary, who will fill out the rest of the notarization section, as described below.

Notarization

Notarization for copyright assignments is recommended. The purpose of notarization is to verify the signature and identity of the person executing the agreement. You can usually locate a notary public through your local yellow pages. To include notarization, add the following statement at the end of the agreement.

On this _____ day of _____ , year _____ , before me, _____ , the undersigned Notary Public, personally appeared _____ and proved to me based on satisfactory evidence to be the person(s) who executed this instrument.

Witness my hand and official seal.

_____

Notary Public

Sometimes this section does not have to be added, as the notary may have a stamp that includes all such information. Wait to have the assignor sign the agreement until he or she is in the presence of the notary.

- If there is more than one assignor, or if the assignor is married in a community property state, signing the agreement may involve a few more considerations.

Multiple assignors. If there are multiple copyright owners, you will need the signature of all owners for your assignment. There are many ways that a copyright can have co-owners. For example, the work may have been created by joint authors or may have been bequeathed under a will to several children who became co-owners. If you are unsure whether there are multiple co-owners, you can research this using the techniques in Chapter 13.

Spousal consent in community property states. A community property state is one in which any property acquired by either spouse during marriage (other than by gift or inheritance), belongs to the husband and wife equally. Copyrights may be co-owned by a spouse in community property states, though court cases on the subject are conflicting. A court in California has held that a spouse in a community property state has a co-ownership interest in the other spouse's copyrighted work. (*In re Marriage of Worth*, 195 Cal.App.3d 768, 241 Cal.Rptr. 185 (1987).) The safest route for an assignor who lives in a community property state is to obtain their spouse's consent to any assignment. The provision below can be added to the assignment and should be notarized.

Spousal Consent Provision

I am the spouse of Assignor and acknowledge that I have read and understand this Agreement. I am aware that my spouse agrees to assign all interest in the Work, including any community property interest or other equitable property interest that I may have in it. I consent to the assignment and agree that my interest, if any, in the Work is subject to the provisions of this Agreement. I will take no action to hinder the Agreement or the underlying assignment of rights.

___[Spouse's signature]_____

Musician Assignment Agreement

If you are hiring a musician to record a composition—for instance, you hire a guitarist to record musical phrases for a video game—you may want to use a more detailed assignment agreement, such as the one offered below. The assignment is for the musician's recorded performance; not for the song. As explained in Chapter 5, there are two separate music copyrights: one in the musical composition or song (musical work) and another in the way in which the song is recorded (sound recording). If the musician has composed the song, you additionally would use the assignment above to transfer the rights to the composition itself as well as to the sound recordings.

FORM
You can download this form (and all other forms in this book) from Nolo.com; for details, see the appendix.

Explanation for Musician Assignment Agreement

- Since the musician is assigning all rights in the performance, the **Grant** section is as broad as possible, and the musician will not retain any rights to the recorded performance.
- The **Warranty and Release** section is an assurance that the musician owns the rights being granted. For example, some musicians are signed to exclusive recording agreements and a record company owns all of their performances, or the musician may be prohibited from recording altogether. The warranty also provides a promise not to sue the company for legal claims such as copyright infringement. The warranty section also includes additional statements that "Company is permitted, although not obligated, to include musician's name as a credit in connection with the performance," and "Company is not obligated to utilize any of the rights granted in this Agreement." These provisions give the company the ability to ditch the performance, if necessary, and to avoid liability in the event that it does not credit the musician.

Musician Assignment Agreement

This Musician Assignment Agreement (the "Agreement") is made between

_____ ("Company")

and _____ ("Musician").

Grant

Musician has performed or recorded performance(s) for the Company in conjunction with the Company recording under the titles:

_____

_____

_____

In consideration of the payments provided in this Agreement, Musician assigns all rights, including all rights under copyright law, in the recorded performance to the Company, its assigns, licensees, or successors and grants the right to use the recorded performance for any purposes and in all forms and media and waives any claim to moral rights.

Payment

Company shall pay Musician as follows: $ _____ .

Warranty and Release

Musician has the authority to grant the rights under this Agreement and Musician releases Company and Company's assigns, licensees, and successors from any claims that may arise regarding the use of the performance, including any claims of infringement of moral rights, rights of publicity, or copyright. Company is permitted, although not obligated, to include musician's name as a credit in connection with the performance.

Company is not obligated to utilize any of the rights granted in this Agreement.

Musician has read and understood this agreement and is over the age of 18. This Agreement expresses the complete understanding of the parties.

Musician's Signature: _____

Musician's Name: _____

Musician's Address: _____

Date: _____

- It is unusual that the musician would be a minor, but in that event, the musician's parent or guardian should sign a consent similar to the Parent/ Guardian Consent in the model release in Chapter 12, "Releases."

Arbitration and Mediation

An arbitration and/or mediation clause provides alternate methods of resolving any disputes that may arise, rather than filing a lawsuit. Although one is not included in the artist or musician assignments, you may, if you wish, include the following provision in either agreement. (For a more detailed explanation of arbitration and mediation, review Chapter 11.)

Mediation; Arbitration. If a dispute arises under this Agreement, the parties agree to first try to resolve the dispute with the help of a mutually agreed-upon mediator in the State of _____ .
Any costs and fees other than attorneys' fees shall be shared equally by the parties. If it proves impossible to arrive at a mutually satisfactory solution, the parties agree to submit the dispute to binding arbitration in the same city or region, conducted on a confidential basis pursuant to the Commercial Arbitration Rules of the American Arbitration Association.

Dear Rich: ## Getting Music Rights for Video

I am in need of a rights transfer document but don't know exactly which agreement/ form will serve my need. I have a video that needs music put to it and I have found a freelancer to do it. So I need him to sign a transfer of rights before he works on the video so that we can copyright it under our name without ever running into a legal issue. Does a patent, copyright, trademark need to be registered by the original artist before an assignment can be signed?

If someone is commissioned to create a contribution for an audiovisual work (a movie, video, etc.) then that would qualify as a work made for hire under copyright law. And if you want to list your company as the "author," you'll have that option under the work-made-for-hire arrangement. Our publisher sells books that include work-made-for-hire agreements. You can probably fashion one yourself as long as you include the following provision:

> Contractor agrees that, for consideration that is acknowledged, any works of authorship commissioned pursuant to this Agreement (the "Works") shall be considered works made for hire as that term is defined under U.S. copyright law. To the extent that any such Work created for Company by Contractor is not a work made for hire belonging to Company, Contractor hereby assigns and transfers to Company all rights Contractor has or may acquire to all such Works. Contractor agrees to sign and deliver to Company, either during or subsequent to the term of this Agreement, such other documents as Company considers desirable to evidence the assignment of copyright.

You'll also need to add some other details, like an assurance that the material isn't taken from somewhere else, information about payment, and other typical contract stuff. The agreement should be signed before the work is completed.

Do you need to register a patent, copyright, or trademark before assigning it? Just to be clear, we're only talking about copyrights. No registration is required for the work-made-for-hire-agreement or for an assignment of copyright. A registration isn't necessary for assigning a trademark, either. You would need to have acquired a patent before assigning it, since patents (unlike copyrights and trademarks) don't exist until the government says, "Okay!" You can, however, assign a patent application on the underlying technology rights. That's enough blah blah blah for today—the Dear Rich Staff has got to go get melancholy with Frank.

Artwork Assignment Agreement

The following agreement provides for assignment of artwork, but it can be modified for photography as well. The assignment includes optional provisions for payment of expenses and dispute resolution.

FORM

You can download this form (and all other forms in this book) from Nolo.com; for details, see the appendix.

Artwork Assignment Agreement

This Artwork Assignment Agreement (the "Agreement") is made between
_____ ("Company") and
_____ ("Artist").

Services

Artist agrees to perform the following services: _____
_____ and create the following artwork (the "Art")
entitled: _____ .

The Art shall be completed by the following date: _____ .

During the process, Artist shall keep the Company informed of work in progress and shall furnish test prints of the Art prior to completion.

Payment

Company agrees to pay Artist as follows:

$ _____ for performance of the art services and acquisition of the rights provided below.

Grant of Rights

Artist assigns to the Company all copyright to the Art and agrees to cooperate in the preparation of any documents necessary to demonstrate this assignment of rights. Artist retains the right to display the work as part of Artist's portfolio and to reproduce the artwork in connection with the promotion of Artist's services.

Expenses

Company agrees to reimburse Artist for all reasonable production expenses, including halftones, stats, photography, disks, illustrations, or related costs. These expenses shall be itemized on invoices and in no event shall any expense exceed $50 without approval from the Company.

Credit

Credit for Artist shall be included on reproductions of the Art as follows: _____

_____

Artist Warranties

Artist is the owner of all rights to the Art and warrants that the Art does not infringe any intellectual property rights or violate any laws.

Artist's Signature: _____

Artist's Name: _____

Artist's Address: _____

_____

Date: _____

Company Authorized Signature: _____

Name and Title: _____

Address: _____

_____

Date: _____

Explanation of Artwork Assignment Agreement

- Since the artist is assigning all rights in the performance, the **Grant of Rights** section is as broad as possible, and the artist will not retain any rights to the artwork.
- Use the **Services** section if the artist has been hired to perform a specific job. If the artwork has already been completed, this provision is not needed. Strike it or enter "NA" for "not applicable."
- The **Artist Warranties** are promises that the artist owns the rights being granted and will not sue the company for legal claims such as copyright infringement. If you wish, you may include an arbitration or mediation section.
- It is unusual that the artist would be a minor, but in that event, the artist's parent or guardian should sign a consent similar to the Parent/ Guardian Consent in the model release in Chapter 12, "Releases."

Dear Rich: **Who Owns Copyright in Clothing Photos?**

I worked for a very large clothing retail company in the corporate office. Photography was not in any way in my job title. One of the marketing managers knew that I did photography and asked if I would shoot some of the clothes that they were trying to sell to another retailer. I first agreed to shoot the products for them to use as line sheets to increase the chances that the other company would buy the products. Then it turned out the president of the company wanted me to do a much larger shoot. The deal went through and the company carried our products. Then I found out that my images were being used in the stores for huge posters and ad campaigns. My company provided them with the posters and banners to put in their stores. I did not sign anything during the shoot or after. My company never did pay me a bonus as they stated they would. I no longer work there and have not received any compensation for that photo shoot. What would professional photographers charge for this type of two-day shoot that was later used for an ad campaign?

Even without a written agreement, an employer owns copyright to everything created by an employee in the ordinary course of employment. For example, do you remember that photograph of the fireman cradling the baby after the Oklahoma City bombing? That was taken by an employee of a gas company whose job was to investigate gas explosions and take photographs of the scene. The gas company employee tried to claim ownership of the photo in order to sell it on T-shirts, but a court ruled the photo was taken within the ordinary course of employment and belonged to the employer.

What's the "ordinary course of employment?" Courts sometimes ask three questions: Was it done on the clock? (Yes, in your case.) Did you take any actions or say anything that indicated that your employer owned the copyright? (We're not sure about that.) Was it part of your job description—that is, was it one of your duties as an employee to take photographs of the goods? (Apparently not, according to your letter.) Based on these questions, the Dear Rich Staff thinks you have a reasonable argument to claim copyright ownership, but it is probably a close call, primarily because the photographs were taken on company time, at the company's facility, and with contributions and supervision from the company. We're also concerned about that bonus you discussed. If it was negotiated as separate payment for the work, then that could influence your ownership claim. As for what other photographers would charge for similar services, the best answer can be found by checking pricing rates at other photographers' websites, or using one of the popular online pricing tools.

Works Made for Hire

Sometimes for copyright purposes the author of a work is the person who pays for it, not the person who creates it. The resulting work is called a work made for hire, or often simply a "work for hire." The basis for this principle is that a business that authorizes and pays for a work should own the rights to the work.

There are two distinct types of work that may be classified as "made for hire":

- a work created by an employee within the scope of employment, or
- a commissioned work created by an independent contractor (nonemployee) that is the subject of a written work-for-hire agreement and that falls within a special group of categories.

This section discusses these work-for-hire rules for employees and independent contractors in more detail. First, it explains some general rules regarding copyright ownership and duration for works for hire.

Significance of Work-Made-for-Hire Status

If a work qualifies as a work made for hire under one of the two methods described above, the person paying for the work (the hiring party) is both the author and copyright owner. As such, the hiring party must be named as the author on an application for copyright registration.

The work-for-hire status of a work also affects the length of copyright protection and termination rights.

Copyright Duration

Works made for hire created after 1977 are protected for a period of 95 years from first publication or 120 years from creation, whichever is shorter. Therefore, if a website company created a work made for hire in 2000 but did not publish it until 2001, copyright protection would extend to 2096 (95 years from the date of publication).

No Termination Rights

As discussed above, someone who assigns a copyright to someone else may be able to recapture the copyright after 35 years. However, a work made for hire cannot be terminated by the creator. This means that the owner of a work made for hire (the hiring party) is assured that he or she will retain ownership for the full copyright term.

Dear Rich: **Illustrating Book About Chinese Zodiacs**

I'm an artist and my friend is a writer. She wants me to illustrate her book on Chinese zodiac astrology. My art would be heavily displayed in the book. How do we work out my getting paid for my art? Do I charge her a flat fee or take a cut of the earnings?

Consider the following questions before proposing anything to the writer.

- **Is the artwork supplementary or essential?** If the artwork is an essential part of the purchasing decision—as in a home decorating or children's picture book—that would be more likely to justify a cut of the earnings. If the illustrations simply supplement the writing (as in most nonfiction books), flat fees are more common.

- **How much time will it take and what is your time worth?** Estimate the number of hours per drawing. If you were billing an anonymous client for the same work, what would you charge? This would be your starting point in determining what you want to earn back (though of course there may a steep discount for your friend). *The Graphic Artists Guild Handbook* provides assistance with pricing.

- **How likely is it that a commercial publisher will distribute the book?** If this work will be the subject of a book deal, the typical advance (assuming there is one) for a nonfiction book would be between $3,000 and $10,000 (though others indicate these advances are higher, we don't think that's an accurate reflection of today's marketplace). Royalties would be 5% to 10% of the book's income but would only be paid after the advance has been earned back. Nonfiction books usually have a sales life of 12 to 14 months. If a book deal is in the works, and you feel you are entitled to a cut of the earnings, you should seek to become a party to the publishing contract. Otherwise, you must rely on the writer to receive the income and then forward your payment.

- **What does your friend want to do?** Because you're dealing with a friend—not an anonymous client—we'd like to see you work out an arrangement that doesn't jeopardize your personal relationship. You could propose a two-tiered system—for example a reduced flat fee but an additional payment if a book deal is signed.

- **What about the rights?** Are you transferring copyright ownership? Do you want to retain certain rights so that you can continue to use, sell, or display the artwork. Determining rights may affect the price. For example, if you would like the right to sell limited edition prints, or to advertise those prints in the book, you might want to adjust your fees accordingly.

Works Created by Employees

Every copyrightable work created by an employee within the scope of employment is automatically a work made for hire. There are no other requirements, no review of the special categories (outlined below), and no need for a written agreement. For this reason, when sorting out ownership issues, a court will first analyze whether an employer-employee relationship exists.

RESOURCE

For more information on the law regarding independent contractors, see *Working With Independent Contractors,* by Stephen Fishman (Nolo).

Whether an employment relationship exists is determined by weighing the following factors:

- **The tax treatment of the hired party.** If the hiring party pays payroll and employment taxes, this factor weighs strongly in favor of an employment relationship. *This factor is virtually determinative by itself.*
- **The provision of employee benefits.** If vacation or health benefits are granted to the worker, this factor weighs in favor of an employment relationship.
- **The hiring party's right to control the manner and means by which the work is accomplished.** If the hiring party exercises control, this factor weighs in favor of an employment relationship.
- **The skill required in the particular occupation.** If the work to be performed requires a unique skill—for example, sculpting—this factor weighs against an employment relationship.
- **Whether the employer or the worker supplies the instrumentalities and tools of the trade.** If the worker supplies his or her own tools, this factor weighs against an employment relationship.
- **Where the work is done.** If the hiring party determines the location of the work, this factor weighs in favor of an employment relationship.
- **The length of time for which the worker is employed.** The longer the period of work, the more this factor weighs in favor of an employment relationship.
- **Whether the hiring party has the right to assign additional work projects to the worker.** If the hiring party can assign additional tasks—including tasks that do not result in copyrightable works—this factor weighs in favor of an employment relationship.
- **The extent of the worker's discretion over when and how long to work.** If the hiring party controls the working times—particularly if it is a regular work week—this factor weighs in favor of an employment relationship.
- **The method of payment.** If the payment is per job—not per day or week—this factor weighs against an employment relationship.

- **The hired party's role in hiring and paying assistants.** If the worker cannot hire and pay assistants, this factor weighs in favor of an employment relationship.
- **Whether the work is part of the regular business of the hiring party.** If the hiring party does not perform this type of work regularly—for example, taking photographs—this factor weighs against an employment relationship.
- **Whether the worker is in business.** If the worker has a business, this factor weighs against an employment relationship.

Dear Rich:

Can a California Employer Claim Employee Copyrights?

As a condition of working for a large company, I am required to agree to an Intellectual Property and Confidentiality Agreement. The only mention of copyright is in a section that states "all copyrights in works authored by me ... during the term of this Agreement are and shall be the exclusive property of the Employer." Unlike the language pertaining to Work Product or Inventions, there are no qualifiers on copyrights, such as that the works have to be related to the business of the employer, done as part of working for them, etc. It seems to me this means that (hypothetically) an automotive company would then own the copyright to anything I write on the weekends, even if completely unrelated to the company (such as a fiction novel about a dog with superpowers). Is there anything in the (specifically California) law that protects copyrights against this very broad-reaching clause?

We doubt that a California judge would permit an employer to own an employee's superpowered dog novel. Here's why:

Public policy. A contractual provision won't be enforced if the provision violates public policy (public policy is the moral and ethical principles upon which the legal system is created). The provision you mention appears to violate California's public policy, which aims to protect employees from overreaching employers. This policy is evidenced by (1) a California labor statute that prevents employers from claiming nonwork-related inventions (innovations that don't involve employer time or resources), and (2) a law that prohibits noncompete agreements. The public policy behind federal copyright law supports an employee's right to own works unless created within the course of employment.

Unconscionability. A contractual provision also won't be enforced if the provision is unconscionable (grossly unfair). What if the Superdog novel is published, attracts a movie deal, and becomes a blockbuster with sequels? Your agreement might be considered to be unconscionable because your payment (your paycheck) is so disproportionate in value as to demonstrate bad faith (or "unconscionability") in the bargaining process.

Works Created by Independent Contractors

A work created by an independent contractor (unlike a work created by an employee) is not automatically classified as a work made for hire. For an independent contractor's work to qualify as a work made for hire, three requirements must be met:

- The work must be specially ordered or commissioned—for example, the hiring party must request the work; it cannot already be in existence.
- The work must fall within a group of specially enumerated categories (outlined below).
- A written agreement must be signed by both parties indicating that it is a work made for hire.

Ordering the Work and Executing an Agreement

A work-for-hire agreement with an independent contractor should be signed before the work commences. However, at least one court has held that the agreement can be executed after the work is completed, provided that at the time the work was created, the parties intended to enter into such an agreement. In that case, a magazine paid an artist by check and on the back of each check was a statement that indicated the drawings were works made for hire. A court of appeals ruled that the artist's continued signature on the checks over a seven-year period demonstrated that he was aware of and accepted the arrangement. (*Playboy Enterprises, Inc. v. Dumas*, 53 F.3d 549 (2d Cir. 1995).)

Work-Made-for-Hire Categories

An independent contractor's work will be a work for hire only if it falls within one of the following categories:

- a contribution to a collective work (such as a short story for a collection or an introduction to an anthology)
- a part of a motion picture or other audiovisual work
- a translation
- a supplementary work—that is, a work prepared for publication as a supplement to a work by another author for the purpose of introducing, concluding, illustrating, explaining, revising, commenting upon, or assisting in the use of the other work (such as forewords, afterwords, pictorial illustrations, maps, charts, tables, editorial notes, musical arrangements, answer material for tests, bibliographies, appendixes, and indexes)
- a compilation (such as a collection of statistics on stock car racing)
- an instructional text—that is, a literary, pictorial, or graphic work prepared for use in day-to-day instructional activities (such as a textbook, but not a novel used in a literature class)
- a test or answer material for a test, or
- an atlas.

Any work created by an independent contractor that does not fall within one of the above categories cannot be a work made for hire. This is so even if the parties have signed a written agreement stating that the work is a work made for hire.

> EXAMPLE: A painter is commissioned to create a mural for a school. The painter signs an agreement entitled, "Work Made for Hire." The painter (not the school) owns the painting because paintings are not included among the enumerated categories of works by independent contractors that can be works made for hire.

Dear Rich:

Can an Assignment Create a Work for Hire?

If I chose to completely assign my copyright in a personally created work of authorship to a sole proprietorship or single-shareholder S corp—with either of these businesses being owned exclusively by me—would the copyrighted product be considered a work made for hire in determining the duration of its legal protection?

The short answer to your question is "No." Just because a business acquires a copyright does not make it a work made for hire. The Dear Rich Staff reports that work-made-for-hire status is determined by the original act of authorship—that is, who is the author and under what conditions the work is created. If it was created by an employee within the course of employment or by an independent contractor (and it fulfills the IC work-for-hire requirements), it will be a work-made-for-hire forever (or at least for the duration of copyright). In other words, authorship status travels with the copyright no matter who acquires it down the road.

Work-Made-for-Hire Agreement

Below is a simple work-for-hire agreement. Remember that it is always necessary to use this agreement with an independent contractor. Strictly speaking, it is not necessary to use this agreement when a work is to be created by an employee. The employer automatically owns an employee's work created within the course of employment regardless of whether there is a written agreement. However, employers often prefer to use written agreements to make it clear to employees that the employer owns copyright.

This agreement can be used for other workers besides artists. Simply revise the appropriate sections to describe the worker and the work made for hire.

FORM

You can download this form (and all other forms in this book) from Nolo.com; for details, see the appendix.

Work-Made-for-Hire Agreement

This Work-Made-for-Hire Agreement (the "Agreement") is made between _____
_____ ("Company") and
_____ ("Artist").

Services

In consideration of the payments provided in this Agreement, Artist agrees to
perform the following services: _____
_____

Payment

Company agrees to pay Artist as follows: _____
_____ .

Works Made for Hire—Assignment of Intellectual Property Rights

Artist agrees that, for consideration that is acknowledged, any works of authorship
commissioned pursuant to this Agreement (the "Works") shall be considered works
made for hire as that term is defined under U.S. copyright law. To the extent that any
such Work created for Company by Artist is not a work made for hire belonging to
Company, Artist hereby assigns and transfers to Company all rights Artist has or may
acquire to all such Works. Artist agrees to sign and deliver to Company, either during
or subsequent to the term of this Agreement, such other documents as Company
considers desirable to evidence the assignment of copyright.

Artist Warranties

Artist warrants that the Work does not infringe any intellectual property rights or
violate any laws and that the work is original to Artist.

Miscellaneous

This Agreement constitutes the entire understanding between the parties and can
only be modified by written agreement. The laws of the State of _____
_____ shall govern this Agreement. In the event of any dispute
arising under this agreement, the prevailing party shall be entitled to its reasonable
attorneys' fees.

Artist's Signature: _____

Artist's Name: _____

Artist's Address: _____

Date: _____

Company Authorized Signature: _____

Name and Title: _____

Address: _____

Date: _____

Explanation of Work-Made-for-Hire Agreement

- In the **Services** section, insert the work that the artist is supposed to perform, for example: "Create a series of photographs for a KeepClean toothbrush advertisement." Insert the amount to be paid to the artist in the payment section.
- The section **Works Made for Hire—Assignment of Intellectual Property Rights** establishes that the work is made for hire. However, if the work does not meet the requirements of copyright law, a backup provision is added that converts the arrangement to an assignment. This type of provision is commonly used by businesses seeking to make sure that ownership rights have been acquired.
- The **Warranty** provision promises that the artist owns the work and that the work is not an infringement. This is necessary to provide an assurance that the work is not taken from another source.
- This agreement includes some **Miscellaneous** provisions. One provision provides that this is the entire agreement and therefore negates any previous oral or written agreements. In addition, any changes to the agreement must be in writing. Insert the home state of the hiring party in the blank space so that that state's law will govern the interpretation of the agreement in the event of a dispute. The attorney provision provides that the winning party in any lawsuit will get attorneys' fees paid by the loser. For a more detailed explanation of these provisions, read Chapter 11, "Art and Merchandise Licenses."

Dear Rich:

Who Owns My Blog?

Out of frustration with the nonsense taking place in our industry I asked a colleague of mine to set up a blog site for me to blog on. So they did. All the content and photos are mine. My employer provided no support for the site other than my colleague's jumping in every so often to change fonts in my writings when things went haywire. I left my employer and want to take my blog content with me to my new employer. Who owns the content?

The short answer is that we don't know ... but we have a feeling your employer owns it.

Work for hire? As we mentioned in a previous blog entry, if the blog is not something you would create in the course of your employment and you created it on your own time, using your own equipment, then you own it under work-made-for-hire rules. But if you got paid for doing it (wrote it during work time), or used work equipment and it was related to work (sounds like it was since you're talking about your "industry") then your employer owns the blog. Some other factors that may matter are whether you signed an employment agreement discussing ownership of employee works, or whether your employee handbook at work has rules regarding employee-created works.

Trademark and domain name issues. Regardless of the copyright rules expressed above, you're free to start another blog at your new job, provided you're not taking and using any trade secrets from your last job. The Dear Rich Staff believes that the bigger question is whether you can take the blog name (your trademark) and the domain name (the URL or address of your blog). If readers associate the blog with your employer—for example, they access it at your employer's website—then it's likely your employer will claim ownership of the name unless there is some alternative agreement between you and your boss. For example, you could work out a deal where you owned the name of the blog but licensed it to your employer during the course of your employment. If the domain is part of a free blogging service such as Blogger, then things become more confusing, and there may be battle over who has rights to use the Blogger URL.

Help Beyond This Book

U sing the information in this book, you should be able to handle most permission situations yourself. However, it's possible that you could find yourself needing additional information, or professional advice from an attorney. For example, if you used material based on a fair use determination and the copyright owner later enters the picture claiming ownership, it's a good idea to consult an attorney for advice.

By educating yourself with this book and utilizing the resources listed in this chapter, you'll be able to work with an attorney more efficiently, keep your costs down, and better evaluate the attorney's services.

Updates to This Book

Because some of the information in this book may change—website addresses, for example—current update information is provided in the Legal Update section of the Nolo website (www.nolo.com/legal-updates).

Resources for More Detailed Permissions Research

The primary areas of law discussed in this book (copyright, trademark, and the right of publicity) are part of a body of law known as intellectual property law. Most of the resources in this section deal with how to research intellectual property law.

Copyright Information

- The U.S. Copyright Office (www.copyright.gov) can provide a broad range of information including circulars, kits, and other publications related to permission issues. Contact the Copyright Office at: Library of Congress, Washington, DC 20559-6000, or visit its website at www.copyright.gov.

In addition, the following information will connect you with various services at the Copyright Office:

- Forms Hotline: 202-707-9100 (24 hours), 202-707-3000 (9 a.m. to 5 p.m.)
- Publications Sections: LM-455, Copyright Office, Library of Congress, Washington, DC 20559
- Licensing Division Section: LM-458, Copyright Office, Library of Congress, Washington, DC 20559; 202-707-8150.
- The Legal Information Institute at Cornell University Law School (www.law.cornell.edu) provides text of copyright statutes and related cases and trademark and right of publicity statutes and cases.
- Stanford University has an excellent resource site devoted to fair use issues at http://fairuse.stanford.edu.

Trademark Information

- The U.S. Trademark Office is a division of the U.S. Patent and Trademark Office (USPTO); (www.uspto.gov). The USPTO site includes relevant applications and trademark office forms. You can also write to: P.O. Box 1450, Alexandria, VA 22213.
- The Trademark Blog (www.schwimmerlegal.com) provides timely news about trademark law and disputes.

The Right of Publicity

Rothman's Roadmap to the Right of Publicity (www.rightofpublicityroadmap.com) provides an overview of each state's right of publicity laws, as well as news and commentary.

Conducting Legal Research

Throughout this book are references to legal cases and laws. You may want to read these cases and laws or pursue more detailed legal research on your own. For example, you may want to learn more about defamation law within your state. Finding out more on a specific legal question generally involves reading legal books and finding applicable law and cases.

Conducting legal research is not as difficult as it may seem. Nolo publishes a basic legal research guide called *Legal Research: How to Find & Understand the Law*, by the Editors of Nolo. It walks you through the various sources of law, explains how they fit together, and shows you how to use them to answer your legal questions.

Nolo's Legal Encyclopedia

Nolo's website (www.nolo.com) offers an extensive Legal Encyclopedia that includes a section on intellectual property. This is a good place to start for online legal research. You'll find answers to frequently asked questions about patents, copyrights, trademarks, and other related topics, as well as sample chapters of Nolo books and a wide range of articles.

Working With an Attorney

A number of permission situations may lead you to seek an attorney's advice. Attorneys have various specialties, and you will need to select a lawyer who is qualified to provide the advice you need.

Generally, an attorney knowledgeable in intellectual property law can answer most permission questions. Intellectual property attorneys are familiar with copyrights, trademarks, right of publicity, and, to some extent, media disputes based on defamation and the right of privacy.

It's a good idea to try to find an attorney who has expertise in the particular type of intellectual property that applies to your permission situation. Some intellectual property attorneys specialize in one type of intellectual property, either copyrights, trademarks, or patents. If, for example, you are concerned about a potential trademark dispute, you should seek an intellectual property attorney who specializes in trademarks.

In addition to all these specialties, some intellectual property lawyers focus on litigation (lawsuits), but not all intellectual property attorneys are litigators. If you have a license dispute and want to sue someone (or someone has threatened to sue you), you will need an intellectual property attorney who is an experienced litigator. Litigators usually bill on an hourly basis, though sometimes if you are bringing the suit (rather than being sued) they may take a case on "contingency." Under this arrangement, if you win, the attorney receives a percentage, usually one-third to one-half, of any money you recover in the lawsuit. If you lose, the attorney receives nothing—except for out-of-pocket expenses, which can easily run into the thousands even for relatively simple cases. Read the information on fees in the section below carefully.

The American Intellectual Property Law Association (AIPLA) (www.aipla. org) may be able to help you locate attorneys in your area. The Intellectual Property Law Association of the American Bar Association also has a listing of intellectual property attorneys.

Defamation and Invasion of Privacy

If your dispute is based on defamation or invasion of privacy, you may need a media law specialist. In this case, the attorney may not be an intellectual property expert but will be knowledgeable in disputes regarding libel, slander, and other personal claims known as torts, especially as they relate to media industries such as publishing and music. If you are locating an attorney through a bar association referral service, ask for a media law attorney.

Finding an Attorney

The best way to locate an attorney is by referrals through friends or others in your field. It is also possible to locate an attorney through a state, county, or city bar association. Nolo, the publisher of this book also provides a national lawyer directory (www.nolo.com/lawyers) with which you can locate intellectual property attorneys. When interviewing an attorney, ask questions about clientele, work performed, rates, and experience. If you speak with one of the attorney's clients, ask questions about the attorney's response time, billing practices, and temperament.

How to Keep Your Fees Down

Most attorneys bill on an hourly basis ($200 to $300 an hour) and send you a bill at the end of each month. Some attorneys bill on a fixed fee basis where you pay a set fee for certain services—for example, $5,000 for a license negotiation.

Here are some tips to reduce the size of your bills.

Get a Fee Agreement

It's a good idea to get a written fee agreement when dealing with an attorney. The fee agreement is a negotiated arrangement that establishes fixed fees for certain work rather than hourly billings. Read it and understand your rights as a client. Make sure that your fee agreement includes provisions that require an itemized statement along with the bill detailing the work done and time spent and that allow you to drop the attorney at any time. If you can't get fixed billings, ask your attorney to estimate fees for work and ask for an explanation if the bill exceeds the estimates.

Keep It Short

If your attorney is being paid on an hourly basis, keep your conversations short (the meter is always running) and avoid making several calls a day. Consolidate your questions so that you can ask them all in one conversation.

Mad at Your Lawyer?

In many states, such as California, a client always has the right to terminate the working relationship with their attorney—although this does not terminate the obligation to pay the attorney. If you don't respect and trust your attorney's professional abilities, you should find a new attorney and terminate the relationship. Beware, though: Switching attorneys is a nuisance and may cost you time and money.

What Is a Retainer?

A retainer is an advance payment to an attorney. The attorney places the retainer in a bank account (in some states, this must be an interest-bearing account) and then deducts money from the retainer at the end of each month to pay your bill. When the retainer is depleted, the attorney may ask for a new retainer. If the retainer is not used up at the end of the services, the attorney must return what's left. The amount of the retainer usually depends on the project. Retainers for litigation, for instance, are often between $2,000 and $5,000.

Review Bills Carefully

Your legal bill should be prompt and clear. Do not accept summary billings such as the single phrase "litigation work" used to explain a block of time for which you are billed a great deal of money. Every item should be explained with the rate and hours billed. Late billings are not acceptable, especially in litigation. When you get bills you don't understand, ask the attorney for an explanation—and ask the attorney not to bill you for the explanation.

Watch Out for Hidden Expenses

Find out what expenses you must cover. This is especially important if you're hiring a lawyer on contingency, since you must often pay the lawyer's costs even if you lose the case, which can come as a nasty surprise. Watch out if your attorney wants to bill for services such as document preparation. This means you will be paying the administrative assistant's salary.

Beware of Litigation

Lawsuits take months or years to resolve and cost $10,000 or more. Typically, the lawyers profit the most. If you're in a dispute, ask your attorney about dispute resolution methods such as arbitration and mediation. Many times these procedures save money and are more efficient than litigation.

If those methods don't work or aren't available, ask your attorney for an assessment of your odds and the potential costs before filing a lawsuit. Get this assessment in plain English. If a lawyer can't explain your situation to you clearly, they probably won't be able to explain it to a judge or jury clearly either.

How to Use the Downloadable Forms on the Nolo Website

This book comes with e-forms that you can access online at
www.nolo.com/back-of-book/RIPER.html
To use the files, your computer must have specific software programs installed. All the files are in RTF format. You can open, edit, save, and print these form files with most word processing programs such as Microsoft *Word*, Windows *WordPad*, and recent versions of *WordPerfect*.

Editing RTFs

Here are some general instructions about editing RTF forms in your word processing program. Refer to the book's instructions and sample agreements for help about what should go in each blank:

- **Underlines.** Underlines indicate where to enter information. After filling in the needed text, delete the underline. In most word processing programs you can do this by highlighting the underlined portion and typing CTRL-U.
- **Bracketed and italicized text.** Bracketed and italicized text indicates instructions. Be sure to remove all instructional text before you finalize your document.
- **Optional text.** Optional text gives you the choice to include or exclude text. Delete any optional text you don't want to use. Renumber numbered items, if necessary.
- **Alternative text.** Alternative text gives you the choice between two or more text options. Delete those options you don't want to use. Renumber numbered items, if necessary.
- **Signature lines.** Signature lines should appear on a page with at least some text from the document itself.

Every word processing program uses different commands to open, format, save, and print documents, so refer to your software's help documents for help using your program. Nolo cannot provide technical support for questions about how to use your computer or your software.

CAUTION

In accordance with U.S. copyright laws, the forms provided by this book are for your personal use only.

List of Forms Available on the Nolo Website

The following files are in rich text format (RTF) and are available for download at: **www.nolo.com/back-of-book/RIPER.html**

Form Title	File Name
Text Permission Worksheet	TextWorksheet.rtf
Text Permission Letter Agreement	TextLetter.rtf
Text Permission Agreement	TextAgreement.rtf
Photo Permission Worksheet	PhotoWorksheet.rtf
Photo Permission Agreement	PhotoAgreement.rtf
Artwork Permission Agreement	ArtAgreement.rtf
Agreement to Use Artwork in Motion Picture	ArtFilm.rtf
Lyric Permission Letter Agreement	LyricAgreement.rtf
Notice of Intention to Obtain Compulsory License for Making and Distributing Sound Recordings	SoundNotice.rtf
Music Synchronization and Videogram License Agreement	SynchAgreement.rtf
Master Use and Videogram License	MasterUse.rtf
Linking Agreement	LinkAgreement.rtf
Coursepack Permission Request Form	CoursepackRequest.rtf
Coursepack Permission Agreement	CoursepackAgreement.rtf
Basic Permission to Use a Trademark in a Book or Magazine	TrademarkBook.rtf
Basic Permission to Use a Trademark in a Movie	TrademarkMovie.rtf
Basic Permission to Use a Trademark in a Photograph or Artwork	TrademarkPhoto.rtf
Trademark License Agreement	TrademarkLicense.rtf
Merchandise License Agreement	MerchLicense.rtf

Form Title	File Name
Merchandise License Worksheet	MerchWorksheet.rtf
Short-Form Merchandise License Agreement	ShortMerch.rtf
Unlimited Personal Release Agreement	UnlimitedRelease.rtf
Limited Personal Release Agreement	LimitedRelease.rtf
Interview Release Agreement	InterviewRelease.rtf
Property Release Agreement	PropertyRelease.rtf
Permissions Tracking Sheet	Tracking.rtf
Basic Copyright Assignment	CopyrightAssign.rtf
Musician Assignment Agreement	MusicAssign.rtf
Artwork Assignment Agreement	ArtAssign.rtf
Work-Made-for-Hire Agreement	WorkAgreement.rtf

Index